nurturing achievement

£23.99

Introduction to
Early Years
Education
and Care

Carolyn Meggitt

HODDER
EDUCATION
AN HACHETTE UK COMPANY

Orders: please contact Bookpoint Ltd, 130 Milton Park, Abingdon, Oxon OX14 4SB. Telephone: (44) 01235 827720. Fax: (44) 01235 400454. Lines are open from 9.00–5.00, Monday to Saturday, with a 24-hour message answering service. You can also order through our website www.hoddereducation.co.uk.

British Library Cataloguing in Publication Data

A catalogue record for this title is available from the British Library

ISBN 978 1 4718 0927 9

First Published 2015

Impression number 10 9 8 7 6 5 4 3 2 1

Year 2018 2017 2016 2015

Copyright © Carolyn Meggitt, 2015

Hachette UK's policy is to use papers that are natural, renewable and recyclable products and made from wood grown in sustainable forests. The logging and manufacturing processes are expected to conform to the environmental regulations of the country of origin.

Cover photo © Hodder Education

Typeset by 11.5/14 Palatino LT Std Roman by Integra Software Services Pvt. Ltd, Pondicherry, India.

Printed in Great Britain for Hodder Education, an Hachette UK company.

Contents

How to use this book

This book contains all the units you need to master the skills and knowledge for the new CACHE Level 2 Certificate in an Introduction to Early Years Education and Care qualification. It is divided into mandatory and optional units.

Key features of the book

> ### LO2 Understand hygienic practice in preparing formula feeds
>
> ### AC 2.1 Hygienic practice when preparing formula feeds and sterilising equipment

Understand all the requirements of the new qualification with clearly stated learning outcomes and assessment criteria fully mapped to the specification.

> ### Learning outcomes
>
> By the end of this unit, you will:
>
> 1 Understand the physical care needs of children.

Prepare for what you are going to cover in the unit.

> ### Key term
>
> **routine** The usual way tasks or activities are arranged.

Understand important terms.

> ### AC.1.4 Reflective practice
>
> Think about the way physical care routines are carried out in your setting. Are parental wishes listened to and acted upon? What do

Learn to reflect on your own skills and experiences.

> ### In practice
>
> **Receiving children into the setting**
> Find out about the system for receiving children in your setting:

Apply your knowledge in the work setting.

> ### Messy play safety
>
> ● Check that paints, glues and other substances are designed for children.

Safety instructions for common setting activities.

Case study

Using everyday events for learning
At lunchtime, a group of sitting babies and toddlers were encouraged to choose their

See how concepts are applied in settings with real life scenarios.

AC 1.1 Activity

Discuss the importance of routines when providing for children's physical

Short tasks to help enhance your understanding of assessment criteria.

Research activity

Caring for a baby's teeth
Prepare a leaflet for parents showing how teeth develop in a young baby and how to ensure their healthy development.

Enhance your understanding of topics with research-led activities encouraging you to explore an area in more detail.

Discussion point
Toilet training
In class, discuss the problems that can arise with toilet training and compare the

Activities that encourage debate and discussion in the classroom.

Guidelines for good practice

Caring for teeth
1 Use a small amount (a smear) of baby toothpaste on a soft baby toothbrush or

Helpful tips and guidelines to follow to develop your professional skills.

AC 1.3 Progress check

Think about how you would give physical care in a non-routine situation.

Summarise key points and underpinning knowledge.

Assessment practice

1 What are physical care needs?
2 Explain the importance of routines

Test your knowledge with questions linked to assessment criteria to help you generate evidence.

Useful resources

The Lullaby Trust
An organisation that offers confidential support to family, friends and carers

Includes references to websites, books and other various sources for further reading and research.

Acknowledgements

I would like to thank the following people for their contributions: Laura Meggitt (Teacher) for her valuable insights and for providing many of the early years case studies; Kirsty Meggitt (Recruitment Consultant) for help with the section on SMART targets in Unit 9.

Many thanks to the staff at The Imagination Den at Twickenham for allowing David Meggitt to take the photos relating to messy play on pages 298–302. The Imagination Den was set up in 2013 and offers an inclusive sensory experience where children are given opportunities to explore different materials and to use their own creativity.

I would also like to thank the editorial team at Hodder Education – Stephen Halder, Publisher; Jane Adams, Desk Editor; and Kate Short, freelance Copyeditor, for all their hard work and support.

Photo and artwork credits

Mandatory units

Unit 1.3

Support physical care routines for children

Learning outcomes

By the end of this unit, you will:

1 Understand the physical care needs of children.
2 Understand hygienic practice in preparing formula feeds.
3 Understand hygienic practice in relation to control of infection.

4 Be able to use hygienic practice to minimise the spread of infection.
5 Understand rest and sleep needs of children.
6 Understand childhood immunisation.
7 Be able to support children in personal physical care routines.

LO1 Understand the physical care needs of children

From the moment they are born, all children depend completely on an adult to meet almost all their needs, but the way in which these needs are met will be different, depending on family background, culture and the personalities of the child and the caring adult.

For healthy growth and development (that is, physical, intellectual, emotional and social development), certain basic needs must be met. These are:

- food
- protection from infection and injury
- shelter, warmth and clothing
- access to health care
- cleanliness
- intellectual stimulation
- fresh air and sunlight
- appreciation, praise and recognition for effort or achievements
- sleep, rest and activity
- relationships and social contacts
- love, consistent and continuous affection
- security and nurture.

At each stage of development, children will have different skills and abilities. Although children do not make significant progress in self-care until the toddler years, there are signs of growing independence much earlier.

At about eight months, babies begin to understand how objects relate to one another and may begin using them for their intended purpose: for example, brushing their hair, 'chatting' on a toy phone, etc.

At around 10–11 months, babies start learning how to drink out of a cup and will also begin to hold out their arms or legs to help when getting dressed.

By around 12–15 months, babies can hold a cup in both hands and drink from it, and they will recognise themselves in the mirror.

By 18 months, most children go through a period of saying 'no'; it is their way of asserting their new feelings of self-identity.

Between one and four years, children can:

- use a fork and spoon: most children have mastered this skill by 17 or 18 months.

- take off their own clothes: children usually learn to do this between 13 and 20 months.
- brush their teeth: they may start wanting to help with this task as early as 16 months, but probably will not be able to do it on their own until they are between three and four.
- wash and dry their hands: this skill develops between 19 and 30 months and is something children should learn before or at the same time as using the toilet.
- get dressed: they may be able to put on loose clothing as early as 20 months, but will need a few more months before they can manage a T-shirt and another year or two after that before they are able to get dressed all by themselves. By 27 months, they will probably be able to pull off their shoes.
- use the toilet: most children are not physically ready to start toilet training until they are at least 18–24 months old, and some will not be ready to begin for as much as a year after that. Two key signs of readiness include being able to pull their own pants up and down, and knowing when they have to go before it happens.
- prepare their own breakfast: children as young as three may be able to get themselves a bowl of cereal when they are hungry, and most can do it by the time they are four and a half.

By the age of four or five, children can eat skilfully with a knife and fork and can undress and dress themselves, except for laces, ties and back buttons. By six or seven years old, children are completely independent in washing, dressing and toileting skills.

AC 1.1/AC 1.2 Routine physical care needs for children and the role of the early years practitioner

Your role in supporting personal care routines

One aspect of children's need for love and security is the need for **routine**. This is why having daily routines is so important in all aspects of childcare. By meeting children's need for routine, parents and carers are helping the child:

- to feel acknowledged
- to feel independent
- to increase self-esteem.

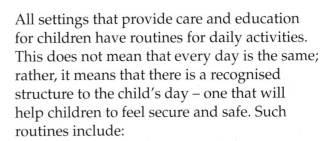

Key term

routine The usual way tasks or activities are arranged.

All settings that provide care and education for children have routines for daily activities. This does not mean that every day is the same; rather, it means that there is a recognised structure to the child's day – one that will help children to feel secure and safe. Such routines include:

- hygiene: changing nappies and toileting older children; ensuring there is a hand-washing routine after messy activities and before eating and drinking
- health and safety: tidying away toys and activity equipment; making regular checks on equipment for hazards
- safety at home times and trips away from the setting: ensuring there is a correct ratio of adults to children, permission from parents and contact numbers, etc.
- meal and snack times: serving of meals and drinks under close supervision
- sleep and rest
- outdoor play.

Supporting hygiene routines

All children benefit from regular routines in daily care. You need to encourage children to become independent by helping them to learn how to take care of themselves. Ways of helping children to become independent include:

- teaching them how to wash and to dry their hands before eating or drinking
- making sure that children always wash and dry their hands after going to the toilet and after playing outdoors

- providing children with their own combs and brushes and encouraging them to use them every day
- providing a soft toothbrush and teaching children how and when to brush their teeth
- ensuring that you are a good role model for children; for example, when you cough or sneeze, always cover your mouth
- devising activities that develop awareness in children of the importance of hygiene routines; for example, inviting a dental nurse to the setting to talk to children about daily teeth care
- making sure that children are provided with a healthy diet and that there are opportunities for activity, rest and sleep throughout the nursery or school day.

Meeting the care needs of children in ways that maintain their security and respect their privacy

It is important that children have their rights to privacy respected when having their care needs met. Intimate, personal care such as nappy changing, toileting, dressing and undressing should be coordinated by a key person. When they are at the right level of development, young children should be asked to consent to offers of intimate care. You might say, for example, to a toddler in the toilet: 'Would you like me to help pull your pants down?' rather than just going ahead and doing it. Similarly, a child who has had a toileting accident should be encouraged sympathetically to help when changing his or her clothing.

Planning routines to meet individual needs

Anyone looking after children should be able to adapt to their individual needs, which will change from day to day. You therefore need to be flexible in your approach and allow, whenever feasible, the individual child to set the pattern for the day – as long as all the child's needs are met. Obviously, parents

and carers have their own routines and hygiene practices and these should always be respected. (For example, Muslims prefer to wash under running water and Rastafarians wear their hair braided and so may not use a comb or brush.)

Whenever you are caring for children, you should always treat each child as an individual. This means that you should be aware of their individual needs at all times.

- Sometimes a child may have special or additional needs.
- Children may need specialist equipment or extra help with play activities.
- Routines may need to be adapted to take into account individual needs and preferences.

In practice

Everyday routines for babies and young children

- Be patient – even when pressed for time, try to show children that you are relaxed and unhurried.
- Allow time for children to experiment with different ways of doing things.
- If you work directly with parents, encourage them to make a little extra time in the morning and evening for children to dress and undress themselves. Children could be encouraged to choose their clothes the night before from a limited choice; the choosing of clothes to wear is often fertile ground for disagreements and battles of will.
- Try not to take over if children are struggling, since this deprives them of the sense of achievement and satisfaction of success.
- Show children how to do something and then let them get on with it. If they ask for help, they should be shown again. If adults keep doing things for children that they could do for themselves, they are in danger of creating 'learned helplessness'.
- Offer praise and encouragement when children are trying hard, not just when they succeed in a task.

Children like to feel independent, but sometimes they need an adult's encouragement to feel that they are capable and that adults believe that they can do it. Teaching independence with self-care skills such as hand washing, brushing teeth, and dressing and undressing is an important step in development. It can be achieved when children are supported in a positive and encouraging way.

Nappy changing

Nappies must be changed regularly to avoid nappy rash and should always be changed immediately after they have been soiled. You must wear appropriate personal and protective equipment (PPE) when changing nappies, such as disposable gloves and aprons. See AC 3.1 for more on PPE.

Whenever possible, the **key person** should change the child's nappy as this helps to develop a close, trusting relationship and enables the key person to report any concerns to the parents. Young babies will need several nappy changes each day, whenever the nappy is wet or soiled. As with any regular routine, have everything ready before you begin:

- a plastic-covered, padded changing mat
- a bowl of warm water (or baby wipes)
- baby lotion
- barrier cream, such as zinc and castor oil cream
- nappy sacks for dirty nappies
- cotton wool
- baby bath liquid
- new, clean nappy.

Key term

key person In early years settings, each child is assigned to a particular adult, known as the key person. The role of the key person is to develop a special relationship with the child in order to help the child feel safe and secure in the setting. The key person will also liaise closely with each child's parents.

It is important to pay attention to the differences between boys and girls when cleaning the nappy area – see the guidelines in the box below. If you are using a special changing table or bed, make sure the baby cannot fall off. Never leave the baby unattended on a high surface. As long as there are no draughts and the room is warm, the changing mat can be placed on the floor.

Guidelines for good practice

Cleaning the nappy area

1 Disposable gloves and disposable plastic aprons must be worn.
2 Wash your hands and put the baby on the changing mat or secure changing unit.
3 Undo the clothing and open out the nappy. It is quite common for baby boys to urinate just as you remove the nappy, so pause for a few seconds with the nappy held over the penis.
4 Clean off as much of the faeces as possible with the soiled nappy. Safely dispose of the nappy and soiled wipes in line with your setting's hygiene policy.
5 Boys: moisten cotton wool with water or lotion and begin by wiping his tummy across, starting at his navel. Using fresh cotton wool or baby wipes, clean the creases at the top of his legs, working down towards his anus and back. Wipe all over the testicles, holding his penis out of the way. Clean under the penis. Never try to pull back the foreskin. Lift his legs using one hand (finger between his ankles) and wipe away from his anus, to buttocks and to back of thighs.
6 Girls: use wet cotton wool or baby wipes to clean inside all the skin creases at the top of her legs. Wipe down towards her bottom. Lift her legs using one hand (finger between her ankles) and clean her buttocks and thighs with fresh cotton wool, working inwards towards the anus. Keep clear of her vagina and never clean inside the lips of the vulva.
7 Dry the skin creases and the rest of the nappy area thoroughly. Let the baby kick freely and then apply barrier cream if required.

Guidelines for good practice

Procedure for changing nappies in a group setting

Nappy changing is an important time and you should ensure that the baby feels secure and happy. Singing and simple playful games should be incorporated into the procedure to make it an enjoyable experience. Every setting will have its own procedure for changing nappies. The following is an example:

- Nappies should be checked and changed at regular periods throughout the day.
- A baby should never knowingly be left in a soiled nappy.
- Collect the nappy and the cream needed. Put on apron and gloves. Ensure that you have warm water and wipes.
- Follow the procedures for nappy changing in close liaison with parents/carers.
- Carefully put the baby on the changing mat, talking to them and reassuring them.

- Once the baby has been changed, dispose of the soiled nappy and discard the gloves in accordance with the policy and procedures of the setting.
- Thoroughly clean the nappy mat and the apron with an antibacterial spray.
- Wash your hands to avoid cross-contamination.
- Record the nappy change on the baby's nappy chart, noting the time, whether it was wet or dry or if there were any faeces from a bowel movement. Also note any change you have observed – such as colour or consistency of the stools, or if the baby had difficulty in passing the stool. Also, note if there is any skin irritation or rash present.
- Check nappy mats for any tears or breaks in the fabric and replace if necessary.

NB Never leave a baby or toddler unsupervised on the changing mat.

For information on disposing of waste in the early years setting, see your setting's health and safety policy on disposal of waste.

Toilet training

Newborn babies automatically pass the waste products from eating – in other words, although they may appear to be exerting a physical effort when passing a stool or motion, they have no control over the action. Parents used to boast with pride that all their children were potty-trained at nine months, but the reality is that they were lucky in their timing! Up to the age of 18 months, emptying the bladder and bowel is still a totally automatic reaction – the child's central nervous system (CNS) is still not sufficiently mature to make the connection between the action and its results.

Recognising that a child is ready to move out of nappies

There is no point in attempting to start toilet training until the toddler shows that he or she is ready, and this rarely occurs before the age of 18 months. The usual signs are as follows:

- Child shows an increased interest when passing urine or a motion: they may pretend-play on the potty with their toys.
- They may tell the carer when they have passed urine or had a bowel motion, or look very uncomfortable when they have done so.
- They may start to be more regular with bowel motions, or wet nappies may become rarer; this is a sign that the bladder is developing.
- They can stand on their feet and sit on a potty seat or a toilet. Some experts assess a child's readiness by their ability to climb stairs using alternate feet – that is, one foot per step.

When to start toilet training

Toilet training should be approached in a relaxed, unhurried manner. If the potty is introduced too early or if a child is forced to sit on it for long periods of time, he or she may rebel and the whole issue of toilet training will become a battleground.

Toilet training can be over in a few days or may take some months. Becoming dry at night takes longer, but most children manage this before the age of five years. Before attempting to toilet train a child, make sure that he has shown that he is ready to be trained. Remember that, as with all development milestones, there is a wide variation in the age range at which children achieve bowel and bladder control.

It is important to encourage self-care skills when children are using the toilet by themselves. They should be encouraged to pull their own pants down and shown how to wipe their bottoms – for example, showing girls how to wipe from the front to the back. You also need children to learn that going to the toilet is a private activity and withdraw by partially closing the door; you should remain nearby in case help is needed.

Dealing with accidents

Even once a child has become used to using the potty or toilet, there will be occasions when they have an 'accident' – that is, they wet or soil themselves. This happens more often during

Guidelines for good practice

Toilet training

- Be positive and supportive to the child's efforts: be relaxed about toilet training and be prepared for accidents.
- Structure the physical environment to help training: have the potty close at hand so that the child becomes familiar with it and can include it in his or her play. It helps if the child sees other children using the toilet or potty. It is also helpful if children are dressed in clothes that are easy for them to manage by themselves, such as pull-up trousers rather than dungarees.
- Work in partnership with parents and carers: it is important to work closely with parents so that everyone takes a similar approach to toilet training. Otherwise the child may become anxious. If a parent starts training their toddler when there is a new baby due, be prepared for some accidents. Many children react to a new arrival by regressing to baby behaviour.
- Encourage and praise: always praise the child when he or she succeeds and do not show anger or disapproval if the opposite occurs; the child may be upset by an accident. It is important not to over-encourage children as this can make them anxious about letting you down.
- Treat a child with respect: do not show any disgust for the child's faeces, or the child might feel guilty. He or she will regard using the potty as an achievement and will be proud of them. Children have no natural shame about their bodily functions (unless adults make them ashamed).
- Establish a routine: offer the potty regularly so that the child becomes used to the idea of a routine, and learn to read the signs that a child needs to use it. Cover the potty and flush the contents down the toilet. Always wear disposable gloves. Encourage good hygiene right from the start, by washing the child's hands after every use of the potty.
- Flexible, personalised approach: some children feel insecure when sitting on a potty with no nappy on – try it first still wearing a nappy or pants if the child shows reluctance. The child may prefer to try the 'big' toilet seat straightaway; a toddler seat fixed onto the normal seat makes this easier. Boys need to learn to stand in front of the toilet and aim at the bowl before passing any urine; you could put a piece of toilet paper in the bowl for him to aim at. Some children are frightened when the toilet is flushed; be tactful and sympathetic. You could wait until the child has left the room before you flush.
- Provide plenty of fluids and fibre to prevent hard stools: children need to drink plenty of water or other drinks in order for them to learn what having a full bladder feels like. They also need to be given foods that contain fibre (such as fruit and vegetables) to prevent constipation.

the early stages of toilet training, as the child may lack the awareness and control needed to allow enough time to get to the potty. Older children may become so absorbed in their play that they simply forget to go to the toilet.

You can help children when they have an accident by:

- remaining calm and reassuring the child; let the child know that it is not a big problem, just something that happens from time to time
- reassuring the child in a friendly tone of voice and offering a cuddle if he or she seems distressed
- being discreet – deal with the matter swiftly; wash and change the child out of view of others and with the minimum of fuss
- supervising an older child discreetly and encouraging them to manage the incident themselves, if they wish to do so
- following safety procedures in the setting – for example, wear disposable gloves and deal appropriately with soiled clothing and waste.

Progress check

Toilet training
Arrange to interview a parent or carer who has recently toilet-trained a child.

- Find out what methods they used and if they encountered any problems.
- Write a report of the methods used.

In small groups, make a colourful, eye-catching wall display that provides tips for parents and carers on toilet training.

Discussion point
Toilet training
In class, discuss the problems that can arise with toilet training and compare the strategies used by different families.

Washing and bath time
Hand washing
Babies and toddlers need to have their hands washed frequently. This is because they are constantly picking things up and putting their hands in their mouths, and they may also pick up an infection. It is important to build regular hand washing into routine care – washing their hands before and after eating.

Hand washing is an important skill that children need to learn. It can be made into a fun activity by singing 'This is the way we wash/dry our hands … on a cold/hot and frosty/sunny morning.' Children soon learn that hand washing is a routine task that must always be done after going to the toilet, before meals and after playing outdoors.

Washing the face
Most young children dislike having their faces washed as they feel they are being suffocated. Always use a clean cloth and wipe each part of the face separately and gently. Dry thoroughly with a soft towel.

Topping and tailing
A young baby does not have to be bathed every day because only her bottom, face, neck and skin creases get dirty, and her skin may tend to become dry. If a bath is not given daily, the baby should have the important body parts cleansed thoroughly – a process known as 'topping and tailing'. This process limits the amount of undressing and helps to maintain good skin condition. Whatever routine is followed, the newborn baby needs to be handled gently but firmly, and with confidence. Most babies learn to enjoy the sensation of water and are greatly affected by your attitude. The more relaxed and unhurried you are, the more enjoyable the whole experience will be.

Guidelines for good practice

A topping and tailing routine
- Wash your hands.
- Remove the baby's outer clothes, leaving on her vest and nappy.
- Wrap the baby in the towel, keeping her arms inside.
- Using two separate pieces of cotton wool (one for each eye; this will prevent any infection passing from one eye to the other), squeezed in the boiled water, gently wipe the baby's eyes in one movement from the inner corner outwards.
- Gently wipe all around the face and behind the ears. Lift the chin and wipe gently under the folds of skin. Dry each area thoroughly by patting with a soft towel or dry cotton wool.
- Unwrap the towel and take the baby's vest off. Raise each arm separately and wipe the armpit carefully as the folds of skin rub together here and can become quite sore – again dry thoroughly and dust with baby powder if used.
- Wipe and dry the baby's hands.
- Take the nappy off and place in lidded bucket.
- Clean the baby's bottom with moist swabs, then wash with soap and water; rinse well with flannel or sponge, pat dry and apply protective cream if necessary.
- Put on clean nappy and clothes.

Babies do not like having their skin exposed to the air, so should be undressed for the shortest possible time. Always ensure the room is warm, no less than 20°C (68°F), and there are no draughts. Warm a large, soft towel on a not-too-hot radiator and have it ready to wrap the baby afterwards.

Collect all the equipment you will need before you start:

- changing mat
- water that has been boiled and allowed to cool
- cotton-wool swabs
- lidded buckets for soiled nappies and used swabs, and clothes
- bowl for warm water
- protective cream such as Vaseline
- clean clothes and a nappy.

Bathing the baby

When the bath is given will depend on family routines, but it is best not to bath the baby immediately after a feed, as she may be sick. Some babies love being bathed; others dislike even being undressed. Bath time has several benefits for babies, as it provides:

- the opportunity to kick and exercise
- the opportunity to clean and refresh the skin and hair
- the opportunity for the carer to observe any skin problems, such as rashes, bruises, etc.
- a valuable time for communication between the baby and the carer
- a time for relaxation and enjoyment.

Before you start, ensure the room is warm and draught-free, and collect all necessary equipment:

- small bowl of boiled water and cotton swabs (as for 'topping and tailing' procedure)
- baby bath filled with warm water – test temperature with your elbow, not with hands as these are insensitive to high temperatures; the water should feel warm but not hot
- changing mat
- lidded buckets
- two warmed towels
- clean nappy and clothes
- brush and comb
- toiletries and nail scissors.

Guidelines for good practice

A bathing routine

- Undress the baby except for her nappy and wrap her in a towel while you clean her face, as for 'topping and tailing'.
- Wash her hair before putting her in the bath: support her head and neck with one hand, hold her over the bath and wash her head with baby shampoo or soap; rinse her head thoroughly and dry with second towel.
- Unwrap the towel around her body, remove her nappy and place it in the bucket.
- Remove any soiling from the baby's bottom with cotton wool; remember to clean baby girls from front to back to avoid germs from faeces entering the urethra or vagina.
- Lay the baby in the crook of one arm and gently soap her body front and back with baby soap. (If preferred, use baby bath liquid added to the bath beforehand.)
- Lift the baby off the towel and gently lower her into the water, holding her with one arm around the back of her neck and shoulders and holding the far arm to stop her slipping.
- Talk to the baby and gently swish the water to rinse off the soap, paying particular attention to all skin creases – under arms, between legs and behind knees. Allow time for the baby to splash and kick, but avoid chilling.
- Lift the baby out and wrap in a warm towel; dry her thoroughly by patting, not rubbing.
- Baby oil or moisturiser may now be applied to the skin; do not use talcum powder with oils as it will form lumps and cause irritation.
- Check if fingernails and toenails need cutting. Always use blunt-ended nail scissors and avoid cutting nails too short.
- Dress the baby in a clean nappy and clothes.

Guidelines for good practice

Keeping babies clean

- Cultural preferences in skin care should be observed; cocoa butter or special moisturisers may be applied to babies with black skin and their bodies may be massaged with oil after bathing.
- Always put cold water in the bath before adding hot – many babies have been severely scalded by contact with the hot surface of the bath.
- Do not wear dangling earrings or sharp brooches and keep your own nails short and clean.
- Never leave a baby or child under ten years alone in the bath, even for a few seconds.
- Do not top up with hot water while the baby is in the bath; make sure that taps are turned off tightly as even small drops of hot water can cause scalds.
- From a few months old, babies may be bathed in the big bath, keeping the water shallow and following the same guidelines regarding temperature and safety. A non-slip mat placed in the bottom of the bath will prevent slipping.
- Avoid talcum powder because of the risk of inhalation or allergy; if it is used, place on your hands first and then gently smooth it on to completely dry skin.
- Do not use cotton-wool buds – they are not necessary and can be dangerous when poked inside a baby's ears or nose, which are self-cleansing anyway.
- Nail care should be included in the bathing routine. A young baby's nails should be cut when necessary. Do this after a bath when they are soft.
- Hair should be washed daily in the first few months, but shampoo is not necessary every day. A little bath lotion added to the bath water could be gradually worked into the baby's scalp until a lather forms and may then be rinsed off using a wrung-out flannel.
- If the baby dislikes having her hair washed, try to keep hair washing separate from bath time so that the two are not associated as unpleasant events.

Caring for children's skin

As well as ensuring that babies and children's skin is kept clean, it is also important that they are protected from the sun.

Protection from sun

Babies benefit from being outside in the fresh air for a while every day. When air is trapped in a building it becomes stale, the level of humidity rises and there is an increased risk of infections spreading. When working in nurseries, practitioners should ensure that rooms are well ventilated and that there are opportunities for babies to go outside. Sunlight is beneficial too, but care should be taken with babies and young children:

- Keep all children out of the sun when it is at its most dangerous, between 11 a.m. and 3 p.m. Those caring for young children should plan outdoor activities to avoid this time unless children are well protected by hats and sun protection cream. Permission must be obtained from the child's parent or guardian before applying sun creams.
- Specialists advise keeping babies up to nine months of age out of direct sunlight altogether to prevent the risk of developing skin cancer in later life.
- Use sun hats with a wide brim that will protect face, neck and shoulders on older babies.
- Use sun protection cream on all sun-exposed areas.
- Use sunshades or canopies on buggies and prams.

Caring for a child with eczema

Eczema (pronounced 'ecks-suh-muh', from the Greek 'to boil over') is an itchy and often unsightly skin condition that affects millions of people to some degree. The most common type which affects children is atopic eczema. About one in eight of all children will show symptoms at some time, ranging from a mild rash lasting a few months, to severe symptoms that persist for years.

- Eczema is not infectious – you can't 'catch' eczema from someone.
- It often starts as an irritating red patch in the creases of the elbows or knees, or on the face.
- It can spread quickly to surrounding skin that becomes cracked, moist and red.
- In severe cases it can blister and weep clear fluid if scratched.
- Later, the skin becomes thickened and scaly.
- Skin damaged by eczema is more likely to become infected, particularly by a bacterium called *Staphylococcus aureus*, which produces yellow crusts or pus-filled spots.

Causes

There is no single known cause, but certain factors predispose a child to suffer from eczema:

- an allergy to certain foods, such as cows' milk
- an allergy to airborne substances like pollen, house dust, scales from animal hair or feathers, or fungus spores
- environmental factors, such as humidity or cold weather
- a family history of allergy
- emotional or physical stress.

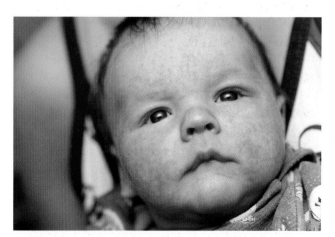

Figure 1.3.1 Eczema appears as a dry, scaly rash that becomes red and may start to 'weep'

Guidelines for good practice

Managing eczema

In mild cases where the child's life is not disrupted, the following measures are usually advised:

- Do not let the child's skin become dry: apply a moisturising cream or emollient to the skin several times a day. Aqueous cream is a good moisturiser and can also be used for washing instead of soap. Apply the cream with downward strokes – do not rub it up and down. (Try to put some cream on when you feed the baby or change a nappy.)
- Identify triggers: identify anything that irritates the skin or makes the problem worse; for example, soap powder, pets and other animals, chemical sprays, cigarette smoke or certain types of clothing.
- Avoid irritants: avoid substances that dry or irritate the baby's skin, such as soap, baby bath, bubble bath or detergents; bathe the child in lukewarm water with a suitable

skin oil added. Avoid wool and synthetics – cotton clothing is best.
- Prevent scratching: use cotton mittens for small children at night; keep the child's nails short.
- Avoid certain foods: do not cut out important foods, such as milk, dairy products, wheat or eggs, without consulting the GP or health visitor. However, citrus fruits, tomatoes and juice can be avoided if they cause a reaction.
- House dust mites: the faeces of the house dust mite can sometimes make eczema worse. If the child has fluffy or furry toys in the bedroom, the house dust mite collects on them. Limit these toys to one or two favourites, and either wash them weekly at 60°C or put them in a plastic bag in the freezer for 24 hours to kill the house dust mite.
- Apply steroid creams as prescribed by the GP: these must be used sparingly as overuse can harm the skin.

In severe cases, the GP will refer the child to a skin specialist (known as a dermatologist).

Caring for children's teeth

Although not yet visible, the teeth of a newborn baby are already developing inside the gums. A baby's first teeth are called milk teeth and these begin to appear at around six months. Dental care should begin as soon as the first tooth appears, with visits to the dentist starting in the child's second year. Teeth need cleaning as soon as they appear because plaque sticks to the teeth and will cause decay if not removed. Caring for the first teeth, even though they are temporary, is important for the following reasons:

1 This develops a good hygiene habit which will continue throughout life.
2 Babies need their first teeth so that they can chew food properly.
3 First teeth guide the permanent teeth into position. If first teeth are missing, the permanent teeth may grow crooked.
4 Painful teeth may prevent chewing and cause eating problems.
5 Clean, white, shining teeth look good.

It is essential to establish a tooth-brushing routine. Children should brush after meals, after snacks and before bedtime, so that it becomes a lifelong habit. Offering children a choice during routines increases the likelihood that they will do the activity and gives them a sense of control. So, for example, when brushing teeth, you could say, 'Do you want to use the minty toothpaste or the strawberry toothpaste?'

Guidelines for good practice

Caring for teeth

1 Use a small amount (a smear) of baby toothpaste on a soft baby toothbrush or on a piece of fine cloth (such as muslin) to clean the plaque from the teeth. Gently smooth the paste onto the baby's teeth and rub lightly. Rinse the brush in clear water and clean her mouth.
2 Brush twice a day – after breakfast and before bed.
3 After their first birthday, children can be taught to brush their own teeth, but they will need careful supervision.
4 Children should be shown when and how to brush – that is, up and down away from the gum. They may need help to clean the back molars.
5 Avoid sugary drinks, sweets and snacks between feeds or meal times.

Research activity

Caring for a baby's teeth

Prepare a leaflet for parents showing how teeth develop in a young baby and how to ensure their healthy development. Include tips on how to make caring for teeth an enjoyable, routine activity.

Caring for children's hair

Most parents will style their own children's hair. If we need to care for their hair while they are in the setting, it is important to follow the parents' preferences; for example, using a wide-toothed comb, or using hair oil rather than shampoo.

Head lice

Head lice are a common affliction. Anybody can 'catch' head lice, but they are particularly prevalent among young children, probably because they tend to put their heads together when playing.

Features of head lice

- They are tiny insects with six legs.
- Head lice only live on human beings; they cannot be caught from animals.
- They have mouths like small needles, which they stick into the scalp and use to drink the blood.
- They are unable to fly, hop or jump.
- Head lice are not the same as nits, which are the egg cases or shells laid by lice. Nits may be found 'glued' on to the hair shafts; they are smaller than a pinhead and are pearly white.
- Head lice are between 1 and 4 mm in size, slightly larger than a pin head (see Figure 1.3.2).
- Head lice live on or very close to the scalp, and they do not wander down the hair shafts for very long.
- Head lice do not discriminate between clean and dirty hair, but tend to prefer smooth, straight hair.
- They are caught just by coming into contact with someone who is infested. When heads touch, the lice simply walk from one head to the other.

Many people only realise that they have head lice when the itching starts, usually after two to three months. The itching is due to an allergy, not to the louse bites themselves. Sometimes a rash may be seen on the scalp, or lice droppings (a black powder, like fine pepper) may be seen on pillowcases.

Figure 1.3.2 Head lice

Treatment

The Community Hygiene Concern charity (www.chc.org) has developed the *Bug Buster Kit*. This contains specially designed combs that can rid a child of head lice without having to subject them to chemical treatments. This method has been approved by the Department of Health.

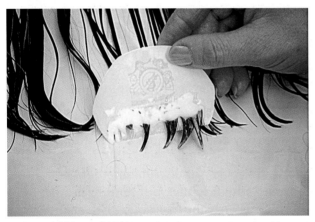

Figure 1.3.3 Using the Bug Buster Kit

Prevention

The best way to stop infection is for families to learn how to check their own heads. This way, parents can find any lice before they have a chance to breed. Families can then treat the lice and stop them being passed around.

Participation in the national Bug Busting Days run by CHC helps to prevent head lice from circulating.

Meal times

Meal and snack times should be enjoyable occasions for both staff and children. The following safety guidelines should be followed to ensure health and safety at these times:

- **Hygiene**: wipe all surfaces where food will be served, before and after meals and snacks. Make sure that children have washed and dried their hands before eating.
- **Serving food**: check that the food you are giving children is appropriate for them; check they have no allergies – for example, to milk or wheat. Never give peanuts to children under four years old as they can easily choke or inhale them into their lungs, causing infection and lung damage. Food should be cut up into manageable pieces and should be served at the correct temperature – not too hot or too cold.
- **Seating**: babies should be securely strapped into high chairs, using a five-point harness.
- **Supervision**: supervise children carefully. Never leave children unattended with drinks or food in case they choke. Never leave a baby alone eating finger foods. Babies can choke silently when eating soft foods such as pieces of banana, so you should make sure that you know what to do if choking occurs. Never leave babies propped up with a bottle or feeding beaker.
- **Routines for meal times**: for toddlers, this should include allowing time for them to feed themselves and planning to make the experience as enjoyable as possible. Special dietary needs and parental preferences must always be taken into account.
- **Feeding babies**: the advantage of family groups in early childhood settings is that babies can easily be part of meal times.

When a whole row of babies all need feeding together, there are often tears and staff become anxious and frustrated because it seems impossible to get each baby fed quickly enough. Meals become times of stress instead of times of pleasure.

Babies learn more if they are given finger foods as soon as this is appropriate. A carrot stick is a wonderful learning experience and makes a good contrast with a metal teaspoon. Observing a baby's learning at meal times is fascinating – for example, does the baby pass the spoon from one hand to the other? Is the spoon held with a palmar grip? Does the baby try to pick up the carrot stick with a pincer grip?

Case study

Using everyday events for learning
At lunchtime, a group of sitting babies and toddlers were encouraged to choose their pudding. A plate of freshly prepared fruit was placed on the table. A tiny portion was given to the babies to try out. Several children showed they wanted more through their movements. The key worker passed the plate to the babies, who were allowed to take more for themselves. This encouraged:

● learning that one portion of fruit is the same as the next
● physical coordination
● a feeling of control over what happens
● decision-making.

AC 1.1   Activity

Discuss the importance of routines when providing for children's physical care needs.

AC 1.2   Activity

Explain your role when attending to the physical care needs of babies and children during nappy changing, washing and bathing, and meal times.

AC 1.3 Situations in which non-routine physical care is required

There are various occasions when you will need to give physical care to a child that is not part of the normal routine. These include:

● when a child has had a toileting accident
● when a child has been sick
● when a child develops a sudden illness, possibly along with a fever that needs to be reduced by tepid sponging
● when a child comes into the setting in a state of physical neglect.

In these circumstances, you will need to provide respectful and personalised care, always being aware of the child's individual needs and preferences.

AC 1.3   Progress check

Think about how you would give physical care in a non-routine situation.

AC 1.4 The benefits of working with parents/carers in relation to individual physical care routines

Parents develop their own way of caring for their child that reflects their culture and personal preferences. It is important to consult parents and carers about these ideas and preferences. This involves respecting their decisions and acknowledging them as being the people who know their child best. Practitioners can then use this knowledge to plan individualised and culturally sensitive care.

While each setting must adopt physical care routines that benefit every child, there may be instances when parental wishes and preferences can be taken into account. For example:

● parents may request that their child has a rest or sleep at a set time each day
● parents may use towelling nappies for their baby
● parents may be using baby-led weaning techniques.

Each parent's preferences should be considered and, where possible, should be accommodated.

AC.1.4   Reflective practice

Think about the way physical care routines are carried out in your setting. Are parental wishes listened to and acted upon? What do you consider the benefits are of working in partnership with parents in this context?

LO2 Understand hygienic practice in preparing formula feeds

AC 2.1 Hygienic practice when preparing formula feeds and sterilising equipment

Hygienic practice is very important when working with babies. A baby's immune system is not as strong or as well developed as an adult's. This means that babies are much more likely to get ill and develop infections. Therefore, good hygiene is essential when making up a formula feed and when sterilising equipment. Hygienic practice is making sure that all equipment and surfaces that you use when feeding are clean and sterile. You must also make sure that your hands are thoroughly washed and clean before touching the equipment.

Guidelines for good practice

Bottle-feeding

- Always wash hands thoroughly before preparing feeds for babies.
- As manufacturers' instructions vary as to how much water and powder to use, it is important to follow the instructions on the product very carefully.
- Do not add extra powdered infant formula when making up a feed. This can make the baby constipated and may cause dehydration. Also, making the feed stronger than the instructions state could result in too high a salt intake, which can lead to severe illness. Too little powdered infant formula may not provide the baby with enough nourishment.
- Never add sugar or salt to the milk.
- Never warm up infant formula in a microwave as it can heat the feed unevenly and may burn the baby's mouth.
- Always check the temperature of the milk before giving it to a baby.
- Always check that the teat has a hole of the right size for the baby you are feeding and check that it is not blocked.
- Never prop up a baby with a bottle – choking is a real danger.

Sterilising equipment

There are several ways to sterilise feeding equipment. For example:

- using a cold-water sterilising solution
- steam sterilising
- sterilising by boiling.

Remember, before sterilising, always:

- clean the feeding bottles, teats, caps and covers in hot, soapy water as soon as possible after a feed, using a clean bottle brush; teats can be cleaned using a special teat cleaner; turn teats inside-out to ensure all milk deposits are removed and wash in the same way as the bottles
- rinse all the equipment in clean, cold running water.

Using a cold-water sterilising solution

- Follow the manufacturer's instructions.
- Change the sterilising solution every 24 hours.
- Leave feeding equipment in the sterilising solution for at least 30 minutes.
- Make sure there are no air bubbles trapped in the bottles or teats when putting them in the sterilising solution.
- Keep all the equipment under the solution with a floating cover.

Steam sterilising (electric steriliser or microwave)

- It is important to follow the manufacturer's instructions as there are several different types of sterilisers.
- Make sure the openings of the bottles and teats are facing down in the steriliser.
- Manufacturers will give guidelines on how long you can leave equipment that you are not using immediately (straight after sterilising) before it needs to be re-sterilised.

Sterilising by boiling

- When using this method, care must be taken to ensure safety and prevent scalds or burns. Hot pans and liquids should not be left unattended, especially if children are present.

- Make sure that whatever you sterilise in this way is safe to boil.
- Boil the feeding equipment in water for at least ten minutes, making sure that all items stay under the surface of the water.
- Remember that teats tend to get damaged faster with this method. Regularly check that teats and bottles are not torn, cracked or damaged.
- Wash your hands thoroughly. Clean and disinfect the surface where you will put together the bottle and teat.
- It is best to remove the bottles just before they are used.

NB Once sterilised, if the bottles are not being used immediately, they should be put together fully with the teat and lid in place. This is to prevent the inside of the sterilised bottle from being contaminated, along with the inside and outside of the teat.

AC 2.1 **Activity**

Describe the procedures for preparing formula feeds and for sterilising equipment. What makes good hygienic practice for preparing formula feeds and for sterilising equipment?

AC 2.2 How poor hygiene may affect the health of babies when preparing formula feeds

Harmful germs are always present on all equipment that you use when preparing formula feeds. Children and adults have developed immune systems that can protect them from these germs, but babies' immune systems are not as strong. Good hygiene practice is vital, so that these germs are killed before they come into contact with the baby. Poor hygiene practice will put the baby at risk of developing illness and infections from these germs. So, the guidelines below must be followed at all times:

- All equipment used to feed the baby must be sterilised.

- Bottles, teats and any other feeding equipment need to be cleaned and sterilised before each feed to reduce the chances of the baby falling sick or getting diarrhoea.
- Use boiled drinking water from the tap to make up a feed.
- Do not use bottled water. This is not recommended for making up feeds as it is not sterile and may contain too much salt (sodium) or sulphate. If you have to use bottled water to make up a feed, check the label to make sure the sodium (also written as 'Na') level is less than 200 milligrams (mg) per litre, and the sulphate (also written as SO or SO4) content is no higher than 250 mg per litre. Bottled water is not usually sterile, so it will still need to be boiled, like tap water, before you prepare the feed.

Bacteria in infant formula

Even when tins and packets of powdered infant formula are sealed, they can sometimes contain bacteria such as *Cronobacter sakazakii* and, more rarely, *Salmonella*. Although these bacteria are very rare, the infections they cause can be life-threatening. Bacteria multiply very quickly at room temperature. Even when the feed is kept in a fridge, bacteria can survive and multiply, although they do this more slowly.

To reduce the risk of infection:

- always make up each feed as the baby needs it
- always use boiled water at a temperature of at least 70 °C, but remember to let the feed cool before you give it to the baby (water at this temperature will kill any harmful bacteria that may be present).

AC 2.2 **Activity**

What are the risks to the health of babies if formula feed preparation and sterilisation of equipment are not carried out with strict adherence to hygienic practice?

LO3 Understand hygienic practice in relation to control of infection

AC 3.1 The role of the early years practitioner in relation to hygienic practice

Cross-infection is the spread of infection from one person to another. Infections are very common in childhood and are responsible for the majority of illnesses that occur in babies and children under the age of five years. A particular concern for early years settings is that young children often lack basic hygiene skills and must rely on others for their care. Shared toilets and washing facilities, toys, equipment and utensils further increase cross-infection risks. Repeated close physical contact with other children, adults and at-risk areas of the environment (such as toilet facilities) increases the risk of acquiring infections.

What is cross-infection?

Infections are caused by bacteria, fungi and viruses. These disease-causing germs (which are also known as pathogenic organisms) can spread in various ways, the main methods being:

- airborne: the germs are carried by the air, such as the chickenpox virus
- droplet spread: infectious droplets of moisture are coughed or breathed out during infection; they settle on surfaces and may be transferred to another person's eyes or mouth, usually by their hands
- direct contact: the germs are spread by touching someone who has the infection, such as scabies or impetigo
- indirect contact: the germs are spread by coming into contact with dirty equipment or other materials.

The importance of hand washing

Effective hand washing is an essential way of preventing cross-infection in early years settings.

How you should wash your hands

We all think we know how to wash our hands, but many of us do not do it properly. Figure 1.3.4 shows how we often miss certain parts of our hands when washing them.

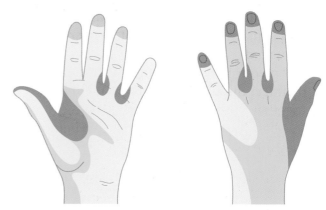

Figure 1.3.4 Parts commonly missed when hand washing

Guidelines for good practice

Effective hand washing

1 Wet your hands thoroughly under warm running water and squirt liquid soap onto the palm of one hand.
2 Rub your hands together to make a lather.
3 Rub the palm of one hand along the back of the other and along the fingers. Then do the same with the other hand.
4 Rub in between each of your fingers on both hands and around your thumbs.
5 Rinse off the soap with clean running water.
6 Dry hands thoroughly on a clean dry towel or paper towel, or under an air dryer.

When you should wash your hands

You should wash your hands before:

- starting work – this is particularly important when working in any caring environment
- preparing food
- eating
- putting a plaster on a child or giving medicines, etc.
- looking after babies and young children.

You should wash your hands between handling raw foods (meat, fish, poultry and eggs) and touching any other food or kitchen utensils, and after:

- handling raw foods, particularly meat, fish and poultry and raw eggs in their shells
- going to the toilet
- coughing or sneezing (into your hands or a tissue)
- touching your hair or face
- playing outside
- touching rubbish/waste bins, cleaning cat litter boxes or using chemical cleansers
- changing nappies
- caring for someone who is ill, especially with tummy upsets
- handling and stroking pets or farm animals, or gardening, even if you wear gloves
- smoking.

Food hygiene

The term 'food hygiene' refers to the practices that should be followed to ensure that food is safe and wholesome throughout all the stages of production to the point of sale or consumption.

Food hygiene is important to everyone. The food we eat is one of the key factors in good health. If you are working with children, you will almost always be involved in handling food in some way. Examples include:

- preparing and serving snacks or meals for children in a nursery or other setting
- preparing and serving snacks or meals in the child's own home
- supervising meal times in a school.

The causes of food poisoning

Any infectious disease that results from consuming food or drink is known as food poisoning. The term is most often used to describe the illness, usually diarrhoea and/or vomiting, caused by bacteria, viruses or parasites.

Most cases of food poisoning result from eating large numbers of pathogenic (or harmful) bacteria which are living on the food. Most food poisoning is preventable, although it is not possible to eliminate the risk completely.

Good working practices

If you handle food as part of your job, you are responsible for ensuring that food does not become **contaminated**.

You need to understand how current legislation affects your work and to follow good working practices. These include the following:

- Keep yourself clean by following the rules of personal hygiene.
- Know how to store and prepare food safely and hygienically.
- Ensure that areas for serving food are clean and safe.
- Protect food from anything that could cause harm.
- Be alert to food safety hazards.
- Ensure that children are given the opportunity to wash their hands before a meal.

> **Key term**
>
> **contaminate** To make unclean by contact or mixture.

Dealing with spillages

When dealing with water spillages:

- ensure when clearing them up that the surface is left completely dry
- ensure that no water is left on the surface.

When dealing with body fluids:

- before clearing them away, ensure that you are wearing the correct PPE, including disposable gloves and a disposable apron
- mop up any spillages using a diluted bleach solution or use the resources provided under your setting's policy
- clean the surface until it is completely dry.

Safe disposal of waste

All types of waste (nappies, used tissues and food scraps) can contain germs and must be disposed of promptly and correctly. Children should not be able to gain access to any waste bins. For more on how legislation affects your work, see Unit 3.

Using correct personal protective equipment (PPE)

The term 'PPE' includes single-use disposable gloves and single-use disposable plastic aprons. You will need to use PPE if you come into contact with blood and body fluids.

- Always wash your hands before putting on and after taking off PPE.
- Disposable gloves and disposable plastic aprons must be worn where there is a risk of splashing or contamination with blood or body fluids – for example, dealing with a nosebleed or nappy changing.
- Some larger settings supply disposable aprons in different colours – for example, red for dealing with blood.

AC 3.1   Progress check

Check your setting's policy for the following procedures: hand washing, food hygiene, dealing with spillages safely, safe disposal of waste, using correct personal protective equipment.

LO4 Be able to use hygienic practice to minimise the spread of infection

AC 4.1 Hygienic practice in relation to minimising the spread of infection

Having read and understood the information for AC 3.1, you will be expected to use hygienic practice at all times to minimise the spread of infection.

LO5 Understand rest and sleep needs of children

AC 5.1 The rest and sleep needs of children aged six weeks to seven years

Everyone needs sleep, but the amount that babies sleep varies enormously and depends on the maturity of the brain (the pre-term baby may sleep for long periods) and on the need for food. Sleep is divided into two distinct states:

- rapid eye movement (REM), which is termed active sleep
- non-rapid eye movement (NREM), which is termed quiet sleep.

In REM sleep, the mind is active and is processing daytime emotional experiences. In NREM sleep, the body rests and restoration occurs. In babies under one year, more of the sleep is active (REM). It is important not to wake babies during deep sleep, as it plays a vital part in restoring energy levels.

The importance of rest and sleep

Rest and sleep are important for our health and well-being. By the end of the first year, most babies are having two short sleeps during the day – before or after lunch and in the afternoon – and sleeping through the night, although there is much variation between children. It is important to have 'quiet periods', even if the baby does not want to sleep.

When we sleep, we rest and gain energy for a new day. But sleep does more than that. When we dream, we process all the events of our daily life. After a night without enough sleep, we often feel exhausted and irritable, but after a good night's sleep we feel rested, refreshed and full of energy. It is important to parents that their child sleeps through the night as it influences the entire family's life and well-being. Children need more sleep than adults because the brain is developing and maturing and they are growing physically as well. Sleep is important to child health because:

- it rests and restores our bodies
- it enables the brain and the body's metabolic processes to recover (these processes are responsible for producing energy and growth)
- during sleep, growth hormone is released; this renews tissues and produces new bone and red blood cells
- dreaming is believed to help the brain sort out information stored in the memory during waking hours.

Children vary enormously in their need for sleep and rest. Some children seem able to rush around all day with very little rest; others will need to 'recharge their batteries' by having frequent periods of rest. You need to be able to recognise the signs that a child is tired. These may include:

- looking tired – dark rings under the eyes and yawning
- asking for their comfort object
- constant rubbing of the eyes
- twiddling the hair and fidgeting with objects
- showing no interest in activities and their surroundings
- being particularly emotional – crying or being stubborn
- withdrawing into themselves – sucking thumb and appearing listless.

Getting the right rest is crucial for the learning of babies and young children. Not all babies will need to sleep at the same time, and it is very worrying to find practices where all babies are expected to have their nappies changed at the same time and to sleep at the same time. These are very individual things. It is important for babies to feel that they are near someone when they sleep. Some babies sleep best on a mat, with a cover to keep them warm, on the floor of a quiet area that is gated. Others sleep better in a darkened room in a cot kept for them. This area should not contain too much stimulation. It is important to relax and let go when falling asleep. Neutral colouring is best and the room should not be cluttered.

It is also important to keep to the sleep-time rituals and patterns that are familiar to the baby at home. Some babies need to have a cuddle, being lowered into their cot as they fall asleep. Others might never go to sleep on a lap, but might need to be in a cot, or in a quiet room, or with their teddy, in order to fall asleep.

Sleep and rest needs at different ages
A baby aged six weeks
Newborn babies tend to sleep a great deal. At around six weeks old, a baby will probably sleep for shorter spells during the day and longer periods at night. The baby will have more deep, non-REM sleep and less light sleep, but will probably still wake for at least one feed at night. Sleep and rest periods are spread throughout the 24-hour period, usually comprising four or five 2.5–3-hour periods of rest and sleep.

A baby aged six weeks needs to sleep and rest for approximately 15 hours in a 24-hour period.

A baby aged seven months
From four and a half months onwards, most babies are capable of sleeping for eight hours at night without needing a feed. By seven months, babies may have two or three daytime sleeps, of 1.5–2 hours each.

A baby aged seven months needs 13–14 hours' sleep and rest in a 24-hour period.

A baby aged 15 months
At 12–24 months, babies tend to sleep for approximately 11 hours at night. The rest of their sleep will be in daytime naps. At around 15–18 months, many babies have just one longer daytime sleep, rather than two shorter naps.

A baby aged 15 months needs 14 hours' sleep and rest in a 24-hour period.

A child aged two-and-a-half years
Most children between the ages of two and three years still need one nap a day, which may range from one hour to three and a half hours. At this age, children usually go to bed between 7 and 9 pm and wake up between 6 and 8 am.

A child aged two-and-a-half years needs a total of 13 hours' sleep and rest in a 24-hour period.

A child aged four to five years
By the age of four years, most children meet all their sleep and rest needs at night, although a few may still need a short daytime rest or sleep.

A child aged four to five years needs a total of 11–11.5 hours' sleep and rest in a 24-hour period.

A child aged six to seven years

By this age, the need for daytime sleeps has disappeared and all the sleep needs are met at night-time.

A child aged six to seven years needs a total of 10.5–11 hours' sleep and rest in a 24-hour period.

Guidelines for good practice

Establishing a routine for rest and sleep

Children will only sleep if they are actually tired, so it is important that enough activity and exercise are provided. Some children do not have a nap during the day but should be encouraged to rest in a quiet area.

When preparing children for a daytime nap, rest or bedtime sleep, you need to:

- treat each child uniquely; every child will have his or her own needs for sleep and rest
- find out all you can about the individual child's sleep habits; for example, some children like to be patted to sleep, while others need to have their favourite comfort object
- be guided by the wishes of the child's parents or carers; some parents, for example, prefer their child to have a morning nap but not an afternoon nap, as this routine fits in better with the family's routine
- reassure children that they will not be left alone and that you or someone else will be there when they wake up
- keep noise to a minimum and darken the room; make sure that children have been to the lavatory – children need to understand the signals that mean that it is time for them to have a rest or sleep
- provide quiet, relaxing activities for children who are unable, or who do not want, to sleep; for example, jigsaw puzzles, a story tape or reading a book.

Different views about sleep and rest

There are cultural differences in how parents view bedtime and sleep routines. In some cultures, it is normal for children to sleep with parents and to have a much later bedtime as a result. Some families who originate from hot countries where having a sleep in the afternoon is normal tend to let their children stay up in the evening. Such children are more likely to need a sleep while in your care; as long as the overall amount of sleep is sufficient for the child, it does not matter. It is always worth discussing bedtime routines with parents. Some areas have sleep clinics managed by the health visiting service to help parents whose children have difficulty sleeping.

Even after they have established a good sleep routine, children's sleep patterns can become disrupted. There may be a number of factors influencing children's sleep.

Guidelines for good practice

Establishing a bedtime routine for babies

Between three and five months, most babies are ready to settle into a bedtime routine:

- Give the baby a bath or wash and put her in a clean nappy and nightwear.
- Take her to say goodnight to other members of the household.
- Carry her into her room, telling her in a gentle voice that it is time for bed.
- Give the last breast- or bottle-feed in the room where the baby sleeps.
- Sing a song or lullaby to help settle her, while gently rocking her in your arms.
- Wrap her securely and settle her into the cot or cradle, saying goodnight.
- If she likes it, gently 'pat' her to sleep.

The routine can be adapted as the baby grows. The NHS and The Lullaby Trust advises that the safest place for a baby to sleep is in a cot in the parents' room for the first six months.

AC 5.1 Activity

Explain the rest and sleep needs of children at different ages, from six weeks to seven years.

Guidelines for good practice

Advice to parents from the NHS

- Cut smoking in pregnancy – fathers too!
- Do not let anyone smoke in the same room as your baby.
- Place your baby on their back to sleep.
- Do not let your baby get too hot.
- Keep baby's head uncovered: place your baby with their feet to the foot of the cot, to prevent wriggling down under the covers.
- If your baby is unwell, seek medical advice promptly.
- The safest place for your baby to sleep is in a cot in your room for the first six months.
- It is dangerous to share a bed with your baby if you or your partner are smokers (no matter where or when you smoke), have been drinking alcohol, take drugs or medication that make you drowsy, or feel very tired.
- It is very dangerous to sleep together on a sofa, armchair or settee.

AC 5.2 Safety precautions which minimise the risk of sudden infant death syndrome

Sudden infant death syndrome

Sudden infant death syndrome (SIDS) is often called 'cot death'. It is the term applied to the sudden unexplained and unexpected death of an infant. The reasons for cot deaths are complicated and the cause is still unknown. Although cot death is the commonest cause of death in babies up to one year old, it is still very rare, occurring in approximately two out of every 1,000 babies. Recent research has identified various risk factors, and the Lullaby Trust has written the following guidelines.

Figure 1.3.5 Preventing SIDS: the feet-to-foot position – feet at foot of bed

Guidelines for good practice

Reducing the risk of SIDS

- The chance of SIDS is higher in babies who get too hot. The room where an infant sleeps should be at a temperature that is comfortable for lightly clothed adults (16–20°C). Use a room thermometer if necessary and check the baby's temperature by feeling her tummy, making sure your hands are warm beforehand.
- Babies should never wear hats indoors, as small babies gain and lose heat very quickly through their heads.
- If the baby is a natural tummy-sleeper, keep turning her over onto her back. A musical mobile may help to keep her happy while lying on her back.

- Place the baby on a firm, flat mattress that is clean and in good condition. Always invest in a brand new mattress if the baby's cot is second-hand. Avoid soft or bulky bedding, including pillows, quilts and duvets.
- Never allow the baby to come into contact with smoky rooms; ask visitors not to smoke in the house. The risk factor increases with the number of cigarettes smoked.
- Learn to recognise the signs and symptoms of illness and know how to respond.
- Learn and practise on a special baby resuscitation mannequin how to perform artificial ventilation and cardiac massage. This should always be practised under the supervision of a qualified first aid trainer.

Sudden infant death syndrome

In groups, prepare a display that details the risk factors in sudden infant death syndrome. Using the information provided, make a poster for each risk factor and state clearly the precautions that should be taken to prevent cot death. Access the NHS website (www.nhs.uk, search 'cot death') for up-to-date recommendations. Also see www.lullabytrust.org.uk.

AC 5.2 **Activity**

Explain the safety precautions which have been proven to minimise the risk of sudden infant death syndrome.

LO6 Understand childhood immunisation

Immunisation is a way of protecting children against serious disease. Once children have been immunised, their bodies can fight diseases that they come into contact with. If a child is not immunised, they will be at risk of catching the disease and will rely on other people immunising their children to avoid becoming infected.

An immunisation programme protects people against specific diseases by reducing the number of people getting the disease and preventing it being passed on. With some diseases – such as smallpox or polio – it is possible to eliminate them completely.

AC 6.1 The reasons for immunisation

How immunity to disease and infection can be acquired

Babies are born with some natural **immunity**. They are:

- able to make their own infection-fighting cells
- further protected by **antibodies** and other substances found in breast milk.

A child's own experiences of infection boost his or her immunity. For some infections (e.g. measles), immunity is lifelong, while for others it is short-lived. Certain illnesses, such as the common cold, are caused by one of several strains of virus, which is why having one cold doesn't automatically prevent another one later. Sometimes the immune system doesn't work properly, as in the case of HIV/AIDS and some other rare conditions. Sometimes it overworks and causes allergy. It can also be affected by emotional distress and physical exhaustion.

There are two types of immunity: active immunity and passive immunity. As discussed above, immunity can be induced by contact with an infection. It can also be induced by **immunisation** against certain infective agents.

Active immunity

Active immunity is when a **vaccine** triggers the **immune system** to produce antibodies against the disease as though the body had been infected with it. This also teaches the body's immune system how to produce the appropriate antibodies quickly. If the immunised person then comes into contact with the disease itself, their immune system will recognise it and immediately produce the antibodies needed to fight it.

Passive immunity

Passive immunity is provided when the body is given antibodies rather than producing them itself. A newborn baby has passive immunity to several diseases, such as measles, mumps and rubella, from antibodies passed from the mother via the placenta. Passive immunity only lasts for a few weeks or months. In the case of measles, mumps and rubella, it may last up to one year in infants – this is why the measles, mumps and rubella (MMR) vaccine is given just after a child's first birthday.

Herd immunity

If enough people in a community are immunised against certain diseases, then it is more difficult for that disease to get passed between those who are not immunised – this is known as herd immunity. Herd immunity does not apply to all diseases because they are not all passed on from person to person. For example, tetanus can only be caught from spores in the ground.

The advantages of immunisation include the following:

- It is the safest way to protect children from particular diseases which may have long-lasting effects.

- Having children immunised at an early age means they are well protected by the time they start playgroup or school, where they are in contact with lots of children.
- It also protects those children who are unable to receive immunisation, by providing what is called herd immunity, which is a partial uptake of immunisation where enough people are immunised to prevent the spread of the disease.
- Children who are not immunised run the risk of catching diseases and having complications.

The disadvantages of immunisation include the possibility of side effects. The possible risks that follow certain childhood immunisations must be weighed up against the risks of complications from the childhood illness. For example, with the MMR vaccine, there is a risk of 1 in 1,000 of febrile convulsions (fits). However, if a child catches the measles disease, the risk of convulsions is 1 in 200.

AC 6.1   Activity

Explain the reasons for immunisation.

Key terms

antibodies Something produced by the immune system to kill bacteria and viruses.

immune system The body's way of detecting and then fighting diseases.

immunisation This protects children (and adults) against harmful infections before they come into contact with them in the community.

immunity A condition of being able to resist a particular infectious disease.

vaccine A substance that stimulates the body's immune system in order to prevent or control a particular infection.

AC 6.2 The immunisation schedule

Table 1.3.1 NHS immunisation schedule for children, 2013/2014

When to immunise	Diseases protected against	Vaccine given	Immunisation site
Two months old	Diphtheria, tetanus, pertussis (whooping cough), polio and *Haemophilus influenzae* type b (Hib)	DTaP/IPV/Hib (Pediacel)	Thigh
	Pneumococcal disease	PCV (Prevenar 13)	Thigh
	Rotavirus	Rotavirus (Rotarix)	By mouth
Three months old	Diphtheria, tetanus, pertussis, polio and Hib	DTaP/IPV/Hib (Pediacel)	Thigh
	Meningococcal group C disease (MenC)	Men C (NeisVac-C or Menjugate)	Thigh
	Rotavirus	Rotavirus (Rotarix)	By mouth
Four months old	Diphtheria, tetanus, pertussis, polio and Hib	DTaP/IPV/Hib (Pediacel)	Thigh
	Pneumococcal disease	PCV (Prevenar 13)	Thigh
Between 12 and 13 months old – within a month of the first birthday	Hib/MenC	Hib/MenC (Menitorix)	Upper arm/thigh
	Pneumococcal disease	PCV (Prevenar 13)	Upper arm/thigh
	Measles, mumps and rubella (German measles)	MMR (Priorix or MMR VaxPRO)	Upper arm/thigh
Two and three and four years old	Influenza (from September)	Flu nasal spray (Fluenz) (annual) (if Fluenz unsuitable, use inactivated flu vaccine)	Nostrils Upper arm
Three years, four months old or soon after	Diphtheria, tetanus, pertussis and polio	dTaP/IPV (Repevax) or DTaP/IPV (Infanrix-IPV)	Upper arm
	Measles, mumps and rubella	MMR (Priorix or MMR VaxPRO) (check first dose has been given)	Upper arm

Not every disease that affects children can be immunised against. There is no routine vaccination for chickenpox or scarlet fever in the UK, although the chickenpox vaccine is offered with the MMR in some other countries. The following diseases are all included in the NHS programme of routine immunisation (2014):

- **Diphtheria**: a bacterial infection which starts with a sore throat but can rapidly get worse, leading to severe breathing difficulties. It can also damage the heart and nervous system.
- **Tetanus**: a bacterial infection caused when germs found in soil and manure get into the body through open cuts and burns. Tetanus is a painful disease which affects the muscles and can cause breathing problems.
- **Pertussis (or whooping cough)**: a bacterial infection that can cause long bouts of coughing and choking, making it hard to breathe. It is not usually serious in older children, but it can be very serious and can kill babies under one year old. It can last for up to ten weeks.
- **Polio**: a highly infectious viral disease spread mainly through close contact with an infected person. The polio virus attacks the nervous system and can paralyse muscles permanently. If it attacks the muscles in the chest, or those that control swallowing, it can be fatal.
- **Hib (*Haemophilus influenzae* type b)**: an infection that can cause a number of major illnesses like blood poisoning, pneumonia and meningitis. All of these illnesses can kill if not treated quickly. The Hib vaccine protects the child against only one type of meningitis (Hib). It does not protect against any other type of meningitis.
- **Meningococcal disease**: one of the serious causes of meningitis – an inflammation of the lining of the brain – and serious blood infections in children. Although fairly rare now, before the introduction of the vaccine it was the most common killer in children aged one to five. The Men C vaccine protects the child against only one type of meningitis (meningococcal).
- **Measles**: a highly contagious virus which causes a high fever and rash. Around 1 in 15 children who get measles are at risk of complications, including chest infections, fits and brain damage. In very serious cases, measles kills. In the year before the MMR vaccine was introduced in the UK (1988), 16 children died from measles.
- **Mumps**: caused by a virus that can lead to fever, headache and painful, swollen glands in the face, neck and jaw. It can result in permanent deafness, viral meningitis (swelling of the lining of the brain) and encephalitis. In rare cases, it causes painful swelling of the testicles in males and the ovaries in females.
- **Pneumococcal disease**: infections caused by the bacterium *Streptococcus pneumonia*. It can cause pneumonia, septicaemia (blood poisoning) and meningitis, and is also one of the most common bacterial causes of ear infections. The bacterium is becoming increasingly resistant to antibiotics in the UK and worldwide.
- **Rotavirus**: a highly infectious stomach bug that typically strikes babies and young children, causing an unpleasant bout of diarrhoea, sometimes with vomiting, tummy ache and fever. Most children recover at home within a few days, but nearly one in five will need to see their doctor, and one in ten of these end up in hospital as a result of complications, such as extreme dehydration. A very small number of children die from rotavirus infection each year.
- **Rubella (German measles)**: an infectious disease caused by the rubella virus. In children, it is usually mild and can go unnoticed. Rubella infection in the first three months of pregnancy causes damage to the unborn baby in nine out of ten cases; it can seriously damage their sight, hearing, heart and brain. In the five years before the MMR vaccine was introduced, about 43 babies a year were born in the UK with 'congenital

rubella syndrome' – that is, the babies had developed the condition at or before birth.

Immunisations are usually carried out in child health clinics. The doctor will discuss any fears the parents may have about particular vaccines. No vaccine is completely risk-free, and parents are asked to sign a consent form prior to immunisations being given. Immunisations are only given if the child is well and may be postponed if the child has had a reaction to any previous immunisation or if the child is taking any medication that might interfere with their ability to fight infection. The effects of the disease are usually far worse than any side effects of a vaccine.

AC 6.2 Activity

Recap the diseases included in the NHS vaccination schedule. Make sure you check with the NHS website for any updates to the schedule.

AC 6.3 Why some children are not immunised

In the UK, the childhood immunisation programme is not compulsory and therefore parental consent has to be obtained before the child is immunised. Although primary immunisation uptake in the UK is relatively high (95 per cent of children are immunised by the age of two years, not including MMR), a small percentage of children are not immunised. Reasons why children may not be immunised include:

- parental preferences, e.g. preference for homeopathy
- religious reasons
- an unwell child when first immunisations were due
- general lack of belief in the validity of immunisation
- fear of being responsible for any possible side effects from the immunisation
- previous diagnosis with the disease.

Fear of side effects

In the past, children with epilepsy or a family history of epilepsy were not given the pertussis (whooping cough) vaccine. There were concerns that the vaccine could directly cause febrile convulsions (or fits caused by fever) and epilepsy. Studies since then have shown there is no link. The whooping cough vaccine is now routinely given to children with epilepsy.

A study in 1998 by Dr Andrew Wakefield suggested that the MMR immunisation could cause autism. This is not the case. The study was flawed and has since been discredited. Extensive research since then has shown that there is no link between MMR and autism. The recent epidemic of measles – mostly in Swansea, Wales – was thought to have been caused by a severe drop in the number of children receiving the MMR jab, possibly because of the now discredited research into links with autism.

AC 6.3 Activity

Explain the reasons why some children are not immunised.

LO7 Be able to support children in personal physical care routines

AC 7.1 Supporting children in personal physical care routines

See ACs 1.2 and 5.1 for further information on personal care routines in relation to toileting, washing and/or bath time, skin, teeth and hair, meal times, resting and/or sleeping.

Good routines can provide valuable opportunities for promoting health and development, whether in a home or group setting. Everyday care routines for babies and young children provide opportunities for the promotion of:

- intellectual and language skills: talking to babies and children when carrying out routine care promotes communication skills and understanding

- emotional development: babies and children feel secure when handled and treated in an affectionate and competent manner
- social skills: young children see and understand that they are treated equally when routines are carried out and will learn the concepts of sharing and taking turns; they will also experience a feeling of belonging, which is very important
- development of independence: good routines allow time and space for toddlers to try to do things for themselves, rather than being rushed by the adult.

Engaging with children during care routines to support their learning and development

Encourage

It is very important that you encourage all attempts when the child is first learning how to do a routine. If you discourage children because it was not done quite right, their attempts at trying might stop.

Practice makes perfect

Remember that young children need a lot of practice (and support) before they are able to carry out new tasks independently. As children gain the skills required for the task, we need to slow down the routine and expect that it might take extra time to complete.

Step by step

Break down routine activities and tasks into easy, manageable steps. For example:

- use a footstool to reach the bathroom basin
- use small steps and a toilet seat to make the child feel more secure when going to the 'big' toilet.

Support

It is important to let children know that you understand their feelings when they are becoming frustrated, and that you will support them so that they feel successful. For example: 'I know it's hard to get your hands really dry; let me help.'

Praise

Praise every little attempt to do any step. Attention to a child's use of a new skill will strengthen that skill. Effective praise is descriptive praise. For example, 'Thank you for putting your cup on the side there – it stopped it from being knocked over' or 'Putting your shoes on all by yourself so quickly was great as now we have more time to play outside.' Children will learn that, when you offer descriptive praise (rather than just saying 'Clever boy'), you are teaching them what you like and why you liked it. They are more likely to do it again.

Modelling

First, model how to do the step and then say, 'Now you show me'. Show one step at a time, allowing time for the child to process the information and imitate what you did before moving to the next step.

Daily and weekly routines

Routines should be planned and organised around the needs of individual babies and children. The routines should ensure that each baby or child has all his or her personal care needs met in a positive environment. Factors to take into consideration when planning and implementing routines include:

- sleep, rest and stimulation
- feeding
- nappy changes
- play preferences
- consultation with each child's parents or carers
- stage of development.

AC 7.1 Activity

Make sure you know about the policies and procedures in your setting relating to care routines. Think of ways in which you can support individual children during routine care activities.

Assessment practice

1 What are physical care needs?
2 Explain the importance of routines when promoting the physical care of babies and young children.
3 Under what circumstances might non-routine physical care be required?
4 Find out your setting's policy and procedures for the safe, hygienic preparation of formula feeds.
5 How can poor hygiene affect the health of babies in relation to the preparation of formula feeds and sterilisation of equipment?
6 Why are sleep and rest so important for babies and young children?
7 How can you ensure that a child's needs for sleep and rest are provided for within the setting?
8 What is sudden infant death syndrome (SIDS)? Explain how you can minimise the risk of sudden infant death syndrome.
9 Which childhood illnesses can be prevented by immunisation?
10 What is the current immunisation schedule for babies and young children in the UK?
11 Give four reasons why some children are not immunised.
12 Describe how you have been able to support children in personal care routines in your setting.

Useful resources

The Lullaby Trust

An organisation that offers confidential support to family, friends and carers affected by the sudden and unexpected death of a baby or toddler.

NHS

The NHS has advice about reducing a baby's risk of SIDS.

www.nhs.uk/conditions/pregnancy-and-baby/pages/reducing-risk-cot-death.aspx

The NHS website contains an explanation of the discredited study by Dr Andrew Wakefield into MMR immunisation.

www.nhs.uk/news/2010/01January/Pages/MMR-vaccine-autism-scare-doctor.aspx

Unit 2

Understand legislation relating to the safeguarding, protection and welfare of children

Learning outcomes

By the end of this unit, you will:

1 Understand legislation and guidelines for the safeguarding, protection and welfare of children.
2 Understand policies and procedures for the safeguarding, protection and welfare of children.

3 Understand how to respond to evidence or concerns that a child has been abused or harmed.

LO1 Understand legislation and guidelines for the safeguarding, protection and welfare of children

Safeguarding is a term which means more than just protecting children from harm. The Department for Education's statutory guidance *Working Together to Safeguard Children* (2013) defines safeguarding as:

● protecting children from maltreatment
● preventing impairment of children's health and development
● ensuring that children grow up in circumstances consistent with the provision of safe and effective care and taking action to enable all children to have the best outcomes.

Safeguarding children's welfare in the context of child protection means protecting them from physical, emotional or sexual abuse, or neglect. It also means helping children to grow up into confident, healthy and happy adults. Although child abuse is not common, it is important to recognise that there are children who are victims of abuse in one way or another.

There is one aspect of work with babies, toddlers and young children that must always come first: the requirement to keep them safe, and to protect them from significant harm.

All those who come into contact with children and families in their everyday work have a duty to safeguard and promote the welfare of children.

AC 1.1 List current legislation and guidelines for the safeguarding, protection and welfare of children

Working Together to Safeguard Children (2013)

This document applies to those working in education, health and social services, as well as the police and the probation service. It is relevant to those working with children and their families in the statutory, independent and voluntary sectors. The document covers the following:

- a summary of the nature and impact of child abuse and neglect
- how to operate best practice in child protection procedures
- the roles and responsibilities of different agencies and practitioners
- the role of Local Safeguarding Children Boards (LSCBs)
- the processes to be followed when there are concerns about a child
- the action to be taken to safeguard and promote the welfare of children experiencing, or at risk of, significant harm
- the important principles to be followed when working with children and families
- training requirements for effective child protection.

This document streamlines previous guidance documents to clarify the responsibilities of professionals towards safeguarding children and to strengthen the focus away from processes and onto the needs of the child.

It replaces:

- *Working Together to Safeguard Children* (2010)
- Framework for the assessment of children in need and their families (2000), and
- Statutory guidance on making arrangements to safeguard and promote the welfare of children under section 11 of the Children Act 2004 (2007).

What to do if you're worried a child is being abused (2006) is a guide for professionals working with children that explains the processes and systems contained in *Working Together to Safeguard Children*.

Figure 2.1 Practitioners and parents must work together to ensure the safety of children

The Disclosure and Barring Service (DBS)

The Disclosure and Barring Service helps employers make safer recruitment decisions and stop unsuitable people from working with vulnerable groups, including children. The DBS acts as a central access point for criminal records checks for all those applying to work with children and young people.

The Children Act 2004

This Act placed a duty on local authorities and their partners (including the police, health service providers and the youth justice system) to cooperate in promoting the well-being of children and young people and to make arrangements to safeguard and promote the welfare of children.

The Act gave the new Local Safeguarding Children Boards powers of investigation and review procedures which they use to review all child deaths in their area, as required by the *Working Together to Safeguard Children* statutory guidance. The Act also revised the legislation on physical punishment by making it an offence to hit a child if it causes mental harm or leaves a lasting mark on the skin. This repealed the section of the Children and Young Persons Act 1933 which provided parents with the defence of 'reasonable chastisement'.

> ### Key term
>
> **Local Safeguarding Children Boards**
> Organisations set up for each local authority area in order to make sure there is an agreement and plan for organisations that work with children to effectively work together to safeguard children.

> ### AC 1.1 Progress check
>
> Make sure you know about the legislation and guidelines for the safeguarding, protection and welfare of children. Those who work regularly with children and who may be asked to contribute to assessments of children in need should read the relevant sections of *Working Together to Safeguard Children*.

AC 1.2 Identify policies and procedures relating to the safeguarding, protection and welfare of children

All workplace policies and **procedures** must be drawn up within the framework of current legislation, and in relation to the safeguarding of children must include the following points:

- a **policy**, reviewed annually, that sets out the responsibilities for practitioners for the protection of children and young people under the age of 18
- training on safeguarding for all those working in or involved with the setting
- a named senior staff member with responsibility for safeguarding arrangements
- a duty to inform the Independent Safeguarding Authority of any person involved with the setting who is a threat to children and young people
- arrangements to work with the Local Safeguarding Children Board
- procedures that include risk assessment within the setting to ensure that the policy works in practice.

The DBS checks on all adults who have regular unsupervised access to children under the age of 18.

> ### Key terms
>
> **policy** A safeguarding policy is a statement that makes it clear to staff, parents and children what the organisation or group thinks about safeguarding, and what it will do to keep children safe.
>
> **procedure** In addition to the policy, each early years setting will need clear procedures about what to do when there is a concern about a child.

Procedures should include:

- keeping a clear, written record of any concern identified
- reporting any concerns to a line manager, or the designated member of staff who

is responsible for safeguarding, who will then decide what (if any) further action is required

- guidelines about how and whether to discuss the concern with the child and/or family.

Policies and procedures are usually kept in the staff room or manager's office. It is the employer's duty to ensure that each member of staff knows about the policies and procedures within the setting. If you come across any policy matter that you are unsure about, you should know where to find the relevant document in order to find out what is expected of you in practice.

Every adult working in the setting must be a suitable person to work with young children, and must have a full DBS clearance (see page 33). This includes students on placements and regular volunteers.

AC 1.2 Progress check ✔

Find out what is meant by the legal term 'suitable person' in relation to the care of young children.

Familiarise yourself with the safeguarding policy in your placement.

AC 1.3 Explain the term 'whistleblowing'

Whistleblowing is an important aspect of safeguarding where staff, volunteers and students are encouraged to share genuine concerns about a colleague's behaviour. The behaviour may not be child abuse but the colleague may not be following the policies and procedures or could be pushing the boundaries beyond normal limits.

Whistleblowing is very different from a complaint or a grievance. The term whistleblowing generally applies when you are acting as a witness to misconduct that you have seen and that threatens other people, children or the reputation of the workforce.

The Public Interest Disclosure Act 1998, known as the 'Whistleblowing Act', is intended to protect the public interest by providing a remedy for individuals who suffer workplace reprisal for raising a genuine concern, whether it is a concern about child safeguarding and welfare systems, financial malpractice, danger, illegality, or other wrongdoing.

LO2 Understand policies and procedures for the safeguarding, protection and welfare of children

AC 2.1 Explain roles and responsibilities in relation to the safeguarding, protection and welfare of children

There are no specific mandatory laws in the UK that require professionals to report any suspicions they may have of child abuse to the authorities. (In Northern Ireland, however, it is an offence not to report an arrestable crime to the police, which by definition includes crimes against children.) In England, government guidance *Working Together to Safeguard Children* (Department for Education, 2013) states that:

'Everybody who works or has contact with children, parents and other adults in contact with children should be able to recognise, and know how to act upon, evidence that a child's health or development is or may be being impaired – especially when they are suffering, or likely to suffer, significant harm.'

The guidelines also state that all staff members who have or become aware of concerns about the safety or welfare of a child or children should know:

- whom to contact in what circumstances, and how; and
- when and how to make a referral to local authority children's social care services or the police.

If there are any child welfare concerns, 'relevant information about the child and family should be discussed with a manager, or a named or designated health professional or a designated member of staff depending on the organisational setting'.

Guidelines for good practice

Safeguarding children in early years settings and schools

- An early years setting or school keeps children safe by having good procedures around safer recruitment and management, and its general operating policy (for example, if children are encouraged to speak out when they feel unhappy or uncomfortable, they will be much less vulnerable to abuse); and by
- ensuring that children's intimate care (nappy-changing, toileting, dressing and undressing) is coordinated by a key person. This reinforces the child's right to privacy and the child would not then expect just anyone to take them aside and undress them.

Following the procedures for safeguarding children

All the legislation and guidance in recent decades, including the Children Act 2004, make it clear that the child's interests must come first. All professionals must work together to promote the child's welfare before all else. For example, imagine that you found out that a father had slapped his child on the face, leaving a mark. You may have developed a very close relationship with this parent and you may be very sympathetic to the difficulties he is experiencing. You may feel that this incident is a 'one-off', that he genuinely loves and cares for the child, and that he would be

devastated if you did not keep this to yourself. All the same, you are required to put the child's interests before your feelings about the family.

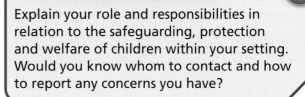

AC 2.1 Progress check

Explain your role and responsibilities in relation to the safeguarding, protection and welfare of children within your setting. Would you know whom to contact and how to report any concerns you have?

AC 2.2 Explain the boundaries of confidentiality in relation to the safeguarding, protection and welfare of children

Confidentiality and 'need to know'

In general, you must keep sensitive information confidential. If information circulates too freely, parents can feel very exposed and vulnerable. They may stop sharing information with staff.

Figure 2.2 Parents need to know that the information they share is confidential

Guidelines for good practice

Confidentiality

- **Where appropriate, seek consent before you share information** – you might find out on a home visit that a child's mother has a serious mental health difficulty, which is well managed by medication and therapy. However, the medication can make her feel rather tired first thing in the morning, and she tells you that she can struggle to take on information or hold a conversation then. So you might say, 'I'll need to tell my manager this, but shall we also let the staff team know, so they can talk with you at the end of the day and not in the morning?' The parent can then give or withhold consent freely.
- **Never disclose any information about a child's welfare in an inappropriate way** to people outside the setting or school – for example, you would not tell friends or family about a child protection conference you had attended.
- **Put the child's interests first** – if sharing information will help to ensure a child's safety, you must do this. In nearly all cases, you would start by explaining to the parent why you wish to share the information and how this would help the child. If a parent refuses, ask for advice and guidance from the named person for safeguarding or the manager/head of the setting. If a parent says something like, 'I did smack her round the head, but you won't tell anyone, will you? They'll take her into care,' you will need to explain clearly that you are legally required to pass on information like this.

Key term

key person system A system within an early years setting in which care of each child is assigned to a particular adult, known as the key person. The role of the key person is to develop a special relationship with the child, in order to help the child to feel safe and secure in the setting. The key person will also liaise closely with each child's parents.

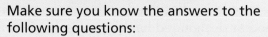

AC 2.2 Progress check

Make sure you know the answers to the following questions:

- Why should you ask a parent for consent before sharing confidential information with another professional?
- Under what sort of circumstances would you share information without consent?

Explain the boundaries of confidentiality in relation to the safeguarding of children.

AC 2.3 Explain benefits of working with others in the context of safeguarding, protection and welfare of children

Different professionals and agencies should work together to help the child and family early on when there are difficulties. They should not wait until something serious happens before taking action. For example, a health visitor might notice that a mother is getting very stressed by the behaviour of her toddler and is struggling to cope. **Early intervention** might involve talking to the mother, showing empathy and perhaps finding some support for her at the local Children's Centre or setting up a programme of home visits. This would be much better than waiting to see if the situation becomes worse before doing anything. Although there is still a common view that social workers intervene to take children away from their families, in reality the vast majority of social work is about helping different agencies work together to support the family, so that the child's safety and well-being are assured.

Key term

early intervention This approach seeks to offer extra help and support to a family before the child starts to lag behind in development or to experience neglect or abuse. Early intervention is about working cooperatively with parents and carers, giving them a chance to make choices about which services they need.

Initial assessments

Initial assessments are undertaken by specialist children's social workers in response to referrals made by, for example, schools, doctors, nurses and early years settings. The initial assessment informs the decision of what to do next. Possible decisions include the following:

- **Offering services to support the child and family**, if it is judged that the child is not at immediate risk of harm but is at risk of poor developmental outcomes.
- **Urgent action to protect the child from harm** (e.g. apply for a court order to take the child into care). Social workers cannot take children away from their parents: only the courts can direct this. However, a police officer can take a child into police protection in an emergency.
- **Holding a strategy discussion**. This would happen where the assessment indicates that the child may be suffering significant harm. Other professionals, like GPs, health visitors, teachers and early years practitioners who know the child and family, may be invited to this discussion. Specialist police officers must always be represented in strategy discussions. Where appropriate, a child protection conference will be arranged.

It is important to remember that staff in early years settings and schools should *not* investigate possible abuse or neglect. The role of the early years practitioner is to refer concerns to children's social care, to contribute to the initial assessment and to attend meetings as requested.

The initial assessment can lead to:

- further work and assessment being undertaken by specialist children's social workers (called the Core Assessment)
- help being offered to the child and family on a voluntary basis, usually coordinated under the Common Assessment Framework (CAF)
- a child protection conference being convened. Key staff working with the family, and the child's parents, will be invited to this conference. The meeting will be organised by an independent chair who has not previously been involved in the case in any way, and who reports to the director of Children's Services.

Child protection conference

The child protection conference seeks to establish, on the basis of evidence from the referral and the initial assessment, whether the child has suffered ill treatment, or whether his health or development has been affected as a result of physical, emotional or sexual abuse or neglect. A professional judgement must be made about whether further ill treatment or impairment is likely to occur. It is possible to hold a child protection conference pre-birth if there are significant concerns that the newborn baby will be at risk of immediate harm (for example, in a family where there has been significant previous child abuse, or where a mother has abused drugs or alcohol during pregnancy).

If this is established, then the child will be made the subject of an inter-agency child protection plan. The child's early years setting or school should be involved in the preparation of the plan. The role of the school or early years setting to safeguard the child, and promote the child's welfare, should be clearly identified. Examples of this role might include:

- carefully monitoring the child's heath or well-being in the setting on a daily basis
- making referrals to specialist agencies – for example, educational psychology
- offering support and services to the parents – for example, a parenting class run at the setting
- monitoring the child's progress against the planned outcomes in the agreed plan.

Figure 2.3 Parenting classes can be part of the safeguarding role of the early years setting

The Core Group

The Core Group of professionals and the child's parents must meet within ten working days of a child being made subject to a child protection plan. The group will be called together by the child's social worker in the role of the lead professional (sometimes called the key worker), and will then meet regularly as required. This group should include a member of staff from the child's early years setting or school. The Core Group develops the child protection plan into a more detailed working plan, outlining who will do what and by when. Both this working plan and the overall child protection plan should be based on the assessments undertaken by the specialist social worker and others, and should address the issues arising in relation to:

- the child's developmental needs
- parenting capacity
- family and environmental factors.

There should be a review of the child protection conference within three months of the initial conference. Further reviews should be held at least every six months while the child remains subject to a child protection plan.

The plan may be ended if it is judged that there have been significant improvements to the well-being and safety of the child. These improvements might have taken place as a result of:

- a change in circumstances (for example, the abusing parent has moved out of the family home and no longer has unsupervised contact with the child)
- the family responding positively to the requirements set out in the plan, and following advice given
- the child being given the medical or other treatment she needs.

At this stage, there might be no further involvement from Children's Services, or the family may continue to be offered further help and support by the different agencies, usually coordinated under the Common Assessment Framework (CAF). This only happens once Children's Services are satisfied that their involvement is not required because the child is no longer considered to be 'in need'.

AC 2.3   Progress check

- What is the Common Assessment Framework (CAF) and how can it help children and their families?
- How would you define a child in need?
- Who can take children into protective care if they are in immediate danger?
- Why might a child be made subject to an inter-agency child protection plan?
- If early years practitioners suspect a child is being abused, should they investigate their concerns?

LO3 Understand how to respond to evidence or concerns that a child has been abused or harmed

Early years practitioners are good at recognising when all is not well with a child. Historically, the biggest difficulty has not been in recognising problems, but in communicating concerns to others (including the child's parents) and acting on them. Often practitioners worry about the consequences of passing on information, and worry that it might lead to the family being split up. It is important to remember that in the vast majority of cases the different services will work with the family to ensure the child's safety. But the decision about what is best for the child should be made by a trained social worker, acting on the best possible information. When practitioners feel worried but do not communicate their concerns to others, a child can be put in danger.

AC 3.1 Describe signs, symptoms, indicators and behaviours that may cause concern

Types of child abuse

The categories of child abuse are:

- physical abuse
- emotional abuse
- neglect
- sexual abuse.

Physical abuse

Physical abuse, or non-accidental injury (NAI), involves someone deliberately harming a child. This may take the form of:

- bruising – from being slapped, punched, shaken or squeezed
- cuts – scratches, bite marks, a torn frenulum (the web of skin inside the upper lip)
- fractures – skull and limb fractures from being thrown against hard objects
- burns and scalds – from cigarettes, irons, baths and kettles.

Often the particular injuries can be explained easily, but you should always be suspicious if a child has any bruise or mark that shows the particular pattern of an object (e.g. a belt strap mark, teeth marks or the imprint of an iron). Also look out for behavioural disturbances in the child, such as aggressiveness towards others or a withdrawn attitude.

Emotional abuse

Emotional abuse occurs when a child consistently faces threatening ill treatment from an adult. This can take the form of verbal abuse, ridiculing, mocking and insulting the child. It is difficult to find out how common this form of abuse is, because it is hard to detect. However, signs of emotional abuse include:

- withdrawn behaviour – a child may not join in with others or not appear to be having fun
- attention-seeking behaviour
- low self-esteem and confidence
- stammering and stuttering
- tantrums beyond the expected age
- telling lies, and even stealing
- tearfulness.

Emotional neglect means that children do not receive love and affection from the adult. They may often be left alone without the company and support of someone who loves them.

Neglect

Physical neglect occurs when the adult fails to give their child what they need to develop physically. They often leave children alone and unattended. Signs of physical neglect include:

- being underweight for their age and not thriving
- unwashed clothes, which are often dirty and smelly
- poor skin tone, dull, matted hair and bad breath; a baby may have a persistent rash from infrequent nappy changing
- being constantly tired, hungry and listless or lacking in energy
- frequent health problems, and prone to accidents
- low self-esteem and poor social relationships – delay in all areas of development is likely because of lack of stimulation.

Sexual abuse

There is much more awareness today about the existence of sexual abuse. Sexual abuse means that the adult uses the child to gratify their sexual needs. This could involve sexual intercourse or anal intercourse. It may involve watching pornographic material with the child. Sexual abuse might also mean children being encouraged in sexually explicit behaviour or oral sex, masturbation or the fondling of sexual parts. Signs of sexual abuse include the following:

- bruises or scratches as in a non-accidental injury or physical injury
- itching or pain in the genital area
- wetting or soiling themselves
- discharge from the penis or vagina
- poor self-esteem and lack of confidence
- regressing and wanting to be treated like a baby
- poor sleeping and eating patterns
- withdrawn and solitary behaviour.

Recognising the signs of child abuse

The National Society for the Prevention of Cruelty to Children (NSPCC) states: 'Children and young people often find it very difficult to talk about the abuse they are experiencing. So adults have a vital role to play in looking out for the possible signs.'

The following section draws on the NSPCC's guide *Learn how to recognise the signs of child abuse*. It is not always possible to be completely certain that a child is being abused, but there are signs and indicators that all early years practitioners should look out for:

- a baby or toddler who is always crying
- a child who often has injuries or bruises
- a child who is often very withdrawn. Withdrawn children are not simply quiet or shy – they shrink from adult attention, lack interest in their surroundings and try to occupy themselves without being noticed
- a child who is often in very dirty clothes, looks unwashed for a period of time or is very smelly
- a child who is frequently very hungry
- a child who is often not appropriately dressed for the weather or time of year. This would include children who often come to the setting in thin T-shirts, shorts or dresses through the winter. It would also include children who come into the setting on a hot day in very warm clothes
- any indication that a child is being left home alone, or left unsupervised in risky circumstances at home

- a child who does not receive the medical treatment he or she needs
- a child who is mocked, sworn at, constantly joked about and made to feel foolish or useless
- a child who expresses fear about particular adults, or seems reluctant to be picked up by a particular adult or afraid to be left alone with that person
- a child with very strong mood swings – anxiety, depression, uncontained anger or severe aggression
- a child whose sexual knowledge, use of sexual words or sexual behaviour is not appropriate for their age or development
- a child who is witnessing domestic violence
- a child who is witnessing significant drug or alcohol abuse.

There may be valid explanations for some of these signs. Equally, there are many other indications of possible abuse, and other circumstances that could be unsafe for a child. The NSPCC advises: 'The most important thing to remember is that if you have a gut feeling that something is not right, trust your judgement and take action.'

Research activity

You can read the full NSPCC guide *Learn how to recognise the signs of child abuse* at **www.nspcc.org.uk**.

Guidelines for good practice

Remember that when practitioners feel worried but do not communicate their concerns to others, a child can be put in danger. Make sure to:

- use your observational skills to learn how to recognise the indicators that may cause concern
- understand what is expected behaviour for children
- be aware of any unusual signs and symptoms that could indicate abuse.

If possible, arrange to attend a course to further your understanding of this complex subject.

AC 3.2 Actions to take if harm or abuse is suspected and/or alleged

It is very important in all suspected cases of abuse that early years practitioners follow procedures that are regarded as good practice and which fulfil the legal requirements. This includes suspicions of child abuse or neglect from your own observations, as well as allegations, either from a child who tells you they have been abused or a parent or other adult who communicates their concerns about abuse of a child to you.

You need to be aware of the indicators of child abuse as outlined above. However, it is important not to jump to conclusions. If you have any cause for concern, you should always talk to your immediate superior or to the head of the nursery or school. Every childcare setting has a policy for dealing with suspected child abuse.

If you suspect child abuse in the home setting, then you should contact your local social services or the NSPCC.

If you have any reason to think that a child might be at risk of harm, you should first report your concerns to your line manager or teacher.

Figure 2.4 Always reassure children and make sure to listen more than speak

Allegation of abuse

If a child tells you he or she has been abused, this is an allegation of abuse or a safeguarding allegation. (It used to be known as disclosure.)

You should do the following:

- Reassure the child, saying that you are glad that they have told you about this.
- Believe the child; tell the child that you will do your best to protect them, but do not promise that you can do that.
- Remember that the child is not to blame, and that it is important that you make the child understand this.
- Do a lot of listening; do not ask questions.
- Report your conversation with the child to your immediate superior.
- Write down what was said by the child as soon as possible after the conversation.

Guidelines for good practice

Recording suspicions of abuse and allegations

As soon as possible after the observation or conversation, you should:

- record the child's name
- record the child's address
- record the age of the child
- record the date and time of the observation or the disclosure
- make a concise, objective and factual record of the observation: for example, if a child has physical injuries, these should be clearly recorded on a body outline figure. You should only record the facts as you see them and not draw any conclusions about the possible cause of the injury
- make an objective record of the disclosure: write down what the child or adult has told you, using their own words. Note also your own responses. Avoid making judgements and interpretations
- record the name of the person to whom the concern was reported, with date and time
- record the names of any other person present at the time.

Confidentiality

These records must be signed and dated and kept in a separate confidential file. As a general rule, information about a child protection issue should only be shared with people on a 'need to know' basis. This means that only staff working directly with the child or the parents will have access to any information about a disclosure or investigation. Gossip and hearsay must be avoided. Names and identities must never be disclosed outside the group designated as having a 'need to know'.

Guidelines for good practice

Reporting child abuse or neglect

- Discuss your concerns as a matter of urgency with the named member of staff for safeguarding, however busy that person seems to be.
- Report the indicators that have led you to suspect child abuse or neglect to your designated safeguarding and child protection officer. Your line manager will help you to follow the correct procedures, but you should know them too.
- You will need to continue to keep carefully written observations. This is because you may be required to make a report, and for this you must have written evidence.
- In most cases, the named member of staff will discuss the concerns with the parent and then make a judgement about what to do next. You should be told what action (if any) is being taken, and why.
- If you have raised a concern and you think that the action being taken is inadequate, meet the named person again. Explain your opinion, referring to what you have observed or heard. Although such conversations are very difficult, they are essential if we are to uphold the principle that the child's welfare and safety come first.
- If you are a student, discuss your concerns in confidence with your tutor. Any worried adult is also entitled to contact Children's Social Care or the NSPCC directly. If you have reason to believe your concern is not being acted on, you should do this.

AC 3.2 Progress check

- What should you remember to do if a child alleges to you? What should you avoid doing?
- Why would early years staff share concerns about a child's welfare or well-being with the child's parents, rather than just keeping a record or making a referral?

AC 3.3 The responsibilities of the early years practitioner in relation to whistleblowing

How to respond to evidence or concerns about a colleague

All early years settings and schools are required to have a policy to deal with allegations made against staff. This will cover cases where a child makes an allegation, or an adult is seen or overheard behaving in an inappropriate way. But there are other examples that might give rise to a concern, without a specific allegation being made. For example:

- a child who seems fearful of a particular member of staff
- a member of staff seeming to try to develop a very close relationship with a child: for example, offering small presents and special treats, or arranging to meet the child outside the setting or school
- a parent expressing a general concern about how a member of staff relates to their child, without being able to say exactly what is wrong.

In cases like these, you will need to discuss your concerns with the named person for safeguarding. Discussions like these are awkward, but it is important to share any concerns you have – the child's welfare is paramount.

Whistleblowing

Sometimes a person inside an organisation knows that something is going wrong and is being covered up. It may be that a person:

- has harmed a child or put a child at risk of harm
- has displayed behaviour involving or related to a child that might constitute a criminal offence, or
- has behaved in a way that raises concern about the adult's suitability to work with children.

If a member of staff has spoken to the manager, head teacher or other appropriate person and made clear that a situation is dangerous and illegal, and no action is taken, it is necessary to 'blow the whistle' and report the concerns directly to an outside body, such as the local Children's Services, Ofsted or the NSPCC. In general, employees who blow the whistle are legally protected against being bullied, sacked or disciplined, if they have acted in good faith.

Case study

Hayley: cause for concern

Hayley has been working at your nursery for two years and has recently qualified as an early years practitioner. You and Chloe have just joined the nursery, which has seen a huge staff turnover in the last year. The room leader, Sarah, is very efficient, but because the nursery manager is on maternity leave, she is increasingly called out of the room. Sarah leaves Hayley in charge as she knows the routine and is qualified. Hayley is very authoritative and quite organised. She has good relationships with parents but she can be sharp with staff, often referring to the fact that she has stuck by the nursery when many members of staff have come and gone. As Hayley is left more and more often in charge, she becomes irritable and frequently loses her temper, often shouting at the children.

One day, a little boy, Jacob, won't sit down to lunch. He gets up and runs around the tables, laughing and treating it as a game. In the end, Hayley loses her temper and grabs him. She forces Jacob hard into a bucket chair and slams the chair forwards towards the table. Unknown to Hayley, Jacob was clutching the chair arms and his fingers get trapped between the chair and the table. He howls and looks frightened. Hayley looks embarrassed, but tells him that he shouldn't have been running around and leaves it at that.

AC 3.3   Progress check

Read the case study above.
1 What concerns would you report to your manager?
2 What do you think could be done to ensure nothing like this happens again?

AC 3.4 Explain why serious case reviews are required

In England, the Local Safeguarding Children Board (LSCB) must undertake a serious case review (SCR) after a child dies and abuse or neglect is believed to be a factor. In addition, serious case reviews are considered in all cases where:

- a child has sustained a potentially life-threatening injury through abuse or neglect, or
- a child has sustained serious and permanent impairment of health or development through abuse or neglect, or
- important lessons for inter-agency working could be learnt.

The government requires that every agency which had a role and responsibility for the child should contribute to the SCR by having an individual management report. The reports are then collated by an overview report author, who must be independent of any of the agencies that had involvement with the child and family. This is all overseen by a review panel of senior staff from the agencies which had no prior involvement with the child, family or decisions taken. The SCR overview report is presented to the Local Safeguarding Children Board, which decides what recommendations are to be acted upon and tracked.

Their purpose is to:

- establish whether there are lessons to be learnt from the case about the way in which professionals and statutory and/ or voluntary agencies work together to safeguard children
- improve inter-agency working and thus provide better safeguards for children.

AC 3.4 Progress check

Research the incidence of serious case reviews in England. Explain why and when serious case reviews are required.

Assessment practice

1. Briefly describe the laws and guidelines which relate to the safeguarding, protection and welfare of children.
2. Select two policy documents relating to the safeguarding of children from your setting. For each document:
   - explain how the policy fulfils the setting's legal obligations
   - explain the course of action outlined in certain situations.
3. What is meant by the term 'whistleblowing'?
4. Explain your role and responsibilities in relation to the safeguarding of children.
5. Describe the boundaries of confidentiality in relation to the safeguarding of children. What is a 'need to know'?
6. How does working with others help in the safeguarding of children?
7. Describe the main signs, symptoms and behavioural indicators that may cause concern.
8. Describe the actions to take if a child alleges or discloses harm or abuse, or if there is reason to suspect any harm or abuse.
9. Outline the responsibilities of the early years practitioner in relation to whistleblowing.
10. Explain the circumstances which give rise to a serious case review being required.

Useful resources

Lindon, J. (2009) *Safeguarding Children and Young People*, London; Hodder Education

Munro, E. (2011) *The Munro Review of Child Protection*: *Final Report: A Child-Centred System*, London; Department for Education

The British Association for the Study and Prevention of Child Abuse and Neglect (BASPCAN)

BASPCAN is a registered charity that aims to prevent physical, emotional and sexual abuse and neglect of children by promoting the physical, emotional and social well-being of children.

Kidscape

Kidscape is the first charity in the UK established specifically to prevent bullying and child sexual abuse.

www.kidscape.org.uk

National Society for the Prevention of Cruelty to Children (NSPCC)

The NSPCC campaigns against cruelty to children and runs ChildLine, the free, confidential helpline for children and young people. The NSPCC also offers services to support children and families, and can investigate cases where child abuse is suspected.

Working Together to Safeguard Children

This is the government's guide to inter-agency working to safeguard and promote the welfare of children.

www.gov.uk/government/publications/ working-together-to-safeguard-children

Unit 2.1

An introduction to the role of the early years practitioner

Learning outcomes

By the end of this unit, you will:

1 Understand the role of the early years practitioner.
2 Be able to communicate to meet individuals' needs and preferences.
3 Understand working relationships in early years.
4 Understand why Continuing Professional Development is integral to the role of the early years practitioner.

LO1 Understand the role of the early years practitioner

All those working with children and young people are bound by legislation to respect the rights of children, young people and their families. In addition to the legal aspects, being a professional means that you must ensure that all children feel included, secure and valued; this is the cornerstone of a positive, integrated environment. As a professional, your practice should adhere to any policies and codes of practice in your work setting. Professional practice should include:

- developing positive relationships with parents in order to work effectively with them and their children
- understanding the extent of your responsibilities and being answerable to others for your work

- working effectively as part of a team
- knowing the lines of reporting and how to get clarification about your role and duties
- understanding what is meant by confidentiality and your role in the preserving of confidential or privileged information that parents or others share with you about their children.

AC 1.1 Identify the skills, knowledge and attributes required for the role of the early years practitioner

Above all else, an early years practitioner needs to like children and to enjoy being with them. Caring as a quality is largely invisible, difficult to quantify and more noticeable when absent than when present. The main individual characteristics required are shown in the box below.

Guidelines for good practice

The skills, knowledge and attributes required by an early years practitioner

- **Knowledge**: A secure knowledge of early childhood development and how that leads to successful learning and development at school is essential.
- **Listening**: Attentive listening is a vital part of the caring relationship. Sometimes a child's real needs are communicated more by what is left unsaid than by what is actually said. Facial expressions, posture and other forms of body language all give clues to a child's feelings. A good early years practitioner will be aware of these forms of non-verbal communication.
- **Comforting**: This has a physical side and an emotional side. Physical comfort may be provided in the form of a cuddle at a time of anxiety, or by providing a reassuring safe environment to a distressed child. Touching, listening and talking can all provide emotional comfort as well.
- **Empathy**: This should not be confused with sympathy. Empathy means being able to 'project' yourself into the other person's situation and experience, in order to understand them as fully as possible. Some people find it easy to appreciate how someone else is feeling by imagining themselves in that person's position. A good way of imagining how a strange environment appears to a young child is to kneel on the floor and try to view it from the child's perspective.
- **Sensitivity**: This is the ability to be aware of and responsive to the feelings and needs of another person. Being sensitive to other people's needs requires the carer to anticipate their feelings: for example, those of a child whose mother has been admitted to hospital, or whose pet dog has just died.
- **Patience**: This involves being patient and tolerant of other people's methods of dealing with problems, even when you feel that your own way is better. Patience is also required with children.
- **Respect**: A practitioner should have an awareness of a child's personal rights, dignity and privacy, and must show this at all times. Every child is unique, and so your approach will need to be tailored to each individual's needs.
- **Interpersonal skills**: A caring relationship is a two-way process. Warmth and friendliness help to create a positive atmosphere and to break down barriers. Acceptance is important: you should always look beyond the disability or disruptive behaviour to recognise and accept the person.
- **Self-awareness**: A practitioner is more effective if he or she is able to perceive what effect their behaviour has on other people. Being part of a team enables us to discover how others perceive us and to modify our behaviour in the caring relationship accordingly.
- **Coping with stress**: Caring for others effectively in a full-time capacity requires energy, and it is important to be aware of the possibility of professional burnout. In order to help others, we must first help ourselves: the practitioner who never relaxes or never develops any outside interests is more likely to suffer 'burnout' than one who finds his or her own time and space.

Key term

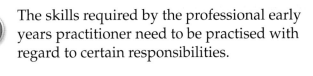

empathy The ability to understand and share the feelings of another.

The skills required by the professional early years practitioner need to be practised with regard to certain responsibilities.

Guidelines for good practice

Your responsibilities as a professional early years practitioner

- **Respect the principles of confidentiality**: Confidentiality is the preservation of confidential (or privileged) information concerning children and their families. It is a complex issue which has at its core the principle of trust. The giving or receiving of sensitive information should be subject to a careful consideration of the needs of the children and their families; for example, a child who is in need of protection has overriding needs which require that all relevant information be given to all the appropriate agencies, such as social workers, doctors, etc. Within the childcare and education setting, it might be appropriate to discuss sensitive issues, but such information must never be shared with anyone outside the setting, unless there are concerns regarding safeguarding.

- **Commitment to meeting the needs of the children**: The needs and rights of all children are the most important thing, and the early years practitioner must seek to meet these needs within the boundaries of the work role. Any personal preferences and prejudices must be put aside; all children should be treated with respect and dignity, irrespective of their ethnic origin, socio-economic group, religion or disability. The equal opportunities code of practice involved will give detailed guidelines, together with the Early Years Foundation Stage (EYFS).

- **Responsibility and accountability in the workplace**: The supervisor, line manager, teacher or parent will have certain expectations about your role, and your responsibilities should be detailed in the job contract. As a professional, you need to carry out all your duties willingly and to be answerable to others for your work. It is vital that all workers know the lines of reporting and how to obtain clarification of their own role and responsibility. If you do not feel confident in carrying out a particular task, either because you do not fully understand it or because you have not been fully trained, then you have a responsibility to state your concerns and ask for guidance.

- **Respect for parents and other adults**: The training you have received will have emphasised the richness and variety of child-rearing practices in the UK. It is an important part of your professional role that you respect the wishes and views of parents and other carers, even when you may disagree with them. You should also recognise that parents are usually the people who know their children best; and in all your dealings with parents and other adults, you must show that you respect their cultural values and religious beliefs (EYFS Positive Relationships – Parents as Partners).

- **Communicate effectively with team members and other professionals**: The training you are receiving emphasises the importance of effective communication in the workplace. You will also be aware of the need to plan in advance for your work with young children: knowledge of children's needs in all developmental areas will enable you to fulfil these within your own structured role.

AC 1.1 Progress check ✓

After reading through this section on what is required in your role as an early years practitioner, it may seem a little daunting. However, by putting the child at the centre of your practice, you can build on all the other skills and attributes. List six personal qualities that you believe to be most important for an early years practitioner.

AC 1.2 Settings that provide early years education and care

The main types of provision for children

Provision for children means the whole range of services that are specifically provided for children. Provision includes health services, social services, education and care services, and leisure and recreation services.

Services for children may be divided into four categories:

1 **Statutory services**. These are provided by the government (or state). The services that are provided are set by laws passed in Parliament.
2 **Voluntary services**. These are provided by organisations such as charities. Volunteers and paid staff provide services in the same way as in the statutory sector. Some or all of their funding comes from donations, and some are paid for by the state.
3 **Private services**. These are profit-making services offered by private providers, and include private nurseries and independent preparatory schools. They are inspected to ensure that the health and safety of the children are maintained and the EYFS is being delivered.
4 **Independent services**. These are provided independently of the state and do not receive government funding; they include independent schools.

Health services for children and their families

Most health services for children are statutory and free. The government's Department of Health is responsible for providing health care through the National Health Service (NHS), which was set up in 1948 to provide free health care to the entire population. Children are entitled to receive free health services provided by:

- GPs or family doctors
- health visitors
- clinics
- hospitals
- dentists
- opticians.

Social services for children

Most social care services for children are statutory and free. Statutory social services were brought together under a director of

Children's Services in each local authority following the Children Act 2004.

Social services provide a range of care and support for children and families, including:

- social workers
- residential childcare
- foster care
- outreach services through Children's Centres.

Education services for children: integrated care and education
Statutory services

Most education services are statutory and free. Statutory education services include the following:

- The **Sure Start programme** (introduced in 1999), which brought together services for pre-school children and their families, including early education, childcare, health and family support.
- The **Early Years Foundation Stage** (EYFS): A comprehensive statutory framework (introduced in 2008 and fully revised in 2012 and updated in 2014) that set the standards for the care, learning and development of young children from birth to five. The EYFS framework is mandatory for all early years providers (from 1 September 2012): this includes maintained schools, non-maintained schools, independent schools, childminders and all providers on the Early Years Register.
- **Children's Centres**: The majority of these were developed from Sure Start local programmes, Neighbourhood Nurseries and Early Excellence Centres. Sure Start Children's Centres are places where children under five years old and their families can receive seamless holistic integrated services and information, and where they can access help from multidisciplinary teams of professionals.

Figure 2.1.1 Children's Centres provide a wide range of services for children and their families

- **Maintained nursery schools**: These offer either full-time or part-time places for children. Traditionally these were for children of three years to the equivalent of the end of the Reception year, but there is now a move towards offering places for children as young as two.
- **Nursery classes and nursery units**: Nursery classes are attached to primary schools. The head teacher of the primary school may or may not be an expert in early years education. Nursery units are usually in a separate building with a separate coordinator.
- **Primary schools**: Children start at primary school between the ages of four and five in a Reception class. Reception is the final part of the EYFS. Pupils then transfer to Year 1 in the September following their fifth birthday, and to Year 2 the following year. These three years are often known as the 'infant school'; Years 1 and 2 cover Key Stage 1 of the National Curriculum. At the end of this time, pupils will move to the junior school. The junior school covers Key Stage 2 of the National Curriculum. Infants and junior are combined into one primary school.

Voluntary services

These services include:

- **Community nurseries**: These are often funded by voluntary organisations such as Barnardo's, the Royal National Institute for the Blind (RNIB), Sense and Scope.
- **Pre-schools and playgroups**: Many (but not all) are affiliated to the Pre-school Learning Alliance, which was set up in 1961 at a time when there was concern from parents at the lack of nursery education available. They usually offer part-time services, and offer perhaps two or three half-day sessions a week, often in a church hall. This type of provision is often the only one available in rural areas.
- **Day schools**, residential special schools or specialist voluntary groups: These support children in mainstream education.

Private services

These services include:

- **Private nurseries**, **nursery schools** and **day nurseries**: These are legally required to be registered and inspected, and to follow the current EYFS statutory framework.
- **Private infant schools**: These are usually called preparatory schools. These schools are also required to follow the EYFS in Reception year.
- **Childminders, nannies and grandparents**: Children are looked after in the childminder's home, or in their own homes by grandparents or nannies. Childminders are offered training and qualifications through PACEY, CACHE

and childminding networks in local authorities. Nannies sometimes live with a family, but not always. Sometimes they look after children from several different families.

Key terms

Scope Scope is a charity that works with disabled people of all ages and their families, across England and Wales.

Sense Sense is a national charity that supports and campaigns for children and adults who are deafblind. Sense provides tailored support, advice and information as well as specialist services to all deafblind people, their families, carers and the professionals who work with them. It also supports people who have a single sensory impairment with additional needs.

Leisure and recreation services

Some of these services are statutory and are provided by the local authority, while others are privately owned and managed:

- sports centres, children's gyms
- music groups
- parks
- adventure playgrounds and soft-play areas
- holiday schemes and activities
- lessons, such as dance and drama
- clubs; for example, Beavers, Cubs and Scouts; Rainbows, Brownies and Guides; Woodcraft Folk
- libraries.

The implications of funding for the statutory and independent sectors

Statutory services

These services are provided free of charge. Some statutory services are provided by central government and are funded from central taxation: for example, the NHS. Others are provided by local government and funded by a combination of local and central taxation:

for example, education and social service departments.

Voluntary services

These organisations (mostly charities) rely on most or all of their funding from donations. They may also provide some of the statutory services, and will be paid by the local authority or government for these services. They are often staffed by volunteers and do not make any profit; any spare income is used to improve the quality of their service.

Private and independent services

These services include private day nurseries, private nursery schools, preparatory schools and kindergartens. They are available for those parents who can afford them, although some financial support is available through government schemes.

Government financial schemes
Childcare Tax Credit

Those parents who are eligible for Tax Credits may be eligible for Childcare Tax Credit, which can help with their childcare costs. This help is based on the parents' income.

Nursery Education Grant (NEG)

The government has introduced a scheme under which all three and four year olds will get a free place at a nursery for at least 15 hours per week. This money is available for public and private nurseries, registered playgroups and childminders who are accredited members of a childminding network. The local authority pays the grant directly to the early education provider up to a certain maximum for three terms. If parents use a nursery for full day care, the grant will pay for part of the day and parents will continue to pay for the rest. From September 2014 in England, approximately 40 per cent of all two year olds are also entitled to access to nursery education.

Figure 2.1.2 Many local authorities provide play facilities for children

Research activity

Choose one of the following services for young children and their families:

- children's gyms or dance lessons
- parent and toddler groups
- adventure playgrounds
- children's clubs.

Find out what services are available in your local area. Your local library will have information to help you.

How are the services run, and how much do they cost?

AC 1.2 Activity

Identify settings in your local area which provide early years education and care. Your local library (Reference section) is a good source of information.

AC 1.3 Describe the relationship between legislation, policies and procedures

Every aspect of early years care and education is subject to legislation in the relevant area of the UK. These laws are reinforced by the use of policies and procedures. Policies describe the requirements for each early years setting, and procedures outline the ways in which policies can be carried out. For example, every setting must conform to the current legislation on health and safety. Each setting has its own policy with regard to meeting those

requirements. The procedures describe how the policy can be carried out.

AC 1.3 Activity

Find out how and when to access the policies and procedures documents in your setting. How are they produced and how do managers ensure they are kept up to date with current legislation? Make a list of the policies and procedures in your setting.

AC 1.4 Describe the role of the early years practitioner in relation to current frameworks

All early years practitioners must work within the EYFS framework. The EYFS:

- **ensures quality and consistency** across early years settings, so that every child makes good progress and no child gets left behind
- **provides a secure foundation** through learning and development opportunities which are planned around the needs and interests of each individual child, assessed and reviewed regularly
- **supports partnership working** between professionals and parents, and between different early years settings
- provides **equality of opportunity and anti-discriminatory practice**, ensuring that every child is included and supported.

The four overarching principles of the EYFS are:

1 a unique child
2 positive relationships
3 a positive environment
4 children develop and learn in different ways and at different rates.

Each principle is supported by four commitments which emphasise inclusive practice (children's entitlements, early support, equality and diversity).

A curriculum that includes all children

Most children learn in a rather uneven way. They have bursts of learning and then they have times when their learning does not seem to move forward (but really they are consolidating their learning during this time). This is why careful observation and assessment for learning of individual children plus a general knowledge of child development are all very important. In the EYFS, observation, inclusion, assessment and record-keeping will be supported by DfES guidance (Enabling Environments, EYFS). Recognising the key developments in a child is a skill, as is recognising the child's pace of learning. Children have their own personalities and moods. They are affected by the weather, the time of day, whether they need food, sleep or the lavatory, the experiences they have, their sense of well-being and their social relationships with children and adults.

Gifted and talented children

People who are talented in certain subjects (like music, dance and mathematics) tend to show promise early in their lives. The most important thing is that adults provide a rich and stimulating learning environment, indoors and outdoors, which encourages children to develop and extend their thinking, understand and talk about their feelings, and understand themselves and others. It is frustrating for gifted children when they are constrained and held back in their learning.

It is also important to remember that however gifted or talented a child may be in a particular respect, he or she is still a child. They need all the things that any child needs, and they should not be put under pressure to behave and learn in advance of their general development.

Children with special educational needs (SEN) and disabilities

Some children will be challenged in their learning, and those working with children with SEN and disabilities will need to be particularly resourceful, imaginative and determined in helping them to learn.

Case study

Children with SEN and disabilities can be underestimated by the adults working with them. For example, most six-year-old children can run confidently across a field. However, in general, visually impaired children in mainstream settings are not expected to try to do this, and so they do not attempt it. No one suggests it to them or offers them help to do it. With the right help, the child might manage it, becoming physically more confident and mobile as a result. The experience of running across a field depends on the child's development, personality and mood. Walking hand-in-hand first might be important. Talking as you go may help. The child may need tips about picking up their feet, and eventually perhaps running towards your voice. If the child tumbles, he will need reassurance, and not an anxious adult. Saying 'Can I help you up?' is more helpful than rushing over and asking 'Are you hurt?'

AC 1.4 Activity

Describe your role in relation to the current learning, development and care requirement frameworks in your area of the UK. In particular, take any opportunities presented to you to attend training sessions relating to frameworks for learning.

AC 1.5 Identify everyday routine tasks which ensure a safe and stimulating setting

How routine tasks help to ensure a safe and stimulating setting

Routines are an important part of the day for babies and young children and can be used not only as valuable learning opportunities, but also as ways to develop young children's independence and imagination. Doing things in the same order helps children to know what to expect when they are in the setting. For example, toddlers may know that, when the practitioner says it is lunchtime, they need to put away their toys, go and wash their hands, sit down at their place at the table and wait for the practitioner to sit down. Most children who have been in the setting for a while remember the basic routines and are more comfortable when the routine is consistent.

Routine tasks include:

- **personal physical care routines** for babies and children not yet able to take care of themselves – such as changing, cleaning, dressing and feeding. Physical care routines are discussed in Unit 1.3.
- **familiar daily routines** – such as hanging up coats, self-registration, hand washing, snack and meal times, tidy-up time, etc.

Although young children have the same *basic* needs, it is important to understand that babies and children are unique individuals – and that, within the routine, you should aim to meet children's needs in an individual way that supports the individual's development and learning. Even though the routines are part of a group setting's framework, routines should not adopt 'one approach for all'; rather, each routine should allow for flexibility to take account of individual preferences.

For example, babies and children have the same basic needs for food, warmth, affection and stimulation. However, there will be many differences in the way that an individual baby likes to be fed and also variations in what they like to eat. Every baby will also have a unique preference for how an adult can comfort them and show them affection.

AC 1.5 Progress check

Choose two routines used in your setting. Write a paragraph stating how each routine promotes development in *each* of the following areas:

- physical
- cognitive
- language and communication
- emotional and social development.

AC 1.6 Describe reasons for adhering to the agreed scope of the job role

If the agreed scope of the job role is not adhered to, or you are uncertain of the exact scope of your role, then:

- children may not be looked after appropriately – in accordance with current frameworks
- children's needs may not be met
- accidents could happen
- you could undertake tasks for which you are ill prepared or even unqualified.

All of this may affect children's learning, care, development and safety, so you must be very clear as to what the scope of your individual role is.

AC 1.6 Progress check

Write down what you think the scope of your role is at your current setting. Share with your supervisor or teacher and discuss if it is accurate. Why is it important that you understand the scope of your role?

LO2 Be able to communicate to meet individuals' needs and preferences

AC 2.1 Identify reasons why people communicate

When working in early years settings, you need to be able to communicate effectively with a wide range of people, such as:

- children
- their parents, families and carers
- colleagues and managers
- different professionals, such as teachers, doctors, nurses and social workers.

Communication may take the form of one-to-one interactions, with a child or a parent, or group interactions such as activities with children, case conferences and staff meetings.

Reasons why people communicate

The main reasons why people communicate in early years settings are given below, with examples:

- **To promote relationships and to offer support**: A social worker arranges regular contact with a family 'in need' and builds up a mutual system of support.
- **To maintain relationships**: A child's key person will ensure that he or she gets to know the child and his or her family, so that a trusting relationship is built and maintained.
- **To exchange information**: A father gives information to the nursery manager about his daughter's dietary requirements. The nursery manager gives the father information about the ways in which the setting will support his child and ensure that she receives the correct diet.
- **To negotiate and liaise with others**: A nursery manager will liaise with other professionals, parent groups and committees to discuss policies and procedures.
- **To express needs and feelings**: Children should be given opportunities to express themselves freely, confident that adults will acknowledge them and meet their needs.

AC 2.1 Activity

Why is communication so important in early years settings?

AC 2.2 Explain how communication affects all aspects of own practice

Although your main job is to care for and educate young children, you will also need to develop positive relationships with adults. These adults will (for the most part) be your colleagues and parents of the children. However, you may also need to interact or communicate with other family members and other professionals involved with the children.

Establishing good relationships in the work setting enables you to support other people and also to expect support from them in times of stress or difficulty. If you work alongside practitioners who you like and respect – and who you know will be there to support you – then you will help to create a positive working environment in which:

- both you and your colleagues experience job satisfaction
- children's **holistic** development is supported
- practitioners work together in a team – with the common aim of providing the best possible service for children
- transitions (such as settling in to a new setting) are managed sensitively
- parents and carers know that they can trust practitioners because information is regularly shared and any concerns are addressed within an environment that encourages open communication.

Key term

holistic Holistic regards the 'whole'. To meet or work with the emotional, social, environmental and symptomatic needs of a person or situation.

Research activity

Different ways of communicating with children

Find out about different methods of communicating with children, such as Makaton, Signalong and PECS. (See the list of useful resources on page 65.)

AC 2.2 Activity

1 Identify the main reasons why people communicate in your work setting. For each reason identified, provide an example of the methods in which communication is carried out.

(For example, in a nursery, one reason people communicate may be: 'To share information with parents or carers about the key person approach'. One method of communication could be a leaflet or brochure produced by the setting and given directly to the parents.)

2 Explain how communication affects relationships in your work setting. For example, you could look at:

a the ways in which colleagues communicate with each other

b how information is shared with other practitioners

c the nature of the relationship between children and their key person.

AC 2.3 Use communication methods that meet individuals' communication needs and preferences

The way in which we communicate with other people should always take account of each individual's needs, wishes and preferences. For example, parents and carers may express a preference to be addressed by their full title, or they may ask to be addressed by their first name.

Empathetic listening

Empathy means being able to 'project' yourself into the other person's situation and experience, in order to understand them as fully as possible. Practitioners need to be able to listen with sympathy and understanding, and give support at the appropriate time. They also need to be able to encourage people who lack confidence that other people will value what they say.

Communicating with parents

You will find that there are many occasions when you are responsible for passing on information clearly to parents. However, parents will also want to talk to you, as well as listen. You will therefore need to develop good listening skills. Try to set a particular time for parents so that they do not take your attention when you are involved with the children. For some parents, this can be very difficult to arrange, especially if they are working.

Factors to consider when promoting effective communication

The key to effective communication is the consideration of **individual needs**. Practitioners need to be flexible in their choice of communication method and to be aware of the need to ask for help if they perceive any barriers to communication. There are many factors to consider when promoting effective face-to-face communication.

Environment

Various environmental factors influence communication, such as:

- the design or layout of the space
- decoration
- lighting
- colour
- furniture
- smells
- noise.

A busy, noisy environment will inhibit effective communication, and practitioners often need to find a quiet place in order for children to feel relaxed and for the practitioner to convey genuine warmth when responding to their needs.

Personal space

The concept of personal space means the distance you are in relation to another person. It is sometimes called proxemics or physical proximity. Psychologists now believe that 'air rage' on planes and other violent outbursts are often caused by 'invasions' of personal body space. In care relationships, those giving care should be conscious of the power they may have over the physical and personal space of the person receiving care.

Communication methods and styles

Good communication involves **listening**, **questioning**, **understanding** and **responding**. It is important to remember that communication does not only happen through the spoken word, but also involves:

● facial expressions and eye contact
● body language: posture and actions or gestures which help to convey meaning
● tone of voice: this can alter the meaning of what has been said; for example, the tone used by other people to say our name instantly tells us whether we are in trouble, being appealed to or just having our attention drawn (particularly if it is our parent!)
● pauses
● turn-taking.

It is thought **non-verbal** communication is as important as talking.

When communicating with other people, it is also important to:

● take account of culture and context, such as situations where English is an additional language
● build a rapport by showing understanding, respect and honesty.

In order to meet individual needs, you will need to know how to choose the most effective method of face-to-face communication. This will include both non-verbal and verbal communication methods.

Non-verbal aspects of communication

Non-verbal communication is widely used by everyone, often without any words being spoken. Waving hello or goodbye, beckoning someone, a smile or 'thumbs up' sign convey messages. Used in conjunction with speech, they aid understanding.

Figure 2.1.3 An open posture encourages communication; A closed posture inhibits communication

Eye contact: Perhaps the most important aspect of non-verbal communication is eye contact. It is extremely difficult to hold a conversation or communicate in any way without it. A practitioner who is listening to a child, parent or carer will therefore use eye contact to express sincerity and empathy – and to show that he or she is attending carefully.

Body language: This refers to the way we stand or sit (upright, slouched, tense, relaxed), the way we hold ourselves, or our posture.

Gestures: Most of us use gestures when we speak: shrugging, shaking the head or perhaps to point to something. Indeed, some people cannot communicate without using their hands and arms!

Touch: Sometimes it may be appropriate to use touch as a gesture of sympathy, reassurance or guidance, or particularly when communicating with a person who is visually impaired.

Facial expressions: Our facial expressions are important in conveying what we mean and how we feel. We judge whether another person has understood what we are saying and how they feel about it by watching facial expressions.

Failure to make eye contact and a 'closed' body stance (arms folded or held across body, hunched body) can make effective communication very difficult. Similarly, an adult with a tense, possibly aggressive, body stance also poses difficulties in communicating effectively. When faced with either of these examples, it is important to interact and respond in a way that reassures him/her.

Barriers to communication

There can be many barriers to communication:

- a visual or hearing impairment
- a different first or 'preferred' language
- strong accent or dialect
- technical or specialist language not being understood
- too much background noise or poor acoustics
- poor lighting so that facial expressions cannot be seen clearly.

Activity

Active listening

Working in threes, with one observer, one sender (parent, in this case) and one receiver (practitioner), carry out a conversation in which the parent talks about his/her difficulty sleeping and his/her tiredness.

- In the first instance, the receiver should not give any eye contact or indication that he or she is listening – no nodding, grunting or murmuring.
- How long can the sender try to make conversation? Discuss how the sender feels.
- Then change to active listening: the receiver should try to adopt an 'open' posture, maintain eye contact (without staring), indicate that he or she is listening and, at an appropriate point in the conversation, reflect back what he or she has been told.
- Change roles so that everyone tries each scenario.

Active listening

Developing good listening skills is very important. Most importantly, **active listening** involves eye contact (or, for visually impaired people, a light touch on the hand or arm to show your presence), an open body position, an interested facial expression and some murmurs of encouragement or nodding to reassure the speaker or sender that attention is being paid. To be an effective listener, you need to concentrate on the sender and understand the message that is being sent. This is different from an ordinary conversation in which you may exchange information about similar experiences and compare them. To ensure that you have understood the message, you should 'reflect back' the main points or concerns using some of the same words and checking before the sender continues.

In the following example, the early years practitioner immediately recalls her own experiences rather than focusing on and responding to the parent:

Parent: I slept very badly last night, I just couldn't get comfortable.

Practitioner: I'm really tired too. My little boy kept crying and I couldn't get him off to sleep till 3 o'clock this morning.

Key term

active listening Active listening is about focusing not only on what is being said, but on the accompanying emotions and feelings that are also being expressed. It provides a safe structure for a child to voice his or her concerns, and to receive feedback from the adult.

Reflective practice

Communicating with children

As practitioners we need to think carefully about what we say and how we say it, and we should also be fully aware of what our body language is communicating.

- Do we look interested when a child is talking to us?
- How do we make sure that the child knows we are listening?
- How do we convey the feeling that what the child is saying and feeling is important to us?
- How could you improve the ways in which you communicate with children?

AC 2.3 | **Activity**

Describe communication methods you have used in your setting or in your learner group that meet individual needs and preferences.

LO3 Understand working relationships in early years

AC 3.1 Explain how a working relationship is different from a personal relationship

A **working relationship** describes a relationship with a work colleague. You do not necessarily have to be close friends with the people you work with and you may need to keep personal opinions and feelings to yourself. Features of a working relationship usually involve each individual working:

- in a business or professional relationship
- as a member of a team
- within agreed guidelines
- within professional codes of conduct, towards the achievement of shared aims and objectives.

A personal relationship is a relationship formed through choice – except for family relationships – with someone whom you like, and whom you may share interests and feelings with. In a personal relationship, there are no sets of rules and procedures to follow and you are able to voice your personal opinions, thoughts and feelings. Features of a personal relationship usually involve each individual forming a bond:

- with a friend
- with a family member
- within a social group.

AC 3.1 | **Activity**

Think about the differences between your own working relationships and your personal relationships.

AC 3.2 Identify different working relationships in early years settings

Working relationships in a team

Effective practice as a team member will depend on liaising with others, and reporting on and reviewing your activities. Conflicts between team members often arise from poor communication – for example, an early years practitioner who fails to report, verbally or in writing, that a parent will be late collecting his or her child on a particular day may cause conflict if a colleague then challenges the parent's conduct.

Most early years practitioners work with colleagues within a team. There are certain benefits for each individual from working in a team. These include:

- the sharing of responsibility, as well as knowledge
- a sense of belonging and a sharing of problems, difficulties and successes
- staff weaknesses being balanced by other people's strengths
- children benefiting from seeing people working well together.

There will always be areas in your work where you experience conflict or stress – these are discussed on page 63.

Developing appropriate relationships with children

In line with the CACHE values, you need to ensure that the child or young person is at the centre of your practice – that their needs are paramount.

Treat children with respect
This means you:

- give only essential directions and allow children to make choices
- set appropriate directions which are realistic and consistent
- ask open-ended questions to encourage language development
- avoid labelling children
- are warm and positive in a way which supports children.

Keep children safe
This means you:

- ensure children are supervised at all times
- ensure children are safe at all times: make sure that all potentially dangerous materials

and objects are kept out of their reach and that consideration is made to a child's stage and individual ability in the use of scissors, knives, etc.

Value and respect children
This means you:

- listen to them
- do not impose your own agendas on them
- do not single out any one child for special attention
- ensure that children maintain control over their own play
- are friendly, courteous and sensitive to their needs
- praise and motivate them; display their work
- speak *to* the child not *at* the child; with young children, this means getting down to their level
- respect their individuality
- develop a sense of trust and caring with each child and young person.

Emotional attachment to children
Early years practitioners are often concerned, or feel that parents are anxious, about young children becoming too attached to staff. However, babies and young children need to form close attachments with significant adults in their lives, and they cannot become too closely attached to an adult. Some young children spend many hours in group settings outside the home – they need and ought to develop attachments to their key person. Parents who work long hours may experience a conflict of emotions. They want their child to be happy and secure in nursery care, but they do not want to feel forgotten or pushed out; parents often feel a real anxiety when their child shows affection for their key person.

Physical contact with babies and young children
Babies and very young children need physical contact – they need to be held and cuddled in order to develop emotionally. Hugging a baby, comforting a child when they are upset,

putting a plaster on them, changing their wet pants – all these are everyday ways in which adults care for young children. However, there is a growing concern among childcare professionals about touching children in their care. Researchers say that there are anxiety and uncertainty about what is acceptable and what is not when it comes to innocent physical contact with children. If teachers and other childcare professionals are no longer allowed to offer comforting hugs – or sometimes even to put on a plaster or sun cream – their relationships with the children they look after will certainly suffer.

Your setting should have policies and procedures that will give clear guidelines on appropriate physical contact with the children or young people in your care. You must pay strict attention to them. What is appropriate physical contact with a baby or toddler, such as hugging them when upset or sitting them on your lap to explain something, will not be seen as appropriate with an older child (the EYFS also gives guidance on this).

Maintaining a professional attitude

It is important to remember that your relationship with the children in your care is a professional one. You should always be friendly and approachable but not try to take the place of the child's parents. Similarly, you should communicate with each child at a level which is appropriate to their stage of development and their holistic needs – you should not yourself behave as a child when interacting with them.

Establishing and maintaining relationships with parents

The parent or carer is a deeply important person to the child, and the relationship between parent and child is always very emotional. Emotional relationships can be a source of great strength, but they can also be challenging. It is important to recognise that parents and staff have different kinds of relationships with the children in their care.

Practitioners need to develop consistent, warm and affectionate relationships with children, especially babies, but they do not seek to replace the parents. Babies need to be with the same people each day to develop social relationships. This is why the EYFS requires all early years settings and schools to implement a key person system.

Parents and staff have one thing in common which is very important: they all want the best for the child. The roles involved are not the same, but they are complementary:

- Staff have knowledge of general child development.
- Parents know their own child the best.

If the partnership between parents, staff and child is going to develop well, each needs to be able to trust and respect the other. The self-esteem and well-being of the people in the partnership – the parents, the staff members and the child – are important when they are working together. How we feel about ourselves influences how we relate to other people.

Parents may have had bad experiences at school, so when their child joins a group setting all those past feelings may come rushing back to the surface. Parents may be anxious and suffer low self-esteem. They might expect your setting to be like the one they went to and this will make them fear for their child. This is often so when parents are required to bring their child to the early years setting under a child protection order. Staff will need to be sensitive to the feelings of parents in this sort of situation. The relationship or 'partnership' with parents is discussed in more depth in Unit 5.

AC 3.2 Activity

Think about the different working relationships within your setting. Consider also relationships formed with other professionals, such as health visitors, special needs coordinators, etc.

AC 3.3 Explain reasons for working in partnership with others

Partnership working enables different services and professionals to join forces in order to prevent problems occurring in the first place. It is an effective way of supporting children and families with additional needs, and helps to secure improved outcomes. Partnership working involves everyone who works with children, whether part-time or full-time. Early years practitioners need to understand the importance of working together in an integrated way and to build it into their everyday practice. Partnership working is also referred to as integrated and multi-agency working.

Key term

partnership working When everyone supporting a child works together effectively to put the child at the centre, to meet their needs and to improve their life.

The importance of partnership working

Before partnership working became the accepted way of working, the parents of a child with special or additional needs would probably face many different appointments with several different people, none of who would have spoken to each other and all of who would expect the parents to give a detailed breakdown of their child's disability. Partnership working is designed to cut across this by bringing together professionals with a range of skills to work across their traditional service boundaries.

AC 3.3 Activity

Explain the reasons for partnership working in your own setting.

AC 3.4 Identify skills and approaches needed for resolving conflict

Children and conflict

Children need to be able to deal with conflict effectively. This is an important life skill and will help children and young people to resolve conflicts in an assertive, but not aggressive, manner. They will be more confident in situations if they feel they can stand up for themselves, without needing others to look out for them. If you see children arguing, try not to step in straightaway. Most conflicts in early childhood relate to sharing and taking turns. For example, if two children are arguing over whose turn it is to use the computer, stay nearby and observe, and allow the children time to sort the dispute out for themselves. Only step in immediately if a child is being hurt, or is at risk of being hurt.

Figure 2.1.4 Children should be allowed to resolve conflict on their own before you intervene

If you do decide to intervene, follow these guidelines:

- Give both children the opportunity to be heard without interruption.
- Invite the children to come up with their own solutions to the problem.
- Acknowledge the feelings and emotions from both sides.
- Suggest one or two solutions if necessary.
- Acknowledge the attempts made to resolve conflict: 'That seems like a good idea, Tom. What do you think, Ivan?'

Stress and conflict in the workplace

Working with young children and their families is demanding. It is work which draws on your personal qualities and skills, and demands emotional engagement – unlike, for example, most office work. This means that the work can be very satisfying, and can lead to feelings of great personal achievement and pleasure in helping others. Equally, during a full-on day, you can start to feel worn down by the demands of the children. Teamwork can offer support, but tensions can quickly build and disputes can flare up between staff members. There may be:

- low morale – individuals may feel unsupported and undervalued in their role
- confusion over individual roles in the hierarchy of the organisation
- stresses associated with the responsibility and accountability for providing care for children who are ill or disadvantaged
- a lack of communication with superiors and colleagues
- ambiguity over which tasks should take priority during the working day
- an excessive workload in both quantitative (i.e. having too much to do) and qualitative (i.e. finding work too difficult) terms
- feelings of personal inadequacy and insecurity, often following destructive criticism of one's work.

Resolving conflict in the workplace

If conflict is not dealt with immediately and effectively, it could flare up into open hostility and then it becomes destructive. However, if managed appropriately, conflict can add to the strength of the team, leading to improved shared understanding. Wherever possible, it is better for practitioners to find their own solutions, with the senior practitioner or manager acting as a facilitator or mediator.

Staff members need time and space to express their feelings and to raise concerns. This alone can often resolve the conflict; therefore, all practitioners need to know:

- who (and when) to approach if they have a problem at work
- that their concerns will be taken seriously.

A senior practitioner or manager needs to:

- encourage open expression of opinions and be trained to handle difficult conversations with staff
- have clear grievance and disciplinary procedures to deal with conflict
- focus on what the individual is saying, rather than on personalities.

AC 3.4 Activity

Think about a situation when you have felt stressed or witnessed a stressful situation in a setting because of conflict within the staff team. Try to analyse the reasons for the conflict and identify the skills and approaches needed for resolving it.

LO4 Understand why Continuing Professional Development is integral to the role of the early years practitioner

AC 4.1 Continuing Professional Development and the early years practitioner

Working in the field of early years care and education can be physically and emotionally exhausting, and professionals will need to consolidate their skills and develop the ability to be reflective in their practice. It is important to keep abreast of all the changes in childcare practices by reading the relevant magazines, such as *Nursery World* and *Early Years Educator*, and by being willing to attend training courses when available. There are greater opportunities than ever before for practitioners to enhance their qualifications up to and beyond degree level. It is clear that the future in early years education and care will favour those who are the best qualified.

Continuing Professional Development

Continuing Professional Development (CPD) should be considered essential in all settings. Having trained practitioners in the early years setting will help to develop and maintain high standards of care and education for the benefit of the children and families while also creating a positive culture of continuous improvement.

As a practitioner, you can ensure that your skills are maintained and your practice is up to date by attending regular training. This will include both core training and CPD.

According to the Early Years Quality Improvement Support Programme, attendance at training should be, on average, more than one session in three months and have a sustained and continuous impact. Ofsted also has an expectation that staff should access training to keep up to date, reflect upon the effectiveness of their practice and strive to improve.

Continuing Professional Development is an ongoing and planned learning and development process. It focuses on what you learn and how you develop but may include a formal process of recording it (through supervision, submission of assignments, etc.). It does not always involve attending a course or completing assignments; for example, CPD could involve doing some work-shadowing, reading some information in a book or on a website, or talking to colleagues about how they handled a difficult situation. The key feature of CPD is to reflect on your learning and think about how it will influence your job or role in the future.

CPD includes:

- all training and development which go beyond the basic 'core' training
- any type of learning that you undertake which increases your knowledge, understanding and experiences of a subject area or role
- any training which improves the quality of the setting and its staff.

Continuing Professional Development is integral to your role as an early years practitioner because it:

- gives you fresh information that may help you to deal with new or complex situations
- can help you achieve your career goals by focusing on learning and development
- will give you confidence in your role
- demonstrates your commitment to developing your skills and expertise in a subject area.

AC 4.1 Activity

How do you share information and develop practice within your own setting? What are the benefits of staff coming together to share CPD opportunities and experiences? Explain why CPD is integral to the role of the early years practitioner.

Assessment practice

1 What do you consider to be the main skills and attributes required for the role of the early years practitioner?
2 Identify six different early years settings in your area, and describe their role in providing care and education.
3 Why is it important to have routines for young children within the setting?
4 Find out about the work role of a qualified early years practitioner. List the main roles and responsibilities described in the job specification.
5 Give five reasons why people communicate with each other.
6 What is body language and why is it so important?
7 How can you select appropriate communication methods to meet individuals' communication needs and preferences?
8 Describe the working relationships within your own setting. How often do you meet your mentor or senior practitioner?
9 Why is it important to work in partnership with others?
10 Why is it important to incorporate Continuing Professional Development into your practice?

Useful resources

Makaton

Makaton was developed to help people with learning disabilities to communicate. It is now widely used with a variety of children with communication difficulties.

www.makaton.org

Picture Exchange Communication (PECS)

PECS uses functional and practical interventions to teach individuals how to communicate, function independently and be successful in their schools, homes, places of employment and the community.

Signalong

Signalong empowers children and adults with impaired communication to understand and express their needs, choices and desires by providing vocabulary for life and learning.

Unit 3

Use legislation relating to the health and safety of children

Learning outcomes

By the end of this unit, you will:

1 Understand legislation and guidelines for health and safety.
2 Understand policies and procedures for health and safety.
3 Be able to identify hazards in an early years environment.

4 Be able to manage risk within an early years environment.
5 Understand how to identify and record accidents, incidents and emergencies.

LO1 Understand legislation and guidelines for health and safety

Every child deserves to learn and develop in an environment that is both safe and secure. Parents who use early years services should be confident knowing that their children will be getting the best possible experiences. There are many regulations, laws and guidelines dealing with health and safety. You need to know where your responsibilities begin and end.

AC 1.1 Current legislation and guidelines relating to the health and safety of children

The most relevant laws relating to health and safety in the childcare setting are listed below:

- Health and Safety at Work Act 1974
- Health and Safety (First Aid) Regulations 1981
- Personal Protective Equipment at Work Regulations 1992
- Control of Substances Hazardous to Health Regulations 2002 (COSHH)
- Manual Handling Operations Regulations 1992

- Food Hygiene Regulations 2006
- Food Information Regulations 2014
- Reporting of Injuries, Diseases and Dangerous Occurrences Regulations 2013 (RIDDOR)
- Care Standards Act 2000
- Fire Precautions (Workplace) Regulations 1997 (amended 1999), The Regulatory Reform (Fire Safety) Order 2005
- Children Act 1989, 2004
- Data Protection Act 1998
- Childcare Act 2006.

Health and Safety at Work Act 1974

Employers have a duty to:

- make their workplace as safe as they are able
- display a Health and Safety Law poster or supply employees with a leaflet with the same information (available from the Health and Safety Executive)
- decide how to manage health and safety; if the business has five or more employees, this must appear on a written health and safety policy.

As an employee, you have a duty to work safely.

If you are given guidance about how to use equipment, you should follow that guidance. You should not work in a way that puts other people in danger.

Regulatory Reform (Fire Safety) Order 2005

The Fire Safety Advice Centre (www.firesafe.org.uk) offers the following advice to nurseries so they can meet this legislation:

- There should be a designated person responsible for fire safety at the setting.
- There should be adequate escape routes, free from obstruction.
- The fire safety officer in the setting is required to carry out a fire risk assessment for all those who are on or around the premises.
- Sufficient numbers of trained staff should be available to enable a safe and efficient evacuation, taking into account the need to assist or carry children.
- There should be an induction process for new staff and regular training and fire drills for all staff and children.
- Fire safety notices and procedures must be written and displayed for all staff and visitors.

Control of Substances Hazardous to Health Regulations 2002 (as amended 2004) (COSHH)

This requires employers to keep a record of substances that could be hazardous to health, where they will be kept, how they will be used and for what purpose, as well as what to do if they contact skin or eyes or are ingested. In a nursery setting, this mainly applies to cleaning chemicals and those used for general maintenance.

Solutions such as bleach or dishwasher powders, some solvent glues and other materials in your setting can be hazardous. You should have a risk assessment that tells you what these things are and what to do to minimise the risks involved. Any new person coming to the team must be made aware of what to do.

Every workplace must have a COSHH file which lists all the hazardous substances used in the setting. The file should detail:

- where they are kept
- how they are labelled
- their effects
- the maximum amount of time it is safe to be exposed to them
- how to deal with an emergency involving one of them.

Never mix products together as they could produce toxic fumes. Some bleaches and cleaning products, for instance, have this effect.

Manual Handling Operations Regulations 1992

This covers jobs that involve lifting. In early years settings, this will apply to lifting and carrying babies and young children, as well as furniture and large play equipment. It requires employers to ensure staff are trained to lift correctly, in order to reduce back strain and injury caused through work tasks.

Reporting of Injuries, Diseases and Dangerous Occurrences Regulations 2013 (RIDDOR)

This requires that the Health and Safety Executive (HSE) is told about serious accidents which result in injuries needing treatment from a doctor. In addition, outbreaks of a serious disease, the death of a child or adult or a dangerous event, such as an explosion, are also reportable.

An accident book must be kept in which incidents that happen to staff are recorded. Accidents to children are recorded in a separate book – see AC 5.3.

If an incident occurs at work that is serious enough to keep an employee off work for seven or more days, employers need to fill in the relevant paperwork and send the report to the HSE. The HSE may investigate serious incidents and give advice on how to improve practice if needed.

Health and Safety (First Aid) Regulations 1981

Employers should make sure that at least one person at each session has an up-to-date first aid qualification and is the 'appointed' first aider. In childcare settings regulated by Ofsted, there is also a requirement for a staff member to be trained in 'Paediatric First Aid'. Methods of dealing with incidents involving adults and children are not the same, particularly where resuscitation is involved. Recommendations change and, for this reason, first aid qualifications must be renewed every three years.

Food Hygiene (England) Regulations 2006

The food hygiene requirements in the statutory framework for the Early Years Foundation Stage state that: 'Managers/ leaders must be confident that those responsible for preparing and handling food are competent to do so. In group provision, all staff involved in preparing and handling food must receive training in food hygiene.'

Everyone involved in preparing food for young children, or helping them to eat, needs to understand the importance of food safety and hygiene, and be aware of the requirements of the Food Hygiene Regulations. These cover what might be seen as common-sense things:

● washing your hands before preparing food
● making sure that the surfaces and utensils you use are clean and hygienic
● making sure that food is stored safely at the correct temperature
● disposing of waste hygienically.

These regulations also include knowledge of safe practices in the use of chopping boards, having separate sinks for hand washing and preparing foods, how to lay out a kitchen and so on. There should always be people available who have completed a Basic Food Hygiene certificate to ensure that guidance is properly carried out.

Food Information Regulations (FIR) 2014

Under this general legislation all early years settings in the UK that provide food for children must correctly state the ingredients in all the food that they prepare. They must also clearly state if any ingredients fall into one of fourteen food categories that are likely to cause allergic reactions. The categories are listed in the legislation and include familiar ingredients, such as nuts and milk, as well as less familiar things like sulphur dioxide, which is used as a preservative. You and your setting must know about these. The legislation also includes plans for nutrition labelling to be extended in 2016 – you must keep up to date with the details of these requirements by checking www.food.gov.uk.

Personal Protective Equipment at Work Regulations 1992

Under these regulations, employers must make sure that suitable protective equipment is provided for employees who are exposed to a health and safety risk while at work. This is considered a last resort, for the risk should be prevented wherever possible. In childcare, the most important piece of personal protective equipment that is provided will be gloves, to be used when dealing with body fluids.

Employees and students should be made aware of the need to use these when changing nappies or dealing with blood spillage or vomit. Good hygiene protects both adults and children.

Data Protection Act 1998

Anyone who keeps records, whether on computers or on paper, should comply with this Act. It should be clear for what purpose the data is being kept. Information about a child should also be accessible to the parent/carer and shared with them. It is not necessary to do this 'on demand'. A convenient time to be able to discuss the information can be arranged. Information should not be kept for longer than necessary, although accident and incident records will need to be kept in case they are needed for reference at some time in the future. Records must also be stored securely.

Children Act 1989, 2004

The Children Act 1989 brought together several sets of guidance and provided the basis for many of the standards we maintain with children. It first defined the amount of space that should be available, as well as outlined some of the principles that we now take for granted:

- The welfare of the child is most important.
- Practitioners should work in partnership with parents.
- Parents should care for their children whenever possible.
- Children's opinions should be taken into account when matters concern them.

The Children Act 2004 did not replace or change much of the 1989 version. However, it placed additional responsibilities on local authorities and partners to work together to safeguard and promote the well-being of children and young people.

Childcare Act 2006

This sets out the statutory assessment of settings within the framework of the Early Years Foundation Stage (EYFS). Among other things, the EYFS covers the adult-to-child ratios for working with children aged under eight. This is based on the age of the children being cared for. The minimum ratios stated in the EYFS are as follows:

- 0–2 years: one adult to every three children
- 2–3 years: one adult to every four children
- 3–8 years: one adult to every eight children.

Some places have slightly different ratios depending on local conditions, such as the number of rooms used or the location of the toilets if not directly off the main room. Local authority nursery classes and schools may also work on a ratio of one adult to 13 children for over threes, where a trained teacher (someone with QTS, EYPS or ETY status) is working directly with the children. Children in Reception classes in maintained schools must have no more than 30 children per qualified teacher.

Munro Review of Child Protection 2011

This government-commissioned detailed review by Professor Eileen Munro recommended a number of further changes to the way in which child protection is organised and the associated inspection framework.

AC 1.1   Progress check

1 Find out what is contained in your setting's health and safety policy.
2 Where is the policy displayed?
3 When was the policy last reviewed?
4 Who is responsible for reviewing the policy?

LO2 Understand policies and procedures for health and safety

Each early years setting will have policies and procedures which reflect the way the setting is run. Policies and procedures convey clear messages to staff members about their roles and responsibilities and set the boundaries within which they are expected to work. Standard sets of policies and procedures may be purchased, but it is important that such 'universal' policies are carefully adapted to reflect precisely what happens in each setting. For example, the procedure for evacuation will be very different between settings, according to the layout of the building and the surrounding physical environment. Policies and procedures must be shared with everyone and each person must be allowed to contribute to them. They should never be compiled by just one person and they should be regularly reviewed. Each setting will develop its own policies and procedures and these may be covered under different headings from those outlined below.

AC 2.1 Policies and procedures relating to the health and safety of children

Supporting children's safety when they move in and out of the setting

Every setting should have clear systems – policies and procedures – in place to ensure the safety of children:

- when being received into the setting
- when departing from the setting
- during outings (off-site visits).

During these times, there is often a lot of movement and activity. When children are received into the setting, several children may arrive at once, parents may be in a rush to get to work and children are keen to join their friends. When leaving the setting, many children will be leaving at the same time, parents may be chatting with others and children will be eager to say goodbye to their friends. During outings, there is usually a great deal of excitement about being in a new place with lots to see and do. Every practitioner should be aware of the policy and procedures in their setting at these times and should be clear about his or her own role and responsibilities.

Receiving children into the setting

All settings must register children on arrival. A daily register of the names of all the children in the setting at any given time is essential, not only in case of an emergency evacuation of the setting, but also so that adequate staff supervision (or staffing ratio) is provided. Many early years settings have door entry phones and a password system for parents and staff to enter the premises. The entrance should be secure so that the door cannot be left open for people to wander in and out. In some settings, one member of staff is at the door, greeting and sharing information with each family as they arrive. Some settings have a designated dropping-off area where a calm atmosphere can be created as parents and carers 'hand over' their child to their key person.

Ensuring safety on departure

Every setting will have a policy about correct procedure when parents and carers come to collect their child. Again, the register must be kept so that it is clear which children are in the setting in case of an emergency. At home time, a member of staff must ensure that every child is collected by the appropriate person: the person registered as the child's own parent or carer, or a person who has written authorisation from the parent or carer. If parents know that they will not be able to collect their child on a particular occasion, they should notify the setting, giving permission for another named person to collect their child. The child's key person should, where possible, be responsible for handover at home times. Within the setting's safeguarding children policy, there should be a written statement of the procedures in place for an uncollected child.

Safety during outings

Any outing away from the children's usual setting (such as trips to farms, parks and theatres) must be planned with safety and security issues as a top priority. When taking part in off-site visits, all practitioners (including volunteers) have a duty to take reasonable care to avoid injury to themselves and others, and to cooperate to ensure that statutory duties and obligations are met. Adults in charge of children during an off-site visit have a duty of care to make sure that the children are safe and healthy. Practitioners have a common law duty to act as a reasonably prudent parent would, and should not hesitate to act in an emergency and to take life-saving action in an extreme situation. As a safeguard to children, volunteer helpers on off-site visits must:

- be appropriate people to supervise children
- be trained in their duties
- not be left with children unsupervised by staff.

Duty of care

Duty of care is the obligations and responsibilities that people in authority have for those in their charge. In early years settings, practitioners owe a duty of care to the children in their care, and also to their parents and families, who expect carers to use their expertise to care for their children.

Unqualified staff or volunteers must not be left in sole charge of children except where it has been previously agreed as part of the risk assessment. Practitioners and volunteers should not be in a situation where they are alone with one child away from the rest of the group.

Risk assessments for outings

There is a legal requirement for settings to carry out risk assessments for outings. See pages 78–80 for information on risk assessments.

The EYFS makes it clear that this should include an assessment of the ratios of adults to children needed for outings, and it must include an assessment of the risks and hazards that might arise for the children. Each type of outing will carry its own particular risks, and practitioners must assess the risks and hazards that may arise and the steps to be taken to remove, minimise and manage them.

Planning the outing

Visit or find out about the venue beforehand and discuss any particular requirements, such as what to do if it rains, or specific lunch arrangements. A risk assessment should include consideration of potential risks in the environment, such as traffic, dogs, ponds or rivers.

Figure 3.1 Children enjoying an outing

A copy of the children's contact information should be taken on the outing, and the person in charge should regularly check the names of the children against the day's attendance list.

Parents should be informed of what is involved on the outing, such as what the child needs to bring (such as packed meal, waterproof coat) and spending money if necessary (state the advised maximum amount). Information about the child's specific needs while out on a trip, such as any medical needs, must be gathered. Parents must sign a consent form that gives the setting permission to take their child off the premises.

- There should always be trained staff on any outing, however local and low-key. Usually help is requested from parents so that adequate supervision is ensured. If the children are under two years old or have special needs, then you would expect to have fewer children per adult than the minimum ratios.
- Swimming trips should be attempted only if the ratio is one adult to one child for children under five years old.
- The younger the children, the more adults are required, particularly if the trip involves crossing roads, when an adult must be available to hold the children's hands.

Make sure that you all count the children regularly. Always accompany children to public toilets, telling a colleague how many children you are taking with you.

If a coach is being hired, check whether it has seat belts for children. By law, all new minibuses and coaches must have seat belts fitted, and minibus drivers must pass a special driving test.

knowledge about health and safety issues. For example, it is hard to imagine that only 25 years ago children were allowed to sit unrestrained in the back of family cars, but the laws since then regarding seat belts and restraints have saved countless lives. All early years settings are bound by the laws described above, and by the EYFS statutory framework. These laws and guidelines provide a framework within which practitioners can work as a team to provide an environment that is as safe and healthy as possible, while still allowing children the freedom to explore their environment in an active way.

The EYFS statutory framework

The EYFS places an obligation on providers to conduct a risk assessment and review it regularly. There is a duty to balance keeping children safe with encouraging them to learn actively.

When children undertake a challenging physical activity successfully, they grow in confidence and capability; their skills develop well for their future when they will have to make risk assessments for themselves.

AC 2.1 Progress check

- Do you know the procedures for arrival and departure in your setting?
- How do you ensure that the person who arrives is authorised to collect the child?
- Do you know what to do if an unknown adult arrives to collect a child?
- Think about the most welcoming and safe way to greet families when they arrive.

AC 2.2 How legislation and guidelines for health and safety inform day-to-day practice

Health and safety legislation is constantly being updated, in response to new research into accident prevention and increased

AC 2.2 Progress check

Health and safety in early years settings
An early years setting or school keeps children healthy and safe by:

- having effective procedures around safety of equipment, hygiene guidelines and accident prevention
- ensuring that all practitioners have an understanding of the legislation that informs good practice
- developing risk assessments that protect children from incurring accidents in the setting.

Find out what your setting's policies and procedures are for accident prevention.

AC 2.3 Roles and responsibilities when keeping children safe

Your setting's health and safety policy will contain the names of staff members responsible for health and safety. All practitioners are responsible for health and safety in any setting. Your responsibilities include:

- taking reasonable care for your own safety and that of others
- working with your employer in respect of health and safety matters
- knowing about the policies and procedures in your particular place of work – these can all be found in the setting's health and safety policy documents
- not intentionally damaging any health and safety equipment or materials provided by the employer
- reporting any hazards as soon as you come across them
- reporting all accidents, incidents and even 'near misses' to your manager.

As you may be handling food, you should also report any incidences of sickness or diarrhoea. If you are unable to contact the sick child's parent or carer (or other emergency contact person), then you will need to seek medical advice. Always ask your supervisor or manager if in doubt.

Apart from your legal responsibilities, knowing how to act and being alert and vigilant at all times can prevent accidents, injury, infections and even death – this could be in relation to you, your fellow workers or the children in your care.

Your role in preventing accidents

The following guidelines will help to ensure that children in your care are protected from some common hazards.

Guidelines for good practice

Your roles and responsibilities in relation to keeping children safe

- to know and work within the policy/procedures of the setting
- to know when and how to respond when concerns are raised
- to appreciate the guidance of the relevant Local Safeguarding Children Board
- to supervise children within set ratios
- to be up to date with safeguarding training
- to appreciate the limits and boundaries of your role and know the reporting process for successful referral
- to have the knowledge and expertise to make clear and appropriate judgements and ensure that they are passed to the most appropriate local agencies, in line with the Munro Review of child protection.
- to identify behavioural changes in the children you care for
- to observe and monitor children to ensure they are growing in confidence
- to work as a key person alongside others and actively engage with the family in order to develop positive relationships and develop trust
- to work as part of a professional team
- to engage in positive partnership working
- to contribute to a safe and stimulating environment where all children develop and learn
- to monitor children's health and general well-being
- to role model positive behaviour
- to be suitably qualified with full DBS clearance
- to promote healthy practice and healthy living
- to protect children from harm from social media, the internet, etc.
- to maintain attendance records
- to maintain safe collection procedures for children.

Guidelines for good practice

Preventing burns and scalds

- Never carry a hot drink through a play area or place a hot drink within reach of children.
- Make sure the kitchen is safe for children – kettle flexes coiled neatly, cooker guards used and saucepan handles turned inwards.
- Make sure the kitchen is inaccessible to children when no member of staff is in it.
- Never smoke in childcare settings and keep matches and lighters out of children's reach.

Preventing poisoning

- Make sure that all household chemicals are out of children's reach.
- Never pour chemicals or detergents into empty soft drink or water bottles.
- Keep all medicines and tablets in a locked cupboard.
- Use childproof containers.
- Teach children not to eat berries or fungi in the garden or park.

Fire safety

- In the case of fire or other emergency, you need to know what to do to evacuate the children and yourselves. You should always practise fire safety.
- Remember that smoking is not allowed in any childcare setting.
- Keep handbags containing matches or lighters securely stored, out of children's reach.

- The nursery cooker should not be left unattended when turned on.
- Fire exits and other doors should be free of obstructions on both sides.
- Ensure you know where the fire extinguishers are kept and how to use them.
- Regularly check electrical equipment for any faults.

Preventing falls

- Babies need to be protected from falls – close supervision is needed. All children will trip and fall at some time, but children should not be put at risk of serious injury.
- Never leave a baby unattended on a table, work surface, bed or sofa.
- Make sure young children cannot climb up near windows – and ensure window catches are used.
- Always clean and dry a floor where children are playing.
- Make sure that clutter is removed from floors.
- Make sure you know how to use safety equipment, such as stair gates, reins and harnesses, adjustable changing tables and car seats.
- Use safety gates when working in home settings.

Being a good role model

You need to set a good example by always taking care with your appearance and your own personal hygiene. Often your early years setting will provide you with a uniform – usually sweatshirt and trousers – but if not, choose your clothing carefully, bearing in mind the sort of activity you are likely to be involved in.

AC 2.3 Progress check

Think about how you can be a positive role model and the responsibilities you have regarding:

- hygienic practice when feeding babies and young children
- promoting hand washing with young children
- reporting any hazards or infectious illnesses.

Guidelines for good practice

Being a good role model for personal hygiene

- Personal hygiene involves regular and thorough cleaning of your skin, hair, teeth and clothes.
- The most important defence against the spread of infection is hand washing; wash your hands frequently – especially before eating, and before and after touching your mouth or nose. You should not use the kitchen sink to wash your hands.
- Parents and carers must wash their hands after they blow the nose or wipe the mouth of a sick child.
- Use paper towels to dry your hands if possible; if cloth towels are used, make sure that they are washed daily in hot water.
- Keep your nails clean and short because long fingernails harbour dirt. Do not wear nail varnish because flakes of varnish could chip off into food you might be preparing.
- Avoid jewellery other than a wedding ring and a watch.
- Avoid contact with the discharge (especially on tissues) of somebody with a runny nose, sore throat or cough.
- Cover any cuts or sores on the hands with a clean, waterproof plaster. Use a new plaster each day.
- Do not share utensils or cups with somebody who has a cold, sore throat or upper respiratory tract infection.
- Wear disposable gloves when changing nappies or when dealing with blood, urine, faeces or vomit.
- Hair should be kept clean, brushed regularly and tied back if long.

LO3 Be able to identify hazards in an early years environment

AC 3.1 Health and safety hazards in an early years environment

On a day-to-day basis, you need to be alert to the changing abilities and safety needs of children and also to identify and address hazards in the childcare setting. Your employer will do this on a formal basis, carrying out regular health and safety **risk assessments** (see pages 78–80). To ensure children's safety, you need to:

- be able to identify a hazard: at every stage of a child's life, you must think again about the hazards that are present and what you can do to eliminate them; this could be play equipment left on the floor, obstructing an exit or small items which have been left within reach of a baby
- be aware of the child's interaction with the environment: this means understanding the different stages of child development – for example, babies explore objects with their mouths and run the risk of choking and young children tend to run everywhere and could trip over toys on the floor
- provide adequate supervision according to each child's age, needs and abilities
- be a good role model, ensuring that the child's environment is kept safe and that you follow the setting's health and safety guidelines
- be able to use the safety equipment provided, e.g. safety gates, window locks, baby harnesses and security intercom systems
- teach children about safety: encourage children to be aware of their own personal safety and the safety of others.

How to identify hazards to the health and safety of children, colleagues and visitors

Practitioners need to be conscious of any risks in the working environment and the potential impact of these risks. They can then plan ahead to avoid hazards and incidents.

Key terms

hazard A source of potential harm or damage, or a situation with potential for harm or damage.

risk The possibility of suffering harm or loss; danger.

risk assessment The assessment that must be carried out in order to identify hazards and find out the safest way to carry out certain tasks and procedures.

Types of hazards

- **Physical hazards** are something that may cause physical harm – like an object left on the floor that someone might trip on, or a sharp object left where children may grab it and cut themselves.
- **Security hazards** are something that might endanger the security of the children or practitioners, for instance a door to the street left open so that strangers can access the premises.
- **Fire hazards** are any objects or set of circumstances that might either cause a fire or endanger people in the event of a fire, e.g. an escape route being blocked by toys.
- **Food safety hazards** are any danger associated with food. This might be undercooked meat, unwashed vegetables, contamination of food that causes an allergy or intolerance, or the risk of choking.
- **Personal safety hazards** are often related to a physical hazard; it can mean any danger to someone's safety. Children do not have a very good concept of their own personal safety so practitioners must plan to minimise it for them.

The environment in which these hazards may occur include the indoor environment, where you probably spend most time, but also the outdoor environment; this may be an outdoor play area or the general outdoors when you go on an outing. The hazards listed below are likely to be different in indoor and outdoor environments.

In the early years setting, a **hazard** may be a substance, a piece of equipment, a work procedure or a child's condition. Examples of hazards in settings include:

- toys and play equipment
- chemical hazards, such as cleaning materials and disinfectants
- biological hazards, such as airborne and blood-borne infections, food hygiene infections
- the handling and moving of equipment and of children
- unsupervised children
- security of entry points and exits
- administration of medicines
- visual or hearing impairments of children.

Risk is defined as the chance or likelihood that harm will occur from the hazard. The likelihood is described as 'the expectancy of harm occurring'. It can range from 'never' to 'certain' and depends on a number of factors.

Example 1: A door

The main entrance to a nursery or primary school may present a hazard. The risks are:

- that a child might escape and run into the road, or go missing
- that a stranger might enter the building.

The likelihood of the hazard of the entrance/ door posing a risk will depend on a number of factors:

- the security of the entrance – for example, can it only be opened by using a key pad or entry phone system, and is the door handle placed high up, out of a child's reach?

- policies and procedures being known to parents and other visitors, such as at collection times.

Example 2: A damaged or uneven floor surface

This may present a hazard. The risk is:

- that someone may trip over and become injured.

The likelihood of the hazard of the damaged floor posing a risk will depend on a number of factors:

- the extent of the unevenness or damage
- the number of people walking over it
- the number of times they walk over it
- whether they are wearing sensible shoes
- the level of lighting.

Babies and young children are at particular risk of harm because they:

- lack any appreciation of danger
- are naturally inquisitive
- love to explore and test the boundaries of their world.

You need to help young children to explore within safe boundaries, but adjust those boundaries according to their capabilities and increasing skill. Useful skills to employ when dealing with inquisitive toddlers include recognising the value of distraction – guiding attention away from something dangerous and towards something potentially more interesting, physically removing the child: 'Harry, come with me – I want to show you something…'.

Even so, no environment, however carefully planned and designed, can ever be totally without risk to children.

Older children face different risks. For example, they are more likely to travel to school independently and need to be aware of the principles of road safety.

Guidelines for good practice

Protecting children from common hazards

- All areas where children play and learn should be checked for hygiene and safety at the start of every session and again at the end of each session – this is often called the safety sweep – but do be alert at all times.
- Look at your setting's written policy for health and hygiene issues.
- Find out from your manager how to clean toys and other equipment, and remember that many objects (plastic toys and soft toys) end up in children's mouths, which is a good way of passing on and picking up an infection.
- Remember that you could also be a risk to children's health. For example, if you have a heavy cold or have suffered from diarrhoea or vomiting within the previous 48 hours, you must not attend work as you could pass on a serious infection to the children.

Safety sweeps

Most practitioners carry out a safety sweep, both indoors and outdoors, on a daily or twice-daily basis – often at the start and end of a session. This is a very useful way to assess risk. The checks are often done informally and are not always recorded, unless the safety sweep has identified a risk that then requires formal assessment. For example, a safety sweep at the beginning of the day may involve checking the outdoor area and asking yourself the following questions:

- Is the 'safer' surfacing in the play area in good condition – for example, no loose or uneven tiles? Rubberised surfaces can get an almost invisible build-up of algae which can make them very slippery when wet, so always check surfaces for slipperiness.
- Are pathways undamaged and free from obstructions?
- Is the area free from litter, glass or any other dangerous objects?
- Is the area free from animal fouling?

A risk assessment would be required if a safety sweep revealed problems regarding any of the above checks. Any faults should be recorded and reported to the relevant person.

LO4 Be able to manage risk within an early years environment

Risk assessment is a method of preventing accidents and ill health by helping people to think about what could go wrong and devising ways to prevent problems. Risk assessments on aspects such as security of the building, fire safety, food safety, toilet hygiene and nappy changing, outings and personal safety of staff should already exist. Other examples of activities where risk assessments are required include:

- cooking activities
- supervising children's use of climbing equipment
- a visit from somebody outside the setting who may be bringing equipment, or a pet animal, to show the children as part of a topic
- making reasonable adjustments for disabled children or children with additional needs, or for staff or visitors.

AC 4.1 Risk assessments within own setting

It is important to note that 'setting' in this context means anywhere you go on trips and outings as well as any outdoor space. It does not just mean the indoor space of the setting. Whatever the reason for the risk assessment, the process remains the same. The Risk Assessment Process identifies five steps that you need to take:

Step 1 Identify risk or hazard – where is it and what is it?

Step 2 Decide who is at risk and how – for example, childcare staff, children, parents, cooks, cleaners.

Step 3 Evaluate the risks and decide on precautions – can you get rid of the risk altogether? If not, how can you control it?

Step 4 Record your findings and implement them – prioritise and make a plan of action if necessary.

Step 5 Monitor and review – how do you know if what has been decided is working or is thorough enough? If it is not working, it will need to be amended, or maybe there is a better solution.

It is usually the responsibility of the manager or person in charge to devise the format of the risk assessment using the above points; he or she must then ensure that they are carried out and that the completed forms are kept to inform procedures that guide your work on a day-to-day basis.

In practice

A risk assessment

Carry out a risk assessment for a visit by a parent who is bringing in her pet rabbit to show the children and talk to them about pets in general. Remember to include possible hazards – for example, allergies, overexcited children, hygiene issues, etc.

AC 4.1   Progress check

Find out how safety is promoted in your setting. Do staff perform regular safety sweeps? Are risk assessments routinely carried out for new activities or scenarios?

AC 4.2 How health and safety risk assessments are monitored and reviewed

It is important to monitor and review risk assessments as there may have been changes within the setting – for example, new equipment introduced or new procedures. After completing an initial risk assessment, a date should be set for the next one.

This could be once a term, twice a year or annually, depending on the size of the setting, the number of staff changes, changes to the physical environment and additional equipment or resources. When new equipment arrives, a new risk assessment should be completed and the findings added to the original document.

AC 4.2 Progress check

The process of review involves answering the following questions:

- Have there been any changes?
- Are there improvements you still need to make?
- Have you or your colleagues identified a problem?
- Have you learnt anything from accidents or near misses?

AC 4.3 Supporting children in own setting to manage risk

An important aspect of teaching children about risk is to encourage them to make their own risk assessments and think about the possible consequences of their actions. Rather than removing all objects and equipment from the environment in case children hurt themselves, adults should teach children how to use them safely. It is important to strike the right balance: protecting children from harm while allowing them the freedom to develop independence and risk awareness.

If a child seems at risk of harming herself in some way, the practitioner must intervene. Then, using language appropriate to the age and understanding of the child, the adult could ask open-ended questions for the child to identify why she could come to harm. In this way, the adult and the child work together to reach a solution and children gain a better understanding of why they were stopped from playing and how to identify dangers. (They can then carry on, if appropriate.)

As children become older, talk to them about keeping safe and how to avoid accidents and injury. Children may also be encouraged to assess risks by being given reasons why they may be asked to do something. For example, when asking children to put the cars and trucks back onto the mat, the adult should explain why it needs to be done and the child learns that if they are not collected someone may trip over them and could hurt themselves.

Case study

Supporting children to assess and manage risk

Four children are playing in a den they have made in the outdoor play area, using a frame and some cloth. The den looks rather crowded and the children are finding it difficult to carry out their play. Matthew, a practitioner, asks them: 'How many children do you think should be in the den? How many of you are in the den? How is it making you feel? What could we do to make it less of a squash?' The children all join in with answers and, after a lively debate, two of the children decide to set up a den for themselves. Matthew helps them fetch the equipment and the play resumes.

1 What are the hazards when too many children are playing in a confined space?
2 How did Matthew support the children in making their own risk assessment?
3 Think of ways in which you could support children in your care to assess and manage risk for themselves.

Figure 3.2 Children playing in a den

AC 4.4 Your role in the setting when managing risk

Step five of the risk assessment process is monitoring and review. This part of the risk assessment process allows practitioners to reflect upon:

- actions taken against the risks that are identified
- the effectiveness of those actions
- any further amendments required.

By building the skills of reflective practice into your everyday work, you will develop the skills of identifying any adjustments that are required in order to minimise risks during an event or experience.

Managing risk means keeping children safe; but you must also provide an enabling learning environment that provides challenges for children. Non-statutory guidance produced by Early Education to support the EYFS, states as a Characteristic of Effective Learning that A Unique Child is one 'seeking challenge' and 'taking a risk, engaging in new experiences, and learning by trial and error'. Adults should 'Encourage children to try new activities and to judge risks for themselves.'

Case study

A breach of health and safety regulations

A child aged 16 months, who had been left unattended for 20 minutes at a nursery, died after getting her neck trapped in the drawstring of a bag. The toddler had been placed in a cot to sleep with a looped drawstring of a bag placed over the side and became entangled in the loops. At the time, she was in the care of a 17-year-old student member of staff while senior managers met upstairs.

Following an inquest verdict of unlawful killing, the nursery owner was prosecuted in the Crown Court, where the judge said staff showed 'gross incompetence' by not acting on warnings from the child's parents that she did often wrap things around her neck, adding: 'This was such an obvious risk that virtually no parent in their own home would have considered it, let alone professionals who should have been responsible.'

It emerged that a proper risk assessment had not been carried out, which would have prohibited the leaving of bags and other potentially dangerous objects within reach of children. Safety rules were poorly understood and inconsistently applied; toddlers were supposed to have been checked every ten minutes. Imposing a £35,000 fine, the judge noted that this was not a case of manslaughter but a breach of health and safety regulations, referring to the tragedy as 'an accident which should have been foreseen'.

1 What factors led to the toddler being unsafe while in nursery care?
2 What sort of risk assessment could have helped to prevent the toddler's death?
3 On a wider subject, do you think that all accidents are preventable?

The guidance also suggests that, for instance, for children aged 22–36 months, adults should 'ensure children's safety, while not unduly inhibiting their risk-taking'.

Practitioners must also remember health and safety needs that may change or be different day-to-day; for instance, the application of sun cream at appropriate times is an important health and safety need that might not exist for some part of the year.

In practice

Find out about your setting's last risk assessment and think about how you can act on it in your day-to-day role.

LO5 Understand how to identify and record accidents, incidents and emergencies

AC 5.1 Accidents and incidents which may occur in a setting

Accidents and incidents can take many forms and may include:

- a child becoming ill while in the setting
- an asthmatic episode
- an accident, such as a trip or fall while playing – resulting in cuts, bruises, fractures or head injury
- non-medical incidents, such as when a child goes missing, fire in the setting and breaches of security.

Routine safety procedures must be in place to ensure the safety of everyone in the setting. These include the procedures for registering children, collecting children and evacuation drills in case of fire or any other emergency.

AC 5.2 Actions to take in the event of accidents, incidents and emergencies

Recognising signs of illness

The responsibility of caring for a child who becomes ill is enormous. It is very important that early years practitioners know the **signs and symptoms of illness** and when to seek medical aid. When a child is taken ill or is injured, it is vital that parents or carers are notified as soon as possible.

Small children are not always able to explain their symptoms and may display non-specific complaints, such as headache, sleeplessness, vomiting or an inability to stand up. Babies have even less certain means of communication and may simply cry in a different way, refuse feeds or become listless and lethargic. With many infectious illnesses, there will be fever.

Key terms

signs of illness Those that can be observed directly – for example, a change in skin colour, a rash or a swelling.

symptoms of illness Those experienced by the child – for example, pain, discomfort or generally feeling unwell. Detection of symptoms relies on the child being able to describe how they are feeling.

Provide comfort and reassurance

If a child becomes ill while at nursery, he or she may have to wait a while to be taken home. In the meantime, you should offer support and reassurance to the child, who may feel frightened or anxious.

- Always notify a senior member of staff if you notice that a child is unwell; that person will then decide if and when to contact the child's parents or carers.
- A member of staff (preferably the child's key person) should remain with the child and keep them as comfortable as possible.

You must deal with any incident of vomiting or diarrhoea swiftly and sympathetically to minimise the child's distress and to preserve their dignity. All settings have an exclusion policy that lets parents know when it is safe for their sick child to return to the group.

What to do in case of serious illness or injury

- Call for help: stay calm and do not panic! Your line manager or designated first-aider will make an assessment and decide whether the injury or illness requires medical help, either a GP or an ambulance. He or she will also contact the parents to let them know about the nature of the illness or injury.
- Stay with the child and comfort and reassure him or her.
- Treat the injury or assess the severity of the illness and treat appropriately. You are not expected to be able to diagnose a sudden illness, but you should know what signs and symptoms require medical treatment.
- Record exactly what happens and what treatment is carried out.

What to do when an accident happens

If a child has had an accident, they are likely to be shocked and may not always cry immediately. They will need calm reassurance as first aid is given, together with an explanation of what is being done to them and why. Parents must be informed and the correct procedures for the setting carried out. If the child needs emergency hospital treatment, parental permission will be needed.

If you work in a setting with others, such as a day care facility or school, there is likely to be a designated person who is qualified in first aid, and they should be called to deal with the situation.

Remember: it is essential that you do not make the situation worse. It is better to do the minimum to ensure the child's safety, such as putting them into the recovery position. The only exception to this is if the child is not breathing or there is no heartbeat.

Recognising the need for urgent medical attention

A child who has sustained a serious injury or illness will need to be seen urgently by a doctor. Serious conditions include:

- a head injury or loss of consciousness
- a wound that continues to bleed after first aid treatment is given

- suspected meningitis (see below)
- an asthma attack not relieved by child's inhaler
- fracture or suspected fracture, burns and scalds, foreign bodies
- life-threatening incidents: for example, seizures, poisoning, choking, **anaphylaxis**, loss of consciousness, respiratory and cardiac arrest.

Key terms

anaphylaxis A severe allergic reaction that affects the whole body. It can lead to **anaphylactic shock**.

anaphylactic shock A potentially fatal immune response when the body system literally shuts down. The most common cause is a severe allergic reaction to nuts, peanuts, an insect sting or certain drugs.

Meningitis

Meningitis is an inflammation of the lining of the brain. It is a very serious illness, but if it is detected and treated early, most children make a full recovery. The early symptoms of meningitis, such as fever, irritability, restlessness, vomiting and refusing feeds, are also common with colds and flu. However, a baby with meningitis can become seriously ill within hours, so it is important to act quickly if meningitis is suspected.

The signs and symptoms of meningitis

In babies under 12 months:

- tense or bulging **fontanelles**
- a stiffening body with involuntary movements, or a floppy body
- blotchy or pale skin
- a high-pitched, moaning cry
- high temperature
- difficult to wake
- refusing to feed
- red or purple spots (anywhere on the body) that do not fade under pressure – do the glass test (see below).

In older children:

- headache
- inability to tolerate light

- neck stiffness and joint pains – the child may arch the neck backwards because of the rigidity of the neck muscles
- fever.

The 'glass test'

Press the side or bottom of a glass firmly against the rash; you will be able to see if the rash fades and loses colour under the pressure. If it does not change colour, summon medical aid immediately. If spots are appearing on the child's body, this could be septicaemia – a very serious bacterial infection described as the 'meningitis rash'.

> ## Key term
>
> **fontanelle** A diamond-shaped soft area at the front of the head, just above the brow. It is covered by a tough membrane and you can often see the baby's pulse beating there under the skin. The fontanelle closes between 12 and 18 months of age.

How to get emergency help

- Assess the situation: stay calm and do not panic.
- Minimise any danger to yourself and to others – for example, make sure someone takes charge of other children at the scene.
- Send for help: notify a doctor, hospital, parents, etc., as appropriate. If in any doubt, call an ambulance: dial 999.
- Be ready to assist the emergency services by providing the following information:
  - your name and the telephone number you are calling from
  - the location of the accident – you should know the address of the setting; if on an outing, try to give as much information as possible (street names, familiar landmarks such as churches or pubs)
  - explain briefly what has happened – this helps the paramedics to act speedily when they arrive
  - tell them what you have done so far to treat the casualty.

First aid for babies and children

Most employers expect specialised training and qualifications in first aid to be completed by employees, in line with legislation. There are now specialist courses, such as St John Ambulance's Early Years First Aid and the British Red Cross's First Aid for Child Carers. The Sure Start Childcare Approval Scheme for nannies requires candidates to hold a relevant Paediatric First Aid Certificate.

Once you have learned how to respond to an emergency, you never lose that knowledge and it means that you could save a life one day.

First aid for an infant or child who is unresponsive and breathing normally

A child's heart and/or breathing can stop as a result of lack of oxygen (e.g. choking, drowning, electric shock, heart attack or other serious injury). If an infant or child has collapsed, you need first to find out if he is conscious or unconscious.

1 Can you get a response? Check if conscious.
  - For an infant: call their name and try tapping them gently on the sole of their foot.
  - For a child: call their name and try tapping them gently on their shoulders.
2 If there is no response, you need to check for breathing. For both infants and children:
  - Open the airway: place one hand on the forehead and gently tilt the head back. Then, using your other hand, lift the child's chin. Take a quick look and remove any visible obstructions from the mouth and nose.
  - Look, listen and feel for normal breathing: place your face next to the child's face and listen for breathing. You can do this while looking along the child's chest and abdomen for any movement. You may also be able to feel the child's breath on your cheek. Allow up to ten seconds to check if the child is breathing or not.

3 If the infant or child is unconscious but breathing normally, place him or her into the recovery position (see below).

The recovery position

If a child is unconscious, this means that they have no muscle control; if lying on their back, their tongue is floppy and may fall back, partially obstructing the airway. Any child who is breathing and who has a pulse should be placed in the recovery position while you wait for medical assistance. This safe position allows fluid and vomit to drain out of the child's mouth so that they are not inhaled into the lungs.

Recovery position for an infant (from birth to one year approx.)

Cradle the infant in your arms, with his head tilted downwards to prevent him from choking on his tongue or inhaling vomit.

Recovery position for a child (from one year onwards)

1 Place arm nearest to you at a right angle, with palm facing up.
2 Move other arm towards you, keeping the back of their hand against their cheek.
3 Get hold of the knee furthest from you and pull up until foot is flat on the floor.
4 Pull the knee towards you, keeping the child's hand pressed against their cheek.
5 Position the leg at a right angle.
6 Make sure that the airway remains open by tilting the head back, then check breathing by feeling and listening for breath.

Continuous assessment and monitoring of an infant or child while in your care

Remember your ABC and continue to monitor the infant or child in your care until you can hand over to a doctor or paramedic.

- A is for AIRWAY: check that the airway remains open. Always monitor a child while in the recovery position.
- B is for BREATHING: check that breathing is normal and regular.
- C is for CIRCULATION: check the pulse (if you are trained and experienced) but ensure you take no more than ten seconds to do this:
  - In a child over one year, feel for the carotid pulse in the neck by placing your fingers in the groove between the Adam's apple and the large muscle running from the side of the neck.
  - In an infant, feel for the brachial pulse on the inner aspect of the upper arm by lightly pressing your fingers towards the bone on the inside of the upper arm, and hold them there for five seconds.

Remember: try to use your second and third fingers when taking a pulse. This is because

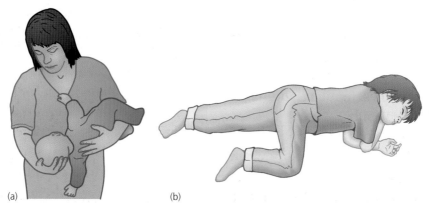

(a)   (b)

Figure 3.3 (a) The recovery position for an infant; (b) The recovery position for a child

both your first finger and your thumb have a pulse that can be confused with the casualty's pulse.

> ### In practice
>
> **Taking the pulse**
> In pairs, practise taking each other's pulse, both the radial pulse, at the wrist, and the carotid pulse, in the neck.

First aid for an infant or child who is unresponsive and not breathing normally

An infant or child who is unresponsive and not breathing normally will need to be given CPR (cardio-pulmonary resuscitation). CPR is a combination of rescue breaths and chest compressions. This keeps the vital organs alive until the ambulance service arrives and starts advanced life support.

Send for help: if you have carried out the checks above and the child is not breathing normally, if you have someone with you, send them to dial 999 for an ambulance immediately. If you are alone, give one minute of CPR, and then call an ambulance. If the casualty is under one year, take the infant with you to call an ambulance.

CPR: resuscitation for an infant who is not breathing (from birth to one year)

1 Open the airway by gently tilting the infant's head back and lifting the chin.
2 Give FIVE rescue breaths by placing your mouth over their mouth and nose, and blow gently for about one second, until you see the chest rise.
3 Place two fingers on the centre of the infant's chest, and give 30 chest compressions by pressing down about a third of the depth.
4 Then give TWO rescue breaths, followed by 30 chest compressions.
5 Continue this cycle of breaths and compressions for one minute.

If not already done, call for an ambulance now and continue the above cycle until help arrives or the infant starts to breathe.

CPR: resuscitation for a child who is not breathing (from one year onwards)

1 Open the airway by gently tilting the child's head back and lifting the chin.
2 Pinch the child's nose. Give FIVE rescue breaths by placing your mouth over their mouth and blow steadily until you see the chest rise.
3 Place one hand on the centre of the child's chest and lean over the child. Give 30 chest compressions by pressing down about a third of the depth of the chest.
4 Then give TWO rescue breaths, followed by 30 chest compressions.
5 Continue this cycle of breaths and compressions for one minute.

If not already done, call for an ambulance now and continue the above cycle until help arrives or the child starts to breathe.

When to administer CPR

CPR should only be carried out when an infant or child is unresponsive and not breathing normally. If the infant or child has any signs of normal breathing, coughing or movement, DO NOT begin to do chest compressions. Doing so may cause the heart to stop beating.

How to administer CPR using an infant and a child manikin

The techniques of giving CPR should never be practised on a child. Infant and child manikins are designed to give a very close experience to the 'real thing' and should always be used to practise on.

Figure 3.4 An infant resuscitation manikin

Choking

Choking is when a child struggles to breathe because of a blockage in the airway. Children under three years are particularly vulnerable to choking because their airways are small and they have not yet developed full control of the muscles of their mouth and throat.

What causes it?

Usually, choking in small children is caused by a small foreign object blocking one of the major airways. This may be a small toy they have put in their mouth and inadvertently swallowed, or a small piece of food they have not chewed properly.

Symptoms

Choking often begins with small coughs or gasps as the child tries to draw in breath around the obstruction or to clear it out. This may be followed by a struggling sound or squeaking whispers as the child tries to communicate their distress. The child may thrash around and drool, and their eyes may water. They may flush red and then turn blue. However, if a small item gets stuck in a baby or toddler's throat, you may not even hear them choking – they could be silently suffocating as the object fills their airway and prevents them from coughing or breathing.

If a child is choking, act quickly!

1 First check inside the child's mouth: if the obstruction is visible, try to hook it out with your finger, but do not risk pushing it further down. If this does not work:
   ● For a baby: lay the baby face down along your forearm, supporting her head and neck with your hand. The baby's head should be lower than her bottom.
   ● For an older baby or toddler: sit down and put the child face down across your knees with head and arms hanging down. Keep the child's head lower than the chest.
2 Give five back blows between the shoulder blades with the heel of your hand.

3 Turn the child over, check the mouth again and remove any visible obstruction.
4 Check for breathing.
5 If the child is not breathing, give five 'rescue breaths' (see ABC of resuscitation).
6 If the airway is still obstructed, give five chest compressions.
7 If the child is still not breathing, repeat the cycle of back slaps, mouth-to-mouth breathing and chest compressions.
8 After two cycles, if the child is not breathing, dial 999 for an ambulance.

Never hold a baby upside down by the ankles and slap his or her back – you could break the baby's neck.

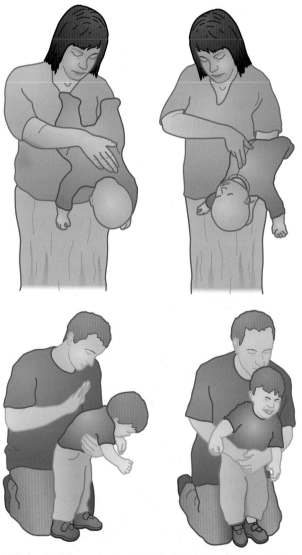

Figure 3.5 How to treat an infant or a child who is choking

Bleeding: cuts, grazes and nosebleeds

Even tiny amounts of blood can seem like a lot to a child. Any bleeding may frighten children because they are too young to realise that the blood loss will stop when clotting occurs. When a child loses a large amount of blood, he or she may suffer shock or even become unconscious.

Minor cuts and grazes

1 Sit or lay the child down and reassure them.
2 Clean the injured area with cold water, using cotton wool or gauze.
3 Apply a dressing if necessary.
4 Do not attempt to pick out pieces of gravel or grit from a graze. Just clean gently and cover with a light dressing.
5 Record the injury and treatment in the accident report book and make sure the parents/carers of the child are informed.

Figure 3.6 Treating a graze

Nosebleeds

1 Sit the child down with her head well forward.
2 Ask her to breathe through her mouth.
3 Pinch the fleshy part of her nose, just below the bridge.
4 Reassure her, and tell her not to try to speak, cough or sniff as this may disturb blood clots.
5 After ten minutes, release the pressure. If the nose is still bleeding, reapply the pressure for further periods of ten minutes.
6 If the nosebleed persists beyond 30 minutes, seek medical aid.

Figure 3.7 Treating a nosebleed

Severe bleeding

When a child is bleeding severely, your main aim is to stem the flow of blood. If you have disposable gloves available, use them. It is important to reduce the risk of cross-infection.

1 Summon medical help: dial 999 or call a doctor.
2 Try to stop the bleeding:
  a apply direct pressure to the wound; wear gloves and use a dressing or a non-fluffy material, such as a clean tea towel
  b elevate the affected part if possible.
3 Apply a dressing. If the blood soaks through, do not remove the dressing, apply another on top, and so on.
4 Keep the child warm and reassure them.
5 Do not give anything to eat or drink.
6 Contact the child's parents or carers.

If the child loses consciousness, follow the ABC procedure for resuscitation.

Note: always record the incident and the treatment given in the accident report book. Always wear disposable gloves if in an early years setting to prevent cross-infection.

Minor burns and scalds

Burns occur when the skin is exposed to direct heat or to chemicals – for example, fire, sunburn, friction, acid, bleach or garden chemicals. Scalds occur when the skin is exposed to hot fluids – for example, boiling water, steam or hot fat.

1 Cool down the area by running it under cool water for at least ten minutes or until the pain eases, or soak in cold water for ten minutes. This will prevent the burn from getting worse.
2 Gently remove any constricting articles from the injured area before it begins to swell.
3 Lightly cover the burned area with a sterile dressing, or you can use cling film, a clean plastic bag or cold, wet cloth (but not wrapping). This will help to protect the sore skin from further irritation and infection.
4 Stay calm and watch for any signs of shock. If the child loses consciousness, open the airway, check her breathing and be prepared to begin rescue breaths.

Do not:

● use adhesive dressings
● apply lotions, ointments or grease to burns or scalds
● break blisters or otherwise interfere.

Figure 3.8 Treating a minor burn or scald

Head injuries

Bruised or bumped heads are quite common in children. The recommended first aid for any head injury is to apply an ice pack to the affected area for ten minutes. First-aiders should be watchful for any deterioration in symptoms, such as a mild headache, feeling sick and mild dizziness, and should seek medical help urgently if any of these symptoms occur.

Children often bump their heads without further consequences but parents should always be informed about head bumps so that they can look out for signs that the injury could be more serious. Most settings have a special 'head bump' letter that is sent out to parents following a head injury, however minor it seems. This letter advises parents how to observe the child for 48 hours following the injury, and what action to take if the child's condition deteriorates. Some settings also put a 'head bump sticker' on the child to alert other members of staff to the problem.

Sprains and strains

For sprains and strains, follow the RICE procedure:

R rest the injured part
I apply ice or a cold compress
C compress the injury
E elevate the injured part.

1 Rest, steady and support the injured part in the most comfortable position for the child.
2 Cool the area by applying an ice pack or a cold compress. (This could be a pack of frozen peas wrapped in cloth.)
3 Apply gentle, even pressure by surrounding the area with a thick layer of foam or cotton wool, secured with a bandage.
4 Raise and support the injured limb, to reduce blood flow to the injury and to minimise bruising.

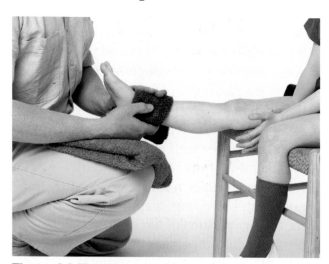

Figure 3.9 Elevate and apply a cold compress

What to do in the event of a non-medical incident or emergency

There are many different types of emergency (apart from a medical emergency when a person is seriously injured or ill) and it is important to know what procedures to follow, for example:

- if a child goes missing
- in case of fire
- if there is a security incident.

Missing children

Strict procedures must be followed to prevent a child from going missing from the setting. However, if a child does go missing, an established procedure must be followed. For example:

- The person in charge will carry out a thorough search of the building and garden.
- The register is checked to make sure that no other child has also gone astray.
- Doors and gates are checked to see if there has been a breach of security whereby a child could wander out.
- The person in charge talks to staff to establish what happened.
- If the child is not found, the parent or carer is contacted and the missing child is reported to the police.

Case study

Missing from a nursery

A two-year-old girl walked out of her pre-school nursery one winter morning, leaving her coat behind, and crossed a busy road as she wandered half a mile to her home. The first that the nursery knew of her disappearance was when her furious father turned up demanding to know why he had found his tearful daughter struggling to open their garden gate.

Fortunately, potentially dangerous events like this are very rare, but they are preventable.

1 How do you think that this could have happened?
2 Consider your own setting and assess whether it could happen there.
3 How could such incidents be prevented?

In case of fire

In the case of fire or other emergency, you need to know what to do to safely evacuate the children and yourselves. You must follow the procedures set out in your setting. In general, though, you should note these rules for fire safety:

- Smoking is not allowed in any early years setting.
- Handbags containing matches or lighters must be locked securely away out of children's reach.
- The nursery cooker should not be left unattended when turned on.
- Fire exits must be clearly signed.
- Fire drills should be carried out regularly; registers must be kept up to date throughout the day.
- Fire exits and other doors should be free of obstructions on both sides.
- Instructions about what to do in the event of a fire must be clearly displayed.
- All members of staff should know where the fire extinguishers are kept and how to use them.
- Electrical equipment should be regularly checked for any faults.

Evacuation procedures

A plan for an escape route and the attendance register must be up to date so that everyone – children and staff – can safely be accounted for at the meeting point of safety. The attendance record must be taken by the person in charge when the building is evacuated. Clearly written instructions for fire drills and how to summon the fire brigade must be posted in a conspicuous place in the setting.

Security issues and violence

Early years settings and schools should be secure environments where children cannot wander off without anyone realising. But they also need to be secure so that strangers cannot enter without a good reason for being there. Occasionally you might encounter a problem with violence, or threats of violence, from a child's parents or carers. Your setting will have a policy that deals with this issue.

AC 5.2 Progress check

AC 5.2   Progress check ✓

List six serious conditions when you must summon medical aid urgently.

AC 5.3 Forms for completion in the event of accidents, incidents and emergencies

All early years settings must follow the guidelines of the Reporting of Injuries, Diseases and Dangerous Occurrences Regulations (RIDDOR) for the reporting of accidents and incidents. (Child protection matters or behavioural incidents between children are not regarded as incidents and there are separate procedures for these.)

The accident report book

Every workplace is, by law, required to have an accident report book and to maintain a record of accidents. The accident report book must be:

- kept safely
- accessible to all staff and volunteers, who should know how to complete it
- reviewed at least half termly to identify any potential or actual hazards.

Information recorded includes:

- name of person injured
- date and time of injury
- where the accident happened (for example, in the garden)
- what exactly happened (for example, Kara fell on the path and grazed her left knee)
- what injuries occurred (for example, a graze)
- what treatment was given (for example, graze was bathed and an adhesive dressing applied)
- name and signature of person dealing with the accident
- signature of witness to the report
- signature of parent or carer.

One copy of the duplicated report form is given to the child's parent or carer; the other copy is kept in the accident report book at the early years setting.

Reporting accidents and incidents

Under the EYFS Safeguarding and Welfare Requirements: Safeguarding and Promoting Children's Welfare, Ofsted must be notified of:

- any food poisoning affecting two or more children looked after on the premises
- any injury requiring treatment by a general practitioner or hospital doctor
- the death of a child or adult as soon as possible or at least within 14 days of the incident occurring.

Local child protection agencies are informed of any serious accident or injury to, or the death of, any child while in the setting's care and they must act on any advice given by those agencies.

When there is an injury requiring general practitioner or hospital treatment to a child, parent, volunteer or visitor or where there is a death of a child or adult on the premises, a report is made to the HSE using the format for the Reporting of Injuries, Diseases and Dangerous Occurrences Regulations.

Reporting to the Health and Safety Executive

In compliance with RIDDOR, a report must be made to the HSE in the following circumstances:

- any accident to a member of staff requiring treatment by a general practitioner or hospital
- any dangerous occurrences – this may be an event that causes injury or fatalities or an event that does not cause an accident but could have done, such as a gas leak.

Any dangerous occurrence is recorded in the setting's incident book.

Reportable incident record

Incidents to be recorded include:

- break-in, burglary, theft of personal or the setting's property
- an intruder gaining unauthorised access to the premises

- fire, flood, gas leak or electrical failure
- attack on member of staff or parent on the premises or nearby
- any racist incident involving staff or family on the centre's premises
- death of a child
- a terrorist attack, or threat of one.

In the incident book, the following information is recorded:

- the date and time of the incident
- nature of the event
- who was affected
- what was done about it or if it was reported to the police, and if so a crime number
- any follow-up or insurance claim made.

Forms relating to health and safety in early years settings

The following forms are required to be kept for each child in all early years settings. They are to be completed when necessary and kept in the child's confidential file. It is your responsibility to find out where the forms are kept and to record relevant information.

- Accident form: a form to record any accident or injury to a child while in the care of the setting – whether on the premises or on an outing. When completed, a copy is given to parents and the original stored in the child's confidential file.
- Treatment record form: a short form to record details of any long-term treatment a child needs, e.g. asthma inhaler. Once completed, a copy is given to parents and the original stored in the first aid box for reference. When no longer required, this is stored in the child's confidential file.
- Medication record form: a short form to record details of any short-term medicine a child needs, e.g. prescription or over-the-counter cough medicines. Once completed, this is stored with the medicine for reference. When treatment has been completed, this is stored in the child's confidential file.
- Parent-administered medication form: a short form to record details of medicine administered prior to the child's arrival and whether they have had this medicine before (i.e. to ascertain the risk of allergic reaction).
- Existing injury form: a short form in which parents can record a recent injury sustained by their child for the setting's information and for the setting to record similar information provided by school/pre-school with a copy being given to parents, e.g. a graze or bruise.
- Register of attendance: a file should be used to record arrival and departure times to the nearest five minutes (rather than the time the parents arrive and depart) and to be completed by a parent or childminder.

Reporting to parents

All accidents, injuries or illnesses that occur to children in a group setting must be reported to the child's parents or primary carers. If the injury is minor (such as a bruise or a small graze to the knee), the nursery or school staff will inform parents when the child is collected at the end of the session, or they may send a notification slip home if someone else collects the child. The parents are notified about:

- the nature of the injury or illness
- any treatment or action taken
- the name of the person who carried out the treatment.

In the case of a major accident, illness or injury, the child's parents or primary carers must be notified as soon as possible. Parents need to know that staff members are dealing with the incident in a caring and professional manner, and they will need to be involved in any decisions regarding treatment.

AC 5.3   Progress check

- List the forms that must be kept at a setting relevant to children's health and safety.
- Make sure you know what to do if a child becomes ill or has an accident.
- Find out where the records are kept and how they should be completed.

Assessment practice

1 Describe the main laws relating to the health and safety of children in your area of the UK.
2 What do the following acronyms stand for: RIDDOR, COSHH and HSE?
3 Why is it important to work within the EYFS framework and to have a good knowledge of the policies and procedures in your setting?
4 Outline your role and responsibilities when keeping children safe.
5 Explain why it is important to manage risk and challenge in the setting.
6 Choose an activity and carry out your own health and safety risk assessment.
7 Describe how health and safety risk assessments are monitored and reviewed.
8 How can you support children in your setting to manage risk?
9 Describe the actions you would take in the event of accidents, incidents and emergencies.
10 What signs and symptoms would lead you to suspect meningitis, and what should you do?
11 Why is it important to record accidents and incidents? Describe the forms that must be completed when dealing with and reporting accidents, incidents and emergencies.

Useful resources

Health and Safety Executive

The Health and Safety Executive (HSE) is the national independent watchdog for work-related health, safety and illness.

British Red Cross

The British Red Cross has some advice on basic first aid skills for children and babies.

www.redcross.org.uk/en/What-we-do/First-aid/Baby-and-Child-First-Aid

Foundation Years

Foundation Years website has some good supporting resources for the 2014 EYFS.

www.foundationyears.org.uk/eyfs-statutory-framework

Unit 3.8

Understand how to plan to meet the needs of the developing child

Learning outcomes

By the end of this unit, you will:

1 Understand approaches to planning when working with children from birth to seven years.

2 Understand how to plan to meet the needs of children.

LO1 Understand approaches to planning when working with children from birth to seven years

AC 1.1 Why the early years practitioner plans to meet individual needs of children

The revised EYFS says: 'Practitioners must consider the individual needs, interests, and stage of development of each child in their care, and must use this information to plan a challenging and enjoyable experience for each child in all of the areas of learning and development.'

Practitioners working directly with young children have an important role. Children remember and look back with pleasure and affection on those who supported their learning in their earliest years. It is important to note that there has been a shift from making curriculum plans (which are too rigid to meet the needs or develop the interests of individual children) to 'curriculum planning', which is flexible and ever changing. The principles on which the curriculum frameworks are based inform the planning, alongside observations of individual children.

This means that the emphasis is on planning within an effective curriculum framework, rather than making a plan using a rigid and prescribed curriculum syllabus.

Your role in planning

As appropriate to your particular role, you will need to plan, implement and evaluate curriculum planning according to the requirements of your setting. When planning, implementing and evaluating curriculum plans, your overall planning aims should be to:

- support all the children you work with
- ensure each child has full access to the relevant curriculum
- encourage all children to join in
- meet children's individual learning and development needs
- build on children's existing knowledge and skills
- help all children achieve their full potential.

Your planning should be flexible enough to allow for children's individual interests and for unplanned, spontaneous opportunities for promoting children's development and learning. For example, an unexpected snowfall can provide a wonderful opportunity to talk about snow and for children to share

Guidelines for good practice

Planning for individual children

1 Observe the child at different times, in different places, indoors and outdoors, at meal times, home time, with different people. What does the child choose to do? What interests the child?

2 Support the learning: are there plenty of opportunities to repeat the experiences that the child has chosen? Is there open and continuous material provision, rather than closed and prescribed activities? Do children have plenty of choice about how they spend their time? What kind of help do the children need? Do adults recognise when help is needed, and do they join children as companions and sensitively engage them in conversations? Do adults know not to interfere when the children are deeply involved?

3 Extend the learning: learning can be extended in two ways:
   ● broadening and deepening the learning – it is important not to automatically think that children constantly need new experiences. They might need to play with the same dinosaurs for several weeks. If they do, this is an opportunity to help them learn the names of different dinosaurs, what they ate and the habitat they lived in. Dinosaur scenarios could be built with sand and water and plants in seed trays, so that children create their own small worlds about dinosaurs. This is often the best way to extend learning.
   ● onwards and upwards – it is important not to rush children into new learning when what they really need is to consolidate what they know. A child might have enjoyed cooking roti or bread rolls. Making a carrot cake is a similar experience, but it involves adding eggs and the mixture is stirred and beaten rather than pummelled. These differences could be talked about, but children will need to make the roti and the carrot cakes so that the conversation will be possible. A book of recipes with pictures is helpful – you could make these and laminate them.

their delight and fascination with this type of weather. A child might bring in their collection of postcards, prompting an unplanned discussion about the collections of other children; this could be developed into a 'mini-topic' on collections if the children are really interested. It is important that children have this freedom of choice to help represent their experiences, feelings and ideas.

AC 1.1 Activity

Why is planning central to your work with children? How can you ensure that your plans are not too rigid and that they allow opportunities to respond to unplanned, spontaneous events?

AC 1.2 Approaches to planning to meet individual needs in the short and long term

Approaches to planning

Rigid plans hold back learning: they do not meet the learning needs or develop the interests of individual children, and lead to an activity-based curriculum which does not help the group or individual children to develop and learn. Planning begins with the observation of the child as a unique, valued and respected individual, with his or her own interests and needs. We could say this is all about getting to know the child, but further general planning is also necessary because there is only so much that children can learn on their own.

Children need an environment that has been carefully thought through, plus the right help from adults in using that environment. This aspect of planning ensures that the learning environment, indoors and outdoors, is balanced in what it offers, so that it helps all children in general, but also caters for individual children.

In this way, the curriculum:

- differentiates for individual children
- is inclusive and embraces diversity
- offers experiences and activities which are appropriate for most children of the age range (the group)
- links with the requirements of legally framed curriculum documents (which include the first three points).

You could use the following sources in your planning:

- the children's interests and preferences
- observations and assessments
- the children's mothers, fathers and carers
- your colleagues in the setting
- other professionals, such as portage workers or health visitors.

Long-term planning

Long-term planning focuses on the following:

- what is known about the general development and learning needs of most children between birth and five years of age
- general provision arising from this first point, in considering what is planned indoors and outdoors
- a general sense of direction, making everyone aware of the principles, values and ideas that support the curriculum
- a particular emphasis for a period of time (perhaps for several months); for example, the way in which children and adults communicate; how to get the most from the outdoor environment; how to support children settling into the setting; creativity; play.

Continuous provision

As part of long-term planning, practitioners need to be fully aware of how the daily routines and the organisation of the inside and outside environment offer children opportunities for development and learning across all the prime and specific areas of learning and development. This can be called 'continuous provision' and accounts for a significant part of the planning process. Continuous provision includes:

- daily and weekly routines
- activities or experiences that children enjoy on a regular basis.

Routines

Routines should also be carefully planned and include:

- the start of the session, including registration/'handover' time for babies from parents/carers to their key person
- snack and meal times
- hand washing and toilet/nappy-changing routines
- story, singing and circle times
- the end of the session – 'handover' from key person to parent/carer.

Medium-term planning

This is the way in which the principles and general framework set by the long-term planning are applied. The medium-term plan will need to be adjusted constantly because it will be influenced by the observations made of individual children.

For children from birth to three years, it needs to include reviews of care routines, key person relationships and the way in which the day is organised to offer play and experiences, including materials and physical resources.

If short-term planning (see below) is effective, many settings find that medium-term planning becomes unnecessary. If the daily plans are good, they often extend over several weeks and become medium-term plans, which are adjusted slightly each day. This is especially so if the curriculum offers continuous open-ended materials, equipment and resources, indoors and outdoors.

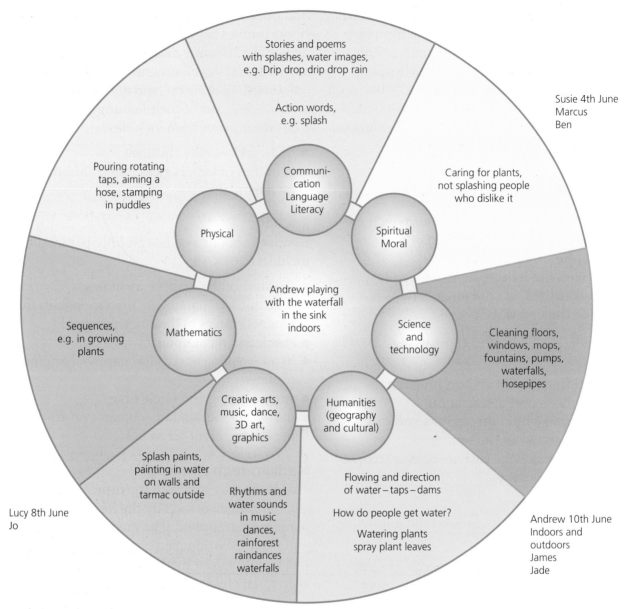

Susie 4th June
Marcus
Ben

Andrew 10th June
Indoors and
outdoors
James
Jade

Lucy 8th June
Jo

Figure 3.8.1 Planning PLOD (possible lines of development)

Short-term planning

This is based on observation sheets of individual children's interests and needs. (If a medium-term plan is used, the observations will inform how to adjust and change the plan so that it is responsive to the individual child's interests and needs.)

One type of plan widely used is called PLOD (possible lines of direction). This was first developed with staff at Redford House Workplace Nursery at Froebel College in Roehampton, and later developed with staff at Pen Green Children's Centre. These plans can be used for one child (as in Figure 3.8.1), or for several children with similar interests.

Individual learning plans

In many settings, observations are recorded in the individual learning plan, sometimes called the individual learning journey. This plan usually shows the different activities,

Case study

Observation and planning

In one setting, observations of the target child (Andrew) over a week showed that a 'waterfall' consisting of three beakers of graded sizes was greatly used. Andrew lined them up next to the tap so that the water fell exactly as he wanted it to. He had a bowl of corks under the waterfall; he aimed the water at them one by one, to make them bob about.

When the tap was turned on, a waterfall was created, which led to much glee and discussion. The long-term plan identified science as a major area for attention.

The practitioner reported this observation of Andrew to other staff members. They decided to put the waterfall out again. In addition, they provided a bigger version in the outside area, using buckets and old water trays. They planned who would be in which areas and aimed for Andrew to learn that water:

- flows
- splashes
- cascades in the outdoor waterfall more than the indoor waterfall
- flows downwards if it can
- makes a trajectory (a moving line)
- has the force to move things that are in its way.

To extend Andrew's interest, the staff planned a visit to the local shopping centre where there is a fountain. They also linked the short-term plans made for Andrew with the medium-term plan (see Figure 3.8.1) and the long-term plan, which had a focus on knowledge and understanding of the world (science).

---

organised into the EYFS areas of learning, and charts the child's development and learning by recording when an activity was introduced. It may also record the child's continued interest in and repetition of the activity and the child's level of competence, noting the skills or abilities demonstrated in each area of learning. Many early years settings now focus on particular children on particular days. This means that every child is observed regularly, and the curriculum is planned in a differentiated way to cater for the interests and needs of individual children.

Individual education plans

Every child with special educational needs should have an individual education plan (IEP).

AC 1.2　Activity

1 Describe approaches to planning to meet individual needs of children, in the short term and the long term.
2 What do you think are the advantages in such planning?

AC 1.3 Planning in relation to current frameworks

EYFS: the observation, assessment and planning cycle

The Early Years Foundation Stage, the core statutory framework for children from birth to the end of their Reception year, should inform all planning. There are no set rules about what planning should look like in the EYFS, nor about what types of planning should be in place. The only requirement is that planning should be fit for the purposes described in the revised document and meet the requirements set out by individual schools, settings or groups of settings. Underpinning all planning should be evaluative questions about its usefulness and whether it makes a difference to teaching and learning in the setting, regardless of whether a child is five months old or five years old.

The child at the centre

Figure 3.8.2 puts the child at the centre of the observation, assessment and planning process. The surrounding layers build up the bigger picture that will influence or be influenced by the observation, assessment and planning process.

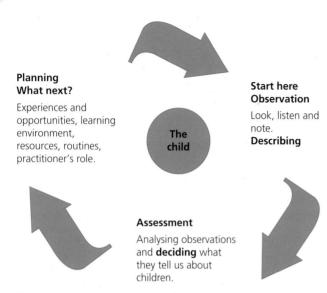

**Planning
What next?**

Experiences and opportunities, learning environment, resources, routines, practitioner's role.

**Start here
Observation**

Look, listen and note.
Describing

The child

Assessment

Analysing observations and **deciding** what they tell us about children.

Figure 3.8.2 The observation, assessment and planning cycle

Starting in the centre, observation, assessment and planning will meet the immediate needs and interests of children in the moment, in the short (daily/weekly) and medium (two to six weeks) term. This will inform longer-term plans and will shape how continuous provision is organised, the organisation of the day, approaches to learning and development, etc.

The outer layers include summaries of children's learning and development, self-evaluation and the EYFS statutory requirements, as well as leadership and management and governance structures. These require certain standards and processes to be in place and will have a direct effect on practice. But they will also be shaped by the children, families and practitioners at the centre.

The KEEP (Key Elements of Effective Practice) planning cycle

Figure 3.8.2 shows how observation and assessment inform the planning process. The cycle is a continuous one and settings adapt their provision to suit the needs of the children and families they are working with at

any one time. It is through close observation, monitoring and assessment that staff can ensure that they introduce appropriate changes in their practice to meet the specific needs of individual children, as well as the whole group. This is particularly relevant to identifying children's schemas, which can be taken into account when planning. It ensures that practitioners plan next steps that take account of a child's development, interests and needs. It marks significant points in a child's learning journey and helps assessment for learning as a continual process.

Key term

schemas Patterns of repeatable behaviour that children show, typically when playing.

Research activity

Case study: Tyrone
This activity will help you to practise using observation and assessment to:

- evaluate the quality of a nursery setting and consider how well it meets the EYFS commitments
- consider a child's starting points in nursery
- consider what you might plan to do next, in order to support the child's development and well-being.

Before you start, have a copy of the EYFS statutory framework to hand, available at this website: www.foundationyears.org.uk/eyfs-statutory-framework/.

Carefully read the case study on Tyrone below, as well as the section below on 'The role of the key person in the EYFS'.

1 How well do you think that this setting is working towards meeting the EYFS commitment to positive relationships?
2 What next steps would you take, if you were Debbie, to continue to meet this commitment?

Case study

Tyrone

Tyrone is six months old, and it is his third day during his settling-in period at nursery. His mother carries him into the nursery and they are both greeted by their key person, Debbie. Tyrone's mother sits down next to Debbie and then places Tyrone on her lap. Debbie starts to sing a song that Tyrone had enjoyed the day before in nursery and he smiles briefly. Tyrone explores the treasure basket that is in front of them briefly, putting a few different objects in his mouth, but he is not really involved in the treasure basket and keeps looking at his mother.

Tyrone's mother says goodbye to him and agrees with Debbie that she will leave him for ten minutes. She says that Tyrone may be hungry, and that she has left some baby rice in his bag. Tyrone starts to cry as his mother is leaving and he reaches towards her, so Debbie has to hold him on her lap. She starts singing again, and this soothes Tyrone a little bit, but he is not happy.

A few minutes later he starts to explore another item in the treasure basket, but his main focus is on the door. Debbie continues to sing and Tyrone moves a little in rhythm with the song. Then he starts to cry again. Debbie soothes him and, wondering if he is hungry, gets out some baby rice. Tyrone angrily rejects the baby rice and pushes the spoon away. When his mother comes back a few minutes later, Tyrone is still crying. She cuddles him, and when she offers him some rice he eats it hungrily.

The role of the key person in the EYFS

- A key person helps the baby or child to become familiar with the setting and to feel confident and safe within it.
- A key person develops a genuine bond with the child and offers a settled, close relationship.
- When children feel happy and secure in this way, they are confident to explore and to try out new things.
- Even when children are older and can hold special people in mind for longer, there is still a need for them to have a key person to depend on in the setting, such as their teacher or a teaching assistant.

We can also use observations to assess children's development, learning and well-being. These assessments help us to think about how we might work with parents and our colleagues to provide further support for children in order to meet their needs, and to build on children's development and learning.

Good-quality observations help you to evaluate your practice and think of next steps for the child. Perhaps most importantly, observations help you to get to know a child, and give a focus for discussions with the child's parents.

AC 1.3 Progress check

Assessing children's development across the EYFS

- Use a single, long observation to inform you about a child's all-round development in the seven areas set out in the EYFS.
- Work as a team to find out whether there are some areas of development and learning that you do not observe often, and think about how you will address this problem.
- Spend time talking to parents, children and colleagues about your observations, so that you gain other perspectives.

LO2 Understand how to plan to meet the needs of children

AC 2.1 Information required for planning to meet the needs of children

Every child needs their practitioners to know:

- what I can do
- how I learn
- what I enjoy
- who I am
- who my special people are.

Some practitioners collect a great deal of information about children, through observations, photographs and collecting drawings. But the value of their work is limited if they just collect information and do not put it to any use. Equally, other practitioners plan activities for children without any thought to what they have observed the children doing. They simply pluck ideas from the air: 'Let's do play dough with glitter on Wednesday; we have not done that for a while.' This makes it unlikely that the children will be able to build on their learning over time.

Planning to meet the needs of children

When children feel their efforts are appreciated and celebrated, they learn more effectively. If adults only praise and recognise results (products of learning), children are more likely to lose heart and become less motivated to learn.

Planning should therefore focus on process and the efforts that children make (processes of learning) as much as the product. An example would be finger-painting rather than handprints, so that children can freely make their own patterns in the paint. At the end, the paint is cleared away, with no pressure on children to produce a product. However, staff might photograph the processes involved in finger-painting and display these on the wall, to remind children of what they did. Or the photos can be stuck in a little booklet in order to create a process book. Children love to share process books later with interested adults, other children and their parents or carers.

Figure 3.8.3 Children who are just discovering paint also need to experiment with it – painting does not have to have an end product

Activity

Making a process book
- Plan and make a process book, showing the sequence of steps needed for children to do finger-painting. This needs to include making the paint, using it and clearing away, with the children participating at each step.
- It is important to have tables at an appropriate height. Children like to stand or work on the floor. They need to be free to move, and often they do not want to sit on chairs (although

these should be provided). It is important to offer experiences and activities that allow children to have a choice about this.
- It is best to use powder paint as it is more flexible and offers more possibilities than mixed paints, which are also much more expensive. There could be paint pots with lids on for new painters; and children who are more experienced can mix their own and use pots without lids.

AC 2.2 Reasons for identifying children's needs, interests and stage of development before planning

Effective planning for children's early learning is based on every child's individual needs, abilities and interests. This is why accurate observations and assessments are so important. These needs have to be integrated into the curriculum requirements for your particular setting and the age groups of the children you work with – for example, the learning and development requirements of the EYFS.

From observations of children, we can build up a picture of their needs and their interests. The focus should always be on the attitudes and dispositions that we want to promote through planned play activities. There has to be flexibility in all planning. Many settings choose a topic to plan activities around – for example, a well-known and popular story, such as *The Gruffalo's Child*. However, children will learn best when they are able to pursue their own particular interests, so you should be able to modify planning and adapt it to take account of individual interests. This does not mean that a well-planned set of themed activities needs to be abandoned; just that allowance should be made to take advantage of a spontaneous expression of interest in something that has just occurred.

AC 2.3 The role of observation in planning

Observation is an essential tool in planning to meet children's needs. Observation is important as it enables practitioners to:

- evaluate individual needs and to share their evaluation with others
- tune in to what interests an individual child and to see how to support and extend their interests
- ensure that their planning and practice are informed by the knowledge gained from observations
- build a fuller picture of each child that informs assessment.

The evaluation of individual needs through observation

Every early years setting must work closely with other professionals and agencies to ensure that each child has the best possible opportunities in their learning. These professionals and agencies are discussed fully in Unit 5.

Observing children as individuals

In order to plan a quality curriculum framework, the first step is to observe children as individuals. Observation helps adults tune in to what interests a child, and to see how to support and extend their interest. When children are interested in the experiences and activities they are offered, they learn more effectively, and adults can add to this and provide children with what they need.

Observation informs planning and practice

Giving children what they need means linking the child's interests with what is needed in the official curriculum framework. The role of the practitioner is to observe, support and extend the child's learning.

Throughout, this book stresses the importance of observation and how it informs the way practitioners can become involved in:

- creating learning environments indoors and outdoors, based on observations of children's interests
- supporting the individual and group interests of children
- extending the interests of individual children, when appropriate
- meeting the needs of children as unique individuals
- sharing and exchanging through rich dialogue and observations with parents/carers.

The final year of the EYFS leads into Key Stage 1. At the time of writing, the EYFS Profile sums up a child's development and learning at the end of the EYFS, using observations that make formative assessments to plot progress. It is a holistic approach, covering the areas of learning set out in the EYFS theme called 'Learning and Development'. However, there are planned changes to these assessments in the EYFS – so make sure you are up to date with the latest requirements.

Looking at the progress of children across the seven areas of learning has proved important. For example, it has been shown that children who achieve well on the goals for physical development are achieving better in pencil control in the literacy goals. There are important discussion points here:

- Early is not necessarily best.
- Narrow approaches constrain rather than help development and learning.
- Learning with quality takes time to embed.
- Children learn through a variety of richly deserved experiences, and so it is often difficult to track down their exact learning journey. Indirect teaching is powerful.
- Adult-led teaching needs to be very sensitive and based on observation, tuning in to the child at the right time in the right way.

Observation informs assessment

See also Unit 11 for information on assessment and observation.

Baseline assessment

When we first meet a child, we need to get to know them and their family/carers. We use our first observations as a way of doing this, along with what parents/carers know and understand.

Formative assessment

As our observations build, we are able to gain a fuller picture of the child, and we quite literally form assessments as we accompany the child on their learning journey.

Summative assessment

At regular points (depending on whether a child has special needs) or when the child is leaving the setting and moving on, we take stock and pause to reflect on an aspect of development and learning, or on the whole child's learning.

Guidelines for good practice

Developing your skills in observation and assessment

The following points will help you to develop your skills of observation, both as you start out on your work with children, and as you develop into an experienced practitioner.

- Plan ahead: think about when most children are likely to be settled enough in what they are doing, so that you can start your observation.
- Think about what exactly you need information about: if you are observing a baby's feeding routine and the baby's responses, you will need to know exactly how much milk the baby has, how the baby likes to be held, what interaction soothes the baby and makes the experience enjoyable, and what happens at the end of the feed. Equally, if you have pages of observations of a child's early writing and lots of examples, then you will need to plan to gather information about an area you know less about.
- Choose your approach with care: if you are building up a profile of a child, you might plan to observe the child over a number of days, choosing different times and places. You can gather information about the start of the day, different types of play inside and out, meal times, settling to sleep or resting, etc. If your focus is assessment for learning, then you need to find times when the child is involved in something worthwhile, so that you will have plenty of material to think about. An observation of a child drifting from one table to the next and looking bored will tell you little about the child's development and learning; it might be better to help the child there and then.
- Respond quickly on the spur of the moment: life with young children is unpredictable, which is what makes it so interesting. You may be busy with a hundred different things but notice out of the corner of your eye that William has gone to the easel and is doing a painting for the first time; or you might be cooking with three children and need to concentrate totally on helping them with the recipe, but also be noticing the things they can do. These are times to write a quick note on a Post-it when you get a moment, or at the end of the session, to add to children's records. Just state very briefly what important thing you saw and always include the date. These are often termed 'wow' moments by practitioners and are usually of great interest to the child's parents.
- Try to observe as accurately as possible: focus on what you see and hear, and try to note everything down with as much detail as possible.
- Take photos or collect examples where possible: subject to the policies of your setting, a series of photos of a child painting will really bring an observation to life. Photocopy a child's early attempts at writing his name, as well as observing how he did this.
- Share your thoughts with others: ask the child to talk to you about what you observed, share the observation with a colleague and talk to the child's parents. You will deepen your understanding by doing this.

AC 2.4 Devising a plan to meet the needs of an individual child

Devising a plan

The following guidelines will help you to develop a plan to meet the developmental needs of an individual child:

- Having used different observational techniques, make an assessment of a child's developmental needs. Remember confidentiality and anti-bias practice.
- Encourage the child to take responsibility for his or her own development plan. Even young children can help in planning activities by suggesting things they enjoy doing.
- Involve parents or carers in the assessment of their children.
- Devise a structure for the plan (your setting may use a regular format for plans). Include the following details:
  - the date and the child's name
  - the aim and purpose
  - the period of time involved, or timescale
  - the activities suggested to meet the child's needs, including a list of resources
  - the targets or goals to use in order to measure the success of the plan
  - the name of the person/s responsible for implementing the plan
  - the date for review of the plan.

Implementing the plan

Many plans are drawn up in consultation with colleagues – either individual plans or those focused more broadly on a whole group or class of children. Practitioners should ensure that they prepare for the plan to be implemented: for example, by organising a time slot, providing equipment and resources, arranging for others to help if necessary, and so on.

Evaluating and revising the plan

The plan should be evaluated by considering whether the targets or aims were fully met or only partially met. You should also **evaluate** it in terms of how enjoyable it was for the child.

Having evaluated the plan, you then need to consider if it could be improved; it is important to let children have a role in reviewing the plan and in suggesting possible changes.

> ### Key term
> **evaluate** Describe and summarise in relation to advantages and disadvantages.

> ### AC 2.4 Progress check
> Describe how you plan provision to promote children's learning and development in your setting. Include examples of any planning sheets you use.

AC 2.5 Why the early years practitioner involves others in planning

Planning work also involves working with other people (for example, parents, carers, colleagues and other professionals) to deliver the appropriate framework for the children in your setting. You should regularly check and discuss the progress of children with parents, carers and colleagues. Seek additional support, especially if children are not progressing as expected – for example, by consulting other professionals as appropriate.

- Observe: remember to observe the children while they are involved in the learning activities and assess whether you need to change or extend these activities to meet their early learning and developmental needs more fully. Children's responses should also be considered when providing support for learning activities.
- Be sensitive to children's needs and preferences: you should take notice of non-verbal responses and preferences demonstrated by the children; these are just as important as what they say. Remember to give the children positive

encouragement and feedback to reinforce and sustain their interest and efforts in the learning process.

- Modifying or extending activities: you can use children's positive or negative responses to modify or extend activities to meet each child's needs more effectively. For example, if the learning intentions prove too easy or too difficult, you may have to set new goals. By breaking down learning activities into smaller tasks, you may help individual children to achieve success more quickly.
- Planning, implementing and evaluating: by changing plans you are continuing a cycle of planning and implementing activities. After the learning activities, you should use all the available relevant information to evaluate the effectiveness of your planning and implementation of the activity; this might include responses from parents, carers, colleagues and other professionals.

Home–setting diaries

These are a useful way of including parents and carers in the observation/assessment/planning cycle.

- They can be completed daily or weekly and include significant events throughout the day for the child concerned.
- They should be easily accessed by parents and enable both practitioners and parents to gain an insight into both the setting and the child's home life and how parents and practitioners can work together to further support the child.
- Some settings use a combined diary and reading record for Reception-aged children. This ensures information can be passed between home and setting in a multipurpose way.
- Other settings may use home–setting diaries only on a short-term basis – for example, for a child who has found it difficult to settle.

Learning journeys

Learning journeys (sometimes referred to as learning journals) are used in early years settings. The term refers to a collection of different documents collected by early years practitioners which:

- provide a picture of a child's development under the areas of learning identified in the EYFS
- consist of photos, artwork, mark-making, etc.
- should be combined with observations made by practitioners, including notes of relevant conversations or comments made by the child.

Practitioners should match any observations to the EYFS curriculum guidance. The aim of a learning journey is to build a unique picture of what each child knows, feels and is able to do – as well as his or her particular interests and learning style. This picture can then be used to identify learning priorities and plan appropriate learning experiences.

AC 2.5 Progress check

Explain why it is important to involve others in planning for the next steps of children's development.

AC 2.6 Reasons for tracking children's progress

Careful observations enable you and your colleagues to make objective assessments concerning children and their individual care needs, behaviour patterns, levels of development, skills/abilities and learning needs and achievements. Assessment of this information can help highlight and celebrate a child's strengths, as well as identify any gaps in their learning. This can then form the basis for the ongoing planning of appropriate care routines, play opportunities and learning activities, and they may also be a useful starting point for future learning goals.

Assessing and recording

You should draw on everyday observations and your knowledge of individual children to inform your assessments. After you have provided play and learning activities, you will need to assess and record the child's progress. Some assessment and recording may occur during the activities, providing continuous assessment of each child's performance (for example, child observations and checklists). Some assessment and recording may occur shortly afterwards (for example, record sheets and formal assessments). It is important to assess and record children's progress so that you can:

- discover if the activity has been successful (have the aims and learning outcomes been met?)
- consider how the activity might be modified/adapted to meet the needs of the child or children
- inform a senior practitioner, teacher, special educational needs coordinator (SENCO) or other professional whether or not a particular activity has been successful.

Methods of recording children's learning and development

Effective recording of children's learning and development should:

- be clear and concise
- be dated and signed or initialled by the practitioner
- be positive in tone and describe children's individual achievements and progress
- reflect the whole child's learning and development
- highlight significant moments within each area of learning
- involve and inform the EYFS team in the setting and also the child's parents and carers
- show clear next steps and the results of the follow-up
- be flexible and take a variety of forms including Post-its, annotated photographs, short observations, learning stories, longer observations, group observations, evidence from home, annotated pictures and collages and quotes
- be manageable and part of each adult's role and daily routine.

Many settings create learning journeys, learning stories, learning diaries and other forms of documentation relating to a child's time in a setting. The purpose of these varies depending on the setting.

Assessment in the 2014 EYFS

Assessment in the 2014 EYFS plays an important part in helping parents and practitioners to understand children's needs and plan activities to meet them, supporting children's progress. It is particularly important that parents are left in no doubt about their child's progress and development, and that learning and development needs are identified early and addressed in partnership with parents and other relevant practitioners. Early years providers must assess young children's progress on an ongoing basis, and also complete assessments at two specific points, as described below.

EYFS Progress Check: summary of development at 24–36 months

Early years practitioners must supply parents or carers with a short written summary of their child's development at 24–36 months. Known as the EYFS Progress Check, the content of this summary of development must be based on the three prime areas of learning: personal, social and emotional development; physical development; and communication and language (see Table 3.8.1). Beyond these areas, it is for practitioners to decide what the summary should include, reflecting the developmental level and needs of each individual child.

The written summary must:

- highlight observations about a child's development, noting areas where a child is progressing well, but particularly focusing on any areas where practitioners are concerned that a child may have a developmental delay, special educational need or disability

- describe the activities and strategies the provider intends to adopt to address any issues or concerns.

Practitioners should discuss with parents how the summary of development can be used to support learning at home. They should also encourage parents to share the summary of progress with other relevant professionals, where necessary.

The concept driving this is the idea that the earlier children receive tailored support to catch up, the stronger their later chances of healthy development. A targeted plan to support a child's future learning and development in the setting will help to ensure a good level of achievement by age five so that the child is well prepared for school.

The EYFS Profile

The second point at which a report on progress is required is the final term of the year in which the child reaches age five, and no later than 30 June in that term. At this point, the EYFS Profile must be completed for each child.

The EYFS Profile:

- provides parents, practitioners and teachers with a well-rounded picture of a child's

knowledge, understanding and abilities, their progress against expected levels and their readiness for school
- helps teachers to plan activities for children starting Key Stage 1
- must reflect ongoing observation and should also take account of all relevant records held by the setting, and of any discussions with parents and other relevant adults.

Each child's level of development must be assessed (and recorded) against the 17 early learning goals. Practitioners must indicate whether children are meeting expected levels of development, exceeding expected levels or not yet reaching expected levels ('expected', 'exceeding' or 'emerging'). The 'expected' levels are the early learning goals (ELGs). See Table 3.8.1.

The Profile must be completed for all children, including those with special educational needs and disabilities. Children will have differing levels of skills and abilities across the Profile and it is important that there is a full assessment of all areas of their development to inform plans for future activities. Parents, carers and practitioners working with the child need to have a clear, rounded picture of all the child's needs.

Table 3.8.1 Early learning goals

Aspect	Expected level of development (ELGs)
Personal, social and emotional development	
Self-confidence and self-awareness	Children are confident to try out new activities and can say why they like some more than others. They are confident to speak in a familiar group and will talk about their ideas, and choose the resources they need for activities they have decided on. They can say when they do or do not need help.
Managing feelings and behaviour	Children can talk about how they and others show feelings and know that not all behaviours are acceptable. They can talk about their own and others' behaviour and its consequences. They can work as part of a group or class and understand and follow the rules. They can adjust their behaviour to different situations and take changes in routine in their stride. ➔

Table 3.8.1 Early learning goals   (*continued*)

Aspect	Expected level of development (ELGs)
Making relationships	Children can play cooperatively, taking turns when playing. They can take account of one another's ideas about how to organise their activity. They can show sensitivity to the needs and feelings of others and form positive relationships with adults and other children.
Physical development	
Moving and handling	Children show good control and coordination in large and small movements. They move confidently in a range of ways, safely negotiating space. They handle equipment and tools effectively, including pencils for writing.
Health and self-care	Children know the importance for good health of physical exercise and a healthy diet and can talk about ways to keep healthy and safe. They can manage their own basic hygiene and personal needs successfully, including dressing and going to the toilet independently.
Communication and language	
Listening and attention	Children listen attentively in a range of situations. They listen to stories, accurately anticipating key events, and respond to what they hear with relevant comments, questions or actions. They can give their attention to what is being said to them and respond appropriately, while remaining involved in an activity.
Understanding	Children can follow instructions involving several ideas or actions. They answer 'how' and 'why' questions about their experiences and in response to stories or events.
Speaking	Children express themselves effectively, showing awareness of listeners' needs. They use past, present and future forms accurately when talking about events that have happened or are to happen in the future. They develop their own narratives and explanations by connecting ideas or events.
Literacy	
Reading	Children read and understand simple sentences in stories and information books, using phonic knowledge to decode regular words and read them aloud accurately. They demonstrate understanding when talking with others about what they have read or what has been read to them.
Writing	Children write their own labels, captions, messages and simple stories which can be read by themselves and others. They use their phonic knowledge to spell words in ways which match their spoken sounds and make use of high-frequency spellings. →

Table 3.8.1 Early learning goals   (*continued*)

Aspect	Expected level of development (ELGs)
Mathematics	
Numbers	Children use numbers up to ten in order to do simple addition and subtraction to solve practical problems. They can find a total by counting on and can calculate how many are left from a larger number by counting back.
Shape, space and measures	Children use everyday language to describe and compare size, weight, capacity, time, position and distance. They know and talk about patterns and the properties of flat and solid shapes.
Understanding the world	
People and communities	Children talk about past and present events in their own lives and the lives of family members. They know that other children do not always enjoy the same things and are sensitive to this. They know about similarities and differences between themselves and others, and among families, communities and traditions.
The world	Children know about similarities and differences in relation to places, objects, materials and living things. They can talk about the features of their own immediate environment and how environments might vary from one another. They can make observations of animals and plants and explain why some things occur, and talk about changes, including in simple experiments.
Technology	Children recognise that a range of technology is used in places such as homes and schools. They select and use technology for particular purposes.
Expressive arts and design	
Exploring and using media and materials	Children sing songs, make music and dance and experiment with ways of changing them. They use and explore a variety of materials, experimenting with colour, design, texture, shape and form.
Being imaginative	Children use what they have learned about media and materials in purposeful and original ways. They represent their own ideas, thoughts and feelings through art and design, music, dance, role play and stories.

AC 2.6   Progress check

Why is it important to track children's progress?

Assessment practice

1 Why is it important to plan to meet the individual needs of children? Give three reasons.
2 What is meant by long-term planning? And short-term planning?
3 What is the role of planning in relation to current frameworks?
4 What information does the early years practitioner need in order to plan to meet the needs of children? How is such information gathered in your setting?
5 Why is it important to identify children's needs, interests and stage of development before you begin planning?
6 Describe four benefits of observation to planning.
7 Devise a plan to meet the needs of an individual child.
8 Why is it important to involve others when planning for the next stage of children's development?
9 Why is it important to track children's progress, and how is this achieved in your setting?

Useful resources

Bartholomew, L. and Bruce, T. (1993) *Getting to Know You: A Guide to Record-keeping in Early Childhood Education and Care*, London: Hodder & Stoughton.

Berk, L.E. (2006) *Child Development* (7th edn), Boston, MA: Pearson International Edition.

Bertram, T. and Pascal, C. (1997) *Effective Early Learning: Case Studies in Improvement*, London: Hodder & Stoughton.

Bruce, T. (2005) *Early Childhood Education and Care* (3rd edn), London: Hodder Arnold.

Dahlberg, G., Moss, P. and Pence, A. (2007) *Beyond Quality in Early Childhood Education and Care: Languages of Evaluation*, London: Routledge.

Elfer, P. and Grenier, J. (2010) 'Personal, social and emotional development', in Bruce, T. (ed.) *Early Childhood: A Guide for Students*, London: Sage.

Early Years Foundation Stage

The government's website includes all the statutory requirements for the EYFS, as well as guidance. Go to the website and search for 'Early Years Foundation Stage'.

www.education.gov.uk

Early Years Foundation Stage Profile videos

Expertly selected video footage of children learning in the EYFS, together with notes and guidance.

Unit 4

Use legislation relating to equality, diversity and inclusive practice

Learning outcomes

By the end of this unit, you will:

1 Understand how legislation and codes of practice inform equality, diversity and inclusive practice.
2 Understand how policies and procedures inform equality, diversity and inclusive practice.

3 Know how to access information, advice and support about equality, diversity and inclusion.
4 Be able to work in ways which support equality, diversity and inclusive practice.

LO1 Understand how legislation and codes of practice inform equality, diversity and inclusive practice

As a practitioner, you have a role to play in ensuring that, in all aspects of your work, every person is given real opportunities to thrive, and that any barriers that prevent them from reaching their full potential are removed. The principles of equality and inclusion are at the heart of work with children in every kind of setting.

AC 1.1 What are meant by equality, diversity, inclusion and discrimination?

Defining important principles

Equality

Equality does not mean that everyone has to be treated the same. People have different needs, situations and ambitions. Early years practitioners have a part to play in supporting children to live in the way that they value and choose, to be 'themselves' and to be different if they wish. Every person should have equality of opportunity.

Diversity

Diversity refers to the differences in values, attitudes, cultures, beliefs, skills and life experience of each individual in any group of people. In the UK, early years curriculum frameworks emphasise the importance of developing every child's sense of identity and promoting a positive sense of pride in each child's family origins. Starting with themselves, young children can develop a sense of belonging to the local community and begin to understand and respect less familiar cultures.

Inclusion

Inclusion is a term used within education to describe the process of ensuring the equality of learning opportunities for all children, whatever their disabilities or disadvantages. This means that all children have the right to have their needs met in the best way for them. They are seen as being part of the community, even if they need particular help to live a full life within the community.

Discrimination

Discrimination occurs when someone is treated less favourably, usually because of a negative view of some of their characteristics.

For example, an individual may be prejudiced in relation to race, age or gender. This negative view is based on assumptions that do not have a factual basis.

Children may discriminate against other children on account of their differences. This often takes the form of name-calling and teasing, and may be directed at children who are either fatter or thinner than others in the group, or who wear different clothes.

Discrimination in the work setting

Stereotypes and labels can lead to discrimination. It is important to avoid labelling or stereotyping people. Stereotyped thinking can prevent you from seeing someone as an individual with particular life experiences and interests, and can lead to negative attitudes, prejudice and discrimination. Examples are:

- Racism or racial discrimination: the belief that some 'races' are superior to others – based on the false idea that different physical characteristics (like skin colour) or ethnic background make some people better than others. An example of racial discrimination is refusing a child a nursery place because they are black.
- Cultural and religious discrimination: examples of these would be failing to address the needs of children from a minority religious or cultural group, such as children from traveller families; or only acknowledging festivals from mainstream culture, such as Christmas and Easter.
- Sexism and sex discrimination: these occur when people of one gender reinforce the

stereotype that they are superior to the other. For example, boys are routinely offered more opportunities for 'rough-and-tumble' play than girls, while some early years workers may encourage girls to perform traditional 'female' tasks, such as cooking and washing.

- Ageism and age discrimination: negative feelings are expressed towards a person or group because of their age. In Western society, it is usually directed towards older people; however, it can affect young people too.
- Disablism and disability discrimination: disabled people are often seen in terms of their disability, rather than as unique individuals who happen to have special needs. Children and young people with disabilities or impairments may be denied equality of opportunity with their non-disabled peers. For example, failing to provide children with special needs with appropriate facilities and services, or organising activities in a nursery setting in a way that ignores the special physical, intellectual and emotional needs of certain children.

There are many other stereotypes that can lead to discrimination, such as those concerning gay and lesbian groups, people from low socio-economic groups and those who practise a minority religion.

Key term

stereotype A way of thinking that assumes that all people who share one characteristic also share another set of characteristics.

Scenarios

Making assumptions

1 Sam, Jason, Laura and Fatima are playing in the role-play area. The nursery teacher asks Sam and Jason to tidy away the train set and trucks, and asks Laura and Fatima to put the dolls and cooking pots away, as it is nearly story time.

   The assumption here is that dolls and cooking utensils are 'girl' playthings, whereas trains and trucks are 'boy' playthings. The teacher is reinforcing this stereotype by separating the tasks by gender.

2 Paul's mother arrives at the school open day. She is in a wheelchair, being pushed by Paul's father. The teacher welcomes the parents and then asks Paul's father if his wife would like a drink and a biscuit.

   This is a common feature of daily life for people who use wheelchairs. They are often ignored and questions are addressed to their companion, often because the other person is embarrassed by the unusual situation and afraid of making a mistake. The assumption here is that the person in the wheelchair would not be able to understand and reply to what is said to them.

3 Members of staff are having a tea break and discussing a new child who has just started at their school. Julie says, 'I can't stand the way these travellers think they can just turn up at school whenever they feel like it – they don't pay taxes, you know, and they live practically on top of rubbish dumps… poor little mite, he doesn't know any different.'

   An assumption has been made which is based on prejudice and stereotyped thinking; in this case, travellers are assumed to be 'scroungers' and to live in unhygienic conditions. Such attitudes will be noticed by all the children in the class and may result in the individual child being treated differently, damaging their self-esteem and leading to feelings of rejection.

4 Harry's mother is a registered heroin addict who has been attending a drug rehabilitation programme for the last few months. Whenever Harry behaves in an aggressive way to other children or to staff, one staff member always makes a jibe about his home life: 'Harry, you may get away with that sort of thing where you come from, but it won't work here. We know all about you.'

   This is an extreme and very unkind form of stereotyping. It is assuming that, because his mother is a drug user, Harry is somehow less worthy of consideration and respect. By drawing attention to his home life, the member of staff is guilty of prejudice and discriminatory behaviour. There is also a breach of the policy of confidentiality.

Key terms

anti-discrimination An approach which challenges unfair or unlawful treatment of individuals or groups based on a specific characteristic of that group, such as colour, age, disability, sexual orientation, etc.

direct discrimination Treating a person less favourably than others in the same or similar circumstances.

diversity The differences in values, attitudes, cultures, beliefs, skills, knowledge and life experience of each individual in any group of people.

equality Making sure that everyone has a chance to take part in society on an equal basis and to be treated appropriately, regardless of his or her gender, race, disability, age, sexual orientation, language, social origin, religious beliefs, marital status and other personal attributes.

inclusion Ensuring that every child, young person, adult or learner is given equality of opportunity to access education and care by meeting his or her specific needs.

inclusive practice The process of identifying, understanding and breaking down barriers to participation and belonging.

indirect discrimination When an organisation has certain practices or procedures that have the effect of disadvantaging particular groups of people.

Case study

The effects of labelling: Harry, my son

When I first met Harry, he was my son. A year later, he was epileptic and developmentally delayed. By 18 months, he had special needs and he was a 'special' child. I was told not to think about his future. My husband and I struggled to come to terms with all this. By the time he was four, Harry had special educational needs and was a 'statemented' child. He was epileptic, dyspraxic, developmentally delayed and had severe and complex communication problems. Two years later, aged six, he was severely epileptic, had cerebral palsy and had communication difficulties. At eight, he had severe epilepsy with associated communication problems; he was showing a marked developmental regression and he had severe learning difficulties. At nine, he came out of segregated schooling and he slowly became my son again. Never again will he be anything but Harry – a son, a brother, a friend, a pupil, a teacher, a person.

1 How many different labels can you identify in this short account?
2 Why do you think Harry's mother felt she had 'lost' her son?

The effects of discrimination on children's development

Discrimination of any kind prevents children from developing feelings of self-worth or self-esteem. The effects of being discriminated against can last the whole of a child's life. In particular, they may:

- be unable to fulfil their potential because they are made to feel that their efforts are not valued or recognised by others
- find it hard to form relationships with others
- be so affected by the stereotypes or labels applied to them that they start to believe in them and so behave in accordance with others' expectations. This then becomes a self-fulfilling prophecy: for example, if a child is repeatedly told that he is clumsy, he may act in a clumsy way even when quite capable of acting otherwise
- feel shame about their own cultural background
- feel that they are in some way to blame for their unfair treatment and so withdraw into themselves
- lack confidence in trying new activities if their attempts are always ridiculed or belittled
- be aggressive towards others: distress or anger can prevent children from playing cooperatively with other children.

Practices that support equality and inclusion and reduce the likelihood of discrimination

Provide positive images

Books and displays should use positive images of:

- children with disabilities
- children from different cultures
- different gender roles, such as men caring for small children and women mending the car.

Consider children with additional or special needs

When you are planning an activity, consider how children with additional needs can participate fully with other children. This might mean providing ramps for wheelchair users, or working with parents to find comfortable ways for a child to sit; for example, a corner with two walls for support, a chair with a seat belt or a wheelchair with a large tray across the arms.

Learn a sign language

You could learn a sign language such as Makaton or Signalong to help communicate with a child who has a hearing impairment or a learning difficulty.

Promote cultural diversity

It is important to support an environment that is inclusive and that promotes cultural diversity.

Guidelines for good practice

Practical ways of encouraging cultural diversity

- Provide a range of activities which celebrate these differences. For example, make children and young people aware of what is involved in celebrations of religious festivals such as Diwali and Chinese New Year, as well as Christmas and Easter, whether or not there are children and young people in the setting who celebrate these occasions.
- Promote a multicultural approach to food provision. For example, parents could be invited into the setting to cook authentic national and regional dishes – Caribbean food, Yorkshire pudding as a dessert, Welsh bara brith, Irish stew, Asian sweets – the list is endless!
- Encourage self-expression in solo and group activities; for example, by providing 'tools' for cooking and eating from other cultures such as woks, chopsticks, griddles.
- Celebrate the diversity of language; use body language, gesture, pictures and actions to convey messages to children and young people whose home language is not English.

Planning activities that promote equality of opportunity

Every child needs to feel accepted, and to feel that they belong, in the setting. Try to find out as much as possible about different cultures, religions and special needs. Activities should be planned which enable each child to:

- feel valued as an individual
- explore a wide range of everyday experiences from different cultures and backgrounds
- express their feelings.

Specific activities may include the following:

1 Play with malleable materials such as play dough, sand or clay; drawing, painting and craft activities help children to express their feelings and are non-sexist activities; include examples from different cultures, such as papier mâché, origami or weaving.

2 Provide toys which offer a range of play opportunities rather than those which are aimed particularly at one sex or the other; for example, provide a wide variety of dressing-up clothes that can be used by girls and boys.

3 Include dressing-up clothes from different cultures and make sure that superhero outfits are available for both sexes, such as Batgirl as well as Batman, or gender-neutral capes.

4 Extend the pretend/role-play area to provide a wide range of play situations, such as an office or shop or a boat.

5 Use books and tell stories in different languages: invite someone whose first language is not English to come and read a popular story – such as 'Goldilocks and the Three Bears' – in their language to the whole group; then repeat the session using the English text, again to the whole group.

6 Play music from a variety of cultures, such as sitar music, pan pipes, bagpipes, and encourage children to listen or dance to the sounds.

7 Plan a display and interest table around one of the major festivals from different cultures, such as Diwali, Hanukkah, Easter or Chinese New Year.

8 Use posters that show everyday things from different countries, such as musical instruments, fruit and vegetables, transport and wildlife.

9 Organise the pretend-play area to include a variety of equipment commonly found in homes in different cultures, such as a tandoor, wok and chopsticks.

10 Provide dolls and other playthings that accurately reflect a variety of skin tones and features.

11 Arrange cookery activities using recipes from other cultures and in different languages; contact the relevant organisations to find out how to promote cooking skills for children with special needs.

12 Consult children about the activities they prefer and try to encourage equality of opportunity.

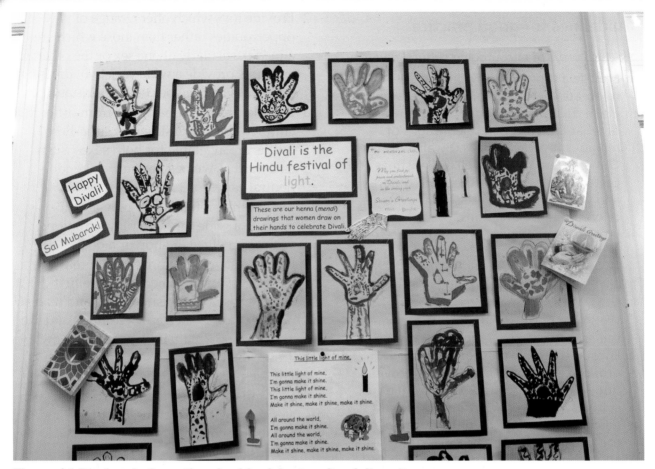

Figure 4.1 Displays in the setting should celebrate cultural diversity

AC.1.1 Reflective practice ?

Promoting equality of opportunity
Think about ways in which you have encouraged equality of opportunity in your work with children or young people. How can you ensure that your practice is not discriminatory? How can you promote equality of opportunity? Write a short account of ways in which you can ensure that no child is treated unfavourably compared with others.

Working in an inclusive way
Every child and young person needs to be included and to have full access to the curriculum and range of experiences, regardless of his or her ethnic background, culture, language, gender or economic background.

AC 1.2 Current legislation and codes of practice relating to equality, diversity and inclusive practice

No law can prevent prejudiced attitudes. However, the law can prohibit discriminatory practices and behaviours that flow from prejudice. You need to be aware of the law as it stands in relation to promoting equality of opportunity.

The laws relating to equality, diversity and discrimination are set out in Table 4.1.

Table 4.1 Legislation and codes of practice relating to equality, diversity and inclusive practice

Legislation and codes of practice	Main points of information
The Equality Act 2010	The Equality Act 2010 replaces all previous equalities legislation, bans unlawful discrimination and helps achieve equal opportunities in and outside the workplace. All early years settings, whether in the statutory, voluntary, independent or private sectors, including childminders, must comply with the Act. The Equality Act 2010 makes sure that people with particular characteristics are protected from discrimination. These are the protected characteristics: ● age ● disability ● gender reassignment ● marriage and civil partnerships ● pregnancy or maternity ● race ● religion or belief ● sex ● sexual orientation (gay, lesbian or bisexual). The Equality Act sets out the different ways in which it is unlawful to treat someone, such as direct and indirect discrimination, harassment, victimisation and failing to make a reasonable adjustment for a disabled person.
The Children and Families Act 2014	From September 2014, government reforms mean that everyone aged from birth to 25 years with special educational needs (SEN) will have a single plan setting out all the support they will receive from education, health and social care, as well as who is responsible for each part of the plan. Also, two-year-olds for whom Disability Living Allowance is paid will be entitled to free early education.
The Special Educational Needs and Disabilities (SEND) Code of Practice 2014	This applies to England only. The Code tells local authorities, schools and others how they must carry out their duties under the new law. It includes changes to the way in which services are planned and provided, through the new EHC Plan (see below).
The Education, Health and Care (EHC) Plan	The EHC Plan replaces the statement of special educational needs. All agencies will jointly plan and commission the services that are needed and will be responsible for monitoring whether these are improving outcomes. The EHC Plan has more parts to it than the statement. In early years provision, it will describe: ● the child's views and future goals ● the outcomes the child is expected to achieve ● health needs linked to the child's special educational needs (SEN) ● health provision the child needs because of their SEN; if health provision is included in a plan, it must be provided ● social care needs and provision linked to the child's SEN; there is a separate law covering social care assessments and provision, but details must be included in the EHC Plan. Each local authority must publish a 'local offer'. This is information about all the support the local authority expects to be available for the children with SEN and disabilities who live in their area. Local authorities must ensure there is a source of independent information and advice available to parents, carers and children with SEN and disabilities.

➡

Table 4.1 Legislation and codes of practice relating to equality, diversity and inclusive practice (*continued*)

Legislation and codes of practice	Main points of information
The Race Relations (Amendment) Act 2000	The general duty of the Act says you must have 'due regard to the need': ● to eliminate unlawful racial discrimination, and ● to promote equality of opportunity and good relations between persons of different racial groups.
The United Nations Convention on the Rights of the Child	As an early years practitioner, you must know and understand the basic requirements of the United Nations Convention on the Rights of the Child. These rights are for children and young people (up to the age of 18 years). (The only two countries in the world that have not signed the Convention are the USA and Somalia.) The rights embodied by the UN Convention which particularly relate to childcare and education are as follows: ● Children have the right to be with their family or with those who will care best for them. ● Children have the right to enough food and clean water for their needs. ● Children have the right to an adequate standard of living. ● Children have the right to health care. ● Children have the right to play. ● Children have the right to be kept safe and not hurt or neglected. ● Disabled children have the right to special care and training. ● Children must not be used as cheap workers or as soldiers. ● Children have the right to free education.

AC 1.2 Progress check

Find out about the legislation covering equality and inclusion and how it relates to your setting: for example, the setting's equal opportunities policy and/or inclusion policy.

LO2 Understand how policies and procedures inform equality, diversity and inclusive practice

AC 2.1 Policies and procedures relating to equality, diversity and inclusive practice

Every setting is bound to work within the framework of the law, and this includes codes of practice and policies that are tailor-made for each setting:

● The Early Years Foundation Stage (EYFS) guidance explains how to put the EYFS into action.
● The SEN Code of Practice provides practical advice and guidance to local education authorities, maintained schools, early education settings and others on carrying out their statutory duties to identify, assess and make provision for children's special educational needs.

Every setting must have a policy on equal opportunities that states how the law is interpreted in that particular setting. The procedures that accompany the policy give guidance on how the policy can be followed.

In practice

Codes of practice and policies

1 How are the laws relating to equality and inclusion reflected in your setting's policy?
2 How does the SEN Code of Practice apply to your setting?
3 How does your setting fulfil its legal responsibility to ensure that every child is included?

AC 2.1 Progress check ✓

Understanding and promoting equality of opportunity
Practitioners should:

- know their equalities lead officer or equalities coordinator
- receive support and training in this area
- work to improve their own practice
- report all incidents of discrimination (an incident is discrimination if it is felt to be discrimination by anyone involved, even an onlooker)
- take active steps to make sure that everyone knows about the services on offer and to involve everyone in all parts of the service.

AC 2.2 Roles and responsibilities when supporting equality, diversity and inclusive practice

Your roles and responsibilities are varied but include:

- to work within the policies and procedures of the setting
- to engage in effective partnership working to enable the child
- to engage actively with the family to appreciate the holistic needs of the child
- to value the individual child
- to develop and sustain a child-centred approach
- to be a positive role model in promoting equality, diversity and inclusive practice
- to provide an inclusive environment which actively welcomes diversity

- to recognise discriminatory practice
- to know how, why and when to challenge discrimination.

Work within the policies and procedures of the setting, engage in effective partnership working to enable the child and engage actively with the family to appreciate the holistic needs of the child

Equality of opportunity is about giving every child full access to the group. You cannot be an expert in every area or be trained to know everything, but you can be a good networker. This means linking people together who might be useful to each other. Get in touch with people who know about:

- welfare rights and social services
- health services
- voluntary organisations and self-help groups.

It is also important to remember that you are part of a multi-professional team and that each member has something different to bring to early childhood work. In addition, parents and family know their child better than anyone else. Use that knowledge and make a point of actively working and talking to the parents about their child's holistic needs.

Value the individual child and develop and sustain a child-centred approach

Have high expectations of the child. When you meet children, whether they are in a mainstream school, a special school or an early childhood setting, make sure that your expectations of what each child can do are high enough. Ensure you consider each child and their individual needs. Set children tasks that help them to make decisions and to exercise choice. It is important to let all children make choices and decisions so that they feel a sense of control in their lives. When people feel they have some control over what they do, they learn better. It gives them greater equality of opportunity. Always adopt a child-centred approach to ensure that the child's individual needs are at the forefront of your mind.

Be a positive role model in promoting equality, diversity and inclusive practice, and provide an inclusive environment which actively welcomes diversity

Ensure you respect yourself and others alike. Try to think why people have different views and customs from your own. Keep thinking about (or reflecting upon) what you do. Think about issues of race, gender, sexual orientation, age, economics, background, disability, assertiveness, culture and special educational needs. Keep changing what you do not like about what you do. Do this without feeling guilt or shame.

Value your knowledge and the things you keep learning about equality and diversity. Consider this an opportunity so that you can look forward and have positive impressions about yourself and other people.

Recognise discriminatory practice; know how, why and when to challenge discrimination, and identify and challenge discrimination in the work setting

The first step in being able to challenge discrimination is to identify when it is taking place. The most obvious and common form of indirect discrimination is when labels are applied to children and young people. While you may believe in private, for example, that Mark is a 'spoilt' child who gets away with the sort of behaviour that you personally think is unacceptable, you should not initiate or join in any discussion that results in Mark being labelled as a 'difficult' or 'spoilt' child. Equally, you may find some children more likeable than others. What is important is that you are fair in your treatment of all the children and young people in your care. You should treat them all with respect and work towards meeting individual needs. Try to develop positive attitudes towards all the children you meet, so that they do not feel the effects of discrimination.

Anti-discriminatory practice is a way of working that challenges words or actions that treat people unfairly (or unlawfully) because of their gender, race, disability, age, sexual orientation, language, social origin, religious beliefs, marital status and other personal attributes.

Discussion point

Exploring assumptions and stereotypes

The following adjectives are often used by adults to describe children:

● noisy	● gentle	● sissy	● lively
● aggressive	● strong	● energetic	● warm
● helpful	● cheeky	● quiet	● babyish
● lazy	● clinging	● moody	● kind
● childish	● emotional	● shy	● smart

Under the three headings 'girls', 'boys', and 'either girls or boys', sort the words from the list above according to whether you think they describe girls, boys or either. Compare this list with a friend.

1 How similar were your choices? Discuss the similarities and differences.
2 Discuss why some words are associated with a particular gender.
3 Does how you sorted the words really apply to all the children you work with or know?

As well as practising anti-discriminatory behaviour yourself, you should never ignore or make excuses for others – children, young people and other adults – if you observe discriminatory or bullying behaviour. The policies and procedures of the setting should always be followed.

Guidelines for good practice

- Make sure that you criticise the behaviour, not the child. Explain why the behaviour is unacceptable, using appropriate language for the child's stage of development. A young child can be told that what they have said or done is hurtful and unfair.
- Support the child who has been the object of discrimination to maintain their self-esteem by showing sympathy and reassurance.
- Refuse to laugh at jokes based on stereotypes. Point out to the person telling the joke that it isn't funny and explain why you object to it.
- Always challenge discriminatory remarks made by colleagues or other adults by telling them that you find their remark or behaviour inappropriate.

AC.2.2 Reflective practice

Try to think why people have different views and customs from your own. Write down some of these different views and think about why people might have them.

LO3 Know how to access information, advice and support about equality, diversity and inclusion

AC 3.1 Sources of information, advice and support about equality, diversity and inclusion

As part of your ongoing personal and professional development, you should always be willing to improve your practice by seeking further information and support from a variety of sources.

Colleagues

In most settings, there is a special needs coordinator (SENCO), whom you can approach for information or support when working with a child or young person with additional needs. It is important to get to know the strengths and personal expertise of individual members in your staff team; you will often find that they can offer useful support, having encountered a similar situation before.

Books and journals

Depending on your area of work, journals and magazines can be valuable in keeping you up to date with what is happening in your sector. Early years practitioners can refer to magazines such as *Nursery World*, *EYE* and *Infant Educator*. Practitioners working with young people can refer to *Children and Young People Now* and *Community Care*. You can find out which books will be useful from your tutor or trainer, and then order them from your local library.

Figure 4.2 There is a variety of sources you can use to keep up to date with developments in the early years sector

Parents and families

Remember that parents, carers and family members can be a valuable resource if you need further information about an individual child's:

- disability or condition
- home language
- special dietary needs or allergies, and preferences
- cultural preferences.

Organisations specialising in equality issues

There are various useful sources of information relating to equality, diversity and discrimination:

- The relevant Acts of Parliament: www.nidirect. gov.uk/government-citizens-and-rights.
- The Equality and Human Rights Commission (EHRC): EHRC has a statutory remit to promote and monitor human rights, and to protect, enforce and promote equality across the seven 'protected' grounds – age, disability, gender, race, religion and belief, sexual orientation and gender reassignment: www.equalityhumanrights.com.
- Early Education: the leading national voluntary organisation for early years practitioners and parents, Early Education promotes the rights of all children to education of the highest quality: www.early-education.org.uk.
- National Children's Bureau (NCB): NCB is a charitable organisation dedicated to advancing the health and well-being of all children and young people across every aspect of their lives, and providing them with a powerful and authoritative voice: www.ncb.org.uk.
- Organisation Mondiale pour l'Education Préscolaire (OMEP): OMEP is an international, non-governmental organisation founded in 1948 to benefit children under the age of eight years throughout the world. OMEP's aim is to promote the optimum conditions for all children, in order to ensure their well-being, development and happiness, both within their family unit and the wider communities in which they live: www.omepuk.org.uk.

AC 3.2 When to access information, advice and support about equality, diversity and inclusion

No one will expect you to know and understand everything, and you may come across situations that you find difficult or challenging. It is your responsibility to seek advice and support from your tutor or line manager, and to use your experience as a valuable learning opportunity

AC 3.2 Progress check

Journals and magazines such as *Nursery World*, *EYE* and *Infant Educator* can be valuable in keeping you up to date with what is happening in your sector. Find out which of these would be useful from your tutor, and then see if your setting or college department has copies. You could also see if they are available in your local library.

LO4 Be able to work in ways which support equality, diversity and inclusive practice

AC 4.1 Interacting with children in a way that values them and meets their individual needs

Interaction that shows respect

It is important that you recognise the differences between children and young people, and that you value those differences. Children and young people should be encouraged not to feel anxious about people who are different from them. We all have different ideas about how we conduct our lives. It is inevitable that each practitioner will encounter many people with vastly different backgrounds, beliefs and outlooks on life. Regardless of your own views, you should always respect the views of others. This involves:

- showing awareness of a child's personal rights, dignity and privacy
- not passing judgement on the way other people live

Guidelines for good practice

Helping children to form positive images of people

- Storytelling: asking storytellers (for example, parents) from different ethnic groups to tell stories in their own languages, as well as in English. This helps children to hear different languages, so that the idea becomes familiar that there are many languages in the world.
- Using arts, crafts and artefacts from different cultures (fabrics, interest tables, books, posters, jigsaws, etc.). This helps children to realise, for example, that not everyone uses a knife, fork or spoon when eating; they might use fingers, or chopsticks, instead. Children are helped to learn that there are different ways of eating, something which might seem strange to them at first.
- Including music and dances from different cultures: listening to them, watching them and perhaps joining in. In every culture children love to stand at the edge while people perform. Children often 'echo-dance'. Watch out the next time you go to a fête: if there are Morris dancers or folk dancers, you are likely to see children watching them and echo-dancing at the sides. Being introduced to different cultures in this way helps children not to reject unfamiliar music. For example, Chinese music has a pentatonic scale (five notes per octave); African music sometimes has five beats in a bar; European music has two, three or four beats but not usually five. A child who has never seen ballet before or a child who has never seen an Indian dance before might find these strange at first.
- Doing cookery from different cultures: you might have multi-language, picture-based cookery books that families can borrow (you might need to make these). For example, there could be a copy of a recipe for roti in English, Urdu and French, or for bread in English, Greek and Swahili; the choice of languages would depend on which are used in the early childhood setting.
- Planning the menu carefully: make sure that the menu includes food that children will enjoy and that is in some way familiar. One of the things young children worry about when they are away from home is whether they will like the food. Food and eating with others are a very emotional experience.

- never allowing children and young people to poke fun at another child or young person
- avoiding stereotyping people on the basis of age, sex, disability, ethnicity or skin colour
- not trying to impose your views on others.

Valuing cultural diversity and respecting difference

Much can be gained from respecting different ways of bringing up children. For example, the Indian tradition of massaging babies is now widely used in British clinics and family centres; the way that African mothers traditionally carry their babies in a sling on their backs is also popular. It is important to understand and respect what the child has been taught to do at home.

Helping children to feel that they belong

Ensure that children who look different, because they are from different cultures or because they have a disability, feel at ease and part of the group. In the early childhood setting, it is important not to have expensive outings or activities, and to invite all parents to take part in the life of the group. No parent or child should be left out because of their economic background. This is an important equality of opportunity issue.

Use of language

We should be careful to be sensitive in our use of language as it is important not to cause offence and to avoid labelling others.

- Avoid the article 'the' when referring to individuals with a specific disability. Grouping all individuals together into a disability category promotes the idea that all of these individuals have common attributes.

  For example: Don't say 'the blind' or 'the disabled'. Do say 'people who are blind' or 'people who are disabled'.

- Avoid using terms that turn the disability into a personal noun. The child should come before the disability or special need.

  For example: Don't say that someone is 'Down's'. Do say 'a child who has cerebral palsy' or 'a young person who has Down's syndrome'.

- Avoid terms that have negative implications, such as 'afflicted with', 'suffers from', 'is a victim of', 'is confined to'. These terms promote negative stereotypes.

  For example: Don't say 'Robbie is confined to a wheelchair – he suffers from muscular dystrophy.' Do say 'Robbie has muscular dystrophy and uses a wheelchair.' (Wheelchairs are liberating to people with disabilities because they provide mobility.)

- Avoid patronising or sensationalising the individual with a disability.

  For example: Don't say 'You would never know he was blind' or 'She dances well for a girl with a prosthetic leg.'

- Avoid reference to the disability at all unless it is necessary. In the same way, racial identification is being eliminated from news stories when it is not significant.

  For example: Itzhak Perlman, the violinist, once said that he would like, just for once, to read a review of his performance that did not mention his disability, especially as it in no way affected his ability to perform.

- Avoid self-projection – that is, always referring to yourself.

  For example: 'I really admire you, because I don't know what I would do if I couldn't walk any more.'

AC.4.1 **Reflective practice**

Interacting with others

Think about the way you interact with people in your setting:

- Have you made an effort to show respect and courtesy?
- Do you act as a positive role model, showing children and young people how you value and respect differences?
- How could you improve the way you interact with others to demonstrate your promotion of equality and diversity?

AC 4.2 The impact of own attitudes, values and behaviour

Inspecting our own attitudes and values

In the UK, there is now legislation on race, gender and disability discrimination, which helps teams of people working together to have an impact on racism, sexism, and disablist attitudes and work practices, however unconscious these may be. In addition, it is important that each of us inspects what we do so that we become aware of our attitudes and values. Only then can we act on the unwittingly discriminatory behaviour that we will almost inevitably find. Discriminatory behaviour occurs when, usually without meaning it, we are sexist, racist or disablist. For example, an early years practitioner might ask for a strong boy to lift the chair. We need to check that what we say we believe matches what we actually do. It doesn't usually! So then we have to do something about it.

Each of us has to work at this all the time, right throughout our lives. It is not useful to feel guilty and dislike yourself if you find you are discriminating against someone. It is useful to do something about it.

The process of inspecting our basic thinking needs to be done on three levels:

1 within the legal framework
2 in the work setting as part of a team
3 as individuals.

AC.4.2   Reflective practice

Giving everyone a voice

It is everyone's responsibility to promote inclusion, but practitioners should actively seek to break down the barriers that prevent those from minority groups having their own voice in the way services are planned and delivered. Think about the following issues within your setting:

- Do you have opportunities within your setting to share ideas about equality issues?
- Do practitioners have a safe space where they can debate and discuss issues of equality, including gender, membership of a minority ethnic group and disability?
- Do you believe your environment is welcoming to all children and their families?
- Do you offer children a secure environment in which to explore their own culture and that of their peers?

As an individual working with children, consider the following questions:

- What expectations do you have of girls that might be different from boys? How does this affect your treatment of both?
- Do you find it easier to deal with girls playing with boys' toys than boys playing with dolls or dressing up in frocks?
- What must it be like to be a boy in the setting? If the workforce were all male, how would it be for the girls?
- Do you know how to challenge prejudice?
- Do you record prejudice-related incidents?
- Do you ensure that children's names are spelt and pronounced correctly?

Assessment practice

1. What is meant by the following terms: equality; diversity; inclusion; discrimination?
2. Describe the legal framework relating to equality, diversity and inclusive practice.
3. List the policies and procedures in your setting relating to equality, diversity and inclusive practice.
4. Describe your role and responsibilities in supporting equality, diversity and inclusive practice.
5. How can you access information, advice and support about how to promote equality of opportunity in your setting?
6. How would you challenge discrimination in the setting?
7. How do you interact with children in a way that values them and meets their individual needs?
8. How do your own attitudes, belief systems and behaviour affect the ways in which you support inclusive practice and principles of equality of opportunity?

Useful resources

Lindon, J. (2006) *Equality in Early Childhood: Linking Theory and Practice*, London: Hodder Arnold.

The Alliance for Inclusive Education
A national campaigning organisation led by disabled people.

Early Support
An organisation that provides materials for families and professionals, including a service audit tool, a family pack and information for parents on certain disabilities and impairments.

KIDS
A charity that works for disabled children, young people and their families.

CACHE
See the CACHE Learner Handbook for this qualification for some more useful information for this unit.

www.cache.org.uk

Unit 5

Understand how to work in partnership

Learning outcomes

By the end of this unit, you will:

1 Understand the principles of partnership working in relation to current frameworks when working with children.
2 Understand how to work in partnership.
3 Understand challenges to partnership working.
4 Understand recording, storing and sharing information in relation to partnership working.

LO1 Understand the principles of partnership working in relation to current frameworks when working with children

Partnership working refers to formal ways of working together. It is often also referred to as integrated or multi-agency working and involves identifying organisations which need to work together for a common purpose, and in setting up a structure for them to come together regularly. A partnership can be formed between a number of individuals, agencies or organisations with a shared interest. There is usually an overarching purpose for partners to work together and a range of specific objectives. Partnerships are often formed to address specific issues and these partnerships may be short or long term.

Key term

partnership working Different services and professionals working together with other teams of people in order to meet the needs of children, young people and their parents or carers. Also called multi-agency working or integrated working.

AC 1.1 Identify reasons for working in partnership

The key principles of partnership working are openness, trust and honesty, agreed shared goals and values, and regular communication between the different services, agencies and teams of professionals. When performed well, partnership working enables agencies and professionals to do the following:

- Maintain a focus on the child by putting them at the centre of everything they do and by involving them. This ensures that everyone communicates about the 'whole' child.
- Improve communication and information sharing: This involves developing strong partnership links with relevant agencies and within the community.
- Support the early intervention process. Early intervention helps to prevent problems occurring in the first place.
- Work in an inclusive way. The needs of every child are valued and supported to ensure active participation in all areas of the setting or curriculum. It also means embedding processes of consultation and engagement with children and families in practice.
- Reduce inappropriate referrals. This involves being knowledgeable and well informed

about the roles and functions of other professionals, and understanding when, why and to who they can make a referral.

- Reduce duplication. This is a key aspect of partnership working – 'ensuring a child only tells their story once'.
- Maintain confidentiality. This means understanding that confidentiality is paramount in helping to build trust and confidence.

AC 1.1   Progress check ✔

Identify the reasons for working in partnership in your own setting.

AC 1.2 Describe partnership working in relation to current frameworks

The EYFS

The EYFS places a specific duty on early years settings to build relationships with parents. The EYFS states that there should be a 'strong partnership between between practitioners and/or carers'.

Keep up to date

There was a major update of the EYFS in 2012 and a further revision in 2014. You should make sure you are familiar with the most recent version of the EYFS.

The Common Assessment Framework (CAF)

The Common Assessment Framework (CAF) is usually used by practitioners to assess the additional needs of a child and his or her family, and to help to identify the services required to meet their needs. The lead professional will usually work with the parents and other agencies to draw up a CAF. It is not always necessary to undertake a CAF for a child – for example, if a child is making good progress and the agencies are communicating well together. The CAF begins with information sharing and assessment of:

- **the child's development**: This is the area in which early years practitioners can usually make the biggest contribution, looking at the child's progress within the framework of the EYFS, including personal, social and emotional development.
- **parents and carers**: This section looks at the care and support offered to the child or young person, including relationships, stimulation and responding to the child's or young person's needs.
- **family and environment**: This takes a wider look at the overall family and environment, and the overall capacity of the parents to support the child's development now and over time.

Drawing on these assessments, the lead professional works with the parents and the **Team Around the Child (TAC)** to put together an integrated plan to support the child's development.

The CAF recognises that a range of factors may affect children's development and vulnerability. A child with complex needs who has supportive parents and a supportive family environment, with good housing and family income, will be much less vulnerable than a child with a lower level of need but who lives in an overcrowded and potentially dangerous flat with a parent suffering from depression. Where a child does not make the expected progress, or where a child is at risk of significant harm, a referral may be made for safeguarding.

The CAF has three elements:

1 **A simple pre-assessment checklist**: to help practitioners identify children or young people who would benefit from a common assessment.

2 **A three-step process** (prepare, discuss, deliver) for undertaking a common assessment: This helps practitioners to collect and understand information about the needs and strengths of the child or young person, based on discussions with

the child or young person, their family and other practitioners as appropriate.

3 **A standard form**: to help practitioners record and, where appropriate, share with others the findings from the assessment, in terms that are helpful in working with the family to find a response to unmet needs.

Discussion point

Partnership working

A mother comes to the setting to collect her child in the afternoon. She reads the weekly menu and looks angry and upset. You ask if anything is the matter, and she says, 'I've had enough. I've just been at the doctor's with Rhianna and been told to cut out cakes and puddings to help her weight. But I can see here that they have cake, custard and all sorts for pudding in nursery.' You try to explain that the nursery's menus have been checked with the dietician and that each meal is properly balanced, but she storms off.

Think about why early years practitioners should work closely with health care professionals in order to help in a situation like this. Discuss your ideas with another learner or in a group.

How should you have handled the situation differently?

Early Support

Early Support is a government programme for coordinated, family-focused services for young children with disabilities and their families in local authorities, hospitals and community-based health services across England. Families receive coordinated support through key person/worker systems, effective sharing of information between agencies, family support plans and family-held records.

AC 1.2   Progress check

Describe partnership working in relation to current frameworks.

LO2 Understand how to work in partnership

Early years practitioners need to understand the importance of working with others in an integrated way and to build it into their everyday practice.

AC 2.1 Explain the roles of others involved in partnership working when meeting children's additional needs, safeguarding children and supporting children's transitions

Professionals who may work together to support children

There are many different services and professionals providing integrated support for children: see Figure 5.1.

Every setting is unique, and the nature of the partnership working will vary accordingly. For example, childminders are primarily home-based and will work with a varying number of professionals and agencies according to the needs of the children who are placed with them.

Meeting children's additional needs

Early Support is an integral part of the delivery of the EYFS for babies and young children under five with disabilities or emerging special educational needs. It helps staff in early years settings to identify needs early and to work in partnership with families and other services to provide the best possible care and support for young children with disabilities. An important part of the Early Support programme is the Family File, which the family holds. The Family File:

- is used by the professionals and the family together, to plan appropriate support to be provided for the child
- informs the family about the different professionals they may meet and what their role is

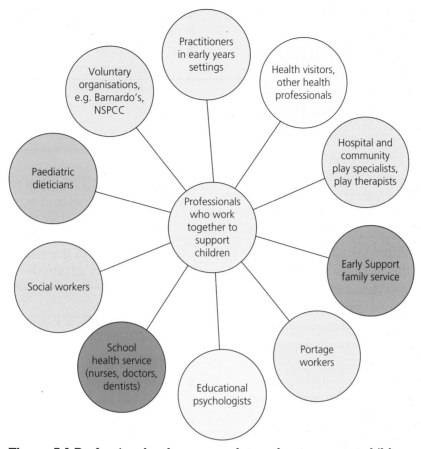

Figure 5.1 Professionals who may work together to support children

- explains how the different health, education and social services can provide support
- allows parents and carers to share information about their child with the professionals they meet, without having to say the same things to every new person
- provides information about sources of financial support and childcare.

Safeguarding children

Safeguarding and promoting the welfare of children depend on effective partnership working between agencies and professionals. Every professional involved in the welfare of children has a duty to safeguard them. The Common Assessment Framework provides opportunities for early intervention in order to prevent more serious issues later on. This aspect of partnership working is discussed in Unit 2.

Referral by social services

When children have been placed in a childcare setting on the advice of a social worker, there may be some resentment from parents. They may feel that their rights and responsibilities have been overridden. It is important that a positive relationship between parents and the setting is established as soon as possible, with a clear understanding that the interest of the child is everyone's main concern. In these situations, there will usually be regular meetings involving parents, staff and other professionals to discuss the child's progress.

Children's transitions

Moving on to different surroundings, a change in caregiver or making friends in a new setting are all transitions for young children. Practitioners in early years settings can support children during transitions by working in partnership with parents. Parents can support staff in getting to know children well, while staff can support parents as they adjust to change.

Transition to school

Schools often have to deal with children who have had no experience of early childhood education or nursery care, as well as with those who have been in day nurseries from a few months old. Some schools have a 'staggered' intake, when children attend on a part-time basis at first, which some parents, especially if they work, find both unnecessary and inconvenient. However, most children take time to adapt to a full school day as this includes a long lunchtime period with less supervision than they are used to and no facilities for an afternoon rest. Transitions and partnership working are discussed in Unit 10, 'Supporting children's development'.

Multi-agency teams

These are made up of practitioners seconded or recruited into the team, making it a more formal arrangement than a multi-agency panel. The team works with universal services (those available to *every* child) to support families and schools, as well as individual children.

> **Key terms**
>
> **agency** In this context, this term covers the range of organisations, services and professional groups who provide services to children and their families.
>
> **seconded** When a practitioner is transferred or 'lent' from their regular occupation to support another role.

Integrated working practices

Examples of integrated working include Sure Start Children's Centres and extended schools, which offer access to a range of integrated, multi-agency services. In Children's Centres, for example, practitioners work in a coordinated way to address the needs of children, young people and families, providing services such as:

- integrated early learning and full day care
- family support
- health services
- outreach services to children and families not attending the centre
- access to training and employment advice.

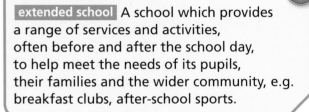

> **Key term**
>
> **extended school** A school which provides a range of services and activities, often before and after the school day, to help meet the needs of its pupils, their families and the wider community, e.g. breakfast clubs, after-school sports.

How multi-agency teams work

Features of multi-agency teams include the following:

- There is a dedicated team leader – also called the **lead professional**.
- There is a good mix of educational, health care and social care staff.
- The people who work in the team think of themselves as team members. They are recruited or seconded into the team, on either a full-time or a part-time basis.
- The team works at a range of levels – not just with individual children and young people, but also small group, family and whole-school work.
- The team is likely to share a base, though some staff may continue to work from their home agencies.
- There are regular team meetings to discuss case working as well as administrative issues.

> **Key term**
>
> **lead professional** The lead professional takes the lead to coordinate provision and acts as a single point of contact for a child and their family when a **Team Around the Child** is required.

Behaviour and Education Support Teams (BESTs)

The Behaviour and Education Support Team (BEST) is one example of multi-agency working.

These are multi-agency teams bringing together a complementary mix of professionals from the fields of health, social care and education. The aim of a BEST is to promote emotional well-being, positive behaviour and school attendance, by identifying and supporting those with, or at risk of developing, emotional and behavioural problems.

BESTs work with children and young people aged five to 18 years, their families and schools. A BEST will aim to intervene early and prevent problems from developing further, and works in targeted primary and secondary schools and in the community, alongside a range of other support structures and services.

A BEST has a complementary mix of education, social care and health skills in order to meet the multifaceted needs of children, young people and their parents.

Schools with BESTs include those with high proportions of pupils with (or at risk of developing) behavioural problems, usually demonstrated in levels of exclusions and attendance.

AC 2.1 Progress check

- Evaluate how your setting uses partnership working in relation to meeting children's additional needs.
- Make sure you know your responsibilities with regard to safeguarding children.
- Through consultation with parents and children, think of ways in which you could develop and improve transition experiences for children and families.

AC 2.2 Explain benefits of working in partnership with parents/carers

Working with parents and carers is an essential aspect of work with children. Parents are the first and primary educators of their children. You can strengthen and build on this responsibility so that parents experience an increase in enjoyment of their children and an understanding of child development. Remember that it takes time and regular communication to build good relationships with parents that are founded on mutual trust and respect.

Early years practitioners need to bear in mind the following facts:

- Every family is different, with different needs and traditions.
- The great majority of parents want to do their best for their child, even if they are not always sure what this might be.
- Each one of us only really knows what it is like to grow up in our own family. Parents almost always like some of the things about their own family and the way they were brought up; but they will just as certainly wish that other aspects of their upbringing had been different.
- Parents usually welcome help when trying out some alternative ways of doing things. They will not want to change too much, though, and they will not want rapid changes forced on them by other people. Early years practitioners need to respect parents' wishes.

The nature of the family has changed in the UK. It has become more complex, mainly due to changes in society – such as moral attitudes towards marriage and changes to the laws concerning divorce. The word 'family' means different things to different people; this depends upon who you are – your own beliefs and attitudes – and your own experiences of family life.

Even social scientists disagree on what defines a family, but a useful definition for the 21st century in the UK is: A family is a 'small social group, consisting of at least one adult and child, usually living together, related by blood, marriage or adoption'.

Figure 5.2 Parents are the first and primary educators of children

Family structures in the UK

The family can include all or some of the following individuals:

- grandparents, uncles and aunts and other relations
- foster parents, step-parents, stepchildren, or only one parent
- two parents living separately
- parents who have chosen to marry or those who have not and are cohabiting
- parents of the same sex bringing up children.

The benefits of working in partnership with parents/carers

Developing a real partnership with parents allows practitioners to learn about the child as an individual and enables the parents to understand and value their own role as their child's primary educator. This equal exchange and understanding brings with it continuity of care for each child, as young children experience a consistent approach at home and across all the settings in which they are cared for and educated.

There are many reasons why it is valuable to involve parents or carers in the work setting:

- Parents know their children better than anyone else.
- Children benefit from the extra attention, particularly one-to-one help.
- A range of different skills can be brought to the work setting, e.g. music, sewing, drawing, cooking, etc.
- Parents and carers who do not share the same language or culture as the work setting can extend the awareness and knowledge of both staff and children about the way other people live, cook and communicate.
- Parents and carers can help by sharing lots of books with children from an early age, and by hearing and helping their child read when they start school.
- Involving parents in the play and learning experiences of their children can help to counteract any negative feelings parents may have about education systems, arising perhaps from memories of their own school days.

In many instances, you will be working under the supervision of others and it is likely that parents will pass confidential information directly to another staff member. However, there may be occasions when you are given information and asked to pass it on, or you may hear or be told confidential information in the course of the daily routine. This issue is dealt with in the section on **confidentiality** (see page 54) and you should follow the guidelines, procedures and practices that apply to your work setting. Remember that lines of management are in place in most work settings and you should follow them if you need to check your understanding or to ask advice. Try to be aware of the ways in which staff members relate to, and communicate with, parents, and try to identify which methods seem to be most effective.

Guidelines for working with parents

- Support parents: Begin by seeing yourself as a resource and support that can be used by parents to further their child's best interests.
- Respect all parents: The vast majority of parents love their children. It is important not to judge parents but to respect their good intentions. Almost every parent wants to do the job well, even if on the surface they do not seem to be interested or loving.
- Recognise the good intentions of parents: Work positively, with this aim as a central focus. Concentrating on the good intentions of parents helps to give them a positive self-image. Just as children need positive images reflected about themselves, so do parents.

The attitude of the staff must therefore be to show parents respect; it is hard bringing up a child.

- Reinforce the parents' sense of dignity and self-esteem: Showing parents respect and reinforcing their dignity demonstrate to them that their child also needs respect and a sense of dignity.
- Using your experience: If you are not a parent, you will not have experienced some of the things that parents have. If you are a parent, you will only know about being a parent to your own child; you will not know what it is like to be a parent of other people's children.

AC 2.2 Progress check

Explain the benefits of working in partnership with parents – to the child, the parent or carer and the setting.

LO3 Understand challenges to partnership working

There will often be many challenges to partnership working. These will vary from one setting – and one particular circumstance – to another.

AC 3.1 Identify barriers to partnership working

There are many potential barriers to effective partnership working. Some are organisational, while others relate to problems with communication.

Information sharing

Problems mostly occur around *when* and *how* to share information. Practitioners may be unclear about their individual roles and responsibilities, and worry that they might misjudge the situation and

be disciplined for sharing information inappropriately. Team meetings need to be arranged at a convenient time and place for everyone; otherwise non-attendance of various professionals can present a barrier to effective working.

Key term

Information sharing The term used to describe the situation whereby practitioners use their professional judgement and experience on a case-by-case basis to decide whether personal information should be shared with other practitioners in order to meet the needs of a child or young person.

Developing a common language

Often there are differences in the cultures of different agencies, and this can lead to difficulties in understanding the terms and language used by other professionals. Already you will have noticed that there is a whole set of acronyms commonly used in settings with children and young people, such as BEST, CAF, EYFS, etc. You do not need to know what they all mean, only the acronyms used in your area of work.

The fear of the 'new'

Some practitioners may feel threatened by new approaches which require them to work differently, across service boundaries. Some may resent being managed by a professional with different skills experiences from their own, and may generally feel out of their 'comfort zone'.

Lack of understanding of different agency roles

If practitioners do not fully understand the roles and responsibilities of other services and practitioners, they may lack confidence in them and worry that a different agency may not treat the matter confidentially; they may even fear that other practitioners may make things worse for the child, young person or family. Not knowing whom to contact for advice and support with information sharing can also create barriers to effective multi-agency working. This often leads to anxiety and a lack of confidence.

Different professional priorities

Team members need to be clear about their goals and their individual roles and responsibilities. Every team member needs to work together to make use of the other professionals' expertise in the best interests of the child and family. It may take time to establish this understanding and to find a way of working together.

Figure 5.3 Supervising other practitioners is sometimes part of working as a team

Parents and carers who may not want to become involved

Many parents will want to become involved in their child's setting, especially if this is an open, welcoming atmosphere and a place to meet other parents. However, there will always be some parents who do not want to participate. There could be a number of reasons for this reluctance. These include:

- working full-time or having other daytime commitments
- feeling that they have nothing of value to contribute
- not being interested in spending time with other people's children
- lacking confidence or feeling shy.

It is important that parents do not feel pressured into becoming involved. You should always respect parents' decisions and not assume that reluctance to be involved shows a lack of interest in their children.

Some early years settings have a drop-in facility for parents that helps support those feeling isolated and experiencing problems, while a family support group, with a skilled family worker on hand, can help people with parenting skills and other issues.

Barriers to communication

- **Time constraints**: There may be several children arriving at the same time, which puts pressure on staff at a busy time. Parents may be in a rush to get away when bringing their children. It is important that you do not interpret this as a lack of interest. Greet them with a friendly nod and pass on any information as briefly as possible.
- **Not seeing parents regularly**: When someone other than the parents brings and fetches the child, staff will need to find other ways to maintain regular communication.
- **Body language and non-verbal communication**: Be aware of how parents may be feeling at a particular time, even when they do not mention anything

Case study

Communicating with parents

1 The parents of three-year-old Thomas have been anxious about their son's appetite since he was ill with a virus. Members of staff at the day nursery have been observing Thomas, keeping written records and photographs, at snack and meal times over a period of a week. They have made sure the food is attractively presented, includes some of Thomas's favourite items and is offered in small portions. They have noticed a great improvement and want to share their findings with his parents and discuss how he is at home.

2 Five-year-old Charlotte has recently become withdrawn from both adults and other children. For the past week or so, she has needed encouragement to complete work tasks which are within her capability and when she has had free-choice activity she has tended to sit alone in the home corner with a soft toy. This represents a change in Charlotte's behaviour and the teacher wants to discuss her concerns with the parents.

- In each case, what method would you use to contact the parents?
- Explain what you would say/write and what you would arrange in order to deal with each situation.

specific; for example, if a parent does not make eye contact, it may be that they are depressed.

- **Written communication**: Unless sent in the post, there is a chance that some letters and other written notes may not reach the parent. Also some parents might have difficulty reading and writing and not want to seek help. The noticeboard can also be used to display a general letter sent to all parents.
- **Making messages clear**: Remember that we understand messages not only from what is said but also from *how* it is said – our tone of voice, gestures and facial expressions can change the meaning of a message. The person on the receiving end of a written message has no such clues. It is important to give careful consideration to the wording of any letter and try to make sure that it cannot be misinterpreted.
- **When English is not the parent's first language**: You can help by signing or – where possible – by involving bilingual staff or translators. Noticeboards can display signs in picture form – for example, showing the activities their child will be doing during the session. Having written information in a number of different languages is also helpful.

AC 3.1 Progress check

Identify barriers to partnership working in your own setting.

AC 3.2 Explain ways to overcome barriers when working in partnership

Effective communication in partnership working

Sharing information through communicating with others is vital for early intervention to ensure that children receive the services they require. It is also essential for safeguarding and protecting the welfare of individuals, and for providing effective and efficient services which are coordinated around the needs of an individual or family. The need for every practitioner to have effective communication and teamwork skills is therefore important.

Effective communication between professionals and agencies is important to make sure that everyone:

- shares information in a clear way that focuses on the individual child or young person
- works towards the same aim: to achieve the best positive outcomes for the child or young person and his or her family.

The EYFS Guidance states: 'It is vital to ensure that everyone is working together to meet the emotional, health and educational needs of children in all settings that they attend and across all services provided.'

Being able to communicate effectively with team members, other professionals and with parents is a very important part of your role as a practitioner. You should always:

- be considerate of others and polite towards them
- recognise the contributions made by other team members – we all like to feel we are valued for the work we do; you can help others to feel valued by being aware of their role and how it has helped you fulfil your own role
- explain clearly to the relevant person any changes in routine or any actions you have taken; for example, as a nanny, always informing a parent when a child you are caring for has refused a meal or been distressed in any way, or reporting any behavioural problem or incident to your line manager in a nursery setting.

Working effectively as a team

To meet the needs of all the children, the staff members must work effectively together as a team. The roles and responsibilities of individual team members will depend on the organisation of the work setting. In your role as a learner, you will be supporting the work of others. You will usually work under the direction (or sometimes supervision) of a nursery manager or teacher, depending on the setting. There may also be professionals from other disciplines (medicine, social services, dentistry, etc.) who are involved with the families and children you work with. A school for children with special educational needs or a nursery that cares for children with physical disabilities will have a multidisciplinary team. This team may include teachers, nursery nurses and assistants, trained special care assistants, physiotherapists, paediatricians and, possibly, social workers.

Effective teamwork is vital in such settings to ensure that:

- everyone knows their individual roles and responsibilities
- parents and primary carers know which team member can deal with any specific concerns.

Key term

paediatrician A qualified doctor who specialises in treating children.

Progress check

Communication in a multi-agency approach
Each profession has its own jargon and set of rules. You do not need to know about these in depth, but you should always be willing to learn from other professionals and to respect the contribution of others working with children and families. You need to:

- be clear about your own role
- be aware of the roles of other professionals
- be confident about your own standards and targets
- be respectful of those that apply to other services.

Reflective practice

The need for clear and effective communication
Think about the examples below and reflect on why clear and effective communication between different professionals is important in providing for the needs of every child and young person:

- A six-year-old child has sickle cell anaemia and attends school but is often in hospital for weeks at a time. Health play specialists, hospital teachers and the child's class teacher are all involved in the child's care and education.
- A child with a severe visual impairment attends a mainstream school and has daily support from a dedicated learning support assistant.
- A young child with special educational needs attends a Children's Centre and is also visited at home by a portage worker.

sickle cell anaemia An inherited condition caused by abnormal red blood cells.

portage worker A home-visiting educational service.

Appropriate communication methods for different circumstances

Informal communication

Ongoing communication with parents and carers is essential to meet the needs of children and young people. For many parents, there can be regular and informal communication when children are brought to, or collected from, the setting. However, it is unusual for both parents to perform this task and, therefore, it is often the same parent who has contact. The methods below can usually work for both parents and practitioners. Finding ways to communicate with parents can sometimes be difficult, especially when staff may not feel confident themselves.

- **Regular contact with the same person**: Always meet and greet parents when they arrive. At the start, it is very important that parents meet the same practitioner – preferably their child's teacher or key person – on a daily basis.
- **A meeting place for parents**: Ideally, there should be a room that parents can use to have a drink and a chat together.

Information that applies in the longer term should ideally be given in writing; for example, information concerning food allergies or medical conditions, such as asthma or eczema. As well as informing staff members, notices may also need to be attached to a child's own equipment or lunchbox, or displayed in particular places, such as food preparation and nappy-changing areas. In a school setting, the class teacher should ensure that any other adults involved in the child's care receive information as appropriate.

Copies of all letters received and sent and a record of all communication should be kept for future reference.

Table 5.1 Exchanging routine written information

Written information	How and when it is used
Formal letter	● Welcome letter prior to admission to the setting ● To give information about parents' evenings or meetings ● To alert parents to the presence of an infectious disease within the setting ● To advise parents about any change of policy or staff changes
Email	● To give information about an event ● To respond to a request from a parent or colleague
Newsletters	● To give information about future events – fundraising fairs, open forums and visiting speakers, etc.
Noticeboards	● To give general information about the setting, local events for parents, support group contact numbers, health and safety information, daily menus, etc.
Activity slips	● To inform parents about what their child has been doing
Admission form	● All parents fill in an admission form when registering their child. This is confidential information and must be kept in a safe place where only staff have access to it ➔

Table 5.1 Exchanging routine written information   (*continued*)

Written information	How and when it is used
Home books	• To record information from both staff and parents. Home books travel between the setting and the home and record details of the child's progress, any medication given, how well they have eaten and slept, etc.
Accident slips	• To record information when a child has been ill or is injured when at the setting
Suggestions box	• Some settings have a suggestions box where parents can contribute their own ideas for improving the service
Policy and procedure documents	• These official documents should be openly available, and parents should be able to discuss them with staff if they have any concerns

Verbal information

Routine information can be – and often is – exchanged verbally. This usually happens at the start and end of the session, when parents and their child's key worker chat informally.

- **Talking with parents**: Always let parents know about their child's positive behaviour and take the opportunity to praise the child in front of their parents. Then if you need to share a concern with them, they will already understand that you are interested in their child's welfare and are not being judgemental. (Many adults associate being called in to see the person in charge with their own experiences of a 'telling-off'.)
- **Recording information and passing on messages**: You will need to record some information the parent has talked to you about – especially if you are likely to forget it! You should always write down a verbal message which affects the child's welfare, so that it can be passed on to other members of staff: for example, if someone else is collecting the child, if a favourite comfort object has been left at home or if the child has experienced a restless night. The person delivering the message also needs confirmation that it will be acted upon. Where there are shift systems in operation,

a strict procedure for passing on messages needs to be established.

- **Telephone calls**: Information received or delivered by telephone should be noted in a diary so that action can be taken.

AC 3.2   Progress check

Encouraging partnership with families
- Do parents feel welcome in the setting? Can you think of ways to make your setting more welcoming to parents?
- Do all parents have the opportunity to contribute to the setting?
- Are parents asked for feedback on any concerns they have about the setting – for example, the outdoor play area?
- Do parents know whom to contact if they wish to seek further advice?
- Are there fun activities, such as fun days, picnics and local visits, to take part in for families to get to know each other outside the setting?

AC 3.3 Give examples of support which may be offered to parents/carers

There are many ways in which the early years practitioner – in particular, the key person – can support parents and carers through working in partnership.

Involving parents in the partnership

- Provide opportunities for parents to contribute to practitioners' developing understanding of the child as a unique individual – through shared observations of their children, in the setting and at home with the parent.
- Encourage parents to help out during sessions, to share their interests or cultures with children and to take part in discussions about the provision.

Sharing information

- Ensure that information about the process of learning is visible for all parents and children.
- Ensure that policies on important areas such as key person, inclusion, behaviour, learning and teaching are made known to parents; parents could also be involved in the drawing up of early years policies.

Supporting parents in developing their own skills

- Many parents find workshops run by the setting a useful way to experience some of the activities their children do, and are able to develop their own skills.

Supporting parents to contribute to planning the learning environment

- Invite the opinions of parents about the general running of the setting and encourage them to evaluate the environment with their child's needs and interests in mind.

Obtaining feedback from parents

An important part of evaluating the complexity of partnership working is making sure that parents are given opportunities to feed back on and to shape services for children and families. Different early years settings will have a range of management systems:

- Maintained nursery schools, and primary schools, will have a legally constituted governing body that includes parent representatives. The governing body will have formal systems for reporting back to all parents and for acting on suggestions and complaints. There will also be systems to survey parents' views on a regular basis.
- Other settings may have a management committee made up of parents and other volunteers. Voluntary and community settings – for example, a pre-school or a community nursery – will often be led by parents of children currently or previously on roll, and be linked to other community and local groups.
- Children's Centres will usually have a parents' forum, a gathering of parents who give feedback on the services offered and shape the future direction of the centre.

> **AC 3.3** **Progress check** ✓
>
> Find ways to obtain feedback from parents about (a) information sharing and (b) the framework of development and learning.

LO4 Understand recording, storing and sharing information in relation to partnership working

AC 4.1 Identify records to be completed in relation to partnership working

Record-keeping

The EYFS requires that:

- settings maintain and regularly update records of children's development and progress
- records are securely stored
- records are accessible to parents on demand.

It is good practice for observations and records to be shared between practitioners in the setting – for example, at planning meetings. This helps to ensure that staff work together to build up a rounded picture of each child's development, well-being and needs.

Involving parents and upholding their rights

The best approach to working with parents is to develop a culture of mutual trust, respect and sharing of information. This will mean making it easy for parents to access their children's records, however they are kept. Parents will expect to be offered regular meetings to discuss their children's progress, when achievements can be celebrated and concerns can be raised and discussed. If you want to encourage parents to look regularly at their children's records, you will need to think about how to make them accessible. A folder full of long written observations is unlikely to engage most parents, especially if the observations are handwritten and hard to read. On the other hand, profile books that are carefully illustrated with photos, as well as including written observations, are much more inviting. Video and slide shows of photos are another way to engage parents. The danger here is that the focus on the child's development, learning and well-being can get lost if parents are presented with something that looks like a scrapbook, family album or holiday slide show, full of posed images of smiling children.

Figure 5.4 Parents should be engaged and a culture of mutual trust, respect and sharing of information should be developed

The EYFS says:

'Parents must be given free access to developmental records about their child (for example, the EYFS Profile). However, a written request must be made for personal files on the children and providers must take into account data protection rules when disclosing records that refer to third parties.'

Preparing reports

As part of your role, you may need to prepare reports. A report is a formal document which presents facts and findings, and can be used as a basis for recommendations. Certain reports that you may write will be a statutory requirement within the EYFS framework, and must be made available to any Ofsted inspection. These include accident reports, reporting of illnesses or injuries and any report of concerns about a child.

Reports you may be required to write include:

- **an accident or incident report**: this is quite straightforward and will involve completing a standardised form
- **a CAF pre-assessment checklist or CAF form**: an official form which is focused and easy to complete
- **a formal report about a project or plan**: for example, a plan to change the use of a room within the setting.

A formal report has a fairly rigid structure and is usually divided into sections, probably with subheadings, performing a very specific task. The language used should be straightforward and to the point, and the report's structure should make it easy to identify the various parts, and to find specific items of information quite quickly. The three general principles of a report are: Why was it done? How was it done? What does it mean?

A formal report usually has the following features:

- **Title page**: include author's name, date and for whom the report is written.
- **Contents list**: list the main sections, sub-sections and any appendices.
- **Introduction**: the background or context to the report and the aims and objectives.
- **Main body or text**: this describes how the study was conducted and gives the facts, findings and results.
- **Conclusions**: this describes what the study has shown, summarising the main points.
- **Any recommendations** for the implementation of a report's findings.

- **Appendices**: include any supporting information here, such as tables, or information that applies only to certain readers.
- **References**: a list of books or articles used or suggestions for further reading.

Information sharing

The government produced a *Guide to information sharing* (2008) for all practitioners working with children and young people. This outlined the important Acts that can be used to develop an information-sharing policy in Children's Services:

- The Data Protection Act 1998: provides a framework to ensure that information is shared appropriately
- The Children Act 2004: on the duty to safeguard and promote the welfare of children
- *Working Together to Safeguard Children* (HMG, 2006): the statutory guidance that sets out how organisations and individuals should work together to safeguard and promote the welfare of children
- *What to do if you're worried a child is being abused* (HMG, 2006)
- The Education and Inspections Act 2006: sets out the duty to promote the well-being of pupils to governing bodies of maintained schools
- The Child Health Promotion Programme (DH, 2008)
- Local Safeguarding Children Board (LSCB) policies, procedures, protocols and guidance.

Recording and storing information

Every setting must provide clear policies and procedures about the recording and storing of information. These are governed by the Data Protection Act 1998. Anyone who keeps records, whether on computers or on paper, should comply with the Data Protection Act. It should be clear to service users (in this case, parents or guardians) for what purpose the data is being kept. Information about a child should also be accessible to his or her parent or carer and shared with them. It is not necessary to do this 'on demand'. A convenient time to be able to discuss the information can be arranged. Information should not be kept for longer than necessary, although accident and incident records will need to be kept for at least three years in case they are needed for reference at some time in the future. Records must also be stored securely.

Electronic recording and storing of information

If information is kept on computers or sent by email, steps must be taken to ensure that it could not fall into the hands of unauthorised people (for example, by the use of encryption software).

The National Electronic Common Assessment Framework (eCAF) enables authorised, trained practitioners from across the children's workforce to electronically store and share CAF information quickly and securely, and to work together to build a holistic picture of a child's needs. The system reduces the need for children and families to repeat their story for different services.

Information should not be kept for longer than necessary, although accident and incident records will need to be kept in case they are needed for reference at some time in the future. Records must also be stored securely.

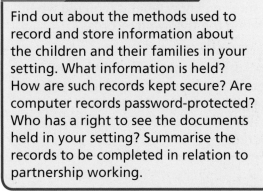

AC 4.1   Progress check

Find out about the methods used to record and store information about the children and their families in your setting. What information is held? How are such records kept secure? Are computer records password-protected? Who has a right to see the documents held in your setting? Summarise the records to be completed in relation to partnership working.

AC 4.2 Explain reasons for accurate and coherent record-keeping

Good practice in the area of record-keeping is based on the following principles. Records and reports should:

- **be legible and grammatically correct**: Handwriting must be neat and care should be taken to ensure that records are free from spelling and grammar errors.
- **help to ensure that children's needs are met**: For example, observation records help to identify children's needs and can inform future practice.
- **help to safeguard the health and well-being of the child**: Any concern about the child's health or well-being should be recorded and reported to the line manager.
- **help to provide continuity of service**, so that another member of staff can take over in the event of the practitioner being ill or unavailable.
- **provide evidence of the practitioner's work**: This will go towards compiling a record of evidence.
- **contain information that practitioners can use** to monitor and evaluate their work in order to improve their practice.
- **help managers to monitor and evaluate** the quality and performance of the service to children and young people.
- **include only factual information**: Opinions and assumptions should not be recorded.

AC 4.2 Progress check ✔

Make sure you know what is required when completing the following records:

- an accident or incident report
- a CAF pre-assessment checklist or CAF form
- a formal report about a project or plan
- observation and planning forms
- developmental records for individual children.

AC 4.3 Explain the reasons for confidentiality when maintaining records

It is essential to maintain confidentiality when working with children and their families, as it imposes a boundary on the amount of personal information and data that can be disclosed without consent. Confidentiality arises where a person disclosing personal information reasonably expects his or her privacy to be protected, such as in a relationship of trust. It is useful to understand fully the meaning of the terms 'consent', 'disclosure' ('allegation') and 'privacy'.

Consent

Consent means agreement to an action based on knowledge of what the action involves and its likely consequences. For example, information on a child should only be collected and stored with the consent of the child's parents or carers – and they should have free access to this information on request. The only exceptions to the rule of consent are the very small number of cases where the child might otherwise be at risk of immediate and significant harm if you shared a piece of information with the parent.

Disclosure (allegation)

A safeguarding allegation means the giving out of information that might commonly be kept confidential, usually voluntarily or to be in compliance with legal regulations or workplace rules. (Allegation used to be known as disclosure.) An example would be a child telling an adult something that causes him or her to be concerned about the child's safety and well-being.

Privacy

Privacy refers to the right of an individual or group to stop information about themselves from becoming known to people other than those to whom they choose to give the information. For example, when former prime minister Tony Blair's ex-nanny wrote a book about life at Number 10, Downing Street, the Blairs took swift legal action to prevent details being leaked to the press. Tony Blair stated; 'We will do whatever it takes to protect…our children's privacy.'

Case study

Confidential information?

During a coffee break, practitioners are openly chatting about Harry, a child that you know. Apparently, the people he lives with are not his parents, but his grandparents – although they look young enough to be his parents. They are bringing Harry up because their daughter (his mother) was judged to be unable to look after her child. This happened a few years ago when Harry was very young, and he had spent some time in social care before his grandparents gained custody. One practitioner noted that Harry always calls them Mummy and Daddy.

1 Is this information confidential? If so, why?
2 Should you inform your line manager of the situation?

AC 4.3 Activity

Explain the reasons why confidentiality is important when maintaining records.

Assessment practice

1 What do you consider to be the main reasons for working in partnership?
2 Describe partnership working in relation to current frameworks.
3 Which policies and procedures are particularly required for partnership working?
4 Explain the roles of others involved in partnership working with reference to your own setting.
5 Evaluate partnership working in relation to (a) safeguarding children, (b) meeting children's additional needs, and (c) children's transitions.
6 What are the benefits of working in partnership with parents/carers?
7 Describe situations when parents/carers may need support.
8 Give four examples of support which may be offered to parents/carers.
9 Describe some common barriers to partnership working and explain what could be done to overcome them.
10 What is your own role in recording, storing and sharing information in relation to partnership working?

Useful resources

National Parent Partnership Network and Parent Partnership Services

National Parent Partnership Network and Parent Partnership Services (PPS) are statutory services offering information, advice and support to parents and carers of children and young people with special educational needs (SEN).

EYFS 2014

This links to the EYFS document on the government website.

www.gov.uk

National Society for the Prevention of Cruelty to Children (NSPCC)

www.nspcc.org.uk

Barnardo's

www.barnardos.org.uk

Unit 6

Supporting children's play

Learning outcomes

By the end of this unit, you will:

1 Understand the play environment.
2 Understand how the early years practitioner supports children's behaviour and socialisation within play environments.

3 Be able to support children's behaviour and socialisation within play environments.
4 Be able to create an enabling play environment which meets the age, stage and needs of children.

LO1 Understand the play environment

AC 1.1 What 'the play environment' means

In an inclusive early years setting that embraces diversity, the layout of a setting and the presentation of material and objects offer a range of experiences and activities across the birth to five years framework. Increasingly, from the time they can walk, younger children integrate with children in the Foundation years for parts of the day, which gives a more natural and family-group feeling. All children are included in settings, regardless of special educational needs and disabilities. All this means that the traditions of wide provision are of central importance in providing an enabling play **environment**.

Key term

environment The provision that is made for children in which they can learn, play and relax. It encompasses both the physical environment (such as the layout, equipment and furniture) and the 'emotional' environment (the atmosphere or ambience that is created).

AC 1.1 Progress check

Explain what is meant by 'environment'.

AC 1.2 Different types of environment

There is a wide variety of play environments in the UK.

AC 1.2 Activity

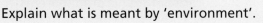

Find out about the types of play environment provided in your local area. Which settings provide integrated education and care for children from birth to five years?

AC 1.3 How environments support play

Creating environments which encourage and support play

Play does not just happen. It is true that babies and young children are biologically disposed to play, but they will not develop their play unless they meet people and experience situations that encourage the development of play. What practitioners provide has a direct impact on play. If practitioners encourage play and create an enabling environment that cultivates play, the quality of children's play will be deeper.

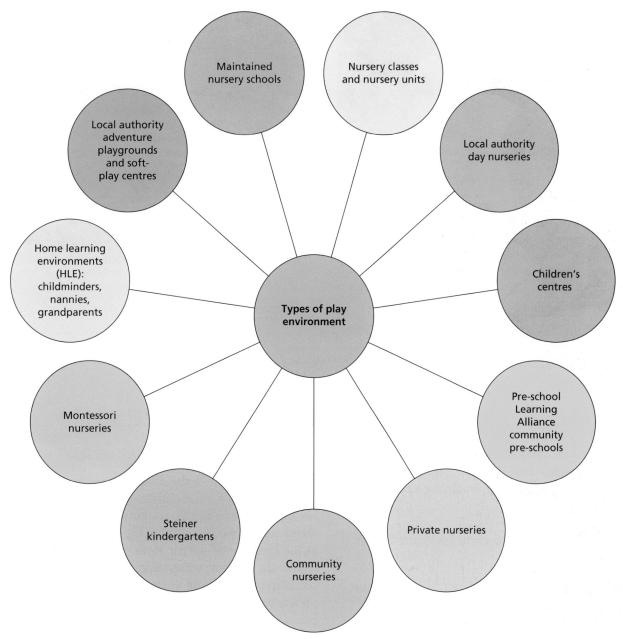

Figure 6.1 Different types of play environment

Continuous provision

There should always be a core of open-ended provision that is continuously offered – this means it is constantly available. Other experiences can be added in or changed, and may not be offered all day every day in the same way.

The following are considered to be types of open-ended continuous provision:

- malleable natural materials (clay, mud, dough)
- home corner for domestic play
- workshop area, with found and recycled material for model-making and mark-making, and including masking tape and scissors that cut (for left- and right-handed children)
- small-world play (doll's house, farm, prehistoric animals, roads, trains)
- sand (wet and dry) and water.

Figure 6.2 The children are involved in parallel (companionship) play: both are digging in the sand and filling holes with water, watching it seep into the sand

Space and places to play indoors: room design

Freedom of movement is central to early childhood. Susan Isaacs, a pioneer in integrated early years provision, thought that children cannot learn if they are made to sit still.

It is hard for children to develop their play if the day is timetabled into rigid slots, with routines that break up the day. If children are allowed to move about freely between the indoor and outdoor areas, research suggests that their play is calmer and of deeper quality.

There is also the advantage that giving children greater choice of where and how they play gives practitioners more time and opportunity to support children's play and choices, rather than organising and directing adult-led 'activities' for most of the day.

Figure 6.3 It is quite a skill to avoid pouring the water over his feet – the child demonstrates this in his play. He also shows us that he is interested in pouring water on the concrete wall of the sandpit, as well as the sand inside the pit. He is noticing that the results are different: water seeps into sand; it splashes off concrete. He might enjoy discussing this later, if photos were taken and he shared them with his key person. Often children do not want to interrupt their play, but they do appreciate reflecting afterwards, and photos are an excellent way to do this in a relaxed way

Space and places to play outdoors: gardens, parks, forests, urban forests

Play does not happen on the order of practitioners. Challenging play helps children to play at their highest levels. Play outdoors gives children opportunities to consolidate and practise skills.

Settings now work hard to make their outdoor area an important part of the play environment. This is vital as it is a requirement of the Early Years Foundation Stage in England.

Children need to interact with nature, so plants, trees, flowers and vegetables are part of this. This encourages bird and insect life. Ideally, children are taken to forests, or to parks with copses of trees, so that they can learn how to be in woodland and open green spaces. These natural spaces strengthen the play and encourage creativity. Den-making is something children all over the world engage in. Dens, mud pies, hoops, beanbags and balls in zones all have a contribution to make to outdoor play.

Open-ended natural materials to play with

These encourage children to think, feel, imagine, socialise and concentrate deeply. This type of material encourages children to think about natural resources in the world (where does clay come from?). Children will tend to use a range of fine motor skills with these materials, such as working at the woodwork bench or making a clay coil pot. Examples of open-ended materials are:

- found materials, such as those used in junk-modelling
- transforming raw materials, like clay and dough
- self-service areas where children can access material themselves (where it is safe for them to do so)
- dressing-up clothes and cookery items in the home area
- wooden blocks.

Carefully chosen and limited use of commercial toys and equipment

It is important to note that toys are often expensive and of doubtful quality in terms of educational experience. Pre-structured toys can only be used in one prescribed way, whereas open-ended material can be used as a prop for all kinds of play scenarios.

A set of wooden unit blocks has more potential for creative and imaginative play than one plastic construction kit. It is best to keep

adding to the wooden blocks, and to choose one construction kit that is as open-ended as possible, so that many different things can be constructed with it, and then to keep adding to that.

AC 1.3 **Progress check**

How is play supported in your setting? Is there continuous provision of open-ended materials? Is the design of indoor and outdoor spaces both functional and attractive?

AC 1.4 How to work with others to create enabling play environments in early years settings

Effective teamwork is essential when planning to provide enabling play environments.

The role of the practitioner is central

The role of the practitioner in supporting children's development and learning, through appropriate materials, equipment and resources, is central to children's experience. A practitioner needs to work with colleagues to plan and create this kind of environment.

Clutter confuses children

There should be nothing in a learning environment, indoors or outdoors, that has not been carefully thought through and well organised. Children need to know what they are allowed to do, and what they are not allowed to do, and the environment needs to signal to children how it should be used and kept. When children feel insecure, they test boundaries.

The space indoors and outdoors should be flexible

Both indoor and outdoor spaces should be flexible, so that they can be set up and transformed for different uses in a variety of ways. Attention should be given to light because the way that it shines into a building changes the atmosphere. If the sun is shining onto a child's face during story time, it will be difficult for the child to become engaged.

The temperature is important

Being too hot or too cold makes it difficult to learn. Outdoors, children need suitable clothing, for all weathers (and so do the adults!), and indoors the rooms should have good air circulation to encourage concentration and reduce the spread of infection.

AC 1.4 **Activity**

How can you work with others to ensure the environment is an enabling one?

LO2 Understand how the early years practitioner supports children's behaviour and socialisation within play environments

AC 2.1 Your role in supporting children's socialisation within play environments

Socialisation involves how children relate socially (and emotionally) to other people. Children need to learn how to deal appropriately with a whole range of emotions, including anger and frustration, within a supportive environment.

An essential aspect of socialisation involves getting young children to behave in socially acceptable ways without damaging their self-esteem: that is, rejecting the children's unacceptable behaviour, not the children themselves. Socialisation begins from birth, as babies interact with the people around them and respond to their environment. More information on the stages of social and emotional development can be found in Unit 10.

Encouraging positive social interactions

Having at least one secure personal relationship with a parent or carer enables children to form other relationships.

Consistent, loving care from a parent or carer who is sensitive to the child's particular needs enables the child to feel secure and to develop self-worth. Children observe the behaviour of parents, carers and other significant adults (such as early years practitioners, play workers, teachers and teaching assistants) and their observations affect the child's own behaviour, including how they relate to others. A child's ability to relate to others may also be affected by:

- special educational needs – for example, communication and/or social interaction difficulties
- family circumstances, such as separation or divorce
- death, abandonment or other permanent separation from parent or main carer.

All children need affection, security, acceptance, encouragement, patience and a stimulating environment. Children deprived of these in the first five to six years of life may find it difficult to relate to other people throughout childhood (and even adulthood). However, children are amazingly resilient and subsequent sustained relationships with caring adults in a supportive environment can help children to overcome early parental separation, rejection or neglect.

Adults who provide inconsistent or inappropriate care may unwittingly encourage inappropriate behaviour in children, which can lead to adults spending less time interacting with the child, resulting in the child having ineffective communication skills as well as difficulties in establishing and maintaining positive relationships with other people. Appropriate social interactions with adults (and other children) will lead to children being able to demonstrate positive ways of relating to others and using appropriate social skills.

AC 2.1 **Activity**

1 Which early social interactions can you remember (for example, at playgroup, nursery, school, clubs, hobbies, on holiday, early friendships)?

2 How do you think these early social interactions influenced your attitudes and actions? For example, did they have positive or negative influences?

AC 2.2 How modelling positive behaviours impacts on children's behaviour

Modelling positive behaviour

Children learn a lot of their behaviour from those around them. Early years practitioners must be good role models and should model positive behaviour. This includes showing respect, being polite, showing consideration for others and waiting with patience.

Modelling positive behaviour is a useful way of helping children to resolve conflicts. For example, when talking to a pair of children who have been fighting, an adult might say, 'I wonder how Jason could have said he wanted the train, instead of grabbing it, or 'Serena, I wonder how you could stop Jason grabbing the train, without hitting him.' It is important to encourage a culture where children can say how they are feeling. Sometimes it may feel like particular children, or a particular child, keep coming to you for help. But it is important that on every occasion you listen with sympathy and sensitively try to help the child. Adults can encourage children to be assertive. For example, they can help children to use phrases like 'I want a turn,' 'Can I go next?' and 'Can I have a turn when you're finished?' Encourage children to respond to things they do not like, by saying 'No,' or 'I do not like that.'

AC 2.2 **Activity**

Think about the behaviours modelled by you and your colleagues in the setting. How could you improve your behaviour when confronted with an aggressive child?

LO3 Be able to support children's behaviour and socialisation within play environments

AC 3.1 Modelling positive behaviour

Children model their attitudes and actions on the behaviour of others. They imitate the actions and speech of those they are closest to, for example, acting at being 'mum', 'dad', 'key person' or 'teacher', copying the actions and mannerisms of adults around the home, childcare setting or school. All practitioners working with children need to be aware of the significant impact they make on children's development, including their behaviour, by providing positive role models. Observing the communication and interactions of parents and other significant adults (such as early years practitioners) affects children's own behaviour, how children deal with their own feelings and how children relate to others. This is why it is so important for adults to be positive role models for children's behaviour.

You need to act as a positive role model for children. You can do this by:

- keeping calm when dealing with problem behaviour
- listening to both sides of the story when there is conflict and apologising if you have made a mistake
- noticing good behaviour and praising it
- being consistent when dealing with inappropriate behaviour

- showing respect to children and other adults, by the way you listen, your facial expression, your body language and by what you say
- making sure that you do not make any negative comments in front of the children.

AC 3.1 Activity

Think about how to model positive behaviour to support children's behaviour and socialisation.

AC 3.2 Planning an activity which supports children's socialisation

How to plan play activities

The best planning comes from knowing the children well. This develops from using the observations practitioners make of children to plan the next step in their play. Children need a variety of activities or experiences, using a range of resources, to enable them to learn and make progress in all areas of development. Planning helps children to use a range of resources and materials. It encourages a 'balanced' day.

Having made decisions about what to provide, it is necessary to plan each activity/experience and consider the following factors:

- aim or purpose
- time needed/group size
- preparation in advance
- preparation at the time
- space/resources/safety
- suitability for age/stage of development
- supervision/adult role
- adaptation for a child with additional needs
- consideration of equal opportunities issues
- opportunities for monitoring and assessing individual children.

Aim or purpose

As for observations, a clear aim is preferable to one that is too wide or vague – for example, 'To develop fine manipulative skills through putting a straw in a carton of drink' or 'To develop listening skills through a "sound" lotto game'.

Almost all activities have many benefits and will help development in more than one area. It is a good idea to identify the main purpose and mention briefly other aspects that are also likely to be involved.

Time needed/group size

Most settings have a daily routine with set times for:

- refreshment, sleep or rest
- outdoor or energetic activity
- assembly or group time
- start and finish times for sessions (these may vary for individual children in a nursery setting).

Knowing how long you are going to need to carry out an activity from start to finish for a group is very important. It helps to decide when it can be done and, if all children are to have the opportunity to do it, how many 'sessions' will be needed. Generally, the younger the children, the fewer you would have in a group – perhaps for a 'messy' activity such as finger painting you may work with just pairs or perhaps just one child. You need to allow time for clearing away, especially if the tables or the area are needed for another activity. Similarly, the children may need to wash ready for lunch or get dressed for going outside/home.

Preparation/resources
In advance

1 The first step is to find out individual children's interests and the setting's current topic or theme, if it has one, and discuss with your supervisor what activity might be appropriate.

2 You should then plan the activity, show the plan to your supervisor and, if it is suitable, agree when you may implement it. Avoid any activity that has been carried out by someone else the day before! At this stage, you can ensure that the space you need (e.g. the book corner or the water tray) will be available. An activity that uses 'permanent' equipment (e.g. Lego, Stickle

Bricks, puzzles) will need setting up – space, layout of equipment, seating if applicable. However, one that uses 'consumable materials' (i.e. ones that are used up and need replacing, such as paper, paint, glue) requires more consideration.

3 Make a comprehensive list of what you need. This should be detailed. For example, not just 'six sheets of paper' but six sheets of A3, black sugar paper (i.e. state size, colour, type).

4 Check that your selected resources are available (another staff member may have reserved the last of the gold paper for a particular display or activity, so do not just go and help yourself!) and collect them in plenty of time. Some may need further preparation – for example, cutting to a smaller size or particular shape, arranging in pots or tubs for easy access, and so on.

5 Check that:
- (for very young children) there are no tiny pieces
- materials are clean
- materials are undamaged
- there are no toxic substances/contents.

For preparation relating to food and cooking activities, see Unit 7.

At the time

1 Always allow time for preparation on the day – arrive early if necessary. Your supervisor will have made arrangements for you to take the agreed number of children at the agreed time. If you are not ready, someone else has to supervise those children and/or find them an alternative activity.

2 Remember to protect tables, surfaces, children and their clothing appropriately.

3 Prepare sufficient quantities of paint, paper, and so on for the group size identified and have them conveniently to hand – you cannot leave a group of young children alone while you go to fetch more paper from the stock cupboard or to mix up more paint!

4 When planning your activity, think about how you will introduce it – what will be your starting point? You might show the children the equipment and ask them about it, or remind them of a previous related experience.

Suitability for age/stage of development

Although you can use books to help you understand what is the 'expected' or 'norm' ability for the age range you are working with, it is more important to base your own planning on what you can see and have experienced in your particular work setting. If you have used your placement time effectively, you will have helped with activities planned by other staff members and become familiar with the resources and with the children.

Remember that children should be active learners and your plan should provide them with 'hands-on' experience. Avoid activities that involve colouring in worksheets or 'sticking' ones that do not allow children to select their own materials and choose how to use the space.

Supervision/practitioner role

Your activity, perhaps a physical one involving large apparatus, may require more than one practitioner to supervise. In this case, it is important not only to check that there are sufficient practitioners available but also that the other practitioner knows your activity's aim and what is involved. If you have written a clear plan, then it can be shared more easily. Try to think ahead about any aspects of your plan that may require an additional practitioner to offering practical help to all children or an individual child.

Adaptation for a child with additional needs and consideration of equal opportunities

As you will be planning for children in your work setting, you will be aware of any children with additional needs – whether the difficulty results from a physical condition, a sensory impairment, a learning difficulty or a behavioural or emotional problem. Take notice of the strategies used by other staff members to allow access to all activities and equipment. This may be straightforward, such as ensuring that you make left-handed or 'dual-handed' scissors available, or more challenging, such as adapting space and materials for a child whose leg is in plaster.

Try to think about adaptations for children with sensory impairment. Visually impaired children will depend heavily on hearing and touch so try to adapt resources or provide extra ones to support their learning (e.g. samples of materials mentioned in stories like 'The Three Little Pigs' – straw, sticks and bricks). Hearing-impaired children will also benefit from learning through touch, but will need visual aids too – perhaps puppets or figures to demonstrate parts of a story or clear pictures sequenced to help with a cooking or construction task.

Always make sure that you have the children's attention, touching a visually impaired child on the arm so it is clear she needs to listen, and ensuring that when talking or giving instructions to a hearing-impaired child, she is able to see the speaker's face. See section on effective communication, in Unit 2.1.

Think about the equal opportunities issues dealt with in Unit 4 (e.g. gender and cultural stereotyping) and make sure that your resources promote positive images.

Opportunities for monitoring and assessing individual children

Your activity will offer opportunities for observing how children use equipment, listen to any instructions, talk about what they are doing and interact with each other. At the end of an activity, make a note about any aspects that presented difficulties, caused frustration or were not sufficiently challenging. Make a note also of those in which the children were particularly successful. This helps staff to keep records, report progress to parents and plan for individual children's future needs.

Evaluating your plan

As well as recording the points mentioned above in relation to the children, you need to consider your own learning. You should try to judge how suitable your activity was and how it might be improved or altered. You can also reflect on your own ability to prepare, explain, to support children and maintain behaviour. Refer to all the factors you had to consider and identify which ones 'worked' (were appropriate) and which were less successful.

For example, would it have been more effective with thicker paint, coloured paper, fatter brushes? Did you allow enough/too much time? Was the cutting task too fiddly for the children to manage independently? How could it have been improved?

Do not be too dismayed if an activity seems to be a disaster, but make sure you understand what went wrong and why!

Planning activities to meet children's needs

When deciding what activities and experiences will be offered to children, staff in a work setting must consider safety, space, children's ages and stage of development, supervision and availability of resources. Most settings plan activities around well-chosen themes or topics. These are usually relevant to the children themselves and, perhaps, the time of year; common ones are 'Ourselves', 'Autumn', 'Festivals' (e.g. Christmas, Diwali, Hanukkah, Chinese New Year), 'Growth' and 'Nursery Rhymes'.

In practice

Supporting socialisation through a play activity

Plan, implement and evaluate a play activity which encourages or extends a child's social and emotional development. Use the assessment from previous observations of the child's social and emotional development as the basis for your planning.

Encourage the child to use a variety of social skills and emotional abilities. For example: positive behaviour; independence (such as using self-help skills or making choices); effective communication skills; sharing resources; expressing needs and/or feelings; understanding the needs and feelings of others.

Consider how you could make sure this activity is fully inclusive. Examples of activities to encourage socialisation include:

● musical activities
● group outings
● imaginary play
● cooking
● playing with natural and malleable materials – sand, water, clay, dough, etc.
● reading in a small group.

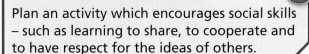

AC 3.2 **Progress check**

Plan an activity which encourages social skills – such as learning to share, to cooperate and to have respect for the ideas of others.

AC 3.3 Carrying out an activity which supports children's socialisation

Having carefully planned your activity, arrange to implement it, using the information in AC 3.2.

AC 3.3 **Progress check**

If possible, carry out an observation of the activity and evaluate it.

AC 3.4 Reflecting on own role in supporting children within play environments

Reflective practice: reflecting on your own role

You should get used to reviewing and reflecting on your experiences as part of your everyday learning. In this way, each experience – whether positive or negative – will contribute to your development and personal growth. Ways to reflect include:

● setting yourself some goals or targets when you start studying, and using your tutor's and your placement supervisor's feedback to monitor your progress
● working out what you have achieved and what you still need to work on
● making a record of your thoughts and reflections to help you to keep track of your ideas and see how far they have developed over a period of time
● recording your thoughts on any difficulties or challenges you are facing
● talking things through with another person, such as another student or a trusted friend
● asking yourself questions about what you did and thinking about how you could have done it better
● using evidence to support or evaluate any decision – for example, observations or notes.

Write it down! It is a good idea to develop the habit of recording your reflections. This will help you to extend your skills in reflective practice.

See AC 2.5 in Unit 9.

Guidelines for good practice

Receiving feedback

- Ask questions: state what you want feedback about. Be specific about what you want to know. Give the speaker time to think about what they want to say.
- Listen: listen attentively – do not interrupt or digress. Ask for clarification if you are not sure you have understood what you have heard. Try not to be defensive or to reject the information. You need to listen, but not necessarily to agree. Take notes of what is said.
- Check: check what you have heard. Repeat back what they have said and ask for

examples of what the speaker means. Give your reactions to the feedback or ask for time to think about it if necessary. Ask for suggestions on what might work better.

- Reflect: feedback is information for you to use – it is not a requirement to change. If you are unsure about the soundness of the feedback, check it out with other people. Work out the options open to you and decide what you want to do. It is up to you to evaluate how accurate and how useful the feedback is.

Key term

appraisal A meeting with your supervisor, mentor or line manager where you review your performance and plan your future objectives and career progression.

LO4 Be able to create an enabling play environment which meets the age, stage and needs of children

AC 4.1 How an enabling play environment meets the age, stage and needs of children

Meeting the needs of babies

It can be very boring to be a baby. This is because babies depend on adults to bring interesting experiences to them. They cannot move about enough to reach for things when sitting, or crawl or walk to get to them.

Bored, unhappy babies cannot learn much and the important period of babyhood when so much learning is possible will then be lost. Studies of child development suggest that the first years of life are of great importance for development and learning, and that this is the time when the child's willingness and ability for future learning are set.

Imagine what it would be like if you spent long periods on your back with only a ceiling to look at, or you were in a pram in the garden with a plastic cover hiding your view of the sky and trees, or you could hear voices, but could not see who was talking because they were standing behind you.

Material provision, equipment and resources for babies

Children from birth to three years enjoy and benefit from the companionship and stimulation of being with older children, but they also become exhausted if they do not have a safe base/haven/nest to return to, where they can be quiet and calm.

Babies need to be cuddled and held on your knee so that they can see things, be talked to and sung to, and be bounced in time with music. They need things to look at, swipe at, grab and hold, chew, suck and mouth, smell, shake and listen to. Babies need objects and people.

Quiet times

Sometimes babies need to be quiet, but they still need to feel that people are near. Of course, it is important that the sun is not in their eyes and that they are comfortable with the temperature and are in a clean nappy.

Babies need times to:

- look at a mobile
- listen to gentle music playing
- hear the birds singing as they lie in a pram under a tree, looking through the branches at the patterns of the leaves against the sky
- sit propped up in a specially designed chair and watch what is going on
- watch other children
- follow voices they know because they spend time with them and love them
- receive warmth and affection.

Floor time

Anyone who observes babies finds that they explore the environment using their senses and movement. They need plenty of opportunities to be on the floor so that they can do this. When lying on their backs, they can watch mobiles or leaves and branches swaying and fluttering in the trees above their pram, and swipe at objects above them with their arms, or kick at them with their legs. But they also need to feel their arms, legs and tummies against the ground. Experts in physical movement development (like JABADAO, the National Centre for Movement, Learning and Health in Leeds) are finding that there are benefits to babies from spending more time on the floor. They need to be given opportunities to crawl as well as to sit and lie down. It is exciting when children take their first steps, but they still need plenty of time down on the floor. This means that there should be plenty of spaces to do this when working with very young children in the first year of their life.

Are there objects a baby can put in his or her mouth, touch and handle, smell, carry about, look at and make sounds with? The floors will need to be clean, as a baby will stop to examine every piece of fluff, dropped crumb or spillage. When the baby crawls outside, he or she will need surfaces such as grass and rougher surfaces. But remember, babies put everything in their mouths.

Tummy time

Babies need time to be on the floor, on their tummies, with interesting natural objects placed in front of them, which they need to reach for. Practitioners can help babies to have things in reach, and at the point where the baby is trying to crawl, keep frustration at bay by making sure there is enough success to keep them trying. It is very difficult for a baby when they are trying to crawl forwards to get something they want, and they find they are moving backwards. Having something to push against can be just the right help at the right time!

Sitting babies – treasure baskets

Elinor Goldschmied pioneered treasure baskets for sitting babies. These are now widely used in most settings. It is very important that they are presented to babies in the correct way or the baby will not get the full benefit of the learning the treasure basket offers. Make sure the basket is the correct shape, height and size. It is distressing for the baby if it tips as they lean on it, or if they are unable to reach the objects on the other side. It is uncomfortable to sit at a basket that is too high (like an adult sitting at a table when the chair is too low for the table height).

The baby needs the companionship of an adult who sits near them (usually on a chair that is near to the ground in height), but who does not join in – simply there as an anchor, smiling when shown objects, but saying nothing. When adults are concentrating (perhaps writing and thinking hard), it interrupts the flow of thought if someone else is making suggestions, asking questions or trying to make conversation with them. Ideally, the treasure basket experience will take place in a quiet area away from the noisier main area. It can be screened off with a clothes horse draped with material, to signal to other, older, more mobile children that this is a quiet area, set aside for sitting babies to concentrate and learn.

The objects should not all be made of plastic, but of natural materials or metals that can be washed and kept clean. This is because plastic does not offer much to the range of senses through which babies learn. As objects become shabby, they should be removed, and there should be new objects to keep the interest of the baby who has regular use of the basket. As your observations of a baby build, you will be able to select objects with that baby's interests in mind. The baby who loves to bang and bash objects will choose different ones from the baby who loves to dangle and shake objects. It is deeply satisfying to try to work out what a baby will particularly enjoy exploring, especially when you have built on your observations successfully.

Babies need enough objects to select from, so the basket should be full enough to encourage this. Examples might be: a small wooden brush, a small cardboard box, a loofah, a wooden spoon, a small metal egg whisk, a bath plug and chain, a small bag of lavender, a large feather.

Of course, you will need to make a risk assessment based on your observations of what a baby needs. Never put an object in the treasure basket that makes you anxious about its safety for a baby, and remember that some babies have allergies. Remember also that some babies are less adventurous than others and will need more support and encouragement to enjoy the treasure basket.

Providing opportunities for rest and sleep

Getting the right rest is crucial for the learning of babies and young children. Not all babies will need to sleep at the same time, and it is worrying to find a practice where all babies are expected to have their nappies changed at the same time and to sleep at the same time. These are very individual things.

It is important for babies to feel that they are near someone when they sleep. Some babies sleep best on a mat on the floor of a quiet area that is gated, with a cover to keep them warm; others sleep better in a darkened room, in a cot kept for them. This area should not be full of stimulation. It is important to relax and let go when falling asleep. Neutral colouring is best, and the room should not be cluttered.

It is also important to keep to the sleep-time rituals and patterns that are familiar to the baby at home. Some babies need to have a cuddle, being lowered into their cot as they fall asleep. Others might never go to sleep on a lap, but need to be in a cot, in a quiet room with their teddy, in order to fall asleep.

Sleep is important for learning. It helps the memory to embed rich learning experiences with people, objects, events and places.

Guidelines for good practice

Material provision, equipment and resources for babies

Expensive equipment is not necessary to create a rich environment in which babies can develop and learn. Babies are helped to develop and learn when they:

- are introduced to treasure baskets
- are offered homemade or commercial toys – for example, baby mirrors, which help their sense of identity (who is that? is that me?); rattles to hold and shake, with and without sounds; wobbly toys and pop-up toys; bath toys that sink and float; a soft toy, such as a teddy bear
- are provided with opportunities to crawl on comfortable surfaces – a mixture of carpets and other surfaces to explore, including grass
- have suitable places to sleep – some babies sleep best in a cot, others in a basket on a floor away from draughts, some tightly tucked in, others with loose bedclothes covering them; babies should never be left to sleep unsupervised
- eat in a family group – this is best for babies, as they are part of the conversation, and they are talked to and given attention in a way that is impossible with a group of babies
- share a book with their key person, which can calm them (they love to look at patterns, grids and circles – see Figure 6.4); books will be chewed and sucked, as babies learn through all their senses.

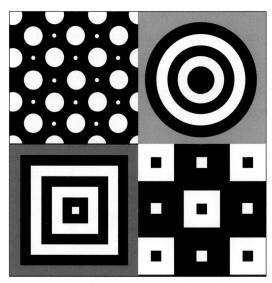

Figure 6.4 Babies love to look at patterns, grids and circles

How an enabling indoor play environment meets the needs of toddlers

The importance of people

Toddlers need practitioners who create a warm, affectionate atmosphere, encourage children to try things, observe and tune in to their learning, and make individual plans to help them learn. Children need to feel valued, appreciated and respected.

When children feel their efforts are appreciated and valued, they develop a positive self-image and a good sense of well-being. This, more than anything else, helps them to learn. The key person in the setting is of great importance in this.

By this age, children are beginning to get a sense of the passing of time through the day as they become familiar with the early childhood setting. They are helped if there is a predictable environment. This does not mean rigid routines, but it does mean having a consistent shape to the day. In this way children can begin to participate fully in the preparation for an experience, the experience itself and the end of the experience. They will feel a sense of closure as they join in clearing things up each day. This means that staff need to work together as a team to create consistent boundaries and

ways of doing things, so that children feel safe, secure and able to develop their intellectual lives. Then they can be explorers and problem-solvers, and they can make and use symbols, with reasoning and enquiring minds.

Heuristic play

Heuristic play is when children play with and explore the properties of objects.

Children need a warm, inviting floor space, without lots of clutter to capture their attention. The space needs to be prepared in advance so that children come upon the carefully spaced piles of objects when they enter the area. All the objects are collected from everyday use, rather than toys.

One pile might include spheres, circular objects and cylinders, such as a cotton reel, a bobble from a hat and a bracelet. Another might be of metal objects, such as tins with smoothed edges or a metal tea caddy. The practitioner sits quietly and provides a calm and concentrating atmosphere that supports the child's explorations without intervening, except to say something like, 'Yes, you have a lovely tin' – but only if the child brings it to them. For more details on heuristic play, see Unit 7, page 171.

Double provision

Through double provision (providing more than one activity at a time), the different needs and interests of children from birth to five years can be attended to with quality. There might be a workshop area, with carefully selected and presented found materials, such as boxes, tubes, dried flowers, moss, twigs, wool, string, masking tape, glue, scissors and card. Here, older children could become involved in making models and constructions, and practitioners can help them to carry out their ideas without losing track of them on the way or becoming frustrated. Children can be helped as they try to join things and make decisions about whether a string knot would be better than masking tape or glue.

Nearby, on the floor, there might be a beautiful basket full of balls of wool and string, which younger and less experienced children can enjoy unravelling and exploring how these behave. Other children might like to return to this earlier way of using string too. Remember that careful supervision is essential to prevent accidents.

It is a good idea to try to offer everything at different levels of difficulty, so that there is something for everyone to find absorbing. Absorbed children behave better, on the whole.

Attractive presentation and tidy-up time indoors and outdoors

If an area is dirty, shabby or in a muddle, it is less attractive to children. Often a well-used area becomes cluttered and untidy halfway through a morning or afternoon, and the children leave it. It is important that practitioners do not neglect these abandoned areas. Children can be encouraged to help tidy it, but practitioners can role-model this mid-session if children are very involved in other areas. At the end of the session, everyone needs to tidy up, though, unless there are good reasons for a child not to, such as being upset or unsettled.

Children should never be nagged or made to feel bad, but they should be encouraged and given specific and appropriate tasks as members of the learning community. Even a toddler enjoys putting rubbish in the bin. It is a question of finding something suitable for each particular child. The important thing is not to overdo the requests for help in tidying, and to remember that it is discriminatory to expect only a few children to do all the tidying.

Movement area

Important play provision for toddlers and children up to at least five years is on the floor! Making a movement corner is as important as making a book corner for brain development, learning and well-being. The floor needs to be clean and carpets should not be scratchy.

Having an interested person sensitively supporting and mirroring is important. Mirroring is a vital pattern for late learning, as research by Colwyn Trevarthen at Edinburgh University shows. Adults who make good play companions are a valuable resource as part of the play provision. The rough-and-tumble play traditional in mammals, including human children, just before sleeping is often engaged in with adults in the family.

> **Discussion point**
>
> **The importance of people in the lives of toddlers**
>
> Having read the sections in this chapter about the importance of people, what do you think are the key messages? Discuss this in a small group, and make a set of commitments to work on in your practice. Write them down and review them in a month's time. Evaluate your progress.

> **In practice**
>
> Audit or reflect on the provision in your setting/placement. If there are gaps in the provision, think about what you would introduce first, and why.

How an enabling indoor play environment meets the needs of children from three to five years

The importance of people

Communication, skilful body movements, play and creative making of symbols are all important aspects of a child's development during this period. Practitioners have a huge role in supporting children with these developments.

Just as babies and toddlers need plenty of time to be in the garden/outdoors, so too do children from three to five years. They also enjoy toddler experiences, alongside increasingly complex experiences. They are beginning to be able to take increasing responsibility for their own risk assessment (at the woodwork bench, when cooking and gardening), but they need adult support or they will not manage to do so.

Children benefit from discussions about safety, and taking care of themselves, others and

Guidelines for good practice

Indoor material provision, equipment and resources for toddlers

Children who are beginning to be confident walkers need:

- stable furniture to pull themselves up on and cruise between
- heuristic play
- a designated space for vigorous movement, with cushions on which to leap and roll about
- wooden and natural material objects to feel, mouth and hold
- simple towers to make and knock down
- finger-painting
- non-toxic crayons and felt-tip pens and paper
- wet and dry silver sand/play sand (not builder's sand)
- play dough – find some good recipes for play dough (some involve cooking, which makes the dough last longer); check the dough is safe to put in the mouth and even to eat, as some children might do this
- opportunities for water play, carefully supervised, at bath time, in paddling pools or with bowls of water – remember, children can drown in very shallow water, so always supervise these activities
- tea sets, toy cars and other play props to encourage pretend symbolic play with a willing adult
- objects to transport in trucks, bags and so on
- boxes to put things into and take things out of
- blankets to cover teddies, dolls and so on (also known as 'enveloping')
- picture books and books with simple texts, and stories and rhymes, such as *Spot the Dog*
- simple dressing-up clothes – mainly hats, shoes and belts for toddlers
- action songs and finger rhymes.

Figure 6.5 Children engaged in imaginative play

equipment. They also need practitioners who give them help in caring for others, thinking of others, looking after the material provision and equipment and making decisions and choices which help their development and learning. Children do not respond well to being judged and disapproved of by adults. They do respond well to being helped to take responsible decisions.

Figure 6.6 Dinosaurs could be the key for this child to learn many different things

Open continuous provision indoors should be provided every day

Everything in the list for continuous, open-ended provision for toddlers (see page 162) should also be provided for children aged three to five years. Children need to be able to experience materials at different levels of complexity, since at times they are operating at their highest levels of possibility, and at other times they need a quieter, less exhausting day. None of us, adult or child, is at our best all day, every day.

It is always useful to move around the environment on your knees or on your back in order to see it from a toddler or baby's view. What would a child see as they move about the environment?

Displays and interest tables indoors

Issues of gender, culture and disability need to be thought through when it comes to setting

up displays. Positive images and multicultural artefacts need to be discussed and planned by staff as a team. Seasonal and cultural festivals and educational visits across the year help children through special and one-off opportunities for exploration.

Displays should respect children's work – do not cut up children's paintings to make an adult's collage. The paintings children do should be mounted and displayed as they are.

The outdoor play environment

How an enabling outdoor play environment meets the needs of babies

Many settings find that when the weather is warm and dry enough, ensuring appropriate supervision, babies and toddlers sleep better outside in cool, fresh air in flatbed cots or prams. They tend to fall asleep more easily and move more gently into wakefulness with clouds or a leafy branch overhead and the sounds of nature and children playing outdoors.

Babies should also be given the opportunity to experience play outdoors:

- Non-mobile babies need to be placed in positions that give them plenty to look at, reach for, swipe at and grasp. Practitioners should carry them to interesting places or sit with them to share interest about the environment.
- Crawling babies need a variety of surfaces to provide different tactile experiences – for example, they will learn that grass is warm, soft and firm but may be wet, whereas paving is hard, cool and smooth. They will also learn how to adapt their newfound movement skills to each different surface.

How an enabling outdoor play environment meets the needs of toddlers

Toddlers who are mastering locomotion and coordination also need several kinds of surfaces to explore and, once they are more confident walkers, they need less predictable surfaces on which to practise their skills.

Guidelines for good practice

Indoor material provision, equipment and resources for children from three to five years

Children from three to five years need access to the following every day:

- wet and dry sand (these are two entirely different learning experiences), with equipment nearby in boxes labelled with words and pictures for children to select
- clean water in a water tray or baby bath, with buckets, guttering, waterwheels, and so on, to make waterfalls, and boxes of equipment labelled with pictures and words
- found and recycled materials in a workshop area, with glue, scissors, masking tape and so on
- book-making area, next to the workshop
- small-world playthings – doll's house, train set, garage, cars, farms, zoos, dinosaurs
- paint/graphics materials in a mark-making area, with a variety of paper and different kinds of pencils, pens and chalks (this might be next to the workshop area)
- malleable clay or dough
- wooden set of free-standing blocks (not plastic, and not bits and pieces from different sets) – unit blocks, hollow blocks and mini hollow blocks (for example, from Community Playthings)
- construction kit (one or two carefully selected types, such as Duplo or Brio)
- book area, which is warm, light and cosy
- domestic play area
- dressing-up clothes (mainly hats and shoes)
- daily cookery with baking materials and equipment
- ICT, digital camera, computer – it is preferable to use computer programs that encourage children to use their imagination, rather than responding to computer-led tasks
- nature table, with magnifiers, growing and living things, such as mustard and cress, hyacinths, wormery, fish tank
- woodwork bench, with glue to join things and tape to bind things together, saws, hammers and a vice
- a range of dolls and soft toys
- music and sounds area, with homemade and commercially produced instruments
- movement area (perhaps next to the music area)
- story props, poetry and song cards
- sewing table
- cooker/food preparation.

Guidelines for good practice

Outdoor material provision, equipment and resources for working with toddlers

Children who are beginning to be confident walkers need:

- a range of surfaces to walk on, and to try to run on
- a large, bouncy ball to kick and throw, bats, hoops and beanbags
- flowers (these are for picking as far as a toddler is concerned); encourage children to pick daisies and dandelions rather than flowers from the flowerbed; they enjoy putting flowers in a vase of water to place on the meal table
- climbing opportunities, always carefully supervised: a small climbing frame or steps
- wheeled trucks to push and pull, pull-along toys, pushchairs for dolls and teddies and other soft toys
- plants and a growing area, and watering cans
- a well-drained sandpit
- a covered pond and fishing nets to use when supervised with an practitioner
- puddles to stamp in wearing wellies
- picnics
- mud pies and a digging area.

How an enabling outdoor play environment meets the needs of children aged three to five years

In her book *Playing Outdoors: Spaces and Places, Risk and Challenge* (2007), Helen Tovey lists the following as important if children are to have a challenging and creative outdoor area. Children need:

- designated spaces (but children should be allowed to rearrange them and use them in a different way)
- connected spaces, which encourage children to join in (sand and water areas)
- elevated spaces (mounds, trees, ramps, steps, climbing frames)
- wild spaces, so that children do not only experience neat and trim tarmac areas
- spaces for exploring and investigating
- spaces for mystery and enchantment (dens)
- natural spaces (digging patches and opportunities to grow flowers and vegetables)
- space for the imagination (providing children with open-ended props, logs, and so on)
- spaces for movement and stillness (climbing, dragging, swinging on bars, jumping, balancing, and so on, as well as sitting in secluded, tucked-away places in peace and calm)
- social spaces (outdoor seats for chatting together)
- fluid places (flexible resources that can be moved about when needed).

Figure 6.7 Raking leaves

Set out resources and equipment minimally – for example, a den with a tea set in it. The children will want to change things about if they are thinking and using the environment well.

Bikes, scooters and carts

Bikes need to be three-wheeled and two-wheeled, with some needing two or three children cooperating in order to make them work. Two-wheeler bikes with no pedals are excellent for children, as they can tilt and balance without having to perform a complex combination of actions. Scooters and carts to push and pull are also important, as are prams and pushchairs for dolls and teddies.

Research activity

Find out what a Forest School in the UK is. Investigate the different approaches to Forest Schools in the UK and in countries such as Germany, Denmark, Norway and Sweden.

AC 4.1   Progress check

Describe how (a) an enabling indoor play environment and (b) an enabling outdoor environment meet the needs of children at different ages and stages

AC 4.2 Creating an enabling play environment

Activity

The enabling play environment: indoors
Focus on just one area in the setting and make a plan that includes the relevant equipment and resources as described in AC 4.1. For example, you could plan a role-play area or a water play area.

The enabling play environment: outdoors
Focus on just one area in the setting and make a plan that includes the relevant equipment and resources as described in AC 4.1. For example, you could plan a simple obstacle course or a small gardening project.

AC 4.2 Progress check

Implement your plans from the Activity box above.

AC 4.3 Reflecting on own role in creating enabling play environments

Using the guidelines for reflecting on your practice in AC 3.4, reflect on your own role in creating enabling play environments.

Assessment practice

1 Explain what is meant by the play environment.
2 Explain how environments support play.
3 Explain how to work collaboratively to provide enabling play environments in early years settings.
4 Describe the role of the early years practitioner in supporting children's socialisation within play environments.
5 Explain how modelling positive behaviours impacts on children's behaviour.
6 Know how to model positive behaviour.
7 Plan an activity which supports children's socialisation.
8 Describe how an enabling play environment meets the age, stage and needs of children.
9 Plan and create an enabling play environment indoors and outdoors.
10 Reflect on your own role in creating enabling play environments in your own setting.

Useful resources

Axline, V. (1971) *Dibs, In Search of Self: Personality Development in Play Therapy*, London: Penguin.

Dowling, M. (2010) *Young Children's Personal, Social and Emotional Development* (3rd edn), London: Sage Publications.

Paley, V.G. (1981) *Wally's Stories*, Cambridge, MA: Harvard University Press.

Sylva, K. and Lunt, I. (1982) *Child Development: A First Course*, Oxford: Blackwell.

Tovey, H. (2007) *Playing Outdoors: Spaces and Places, Risk and Challenge*, Maidenhead: Open University Press.

Anna Freud Centre

The centre was established in 1947 by Anna Freud to support the emotional well-being of children through direct work with children and their families, research and the development of practice, and training mental health practitioners.

www.annafreud.org

HighScope

HighScope is an American approach to early education and care, with several decades of research into its effectiveness. The website includes books, DVDs and news of training events and conferences in the UK.

Kate Greenaway Nursery School and Children's Centre

This website includes news and policies for a centre based in central London.

www.kategreenaway.org

Kidscape

This charity was established specifically to prevent bullying and child sexual abuse. The website includes resources for parents, children and professionals, and details of campaigns and training events.

www.kidscape.org.uk

Treasure baskets and heuristic play

Goldschmeid, E and Jackson S, (1994) *People Under Three young children in day care* (Routledge,Oxon) pp 128-141.

JABADOA

The movement play specialists

www.jabadao.org

Forest Schools

www.forestschoolassociation.org/

www.forestschools.com

Unit 7

Support children's play in early years

Learning outcomes

By the end of this unit, you will:

1 Understand the role of play in children's development.
2 Understand children's rights in relation to play.

3 Understand how children play during different stages of development.
4 Be able to support different types of play for children.

LO1 Understand the role of play in children's development

What is play?

Play is an essential part of every child's life and is vital for the enjoyment of childhood as well as for promoting social, emotional, intellectual and physical development. This unit provides the knowledge and understanding of the value of play in early years in preparation for practical experience.

Play is a word that is widely used in the field of early childhood, but it is very difficult to define. It is probably one of the least understood aspects of an early childhood practitioner's work, yet play is probably one of the most important elements of childhood. A traditional way of talking about play has been to break it into different types.

AC 1.1 Why play is necessary for the development of children

It would be inaccurate to say that play is the only way in which children learn. However, play is a major part of learning. It can open up possibilities to reflect on and apply ideas and imagination, relationships and feelings. It can help children be physically coordinated, capable of flexible thinking, be ethically

thoughtful and to develop a sense of awe and wonder.

Children learn through play. Children need opportunities to learn through:

- learning to predict: children learn to predict that something is about to happen. For example, a baby learns to predict that food will soon appear if a bib is tied around his or her neck.
- learning the consequences of their actions: children understand that they can bring about a result by their own actions. For example, a baby learns that if he or she cries, he or she will be picked up and comforted.
- asking questions: as soon as they can talk, children ask questions to try to make sense of their world and gain information. For example, four-year-old children constantly ask the question 'Why?' whereas two-and-a-half-year-old children constantly ask 'Who?' and 'What?'
- understanding concepts: experiences with real objects help young children to understand concepts and to develop problem-solving skills. For example, mathematical concepts involve understanding number, sequencing, volume and capacity as well as weighing and measuring.

- repetition: children learn by repeating activities over and over again. For example, they can learn a song or nursery rhyme by hearing it sung to them many times.
- imitation: children learn by copying what others do. For example, they learn how to write by copying letters, and in **role play** children copy the way they have observed others behave in certain situations.

Key term

role play A form of pretend play when children engage in, explore and learn about the everyday roles that occur in their familiar experience: the roles carried out by their parents or carers and members of their community.

Discussion point

Discuss the following in a group:

- What are your memories of your childhood play? Did you play?
- Did you make dens in the garden, under a table or with your bedclothes?
- Did you pretend you were in outer space, on a boat, on a desert island, going shopping?
- Did you feel you had hours and hours to play?
- Did you enjoy using inexpensive play props or were your favourite toys expensive, commercially produced toys?

AC 1.1 Progress check

Why is play essential to the overall (holistic) development of children?

LO2 Understand children's rights in relation to play

AC 2.1 The rights of children in relation to play

The United Nations Convention on the Rights of the Child, adopted by the United Nations in 1989, spells out the basic human rights to which every child, everywhere, is entitled.

The Convention sets out in a number of statements, called articles, the rights of all children and young people up to the age of 18. This includes Article 31 – the right to engage in play and recreational activities.

- Article 31:
  1 Recognise the right of the child to rest and leisure, to engage in play and recreational activities appropriate to the age of the child and to participate freely in cultural life and the arts.
  2 Respect and promote the right of the child to participate fully in cultural and artistic life and encourage the provision of appropriate and equal opportunities for cultural, artistic, recreational and leisure activity.
- Article 23 – rights of disabled children: a mentally or physically disabled child should enjoy a full and decent life, in conditions which ensure dignity, promote self-reliance and facilitate the child's active participation in the community. This includes additional care and assistance where appropriate, free of charge whenever possible.
- Article 30 – children of minorities or of indigenous people: the right for children from minority communities to enjoy their own culture, and to practise their own religion and language.

AC 2.2 How settings meet the right for children to play

Supporting children's right to play
Early years settings must work within the frameworks for learning in the UK, which for England is the EYFS. Well-planned play, both indoors and outdoors, is an important part of the EYFS. Children learn by playing and exploring, being active, and through creative and critical thinking, which takes place both indoors and outside.

The EYFS framework applies to children from birth to five years of age. During this Foundation Stage, children might be attending a playgroup, pre-school, nursery school, nursery class, day care setting, Reception class or private nursery, or be with a childminder or nanny. The EYFS explains how and what children will be learning to support their healthy development. Children will be learning skills, acquiring new knowledge and demonstrating their understanding through seven areas of learning and development.

Children should mostly develop the three prime areas first. These are:

● Communication and language
● Physical development
● Personal, social and emotional development.

These prime areas are those most essential for children's healthy development and future learning.

As children grow, the prime areas will help them to develop skills in four specific areas. These are:

● Literacy
● Mathematics
● Understanding the world
● Expressive arts and design.

AC 2.2 Activity

Look at the areas of development and learning as set out in the guidance documents for the EYFS and think about how each area can be planned for in play. How do you think this play meets the rights of children?

LO3 Understand how children play during different stages of development

The stages of play

It used to be thought that there were four stages of social play:

● solitary play
● parallel play
● associative play
● cooperative play.

Recent research shows that children do not develop as if they are climbing up a ladder. Instead, brain studies show that their play develops like a network. Sometimes they will play alone (solitary play). Sometimes they will play with others (parallel, associatively or cooperatively).

It will partly depend on their age, but it will also depend on their mood, others around them, where they are and whether they are tired, hungry or comfortable.

It is certainly easier for toddlers and young children to play together in parallel, associatively or cooperatively if they are in a pair (two children). Larger groups are more of a challenge for young children. Gradually, three or four children might play cooperatively together. This tends to develop from three to four years of age.

Table 7.1 Play and the development of physical coordination

Sit (usually 6–9 months)	• Play with feet (put them in mouth) • Cruise around furniture	• Play with objects using a pincer movement (i.e. finger and thumb) • Transfer toys from one hand to the other • Enjoy dropping objects over the side of the high chair and look to see where they have gone • Play with objects by putting them into the mouth • Enjoy 'treasure baskets' (natural objects and household objects) Provide: • Cups, boxes, pots of different sizes
Crawl (usually 9–12 months)	• When sitting, babies lean forward and pick up objects • Enjoy playing by crawling upstairs or onto low furniture • Love to bounce in time to music	• Pick things up with a pincer movement (finger and thumb) • Pull objects towards themselves • Can point at toys • Clasp hands and love to copy adults' actions in play • Love to play by throwing toys on purpose • Hold toys easily in hands • Put objects in and out of pots and boxes Provide: • Push and pull toys
Walk (but with sudden falling into a sitting position) (12–15 months)	• Can manage stairs with adult supervision • Can stand and kneel without support	• Begin to build towers with wooden blocks • Make lines of objects on the floor • Begin using books and turn several pages at a time • Use both hands but often prefer one • Lot of pointing • Pull toys along and push buttons Provide: • Board books and picture books with lines • Big empty cardboard boxes • Messy play with water paints and sand (be alert for physical safety)
Walk confidently (usually 18 months)	• Can kneel, squat, climb and carry things • Can climb on chairs • Can twist around to sit • Can creep downstairs on tummy going backwards	• Pick up small objects and threads • Build towers • Scribble on paper • Push and pull toys • Enjoy banging toys (e.g. hammer and peg drums) Provide: • Large crayons and paper for drawing →

Table 7.1 Play and the development of physical coordination   (*continued*)

Jump (usually two years)	<ul><li>Can jump on the spot and run, and climb stairs two feet at a time</li><li>Kick but not good at catching ball</li><li>Enjoy space to run and play (trips to the park)</li><li>Enjoy climbing frames (supervised)</li></ul>	<ul><li>Draw circles</li><li>Build tall towers</li><li>Pick up tiny objects</li><li>Turn the pages of books one at a time</li><li>Enjoy toys to ride and climb on</li><li>Enjoy messy play with water paints and sandpits</li></ul>Provide:<ul><li>Duplo, jigsaws, crayons and paper, picture books, puppets, simple dressing-up clothes, hats, belts and shoes</li></ul>
Hop (usually three years)	<ul><li>Jump from low steps</li><li>Walk forwards, backwards and sideways</li><li>Stand and walk on tiptoe</li><li>Stand on one foot</li><li>Try to hop</li><li>Use pedals on tricycle</li><li>Climb stairs one foot at a time</li></ul>	<ul><li>Build taller and taller towers with blocks</li><li>Begin to use pencil grip</li><li>Paint and make lines and circles in drawings</li><li>Use play dough, sand for modelling, paint</li><li>Hold objects to explore</li></ul>Provide:<ul><li>Trip to the park, walks, library, swimming</li><li>Cooking activities, small-world play, gluing, pouring, cutting</li></ul>
Skip (usually four years)	<ul><li>Balance (walking on a line)</li><li>Catch a ball, kick, throw and bounce</li><li>Bend at the waist to pick up objects from the floor</li><li>Climb trees and frames</li><li>Can run up and down stairs one foot at a time</li></ul>	<ul><li>Build tower with blocks that are taller and taller</li><li>Draw people, houses, etc.</li><li>Thread beads</li><li>Enjoy exercise, swimming, climbing (climbing frames and bikes)</li></ul>Provide:<ul><li>Jigsaws, construction toys, wooden blocks, small world, glue and stick, paint, sand, water, clay, play dough, dressing-up clothes, home area play</li><li>Cooking (measuring, pouring and cutting)</li></ul>
Jump, hop, skip and run with coordination (usually five years)	<ul><li>Use a variety of play equipment (slides, swings, climbing frames)</li><li>Enjoy ball games</li><li>Hop and run lightly on toes, and can move rhythmically to music</li><li>Well-developed sense of balance</li></ul>	<ul><li>Sew large stitches</li><li>Draw with people, animals and places, etc.</li><li>Coordinate paintbrushes and pencils, and a variety of tools</li><li>Enjoy outdoor activities (skipping ropes, football – both boys and girls enjoy these)</li><li>Make models, do jigsaws</li></ul>

→

Table 7.1 Play and the development of physical coordination   (*continued*)

Move with increased coordination and balance (usually six–seven years)	• Can ride two-wheeled bicycle • Hop easily with good balance • Can jump off apparatus at school	• Build play scenarios with wooden blocks • Draw play scenarios in drawings and paintings • Hold pencil as adults do • Enjoy ball games • Enjoy vigorous activity (riding a bike, swimming) (NB children should never be forced to take part) • Enjoy board games and computer games • Often (but not always) enjoy work being displayed on interest tables and walls (NB children should never be forced to display their work)

Playing alone

Solitary play: a child plays alone
From six months

Solitary play is play that is undertaken alone, sometimes through choice and at other times because the child finds it hard to join in, or because of his or her developmental stage.

In the first stage of play, beginning at about six months, babies play alone. Babies and toddlers need time and space to play alone, but often appreciate having others around them as they do so.

- Playing alone gives children personal space and time to think, to get to know themselves and like themselves.
- When toddlers play alone, they seek interesting experiences, but need support when frustrated.
- Children of all ages engage in solitary play sometimes; playing alone enables older children to concentrate and practise their skills (e.g. when constructing a model).
- It is important to protect the child's play space and toys from interference by other children.
- Children should be allowed to experience 'ownership' of toys and not be pushed to share before they are ready.

Example

A child might play alone (e.g. with a doll's house) because they want to play out a story that they have in their head. Having other children join the play would stop them being able to do this.

Figure 7.1 Baby playing alone

Onlooker behaviour
From about eight months to three years

Onlooker 'play' is the passive observation of the play of others without actual participation. Before children begin to play with each other, they go through a brief stage of onlooker behaviour:

- Children will stop what they are doing to watch and listen to what other children are doing.
- Older children may also watch others play if they are new to the group and don't yet feel ready to enter into the play.
- Even a child who is already secure in a group may engage in onlooker behaviour – taking a passive interest in what their friends are doing, but not joining in.

Stages of social play: children play together

Parallel play

From two to four years

Parallel play is when children play alongside each other but quite separately and without communicating with each other. Onlooker behaviour evolves into parallel – or side-by-side – play, which includes a lot of imitation and conversation back and forth between the players:

- During this stage, children like to have exactly the same toys as their peers do, but their own play space.
- They are no longer content to play alone, but they are also not ready for the demands of sharing toys or taking turns.
- Older children also enjoy parallel play with their friends.

Example

Two children might both put dolls to bed in the home area. They don't take much notice of each other.

Figure 7.2 Parallel play

Associative play

From three-and-a-half to five years

Associative play is when two or more children actively interact with one another by sharing or borrowing toys, while not doing the same things. Children playing at the parallel stage will begin to become aware of other children. They will often begin to communicate through talking to each other or by becoming aware of each other's games and explaining to each other what they are doing:

- Gradually one child will become involved in the other child's play; this is known as associative (or partnership) play.
- Language becomes much more important, imagination increases and dramatic themes begin to come into the play; this category of play may seem to be cooperative, but this is not the case – at this age, children are still too egocentric to have true cooperation.

Example

Two children might play so that one is the cook in the café and the other is the waitress. They don't seem to care that they have no customers.

Figure 7.3 Associative play

Cooperative play

From four-and-a-half years

Cooperative play is when children begin to 'play' together – to share their play. They become more sociable and take on roles in the play. Children begin to be aware of the needs and the roles of their peers and gradually the play can become complex:

- Rules are sometimes devised and some cooperative play will be revisited over several days.
- Cooperative play continues throughout middle childhood, where it evolves into more stylised games with rules.

- In the early stages of cooperative play, the rules are not as important as the sense of belonging to a group and working towards a common goal.

Figure 7.4 Cooperative play

Example of early (or simple) cooperative play

One child might be the baby and the other might be the parent, as they play going to the shops. They talk about their play ideas: 'You say "mum" and I say "yes, darling."'

Example of later (or complex) cooperative play

A group of children between three and five years old have been on an outing in the local market. When they return, the adult sets up a market stall. Some children become customers and buy things. Others sell things. John has a hearing impairment and uses sign language. Jack understands John's sign to give him three oranges. Other children talk as they play: 'You come and bag these apples.'

AC 3.1 The characteristics of child-initiated play and adult-led play

Child-initiated play

Child-initiated play occurs when children make their own decisions, without suggestion or guidance from adults, about the way in which they use the equipment and resources provided for them. For example, although a practitioner may have chosen which construction materials to set out (e.g. wooden blocks), two children may decide to work together to build a castle for 'small world' figures or 'play people'. This, then, is a child-initiated activity.

Adult-led play

These activities are planned, prepared and, often, initiated by adults. For example, a water activity might be planned that focuses particularly on 'force' or 'pressure'. The adult may have selected the equipment that lends itself to using water under pressure – squeezy bottles, thin plastic tubing, a water pump – and allowed children to use it in their own way, or played alongside the children, talking about what was happening and questioning them so that they express their ideas.

Even when an activity is adult-led it should always involve active participation by the children. Activities that have an 'end product' (e.g. a model or a special occasion card) must allow for children's experimentation and creativity so that each one is different and original. You should not aim to have all the children's work looking the same or 'perfect' (i.e. your idea of what the finished article should look like). Ownership is very important: children need to feel that their work is their own. What children learn from doing the activity – practical skills, understanding of materials, textures, sounds and so on – is far more important than the finished article.

Structured activities

These should be carefully planned to develop a particular aspect of understanding or skill. They are structured in that there are resources, carefully chosen, and usually a sequence of tasks, or steps, that may lead to a desired learning outcome or objective. A practitioner usually leads, supervises and monitors children's responses.

In practice

A simple sorting activity

Aim: to find out if children can identify and sort all the blue objects from a selection of objects of different colours.

Ask the children individually to find something blue and put it in the sorting 'ring' with other blue things – this ensures that all children participate and enables the practitioner to find out if the child has understood the task and can carry it out.

- For this task, the child has to know what 'blue' means and be able to distinguish objects of that colour from others.
- Some children may not realise that there are different shades of blue that are still 'blue'.
- Practitioners working with children on an activity such as this need to talk to them. Asking questions and enjoying a chat together help practitioners check each child's understanding.

AC 3.1   Progress check

What are meant by adult-led play and child-initiated play? Why is it important to recognise these aspects of play?

AC 3.2 How children's play needs and preferences change in relation to their development

What are play needs?

Play needs are individual to each child and are directly related to the age, stage of development and interests or preferences of the child.

Progress check

Play needs include opportunities to:

- play in safe places
- use a variety of objects and materials
- learn about the physical environment
- develop empathy (being able to imagine what someone else feels or thinks)
- take control of their own learning – at their own pace
- develop relationships with others – both other children and adults
- explore their own feelings – and learn how to control them.

Adults often make assumptions about the play needs of children, but these are not always an accurate reflection of what children both want (play preferences) and need (play needs).

Observing children during their play and discussing their play preferences with them will help to ensure that each child's play needs are met.

Having respect for children and valuing their play preferences

Giving attention to children's play activities can range from being a passive observer through to being fully involved in their play. Our own experience of playing as children and our ideas about play are certain to have an influence on the way we think about how children play. Children quickly pick up on the way adults react when they are playing. For example, if you hover over a child who is using the climbing frame for the first time, the child will probably be less adventurous and turn to you for reassurance. Or if you stereotype children's play by always encouraging boys to play as superheroes and girls to play with the prams and dolls, the children may alter their course of play to fit in with your ideas.

One of the most important skills is being able to know when to get involved and when to allow children to carry on playing. The principle behind this is having respect for children and valuing their play preferences. Although you may be involved in planning the play environment, you are not planning the way children play in it. Children need to be able to initiate their own ideas and to be spontaneous.

The play preferences of children from birth to eight years

Babies (from birth to 18 months) are totally dependent on caring adults to provide them with new play experiences. They show a preference for:

- watching movement and listening to rhythmic sounds
- holding rattles, chiming balls and musical toys
- exploring textures – for example, on an activity mat
- playing with stacking beakers and bricks
- exploring objects with their hands and their mouth
- active play with a caring adult
- making noises by banging toys
- playing with empty cardboard boxes
- looking at picture books.

Figure 7.5 Babies enjoy looking at picture books

Children aged 18 months to three years have an increasing desire for independence. They show a preference for:

- playing with things that screw and unscrew
- paints and crayons

- sand and water play
- playing with balls – rolling, kicking and throwing.

Towards the end of this period, they show a preference for:

- toys to ride and climb on
- matching and sorting games
- simple jigsaw puzzles
- puppet play and action rhymes
- musical games
- jumping, running and physical games
- role play.

Children aged three to five play with other children. They show a preference for:

- playing outdoors
- active pretend play with other children
- jigsaw puzzles and making models
- simple craft activities and playing with dough
- playing on the floor with bricks, trains, dolls and boxes, alone and with others
- acting out puppet shows
- imaginative play.

Children aged five and above are learning self-control and enjoy showing what they can do. They show a preference for:

- team games and games with rules
- complicated games on the floor with small-world objects
- more elaborate pretend play with others
- playing cooperatively with other children
- fantasy play
- activities that involve precise movements – such as hopscotch or skipping games.

AC 3.2 Activity

Describe children's play needs and preferences in relation to their stage of development.

LO4 Be able to support different types of play for children

AC 4.1 Benefits of physical play, creative play, imaginative play, sensory play and heuristic play

Physical play

Physical play promotes children's health. It links with all other areas of a child's development. The brain works better if children have plenty of fresh air and exercise. That is why both indoor and outdoor play are very important.

Through physical play, children learn to challenge gender stereotypes. Boys and girls can enjoy playing ball games (e.g. football play scenarios, running and climbing). Children need to be encouraged in these activities. It helps if they wear clothes and shoes that allow freedom of movement.

The benefits of physical play
Physical play helps children to:

- express ideas and feelings: children become aware that they can use their bodies to express themselves by moving in different ways as they respond to their moods and feelings, to music or to imaginative ideas
- explore what their bodies can do and become aware of their increasing abilities, agility and skill: children's awareness of the space around them and what their bodies are capable of can be extended by climbing and balancing on large-scale apparatus, such as a climbing frame, wooden logs and a balancing bar and by using small tricycles, bicycles and carts
- cooperate with others in physical play and games: children become aware of physical play as both an individual and a social activity, in playing alone or alongside others, in playing throwing and catching with a partner, in using a seesaw or push cart or in joining a game with a larger group

- develop increasing control of fine movements of their fingers and hands (fine motor skills): for example, playing musical instruments and making sounds with the body, such as clapping or tapping, help develop fine motor skills in the hands and fingers, while also reinforcing the link between sound and physical movement; helping with household tasks – washing up, pouring drinks, carrying bags – also develops fine motor skills
- develop balance and coordination, as well as an appreciation of distance and speed; energetic play that involves running, jumping and skipping helps children to develop these skills
- develop spatial awareness: for example, dancing and moving around to music develops a spatial awareness while also practising coordination and muscle control.

Creative play

Children must not be expected to 'make something'. Creative play is about experimenting with materials and music. It is not about producing things to go on display, or to be taken home.

Practitioners can encourage creative play by offering children a range of materials and play opportunities in dance, music, drawing, collage, painting, model-making and woodwork, sand (small-world scenarios), water (small-world scenarios) and miniature garden scenarios.

The benefits of creative play
Creative play helps children to express their feelings and ideas about people, objects and events. It helps children to:

- be physically coordinated
- develop language
- develop ideas (concepts)
- develop relationships with people
- be more confident, and it boosts their self-esteem.

Imaginative play

Sometimes called drama or pretend play, imaginative play is where children make play scenarios – for example, about a shop or a boat, a garage, an office or a swimming pool.

There will be nothing left to show anyone when the play finishes. Pretend-play scenarios do not last. This is why it is difficult to explain to parents the importance of pretend play.

What to look out for in imaginative play

- Children use play props – for example, they pretend a box is a fridge, or a stick is a spoon, or a daisy is a fried egg.
- They role play and pretend that they are someone else (e.g. the shopkeeper).
- When they pretend play together, cooperatively, this is called socio-dramatic play.
- Young children pretend play everyday situations: getting up, going to sleep, eating.
- Gradually children develop their pretend-play scenarios to include situations that are not everyday events, and that they may only have heard about but not experienced. This is called fantasy play. They might pretend to go to the moon or go on an aeroplane. It is not impossible that these things will happen to them.
- Superhero play develops when they use unreal situations, like Superman, Power Rangers or cartoon characters.
- Children use imaginative play to act out situations that they have experienced, like going to the supermarket. For example, a group of children made a swimming pool out of wooden blocks. One of them pretended to be the lifeguard and rescued someone from drowning. All the children had visited a swimming pool so this pretend play was based on a real experience.

The benefits of imaginative play

Imaginative play links with the Early Years Foundation Stage Profile and is part of all seven areas of learning. Imaginative play also links with all areas of a child's development:

- emotional development
- social development
- language development
- cognitive (thinking) development
- physical development.

Sensory play

Sensory play includes any activity that stimulates a young child's senses. It is important to remember that children learn best when they can actually touch, see, smell, taste, hear and manipulate the materials in their world. Stimulating the senses sends signals to children's brains that help to strengthen neural pathways that are important for all types of learning. For example, as children explore sensory materials, they develop their sense of touch, which lays the foundation for learning other skills, such as identifying objects by touch and using fine motor skills.

Sensory activities and sensory tables promote exploration and encourage children to use scientific processes while they play, create, investigate and explore.

Examples of sensory play

- Sand and water play: provide interesting objects – pipes, funnels, ladles, scoops, sieves, etc.
- Play dough: provide rolling pins, cutters.
- Play with a variety of malleable materials: shaving cream, cornflour, dried or cooked pasta, dried beans or lentils.
- Natural objects: collect sticks, feathers, fir cones, etc. during a walk in the park or garden.
- Fruits and vegetables: encourage children to touch, smell, taste and play with all the different produce.
- Music activities: singing, dancing, playing musical instruments, etc.

The benefits of sensory play

Spending time stimulating their senses helps children develop cognitively, linguistically, socially and emotionally, physically and creatively:

- Cognitive development: sensory play promotes spatial awareness, mathematical thinking, and scientific exploration and discovery. Sensory play provides opportunities for learning colours, counting, sequencing, sorting and constructing.
- Language development: sensory play encourages children to use descriptive and expressive language, and to find meaning behind words, such as 'slimy' or 'lumpy', which are essentially meaningless when taken out of context. Children also develop pre-writing skills as they focus on hand–eye coordination tasks while using various materials.
- Emotional development: sensory play provides a way for children to relieve their stress and to express their feelings. Pummelling clay or playing with water, for example, can be very soothing and relaxing to a young child. The open-ended nature of sensory play gives children the opportunity to create or recreate pictures, shapes and designs as many times as they like. Sensory play also eliminates the fear and experience of failure, which can negatively impact a child's self-esteem.
- Social skills: when engaged in group sensory play, children often form emotional bonds with other children as they share a common experience. Working closely together at a sand and water table, for example, provides young children with opportunities to observe how their peers handle materials, to share their own ideas and discoveries, and to build relationships. Because playing with play dough or sand does not require the use of language, even very young children can build early social ability through sensory play.
- The development of fine motor skills: in the process of rolling and cutting up play dough or scooping and pouring water and beans, children will develop hand–eye coordination and fine motor control. Children are also developing the skills and muscles they will need for handwriting and other fine manipulative skills.

- Creative development: sensory play allows children to experiment with a large variety of materials in new and creative ways. Play that is open-ended and uninterrupted by adults allows creativity to flourish. The children are able to use the materials in any way they like and are able to enjoy the process with no concern for the end product.

Heuristic play

Heuristic play is the term used to describe children playing and exploring natural materials using all of their senses. (The word 'heuristic' means 'helping to find out or discover'.) The concept was developed by Elinor Goldschmied, a child psychologist, from her work watching how children gain knowledge of the world around them.

Heuristic play is rooted in young children's natural curiosity. As babies grow, they move beyond being content to simply feel and ponder objects, to wanting to find out what can be done with them. Toddlers have an urge to handle things: to gather, fill, dump, stack, knock down, select and manipulate in other ways. Kitchen utensils offer this kind of activity and can occupy a child for surprising stretches of time.

When toddlers make an enjoyable discovery – for instance, when one item fits into another, or an interesting sound is produced – they often repeat the action several times to test the result. This strengthens cognitive development as well as fine muscle control and hand–eye coordination. Treasure basket play was also developed by Elinor Goldschmied to promote heuristic play.

The benefits of heuristic play

Heuristic play:

- supports inclusion
- is often considered to be therapeutic
- supports children's cognitive development, as they learn through discovery and exploration
- offers children the opportunity to test out their own theories and to problem-solve.

In practice

Observing a baby with a natural treasure basket

Babies learn about their environment using all their senses – touch, smell, taste, sight, hearing and movement. A treasure basket is a collection of everyday objects chosen to stimulate the different senses. Babies have the chance to decide for themselves what they want to play with, choosing in turn whichever object they want to explore.

1 Choose a sturdy basket or box – one that does not tip over easily.
2 Fill the basket with lots of natural objects or objects made from natural materials so that the baby has plenty to choose from. For example:

- fir cones
- large seashells
- large walnuts
- fruit or vegetables (e.g. apple, lemon, gourd)
- brushes
- woollen balls
- wooden pegs
- small baskets
- feathers
- large pebbles
- pumice stones.

3 Make sure that everything you choose for the basket is clean and safe. Remember that babies often want to put things in their mouths, so you need to check that all objects are clean and safe.
4 Make sure the baby is seated comfortably and safely, with cushions for support if necessary. Sit nearby and watch to give the baby confidence. Only talk or intervene if the baby clearly needs attention.
5 You should check the contents of the basket regularly, cleaning objects and removing any damaged items.
6 Write an observation of the activity, noting the following:
- the length of time the baby plays with each item
- what he or she does with it
- any facial expressions or sounds made by the baby.

Progress check

Understanding key terms in play

1 Match the category of play in column one with the example in column two.

1 Physical play	A Child using a brush and paint on paper
2 Fantasy play	B Three children are playing in the home area; one is the shopkeeper and the other two are customers
3 Exploratory play	C Child pretending to be a firefighter
4 Manipulative play	D Child playing outdoors on a climbing frame and slide
5 Creative play	E Baby playing with treasure basket which contains natural and everyday objects
6 Imaginative play	F Children playing with beakers and wheels at the water tray
7 Heuristic play	G Child threading beads onto a lace
8 Socio-dramatic play	H Child pretending he is flying to the moon on a broomstick

2 For all the headings in column one (except for heuristic play), think of two more examples of activities which correspond to each type of play.

AC 4.1 Progress check

Describe the benefits of physical play, creative play, imaginative play, sensory play and heuristic play.

AC 4.2 Implementing activities which support different types of children's play

Both your tutor and the staff in your setting will be able to offer ideas and guidance about the types of activities which support each area of play outlined in AC 4.1.

Guidelines for good practice

Planning and implementing activities with young children

- Plan each activity: always plan each activity, taking into account the children's age and stage of development.
- Plan the timing for the activity: allow some flexibility within your timescale to allow for spontaneity.
- Discuss your plan with your supervisor or mentor. Make sure that your setting has the materials and resources required.
- Consider health and safety issues relevant to your activity: for example, how much supervision will be necessary; health and hygiene factors during a cooking activity, etc.
- Prepare the area beforehand: for example, protecting tables, organising water tables and appropriate clothing (e.g. aprons or warm outerwear) for the children.
- Evaluation: after the activity, discuss how well it went with the children and with colleagues. Evaluate it in terms of the benefits to the children and to the setting. Think about how you could improve it next time.

Ideas for activities

Physical play

- Large apparatus: climbing frame, ropes to swing on, planks to walk on with ladders and things to jump off.
- Small apparatus: bats, balls, hoops, beanbags, ropes and pushcarts.
- Games: 'What's the time, Mr. Wolf?' or creating an obstacle course for children riding trikes, or a simple game with beanbags.

Creative play

- Clay, wet sand, dough and recycled materials: children can make models with these materials. Activities will also involve them using sticky tape, scissors, rolling pins, string, wire and other materials.
- Drawing and painting: plain white paper of varied sizes, plus pencils, wax crayons, felt-tip pens, chalks and slates, charcoal, powder paints and different thicknesses of brushes.
- Music: singing and listening to a wide range of music from different cultures; dancing and moving about to music and playing with musical instruments.

Imaginative play

- Dressing-up clothes
- Dolls and puppets
- Small-world play equipment
- Wooden boxes, which can be used as beds, tables, chairs
- An old airer (clothes horse) with a sheet or blanket over it makes good walls for a den – both indoors and outside.

Sensory play

- Sand and water play – both indoors and outdoors
- Play dough
- Play with a variety of malleable materials – 'gloop', finger painting, etc.

Heuristic play

- Treasure baskets (see AC 4.1 above)
- Collections of interesting objects.

AC 4.2 Progress check

Implement your activities and evaluate them.

Assessment practice

1 How is play necessary for the holistic development of children?
2 What are children's rights in relation to play?
3 How do settings meet the right for children to play?
4 What are the characteristics of child-initiated play and adult-directed play?
5 How do children's play needs and preferences change in relation to their stage of development?
6 What are the benefits of physical play, creative play, imaginative play, sensory play and heuristic play?

Useful resources

Play England

Promotes free play opportunities for all children and young people, and works to ensure that the importance of play for children's development is recognised.

www.playengland.org.uk

Treasure baskets and heuristic play

Goldschmeid, E. and Jackson, S. (1994) *People Under Three: young children in day care* (Routledge, Oxon) pp 128–141.

Unit 8

Support the needs of the child in preparing for school

By the end of this unit, you will:

1 Understand 'school readiness' in relation to the role of the early years practitioner.
2 Understand how working in partnership with others contributes to children's school readiness.

3 Be able to support children's language and communication needs in preparation for school readiness.
4 Be able to support children's mathematical development in preparation for school readiness.

LO1 Understand 'school readiness' in relation to the role of the early years practitioner

AC 1.1 What is 'school readiness'?

At the launch of the revised EYFS in 2012, the Children's Minister at the time stated:

'What really matters is making sure a child is able to start school ready to learn, able to make friends and play, ready to ask for what they need and say what they think. These are critical foundations for really getting the best out of school. It's vital we have the right framework to support high quality early years education. Our changes, including the progress check at age two, will support early years professionals and families to give children the best possible start in life.'

The EYFS includes many references to children being 'school ready'. For example:

'The EYFS sets the standards that all early years providers must meet to ensure that children learn and develop well and are kept healthy and safe. It promotes teaching and learning to ensure children's "school readiness" and gives the broad range of knowledge and skills that provide the right foundation for good future progress through school and life.'

However, there are different ideas about exactly what 'school ready' means. Research shows that children who enter school ready to learn appear to achieve more academically. Academic success has been linked to improved social, economic and health outcomes. The concept of school readiness can be used to include:

● the readiness of the individual child
● the school's readiness for children
● the ability of the family and community to support optimal early child development.

The AcE Programme (Accounting Early for Life Long Learning) set out what a child needs early on for lifelong learning and termed this as making the child 'life ready' rather than 'school ready'. The programme describes four underpinning, or 'prime', capacities for a young child as they move into school and later childhood life:

1 Language development and communication skills, including:
● language exploration
● language agency (or use)
● language range
● language processing.

2 Attitudes and dispositions, including:
- independence
- creativity
- self-motivation
- resilience.

3 Social competence and self-esteem, including:
- effective relationships
- empathy
- responsibility
- assertiveness
- self-worth.

4 Emotional well-being, including:
- emotional literacy
- empowerment
- connectedness
- positive self-esteem.

AcE also stresses that progress and the pattern of development of individual children will depend on:

- their particular strengths and interests
- their experiences and culture in the home
- their time and experiences in a range of settings
- their age.

Discussion point

The characteristics of school readiness

Read the following statements about school readiness:

1 'First, school readiness: if there is one theme which predominates in the conversations I have had with primary school teachers in the last year or so it is the difficulty they have in dealing with children who arrive in Reception class totally unprepared to learn. Teachers report to me that a growing number of children cannot form letters or even hold a pencil. Many cannot sit and listen. Many can scarcely communicate orally, let alone frame a question. Many cannot use a knife and fork. Many cannot even go to the lavatory properly. Some express their frustration through displays of inarticulate rage.' (Michael Gove, Secretary of State for Education, 2011)

2 'There is a mischievous mistruth in the belief that doing certain things early helps children get ready for the next stage. The best way to help a child to get ready to be 5 is to let her be 3 when she is 3 and let him be 4 when he is 4, and to hold high expectations of what children in their first 48 months of life might achieve.' (Nutbrown, 1996, p. 54)

3 'In research conducted by the Professional Association for Childcare and Early Years (PACEY), 97% of the childcare professionals surveyed agreed that the term "school ready" should be defined as being children who: (a) are curious about the world, (b) have a desire to learn, (c) can cope emotionally with being separated from their parents, and (d) are relatively independent with their personal care. Only a third of childcare professionals believe that a definition of "school ready" should include a child having a good basic understanding of reading, writing and arithmetic.'

4 Children born in the UK in the summer are entering school a whole year before those who are born after 31 August. Entering school may prove harder for the younger children, particularly if they have some additional challenges, such as those with special educational needs or who are learning a second language.

5 Children who join Key Stage 1 in the first year of statutory schooling may be as little as a month older than children in the final year of the EYFS, in the Reception year. But there are differences between the child-focused EYFS, which facilitates play, choice and autonomy, to learning in Key Stage 1, which is based on a subject-led curriculum, determined and led by the class teacher.

In a group, discuss each statement.

- Try to arrive at a description of the characteristics of school readiness with which the majority in the group agrees.
- Do you agree with the idea that children should start school as early as possible (as in the UK), or do you think the Scandinavian countries are right in leaving formal schooling until much later?

These four capacities in the young child make him or her an effective learner; it is particularly important that the skills are established in the child's formative years, as it becomes increasingly more difficult to learn later on in life. Children should exit the Early Years Foundation Stage equipped with these capacities – or abilities – to be a lifelong learner.

In most of Europe, children start school much later than they do in the UK. In fact, children there are not regarded as being 'ready for school' – in other words, ready for formal teaching and learning – until they are at least six years of age. The latest curriculum frameworks and related guidance in England say that children should be 'made ready' for school by the age of five.

AC 1.1   Progress check

In your own words, how would you describe the main characteristics of school readiness?

AC 1.2 How the early years practitioner supports children to prepare for school

Preparing children for transition to school is not about teaching them to read and write (although some four year olds will be able to read short books and to write some words or even sentences). It is about making sure children are confident and able to deal with the social, practical and behavioural demands of the classroom and the playground. It involves preparing children socially and emotionally as well as intellectually and educationally.

Practitioners need to work with an awareness of, and sensitivity to, each individual child as they are supported in the transition to school.

Guidelines for good practice

Supporting children to prepare for school

- Listen to children: try to find out how the child feels about a move – what they might be excited about or feel anxious about.
- Encourage children to talk: about what they already know and how they think they will adjust to the change.
- Recognise the needs of an individual child and his or her family in relation to attachment needs and separation anxiety. Some will be more vulnerable than others at this time.
- Reassure children that you are there for them: show them that you will always respond to their needs – for example, for a comfort object or a particular routine to provide stability when they are handling separation.
- Show respect for a child's way of making it work for themselves, by listening to the child and to their parents or carers about how they want to handle the separation from each other and adapting your plan to include this information.
- Plan carefully for transition, making sure you collect and make use of all the information from parents and from previous settings.
- Offer support: additional time and support may be needed for those who are younger, less mature or less confident, who are less able, or who have special educational needs or English as an additional language.
- Organise some fun sessions at the setting about getting ready for 'big' school; for example, a school role-play corner with uniforms from local schools.
- Visit the primary 'feeder' schools in the summer term to get a clear idea of the school day and challenges for young children.

AC 1.2   Progress check

Explain how the early years practitioner supports children to prepare for school.

AC 1.3 The holistic needs of the child as they prepare for school

As children grow and develop, different care needs come into focus; this is particularly true when a child differs from the developmental norm. Maslow's hierarchy of needs is a useful tool for considering these needs in a developmental framework.

Maslow's theory of human needs has relevance to child development and care. For example, at the basic level of physiological needs, a child who is cold or hungry will be unable to respond to planned activities. Mia Kellmer Pringle (1920–83) has suggested that there are four significant developmental needs which have to be met from birth. These are: the need for love and security, the need for new experiences, the need for praise and recognition, and the need for responsibility.

The need for love and security

This is probably the most important need as it provides the basis for all later relationships. The young child instinctively wants to move away and become more independent, but separating from the parent figure may be difficult. Each child deals with this challenge in his or her own way.

Security

In their first year, the need for security may be met by having a comfort blanket or a favourite toy – Donald Winnicott (1896–1971) called this a 'transitional object'. For more on the need for security, see Unit 10.

Routine

Another aspect of the child's need for love and security is the need for routine and predictability. This is why having daily routines is so important in childcare. By meeting children's need for routine, carers help the child to feel acknowledged and independent and this increases their self-esteem.

Attachment

Pringle, like John Bowlby (1907–90), recognised children's need to have a steady, durable and caring relationship with empathetic adults. A continuous, reliable, loving relationship first within the family unit, then with a growing number of others, can meet this need. It can give the child a sense of self-worth and identity. In childcare settings, the key person system helps to meet this need.

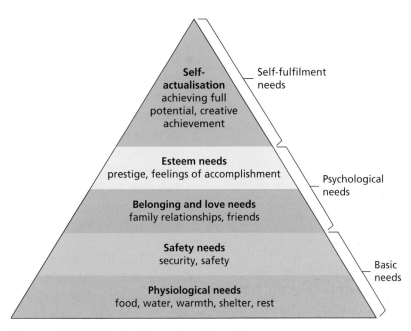

Figure 8.1 Maslow's hierarchy of needs

The need for new experiences

New experiences are necessary for cognitive development. Children learn from their experiences. In early life, it is largely through play and language that the child explores the world and learns to cope with it. As children pass through each stage of development, they often return and work on a previous level in a new way. For experiences to be meaningful, they must extend what children have already learned; they should present children with social, intellectual and physical challenges.

The need for praise and recognition

Growing up requires an enormous amount of learning – emotional, social and intellectual. Strong incentives are necessary for children to continue through the difficulties and conflicts that they will inevitably encounter. The most effective incentives are praise and recognition sustained over time.

Self-fulfilling prophecy

Children feel like failures when they cannot live up to the unrealistic hopes of their parents and are less likely to repeat their efforts. The lower the expectation of the carer, the lower the level of effort and achievement of the child – sometimes called the self-fulfilling prophecy.

Intrinsic motivation

If you make children feel anxious when they have not succeeded, they will avoid activities likely to lead to failure. It is important to praise children appropriately when they try hard or have achieved something new, however small it might seem. This will motivate children to greater effort and lead to the desire to achieve something for its own sake; this is called intrinsic motivation.

The need for responsibility

Being responsible involves knowing what is to be done and how to do it. Children have different levels of understanding at different ages. Your role is to structure the environment to provide challenging tasks according to their different interests and ability levels. The need for responsibility is met by allowing children to gain personal independence. This is done first through learning to look after themselves in matters of everyday care and then through a gradual extension of responsibility over other areas until they have the freedom and ability to decide on their own actions. Cooperation rather than competition allows children more freedom to accept responsibility. You can help by building group work into your planning activities.

Your role in promoting independence and self-care in children

- Encouragement is the most important factor in helping children towards independence.
- Praise: whenever children attempt a new skill, whether they succeed or not, praise them and urge them to try again.
- Don't interfere: try not to step in too quickly to help; it is essential that they have enough time to manage these things on their own, at their own pace. Never pressure children to try something before they are ready.
- Be patient: put up with the experimentation even if it means a lot of mess. The more they practise, the better they will become.
- Set limits: keep a watchful eye on children as they begin to experiment with doing things on their own. Set limits and explain them: tell them why it is dangerous to turn on the oven or use the bread knife.
- Promoting independence at meal times: let babies hold their cup even though you control it; gradually pass the control over to them. As soon as the child can pick up tiny objects with finger and opposing thumb (at around six to nine months), encourage self-feeding with tiny sandwiches, little bits of banana, cooked carrot or grated apple. NB Always supervise because of the dangers of choking.

Promoting independence when dressing

Zips, buttons and hooks are difficult for small children choose clothing with elastic waistbands, Velcro, or ones which slip on with zips and buttons partly closed. Lay out clothing so that children can lift it the right way round: trousers front up, jumpers and dresses front down; this is so that they can sit down and put them on. Help them to put their shoes on, but let them fasten them themselves whenever possible. (Children sit with their knees turned out and naturally put shoes on with the fastenings on the inside where they can see them; that's why they are often on the wrong feet.)

> **AC 1.3 Progress check** ✓
>
> Using the information above, look at the ways in which your setting provides for the holistic needs of children as they prepare for school.

LO2 Understand how working in partnership with others contributes to children's school readiness

AC 2.1 Others who help children prepare for school

The starting point when planning for any transition is to know the children and their families well. This enables teachers to plan an effective programme for transition. Smooth, planned transitions from the EYFS to Key Stage 1 cannot be achieved without wholehearted support from the whole school, and it needs to be seen as a shared responsibility between EYFS staff and their Key Stage 1 colleagues in Year 1.

In Reception, children should:

- be told who their teacher is as early as possible; children feel more secure if they can name and talk about their new teacher
- visit Year 1 to work and play alongside 'buddies' – carefully selected children assigned to look out for children making the transition to Year 1
- draw a picture of themselves on a visit to Year 1, so the Year 1 teacher can use these to make a display to welcome children at the beginning of the September term

- prepare their coat-peg label/tray on a visit to Year 1, ready for the start of the new term
- visit Year 1 in small groups to 'interview' the Year 1 teacher and ask the questions they want to ask (prepared with the Reception teacher).

After transition, children should:

- visit the Reception class in small numbers to share projects or experiences
- have lunch at the same time as Reception so as not to face the noisy whole-school dinner hall
- be initially accompanied to the lunch hall by a familiar adult (not a dinner lady who has other children to supervise)
- feed back on 'things to look forward to' in Year 1, ready for the next cohort of children.

Parents and carers

Parents and carers also need to have their voices heard because they will have a different view of transition, possibly from the experiences of older children in the family, and they should be able to share these experiences with the school.

- Consult parents on their feelings about transition, before and after the event.
- Hold a meeting for parents of children moving to Year 1, to explain the Key Stage 1 approaches to learning.
- Hold a meeting for parents of new Year 1 children after the start of the new term, to explain further the approaches in Year 1 and to see if there are any concerns or queries.
- Hold workshops for parents new to Key Stage 1 to explain how children's learning needs are met across the curriculum.

Reception and Year 1 staff

One visit to the new class is not enough. Children need time to get to know new teachers and new classrooms – and teachers need time to get to know their new children.

- Attend any necessary courses about developmentally appropriate practice that builds on the EYFS.
- Visit each other's classes to become familiar with expectations of children and learning experiences of children when they move on.

- Swap classes and teach for a morning, afternoon or day on a regular basis (thus no supply cover is required).
- Undertake joint observations of selected children and share possible 'next steps' of learning.
- Meet to pass on information from children's records or profiles, including any knowledge gained from home visits.
- Meet to plan for the long- and medium-term stage curriculum coverage.
- Move with the children each year on a rolling programme, so the Reception teacher becomes the Year 1 teacher and the Year 1 teacher takes Reception (this can also apply to support staff).

Case study

In one primary school, every Friday, the Year 1 teachers swapped classes with their Foundation Stage colleagues. In this way, the Year 1 teachers came to understand the ways in which children were learning in the EYFS and what made them confident and motivated to learn. They were then able to plan a programme for the early weeks of children's Year 1 experience which mirrored the children's experiences in the Foundation Stage.

Head teachers and senior management teams

Head teachers and senior management teams need to recognise how important it is for children – and staff – to have time to prepare for transition properly and to ensure that adequate financial resources are set aside to support the process. All senior staff need to understand how children learn in Key Stage 1 so that, when they monitor the quality of teaching and learning, they have appropriate expectations for planning, practice and evidence of learning.

AC 2.1 Progress check ✓

Identify others involved in helping children prepare for school. Find out how the transition from EYFS to Year 1 is carried out in your setting.

AC 2.2 Information required to meet the individual needs of the child during transition

Within every class, there is a wide range of children with an equally diverse range of learning needs and abilities. Some five-year-old learners in the Reception class are ready to learn elements of the Year 1 curriculum. Some children in Year 2 struggle to learn the objectives that are meant for children in Year 1. Children need to be treated as unique individual learners, rather than as a homogeneous group who all happen to be 'in Year 1'.

Schools need to receive the following information from early years settings:

- names and contact details of children moving into Reception
- any additional needs of the children and their families – for example, English as an additional language
- transfer forms – these may include questions such as 'What are the child's key strengths and interests?'
- special educational needs information; if a child has special educational needs, contact the school SENCO as early as possible after confirmation of a place.

Schools also need each individual child's EYFS Profile or equivalent assessment documentation.

The EYFS Profile

All early years providers must complete an EYFS Profile for each child in the final term of the year in which they turn five. For most children, this is the Reception year in primary school. The main purpose is to provide an accurate assessment of individual children at the end of the EYFS. The Profile describes each child's attainment against 17 early learning goals, together with a short narrative about their learning characteristics.

In addition, Year 1 teachers must be given a copy of the Profile report together with 'a short commentary on each child's skills and abilities in relation to the three key characteristics of effective learning. These should inform a dialogue between Reception and Year 1 teachers about each child's stage of development and learning needs and assist with the planning of activities in Year 1.'

There is a duty placed on schools regarding information sharing in the statutory guidance. The EYFS states:

'If a child moves to a new school during the academic year, the original school must send their assessment of the child's level of development against the early learning goals to the relevant school within 15 days of receiving a request.'

AC 2.2 **Progress check** ✓

Describe the information required to enable the school to meet the individual needs of the children during transition.

LO3 Be able to support children's language and communication needs in preparation for school readiness

AC 3.1 What is a 'language-rich environment'?

It the 1970s, researcher Basil Bernstein, in a paper called 'Class, Codes and Control' (1971), introduced the idea that children from working-class backgrounds developed what he called a restricted language code (using a more limited range of words and less complex forms of grammar). He thought that children from middle-class homes developed an elaborated language code (using a wider range of words and more complicated grammar) and as a result they achieved better results academically.

As a result, in both the USA and the UK, programmes of education were developed with the aim of enriching the language and learning environments of young children, so that they would succeed in education.

But during the 1980s–90s, it became clear that there is more to a language-rich environment than it seems. Gordon Wells found that it was important for practitioners working with young children to understand the background and culture of the children and families they were working with. Then they would be able to understand the richness of the child's own language and culture.

Recent research shows that children growing up in Japan who are described as lower class do badly in school compared with children described as upper class. But if the family moved to the USA, they were simply thought of as Japanese. It didn't matter what class they had been described as when they were back in Japan. In the USA, there is a perception that Japanese children study well at school, and this positive attitude towards them seemed to influence them so they did well in school. In other words, positive attitudes from practitioners towards children are essential if children are to develop good language skills.

The importance of context and a language-rich environment

The brain develops important interconnecting networks, which include movement, communication, play, symbol use, problem-solving and understanding why things happen (cause and effect). These become more complex as the networks for learning in the brain develop. Before five years of age, the language system is not yet mature. Reading and writing develop most easily and enjoyably once language is well developed.

AC 3.1 Progress check

What are the main characteristics of a language-rich environment?

AC 3.2 Contributing to a language-rich environment for children from birth to five years

Resources for promoting a language-rich environment

The early years setting should be equipped with a basic set of resources and books appropriate to the ages and developmental needs of the children. Resources should reflect the cultural and linguistic diversity of our society and be organised so that they are equally accessible to all children in the setting, and enable choice and independence. General resources may include:

- visual aids: wall displays including children's work, maps, pictures and posters; interest tables with interesting objects related to topic work; 3D displays of children's work, including construction models; videos; computer graphics; books
- indoor and outdoor play equipment appropriate for the children's ages and levels of development and suitable for children of all abilities
- groups of tables for group work, including literacy and numeracy activities
- groups of tables for 'messy' practical activities (e.g. arts and crafts, design technology), including storage for art/ design materials and equipment such as paint, paint pots, drying rack; sink for washing paint pots and brushes; basin for washing hands
- computers and printers with selection of appropriate software
- CD players with headphones and a selection of CDs
- book/story corner with appropriate range of fiction and non-fiction books, including some dual-language books

- quiet area where children can go for privacy, rest or sleep depending on their individual needs, including cushions, mats or cots, appropriate to the ages of the children
- whiteboard, overhead projector and teaching base in settings supporting children's literacy and numeracy skills, with marker pens, transparencies, textbooks, teaching manuals and other resources needed by staff on a regular basis
- writing and drawing materials, including a variety of writing tools (crayons, pencils, pens, pastels, chalks) and different shapes, sizes and types of paper (plain, coloured, graph)
- specialist resources for specific learning areas stored in the appropriate curriculum resource cupboard/area
- children's work trays to store individual workbooks, folders for topic work, reading books, reading logs, personal named pencils, crayon tins
- area with individual coat pegs for children's coats and PE bags.

The importance of labelling

Very young children respond to labels even before they can read them; they will ask adults what labels say. Using pictures or objects as well as written words helps children to make sense of labels and to develop their own literacy skills.

Labelling introduces young children to one of the important purposes of written language: providing information or directions. Labels encourage children's independence in reading and writing. A special place for children to keep their belongings (whether on a hook, or in a drawer, tray or basket), clearly labelled with each child's name, is an essential part of the effective language-rich environment. With very young children, a picture on the left-hand side of the label helps them to remember to work from left to right in reading and writing activities.

Reflective practice

- How does the environment at your setting stimulate and support children to communicate through meaningful activities and experiences?
- Is the learning environment rich in symbols and signs, words, dance and art which take account of and extend children's cultural experiences?

Your role in contributing to a language-rich environment

It is important that children spend time with people who speak fluently so that they hear the patterns of the language they are trying to learn. A language-rich environment which encourages children to talk is crucial. Hearing other people speak fluently allows the child to experience comprehensible input: if the adult says, 'Oh dear, you've bumped your knee. Shall I rub it better?' and points at the child's knee and makes a rubbing mime, then the child has enough clues to understand what is being said. This is very important for young children, children with language delay and children who are learning English as an additional language.

Children learn by doing, so language is best learned when children are active in their learning. A practitioner might say to a three-year-old child, 'You've got to the top of the slide, haven't you? Are you going to come down now?'

Encouraging conversations and group discussions

Conversations need to:

- be two-way
- involve sharing feelings and ideas
- involve thinking of each other
- be a real exchange of feelings and ideas between children and other children, and between children and adults
- include turn-taking as the conversation flows
- involve thinking about what will be of interest to each other, as well as things that are of interest to oneself.

One-to-one conversations with young children

Young children are beginning to establish a strong sense of self, realising that they are a separate person; this is why their favourite words are often 'no' and 'mine'.

Guidelines for good practice

One-to-one conversations with young children

- Children need to be spoken to as individuals.
- They need to spend time with adults who are patient with them and who listen to them. It is hard for young children to put their feelings and thoughts into words, and it takes time, so adults need to be aware of this. It is very tempting to prompt children and say things for them. Instead, try nodding or saying, 'Hmm'. This gives children time to say what they want to.
- Do not correct what children say. Instead, elaborate on what they have said, giving them the correct pattern. For example, Shanaz, at two years, says, 'I falled down.' The adult replies, 'Yes, you did,

didn't you? You fell down. Never mind, I will help you up.'
- It is important that all children experience unrushed, one-to-one conversations with adults and with other children – for example, when sharing a drink together at the snack table, chatting while using the clay or sharing a book together.
- Value and respect the child's language and culture.
- Have genuine conversations with children, using gestures, eye contact and props.
- Encourage children to listen to and enjoy stories, including those of their own culture.
- Introduce 'book language', such as 'Once upon a time…'.

Researchers have noticed that, although toddlers often turn their backs on their mother (or other adults they are familiar with and have a close relationship with, such as their key person) and say 'No!' to a suggestion, they do in fact take up and imitate the idea offered to them. Adults need to be aware of this, and to realise that when a toddler says 'No!' they really mean they want to do something for themselves, and to make the decision for themselves, rather than feeling controlled. It is all part of developing a strong sense of self.

Small group discussions

Children need help when taking part in group discussions. Groups should consist of no more than four to eight children and wherever possible should be with the key person, whom the children will know well. Having to wait for a turn frustrates young children, as does having to wait until everyone is sitting quietly. It is best to start a song or a dance with plenty of actions, so that everyone can join in from the beginning of the group time. Children are then much more likely to be willing to sit quietly for a story.

In a small group, children can take part in the discussion more easily. Group times should last no longer than 10–15 minutes.

In practice

Nathan (aged six years) is a quiet and shy child who needs lots of encouragement to participate in group discussions. He enjoys books and ICT activities. Suggest ways in which you can encourage his communication skills.

AC 3.2   Progress check ✓

Describe how your setting provides a language-rich environment which encourages opportunities for appropriate activities and experiences to enable children to develop their language and communication skills.

AC 3.3 Planning for activities to encourage speaking, listening, reading, writing and digital literacy

Activities to develop speaking and listening skills

These activities can be divided into five basic categories:

- exploration
- conversation
- description
- discussion
- instruction

Exploration

- Toys and other interesting objects to look at and play with, such as household objects (remember safety)
- Sounds to listen to, including voices, music, songs and rhymes
- Noisemakers, such as commercial and homemade musical instruments
- Bath toys and books
- Construction materials, including wooden bricks, plastic bricks and 'junk' modelling
- Natural materials such as water, sand, clay, dough and cooking ingredients
- Creative materials such as paint, paper and glue
- Outdoor activities and outings, including gardening, visits to parks and museums, swimming
- Animals, including visits to farms and wildlife centres, looking after small pets.

Description

- News time, circle time
- Recording events, outings, visits and visitors
- Books and stories appropriate to age/level of development, including cloth books, board books, activity books, pop-up books, picture books, audio books, textbooks, novels, encyclopaedia.

Conversation

- Talking about their day, experiences and interests in a variety of settings with other children and adults, such as playgroup, nursery, school, after-school clubs, youth clubs

- Talking during imaginative play activities, such as playing with pretend/role-play equipment: for example, dressing-up clothes, home corner, play shop, puppets; playing with dolls, teddies and other cuddly toys; playing with small-scale toys such as toy cars, garages and road systems, train sets, doll's houses
- Talking about special events such as birthdays, new baby, religious festivals
- Talking while doing activities – not necessarily related to the task!

Discussion

- Problem-solving during activities, such as mathematics, science and technology
- Follow-up discussion after an activity or event, such as watching DVD/television or live performance, listening to a story or recorded music
- Cooperative group work
- Games and puzzles.

Instruction

- Preparation before an activity
- Explanation of what to do – verbal and/or written on a board

- Instructions during an activity to keep the children on task
- Extra support for individuals
- Introducing or extending knowledge on a specific skill
- Step-by-step instructions
- Worksheets, workbooks and work cards
- Delivering verbal and/or written messages; carrying out errands.

Activity

Using your own experience
Describe an example activity for each of the five categories, based on your own experiences of working with children.

Activities to develop early reading skills

In order to learn to read, children must recognise that a certain pattern of letters represents a particular sound. They need to build up a set of skills that will help them to make sense of words, signs and symbols.

Table 8.1 Activities to promote early reading skills

Early reading skill	Activities to promote the skill
Shape recognition and matching: the ability to recognise shapes and to differentiate between them is important. Children learn to match shapes and patterns first and this helps them to match letters and, finally, words.	<ul><li>Snap</li><li>Shape sorter</li><li>Picture pairs</li><li>Lotto</li><li>Jigsaws</li><li>Dominoes</li></ul>
Rhyming: research shows that children who can understand about rhyming words have a head start in learning to read and, even more, to spell.	<ul><li>Rhyming games such as 'I spy with my little eye, something that rhymes with cat' (hat or mat)</li><li>Leave off the end of rhymes for the child to complete, e.g. 'Humpty Dumpty sat on a wall, Humpty Dumpty had a great...?'</li><li>Read simple poetry →</li></ul>

Table 8.1 Activities to promote early reading skills   (*continued*)

Early reading skill	Activities to promote the skill
Language skills: the more experience children have of language, the more easily they will learn to read. Children need to hear and join in conversations (with adults and children), and to listen to stories and poetry of all sorts.	• Talking • Reading stories • Encouraging children to talk • Share their favourite stories again and again: repeating phrases helps to build children's language
Concepts of print: this means 'how we look at books' and includes following print the right way (from left to right), turning the pages, looking at pictures.	Children need to learn practical skills: • how to hold a book (the right way up!) • how to turn pages singly • let the child see your finger following the print when reading
Letter skills: children need to learn what sounds the letters can make.	• Begin with letters with an interesting shape that makes them easy to recognise or a letter which is important to the child, such as their own initial • Use the letter sounds rather than letter names, e.g. 'a for ant', not 'ay for ape' • Try a letter hunt: looking for objects which begin with a particular letter
Motor skills: since reading and writing are best taught together, pencil control is important.	• Encourage creativity: drawing and painting with lots of different tools and materials to encourage pencil and brush control • Playing with small toys, especially construction sets, helps to develop fine motor skills
Looking at a variety of **printed materials:** newspapers, magazines, packaging, street and shop names, etc.	• Point out words in the environment, e.g. 'Push', 'Pull', 'Open', 'Closed', etc. • Visit the library to encourage familiarity with the idea of books for everyone
Memory skills: words are made up of sequences of letters and sounds, and children need to remember this before they can read.	• Memory games: such as 'I went to the shops and I bought a…' and pairs (pelmanism) all help to improve children's memory skills and to increase their attention span • Sequencing: book page layout can be reinforced by, for example, laying out the child's clothes to be selected first from left then to the right: vest, pants, top, trousers, socks, shoes

The use of story and rhyme in supporting communication, language and listening
Storytelling
There is a difference between reading stories from a book and storytelling. A love of stories is common to all young children, and by telling stories, rather than reading them, a storyteller can really bring the story to life and make it a more interactive experience for the children. To enhance the experience of storytelling, you can use:

- visual aids or props (objects related to the story)
- sound effects – children could be encouraged to make appropriate sounds
- pictures or photographs
- children's drawings and paintings.

When telling (or reading) a story to a group of children, it is important to arrange seating comfortably, and to ensure that all children can see and hear both you and the book or visual aids. Practitioners should also find opportunities to read or tell stories to individual children or very small groups. Having extra attention at story time allows children to point, to comment and to help with page turning.

Rhyme

Sharing rhymes with young children helps them listen to the patterns of language. Children first begin to notice that certain words have the same sounds at the end (rhyme). Later they notice that many words share a pattern in the way they are spelled. Understanding these links makes learning to read much easier.

Rhyming words help children appreciate beginning and ending sounds – for example, 'cat', 'pat' and 'mat'. Rhyming activities suggested in the EYFS include the following:

- Share, recite and encourage joining in with rhymes, action songs and games. For example, as the children come to join the circle for group time, say the rhyme: 'I know a name which rhymes with hen, he's sitting in the group and his name is…' and encourage the children to provide the name (for example, Ben). For children whose names do not lend themselves to rhyme, say for example, 'I know a girl whose name I can sing, Jodie's coming next and she's in the ring'.
- Encourage repetition, rhythm and rhyme by using tone and intonation. Use rhymes from a variety of cultures, including those shared by parents from home. Increase

children's repertoire of familiar and traditional rhymes.

- Encourage children to use a microphone and recording equipment to record their own rhymes.

Methods of teaching reading

You can help children to read by enjoying a book or poetry card together, without any pressure. Children can see how a book is used, where to begin, how to turn a page and the direction of print, using pictures as clues, finding familiar words and guessing. Being able to guess and predict what the print says is important. Children are usually fascinated by guesses that go wrong, realising this as they learn to link what they read with meaning, and to work out the words using their increasing ability to segment and blend the **graphemes** and **phonemes**. It is important to say, 'What do you think he says next?' Show the child any patterns – for example, a phrase that is repeated – and talk about the letters, words and sentences as you go. Picture cues are very important when learning to read, so talk about these and the clues they give.

> ### Key terms
>
> **grapheme** Distinct units that make up a written language, e.g. letters of the alphabet.
>
> **phoneme** Distinct sounds that make up a spoken language, e.g. 'th' sound in 'that'.

Alphabet books are important as they help children to segment words and to focus on the initial grapheme and phoneme in a word, while offering a meaningful picture to help the child along. Regularly singing the alphabet is helpful too.

Pointing out children with the same letter at the beginning of their names helps, and there can be fascinating discussions about why George is pronounced with a 'j' sound, while Gary is with a 'g' sound.

Children often know favourite stories by heart; this gives children a sense of control and the ability to feel they can predict what the text says. It gives them a can-do feeling, which is crucial in learning. Decide as a team which books you will introduce as core texts, to help children become familiar with them. Note which books are favourites of particular children, and use these with the child in the same way. Above all, remember that learning to read should be fun, and it should hold meaning for the child.

In practice

Stages of reading
Observe children aged three to seven years. Identify which children are emergent, beginner and fluent readers. What are the factors that you use to decide this? What can you do to support children in their enjoyment of books?

Informative displays set at the children's eye level are also an effective way to prompt discussion and conversation about a subject. Such displays might feature posters or photographs with extracts of information and questions about a project in the setting.

Writing

Writing has two aspects:

- what it says – the construction of meaning
- the look of it – the handwriting and letter shapes (transcription).

When children begin to write, they are constructing a code. Most languages have a written code. Writing develops when children begin to use symbols. Often they begin by putting letter-type shapes into their drawings. These gradually get pushed out to the edges of the drawing, to look more like words and sentences. Practitioners need to observe the shapes, sizes and numbers that children experiment with. Children need to be free to experiment, without criticism or pressure. Left-handed children must never be encouraged to write with the right hand. Young children find capital letters, which are more linear, easier to write than lower-case letters, which have more curves, so they tend to experiment with capitals first. It is when children begin to experiment with curves that they are indicating they have more pencil control, so can begin to form letters more easily.

Children need:

- to manipulate and try out different ways of 'writing', using their own personal code – tracing or copying letters undermines this because their own movement patterns and laying down of neural pathways are an important part of the process
- to explore what writing is
- adults to point out print in books and in the environment – for example, on notices and street signs
- adults to talk with them about environmental print, and to pick out their favourite letters (often those in their name). A child's own name is important to them, and they often write the names of people they love, plus the words 'love from'.

Learning to write

Writing and spelling are more difficult to learn than speaking and reading. The child's first word written from memory is usually his or her own name. Most of the activities shown to promote early reading skills will also help children to learn to write. They also need to know how to:

- control the pen or pencil – this involves fine manipulative skills
- form letters, including upper- and lower-case letters
- recognise letter direction, e.g. b,d and p,q
- write in a straight line and to space out words
- punctuate – understanding when writing needs a comma or full stop
- plan what they are going to write in advance
- sit still for some time with the correct posture for writing.

Figure 8.2 Early mark-making

Children learn how to copy letters from as early as two years, and the skills of learning to write develop gradually as they become competent readers.

How writing develops

Children will progress through the different stages at different rates and ages, depending on their experiences and developmental abilities. All children begin their journey into writing by making marks. This early writing follows a sequence of what the child can do.

Stage one

● holds the pencil or crayon in the palm of the hand in a palmar, or fist-like, grasp
● makes early attempts at **mark-making**, which feature lots of random marks, often made over other marks, and often described by adults as scribbles
● cannot usually distinguish between her writing and her picture.

Stage two

● may hold the pencil or crayon in a pincer grip between the thumb and index finger
● makes a definite attempt to make individual marks
● attempts to close shapes making an inside and an outside; these shapes are often circular
● combines shapes and lines; these marks will often represent one word.

Stage three

● copies adults and makes marks going across the page; these are often zigzags and curvy lines
● has a clearer idea of the marks she wants to make
● may use either hand for writing.

Stage four

● forms symbols and some recognisable familiar letters that follow on from one another

- is becoming aware of the left-to-right direction of print and can point to where the print begins
- is becoming aware that writing conveys meaning and may 'read' own writing.

Stage five

- writes a message using familiar letters
- writes some upper- and lower-case letters
- writes her name reliably.

Stage six

- writes most of the alphabet correctly using upper- and lower-case letters
- writes first one or two letters correctly then finishes with a jumbled string of letters
- begins to write capital letters and full stops at the beginning and end of work
- writes a longer sentence and can read it back
- attempts familiar forms of writing such as letters and lists.

Stage seven

- makes individual marks and uses some letters from her own name to communicate a message
- begins to understand that drawing and writing are different
- is becoming aware that print carries a message.

Key term

mark-making When children realise that marks can be used symbolically to carry meaning, in much the same way as the spoken word, they begin to use marks as tools to make their thinking visible.

How to promote mark-making and writing skills

Settings should provide:

- materials for mark-making: these can include a range of pencils, felt tips, different-sized paper, envelopes, little books and recycled cards; also useful are other materials such as alphabet charts, name cards and magnetic letters.
- meaningful contexts: a 'writing-rich' environment where writing and mark-making are encouraged for a wide variety

of purposes or when adults take part in writing with children
- examples of other people writing: these can include activities such as staff completing records, parents and carers leaving messages and visits to the local environment to see adults writing in shops, banks or post offices
- encouragement and praise: all attempts at writing made by children should be positively encouraged. Practitioners help children to understand that their writing is important and valuable if they take time to discuss with children what marks mean.

In practice

Observe a child engaged in a writing activity. Assess the child's writing skills, by commenting on:

- manipulative skills
- concentration
- creativity of the finished piece of writing.

Figure 8.3 Children should be given plenty of opportunities for mark-making

Scribing

Sitting down with children at the mark-making table, at their level, and scribing their messages for them are all important aspects of working sensitively with children. Children do not offer adults their writing for it to be judged and found wanting. They give their effortful early attempts at writing with love, and trust that the adult will appreciate and value them. Then they begin to share with the adult those aspects they found difficult and accept help that is proffered willingly.

Reasons for writing

Children are attracted to activities such as writing labels for the photograph album, as they engage with talking about what they were doing, or about their friends and family. Writing messages such as 'closed' and 'open' for the shop helps children to see the reasons for writing.

Remember, you cannot plan the next steps for a child unless you first observe what interests the child and what engages them in learning. Observation helps practitioners to create a learning environment, indoors and outdoors, which supports the development of writing.

Digital literacy

The use of technology to support language and literacy

The use of information and communication technology in the EYFS is based on the needs of the children, the focus of the learning and whether the technology will add to children's educational opportunities and experiences.

The use of computers

Fine and gross motor skills develop at varying rates, and learning to write can be tedious and difficult as children struggle to form letters. A word processor allows them to compose and revise text without being distracted by the fine motor aspects of letter formation. If computers are used with children in kindergarten, pre-school or other early years settings, the computer should be one of many activity choices they can explore.

- Three- to five-year-olds generally spend about the same amount of time at a computer as they do on other activities such as playing with blocks or drawing. Most children of this age are limited to icons and pictures on the screen for understanding. They are also more interested and less frustrated when an adult is present; their computer use is usually facilitated by the teacher or practitioner.
- Five- to eight-year-olds: as they mature, children use computers more independently, and the teacher's role moves from guidance towards monitoring and active support. Software programs for this age group should be limited in number and appropriate for children's skill level and the intended use. More opportunities for independent use become available with increasing language and literacy skills. For example, simple word processors become important educational tools as children experiment with written language.

Recording equipment

Tape recorders and MP3 players support early literacy experiences by integrating all aspects of literacy: speaking, listening, reading and writing. They allow children to listen to recorded stories or songs, or to follow along in a book as they hear it being read on tape. Children can record family stories, their own made-up stories, poems, and songs, or themselves reading aloud. When adults write down stories from children's dictated words or from the recording equipment, children see how the spoken word can turn into the written word. They can also help children develop their own storytelling ability and an understanding of how sound translates to print.

Cameras

Cameras (film, video or digital) can record children's activities while they are working, as well as performances and special events. Children can tell a story in pictures and write or dictate captions. Photos can be used to share the learning with other children and with parents.

AC 3.3 Activity

Use strategies to plan one activity to support each of the areas outlined above.

AC 3.4 Activities that encourage speaking and listening, reading, writing and digital literacy

Using your plans from AC 3.3, arrange to carry out an activity for each of the areas described above.

LO4 Be able to support children's mathematical development in preparation for school readiness

AC 4.1 How to create an environment which supports children's mathematical development

Mathematical understanding includes the development of:

- abstract thought – through the use of imagination and symbolic representation
- mathematical abilities, such as estimating, predicting or hypothesising
- the language of mathematics (it is now widely agreed that becoming a mathematician is like learning another language).

An environment that supports children's mathematical learning needs to be carefully planned and resourced. Children need both indoor and outdoor environments that provide the following:

- opportunities for mathematical problem-solving; an environment which encourages children to 'have a go' and to be creative when trying to solve problems
- an area for mathematical graphics – or mark-making
- stories, books and rhymes which reflect mathematical ideas, represent concepts and foster imagination

- spaces to go up, over, into, on and through; things to climb on to, up, down and under
- a clock and a timetable for the day that are visible to all children
- the use of routine activities to promote mathematical language and problem-solving
- real-life mathematical ideas represented in role-play resourcing; for example, petrol stations, shops, supermarkets and natural environments, such as beaches and woods
- plans for mathematical learning which reflect and take into account children's current interests.

It is also important to provide a range of resources which ensure that children with additional needs can access them. For example, provide tactile number cards, and number lines with large print for children with impaired vision.

Graphics area (mark-making)

The graphics area – so important for the development of children's literacy – should also include resources for mathematical graphics. For example, include:

- real money
- number lines
- clocks
- stamps
- tape measures and rulers
- raffle tickets
- calculators.

Using everyday routines to support children's mathematical development

There are many opportunities for mathematical learning during the daily routines in a setting.

- Self-registration: children can make a mark or add their names to a list.
- Water play: involve children in setting up the water tray/table and learning about mathematical concepts (see below for more ideas).
- Sandpit or tray: talk to children as they play with water or sand, to encourage them to think about when something is full,

empty or holds more. Which containers shall we use today? Should we put more sand in? How much more? How can we fill it?

- Snack and lunch time: counting out and cutting pieces of fruit; counting items of cutlery and glasses; discussing which shape of cloth would be best to use – round, square or hexagonal. How many children are having lunch today? How many chairs will we need?
- Tidy-up time: is there room for all the hats in the basket? Have we enough space to put all the trikes in the shed? How can we empty the sand tray?

Using the language of mathematics

Using mathematical language comes naturally when playing with children. Throughout the day, one uses words such as 'first', 'next', 'this one is bigger, smaller', etc. The use of open-ended questions also gives young children opportunities to think and to work out the solutions to problems by themselves.

Shape, space and measures: words to use

- shape, round, flat, straight, curved
- roll, stack, slide, pile
- 2D, flat shape, circle, triangle, rectangle, square
- 3D, solid shape, cube, cuboid, sphere, pyramid, cone
- corner, face, side, edge, end
- pattern, repeat, repeating pattern, symmetrical
- first, second, third…, last
- size, bigger, smaller, the same as, copy
- sort, make, build, draw
- fit together, match.

Number: words to use

- number, zero, one, two, three… to 20 and beyond
- add
- take away, leave
- make, sum, total, altogether
- enough, not enough, double

- more, less, count on
- How many more to make…?
- How many are left?

Number lines and tracks

Number lines provide a mental strategy for addition and subtraction. Children make a natural progression from counting to basic addition, but there is an important milestone on the way. This occurs when they realise they don't have to count all the way from one each time. For example, to add three and four, children start out by counting on fingers from one to three, then they count four more to get seven. This method is a natural progression, but involves unnecessary counting of one to three. When children realise this, they start at three and then count on to seven. Number lines are a useful way to accelerate this development. Numbers that can be easily moved on a string are excellent for using flexibly where children can discuss, for example, the numbers they want to hang on the line. The advantages of using number lines include the following:

- Practitioners can easily refer to the number lines to support any number conversation or group activity.
- Often children will look at their age number or door number to initiate a conversation.
- Number lines of different lengths are useful to show children that numbers go beyond ten and to help them see the number sequence and how numerals are written.

AC 4.1 Progress check

- In your setting, can children easily access resources which support their mathematical development?
- Is every area of mathematics covered – that is, number, weight, time, measurement for length, space and money?

Figure 8.4 A hanging number line

AC 4.2 Planning for children's participation in activities that encourage mathematical understanding

Planning activities that encourage number

Children develop their awareness of number through play, exploration and everyday routine activities. To become proficient at counting, children need opportunities to:

- learn the vocabulary of number: comparison words, such as more, less, the same, etc.
- recite numbers in the right order – counting candles on a birthday cake or singing a number song
- count out a given quantity of objects – such as toy animals
- count items in a set

- count things that cannot be seen – such as someone tapping on a drum or playing notes on a recorder
- count physical movements, like the number of hops or steps.

When selecting number songs and rhymes, try to include those that children are familiar with from home. Also make sure that they include:

- counting back and counting forward
- the idea of zero ('no' or 'none'), using action rhymes such as 'Five little ducks'
- counting in pairs, using, for example, '2 ,4, 6, 8, Mary at the cottage gate'
- counting to five, ten and beyond.

Planning activities that encourage shape, size and pattern

Children explore the properties of shapes at home and in the setting. They play with natural objects that differ in size and shape, and they learn the vocabulary of shape: for example, this path is straight and this one is curvy. Children need an environment in which pattern is evident and discussed – in resources, in routines, in music and in the way in which festivals and changing seasons are celebrated. Patterns help children learn to make predictions, to understand what comes next, to make logical connections and to use reasoning skills.

Children need opportunities to:

- investigate the properties of shapes, including 2D shapes (lines, circles, triangles and squares) and 3D shapes (cubes, cylinders, cones and pyramids); rather than just learning the names of shapes, children need to learn about what shapes can and can't do; and which shapes fit together and which shapes don't
- explore and build with 2D and 3D materials: include large objects, such as blocks, cardboard boxes and crates, and smaller ones, such as sets of small bricks, construction kits and shaped blocks
- investigate patterns, which are simply things – numbers, shapes, images – that repeat in a logical way. Examples of activities to investigate pattern include:
  - sorting patterns in wallpaper or fabric samples
  - exploring raindrops in puddles – concentric circles
  - threading activities
  - tessellating games i.e. shape games where patterns interconnect
  - playing with dominoes
  - icing and decorating cakes/biscuits to a counted plan.

Planning activities that encourage weight, volume and capacity

While children are comparing the length, weight, volume or capacity of objects, they are also beginning to gain an understanding of conservation of measures. They understand that the properties of an object – its weight, volume and so on – do not change randomly, even though the appearance of an object might change. Children need opportunities to:

- use the relevant vocabulary: volume – big, little, small, thick, wide, thin; capacity – full, half full, empty, holds, container; weight – weigh, balance, heavy/light, heavier/lighter, heaviest/lightest
- learn how to weigh large and small items; provide a range of scales, such as bucket balances, kitchen scales, stand-on scales and any other weighing machines that will give the children an opportunity to weigh large and small items
- talk about lengths, distances and weight without measuring them; you could encourage a conversation about what a long way it is to the park, or how heavy a box is to carry
- compare two things directly, one against the other: find which dinosaur is the largest, or the longest; and which bowl holds the most by filling one with mini pasta shapes and tipping it into the other bowl
- use measuring tools, such as centimetre tapes, rulers, jugs with measures and litre containers. Using real measuring equipment gives children the opportunity to practise being measurers.

Planning activities that encourage matching and sorting

When children explore their environment they notice how things are alike, and how they are different.

Sorting involves separating objects into groups according to their similarities. Children begin to sort them by characteristics that have meaning to them, such as colour, size, shape, texture and sound. Children then begin matching objects that have the same characteristics. It is easier for children to begin matching pictures after they have had experience matching concrete objects. As children begin to master their matching skills, they will try more complex mathematical activities.

In order to support understanding of matching and sorting, children need opportunities to:

- help with household tasks, such as putting away the shopping or sorting the laundry
- pair or match objects in everyday situations, such as laying the table for tea – making sure that each person has 'one' of each item of cutlery, etc.
- play card-matching games such as Snap or Happy Families. For very young children, play Snap using two separate piles of cards, and show them how to turn the cards over.

AC 4.2 Activity

Make plans to encourage children's participation in activities to develop an understanding of each of the areas above, i.e. number; shape, size and pattern; weight, volume and capacity; and matching and sorting.

AC 4.3 Carrying out activities that encourage mathematical understanding

Using your plans in AC 4.2, arrange to carry out the activities in your setting.

Assessment practice

1 Explain the term 'school readiness'.
2 Explain how the early years practitioner supports children to prepare for school.
3 Describe the holistic needs of the child as they prepare for school.
4 Identify others involved in helping children prepare for school.
5 Describe the information required to enable the school to meet the individual needs of the child during transition.
6 Explain what is meant by a 'language-rich environment'.
7 Describe two activities that support children's learning for each of the following areas: speaking and listening skills; reading; writing; digital literacy.
8 Describe how to create an environment which supports children's mathematical development.
9 Plan activities which support children's understanding of number; shape, size and pattern; weight, volume and capacity; and matching and sorting.
10 Carry out your planned activities, and evaluate how each activity supports children's understanding of number; shape, size and pattern; weight, volume and capacity; and matching and sorting.

Useful resources

Early Education (2012) *Development Matters in the Early Years Foundation Stage (non-statutory guidance)*, London: BAECE (www.early-education.org.uk)

Fisher, J. (2010) *Moving On to Key Stage 1 – Improving Transition from the Early Years Foundation Stage*, Maidenhead: Open University Press.

Likierman, H. and Muter, V. (2006) *Prepare Your Child for School*, London: Vermilion.

Nutbrown, C., ed. (1996) *Respectful Educators – Capable Learners: Children's Rights and Early Education*, London: Sage.

Pound, L. (2008) *Thinking and Learning about Mathematics in the Early Years*, London: Nursery World/Routledge.

Whitehead, M. (2010) *Language and Literacy in the Early Years 0–7* (4th edn), London: Sage.

Gordon Wells (2009) 2nd edition *The Meaning Makers: Learning to Talk and Talking to Learn* (New Perspectives on Language and Education) Multilingual Matters.

Books for children

Once There Were Giants by Martin Waddell and Penny Dale (Walker Books) – as a baby girl grows up and becomes an adult, the 'giants' in her family seem to grow smaller.

Happy Birthday, Sam by Pat Hutchins (HarperCollins).

Sunshine and Moonlight by Jan Ormerod (Frances Lincoln) – these companion titles and classic, wordless picture books look at the daily routines of a young girl in the morning and at night.

The Very Hungry Caterpillar by Eric Carle (Picture Puffin).

NRICH

The NRICH Project aims to enrich the mathematical experiences of all learners. To support this aim, members of the NRICH team work in a wide range of capacities, including providing professional development for teachers wishing to embed rich mathematical tasks into everyday classroom practice.

www.nrich.maths.org

Unit 9

Engage in professional development

Learning outcomes

By the end of this unit, you will:

1 Understand professional development.

2 Be able to use reflective practice to contribute to own personal and professional development.

LO1 Understand professional development

Professional development and reflective practice are both fundamental to those who work with children in a wide range of settings. Engaging in professional development has a positive influence on improving the status of early years practitioners, as well as enabling them to share examples of effective practice with others. Early years settings benefit from employing early years practitioners who are able to reflect on and improve their professional expertise.

AC 1.1 What is 'professional development'?

Professional development is important for anyone working within a profession. Each profession has a set of standards and rules which governs its practice. Professional development:

- concerns the acquisition of skills and knowledge both for personal development and for career advancement
- involves all types of learning opportunities, ranging from college degrees to formal coursework, conferences, study days, specialist courses and informal learning opportunities while in practice.

In relation to early years practice, professional development also includes

mentoring and reflective practice. Being a professional early years practitioner means having sufficient knowledge and understanding of children in relation to their learning and development. It also means being able and willing to challenge everyday practice and to adapt it where necessary through regular analysis of how best to meet children's holistic needs.

There are many skills involved in working with and caring for children that all adults need.

These include:

- the support and experience to reflect and learn from experience
- the confidence and ability to respond in the best possible ways to individual children
- really knowing about the child, trusting that knowledge and the judgements that are based on it
- being prepared to learn from the child – for example, by listening to what a child tells you and observing what they do.

Working in the field of early years can be physically and emotionally exhausting, and professionals will need to consolidate their skills and develop the ability to be reflective in their practice. You also need to be able to give and receive feedback; this is a skill that needs to be practised in order for it to be effective for both parties.

The effect of your own experiences on your practice

Your professional development includes your own 'growth' as a person:

- Your experiences at work and at home can change your attitudes, priorities and ambitions.
- Changes in home circumstances influence decisions you make about your work – for example, the hours you work, where you work and the level of responsibility you take on. If you are without family responsibilities, you may welcome the extra challenge of a training course to develop your career. However, if you have to strike a balance between career and home life and additional time is not available for training, then this might seem a burden.
- Sometimes a personal interest will influence the course of your professional development. For example, you may know a friend's child who is disabled, which sparks an interest in working with children with additional needs.

Self-awareness

An important part of your personal development is self-awareness. Self-awareness means:

- knowing who you are and what you enjoy doing
- being able to recognise your skills, strengths and weaknesses
- being able to recognise your effect on other people.

Key areas for self-awareness include our personality traits, personal values, habits and emotions.

Self-awareness helps you to exploit your strengths and cope with your weaknesses. The process of being self-aware can be uncomfortable when you realise that something you have done or said has had a negative impact on someone else. However, unless we face such self-awareness, we can never really develop and improve our practice. What is important here is that you have a network of colleagues that you can call upon for support and guidance should you require it.

Self-awareness is also crucial for developing effective interpersonal skills and building positive relationships with children and their families. Additionally, being self-aware allows you to identify your own learning needs and the ways in which those learning needs can be met – and then it is involved in your evaluation of whether those needs have been met.

Being non-judgemental

It is very important to be non-judgemental. It is easy to criticise others and to believe that you would approach things in a better way. However, parents and carers can only learn to trust you if they know that you are not judging their actions.

AC 1.1 Activity

Make a list of the areas of practice you would like to develop and find out how to access opportunities for further training and education.

AC 1.2 Professional development opportunities

It is important to keep up to date with the changes in early years practice by reading the relevant magazines and journals, such as *Nursery World* and *Early Years Educator*, and by being willing to attend training courses when available. Nationally and locally, both public services and private companies will offer a variety of opportunities on diverse topics – for example, courses on:

- the EYFS
- Learning and Development
- Leadership and Management
- SEND and Inclusion
- Safeguarding and Welfare Requirements
- Paediatric First Aid.

TACTYC, the Association for the Professional Development of Early Years Educators, is an early years organisation for anyone involved with the education and training of those who work with young children.

You will be working hard to obtain the Level 2 Introduction to Early Years Education and Care and can look forward to developing your career with children. This is called professional development and is important because it:

- enables you to develop greater knowledge and understanding in connection with your work
- offers opportunities to improve skills or gain new ones
- can enable you to experience new situations
- can prepare you for different roles and responsibilities.

The range of professional development available

You may decide to progress to one of the CACHE Level 3 Early Years Educator suite of qualifications, or a Playwork course. Some aspects of professional development are dealt with through in-service training courses, often organised and paid for by your employer. You may receive the training from a member of your own staff or visit a college or recognised training organisation on a part-time basis. Courses can cover anything from dealing with a particular medical condition to developing ways of improving assessment and record-keeping.

Employment opportunities

CACHE Level 2 qualifications provide a stepping stone to Level 3 qualifications. They show that you have a good knowledge and understanding, and the ability to perform various well-defined tasks with some direction and guidance. The knowledge and skills that you learn are applicable to the jobs shown in Table 9.1, where you would be working under supervision.

Table 9.1 Working in the public, voluntary and private sectors

Public sector		
	Areas of work	Types of job
Local education authority	Nursery schools State nurseries Infant, lower and primary schools Schools for children with special needs	Nursery trained teacher Nursery assistant Classroom assistant Special needs classroom assistant
Local government services	Family Centres Children's Centres (run by Social Services) Holiday playschemes	Nursery assistant in Family Centres and children's daycare nurseries Playworker in holiday playschemes and adventure centres
Health authority	Health visiting in the community Hospitals Hospital crèches and nurseries Adventure centres and one o'clock clubs	Health visitor assistant in clinics and in clients' homes Play assistant in hospital children's units Nursery assistant in crèches and nurseries
Voluntary sector		
	Pre-school playgroups After-school clubs Holiday playschemes Nurseries	Nursery assistant After-school club assistant Holiday playscheme worker Playworker

➜

Table 9.1 Working in the public, voluntary and private sectors   (*continued*)

Private sector		
	Day nurseries	Nursery assistants
	Nursery schools	Playworkers or ski nannies
	Crèches (in workplaces, shopping centres or sport and leisure centres)	Mother's Help (childcare and housework)
	Holiday companies (e.g. ski chalets, water sports, cruise ships, hotels)	Au pair (usually unqualified childcare, often young people working abroad and living with the family)
	Families	Nanny (usually qualified in childcare, may live with family)

AC 1.2   Progress check ✓

Using the internet and your local authority website, identify professional development opportunities in your area.

LO2 Be able to use reflective practice to contribute to own personal and professional development

AC 2.1 Creating a curriculum vitae

Preparing a CV

It is always useful to compile a curriculum vitae (CV) and to keep it up to date. The purposes of a CV are to:

- provide a brief outline of your life history
- set out basic factual information in a concise manner
- help in filling out application forms.

Microsoft Word and Open Office both have templates for a CV. The main sections to include are:

- first name and family name
- personal details: date of birth, full postal address, telephone number and email
- education and qualifications: include names of schools and colleges attended, with dates and qualifications obtained

- employment history: list all previous employment, including Saturday and holiday jobs; if you have not worked before, include babysitting experience and college work experience
- other experience: include any voluntary work, involvement in local organisations or groups, sport and leisure interests
- referees: give the names, positions and addresses of two people who are willing to provide references for you. Always ask them first.

CVs should be well-presented and free from any mistakes. Use your spellchecker, and also get a friend to check it through. In general, if you are applying for a post in a school or local authority Children's Centre or day nursery, CVs alone will not be accepted. Read the guidance on job applications very carefully before you complete the forms.

AC 2.1   Progress check ✓

Using the guidelines above, prepare a CV.

AC 2.2 Own professional development needs

The opportunities for learning when working with children are endless. You will increase your knowledge and skills every day through interacting with children and their carers or parents. It is important to take every opportunity to learn more – to increase your skills and understanding. For example, parents and carers will soon recognise when someone has learned about the common pattern of development in their child's age group. They will also appreciate when someone has taken the trouble to learn more about their child's particular condition or home background. You will also learn a lot from colleagues and training opportunities, and should always be willing to share any knowledge you have gained.

The importance of setting targets

Setting targets – or goals – as part of a personal development plan will help you to get more involved in your learning. Remember, your targets are personal – they may be quite different from those of others in your class. Learning targets can help you to:

- decide what is most important to you in your learning
- fit your studies in with your other commitments
- decide on how you will study
- become an active learner
- reflect on your own practice
- think about your personal and professional development.

Your learning targets should:

- include a timescale to show when they should be completed; you could identify a final goal and then break down the steps towards achieving that goal into short-term, medium-term and long-term targets
- identify success criteria – to show how you will know when you have achieved a target
- be realistic
- be relevant to you.

Setting appropriate targets

SMART targets

Each member of a team needs to know exactly what is expected of them. These expectations are called targets or 'objectives'. The targets that are most likely to be achieved are those that are 'SMART', which stands for:

- **Specific**: They must be easy to understand and say exactly what you want to happen.
- **Measurable**: Success can be measured by checking back carefully against the instructions that have been given.
- **Achievable**: The targets can be reached with reasonable effort in the time you are allowed.
- **Relevant**: The targets must be appropriate, building on previous strengths and skills.
- **Time-related**: The targets have clearly set deadlines and are reviewed frequently.

Progress check

Using SMART targets
Look at the following scenarios and see how SMART targets can help individuals and teams to plan and achieve their objectives.

1 Scenario 1: Paula has been asked if she would organise a display for the nursery room. The only instructions she has been given are:
'Paula, can you put up a nice, colourful display in the nursery room, please?'
2 Scenario 2: At a different nursery, Mark has also been asked to organise a display. On Wednesday, he was given these instructions:
'Next Monday we need to create an interactive display for the nursery room. It will be on the theme of autumn. We've already collected some pine cones and autumn leaves, and we also have some good posters, but I'd like you to plan what else we need and let me have a list of resources by tomorrow lunchtime.'

Reviewing, updating and amending targets for professional skills

It is important to review the targets identified in your personal plan at regular intervals. Sometimes you may find that the targets set were unrealistic, either in timescale or in the amount of work involved. An important part of planning and evaluating your plan is knowing when and why to review and amend your targets.

Activity

Using targets for personal and professional development

Write down in two or three sentences what you hope to achieve through your course and how you see it helping you in the future.

- What do you want to be able to do, think, feel, understand or know?
- How would this learning be recognised by others?
- What are the steps you need to take to reach the end result?

Now write your personal plan (see below) and learning targets based on these ideas and using the information in this unit as a guide.

AC 2.3 Working with others to agree own personal development plan

A personal development plan will:

- help you to take responsibility for your own career and professional development
- motivate you to develop your own skills
- help you to be aware of your strengths and weaknesses
- help you to decide what training might be required to fulfil your future plans.

There are five main steps to creating a personal development plan:

1 Think about your skills, strengths and weaknesses: before you can decide which areas you need to develop, you need to identify the skills you already have.

2 Decide which areas you need to develop: think about what you need to do to become more competent in your present work role.

3 Create the plan: think about how you can achieve your objectives – will you need training, to shadow a colleague or to take on a different role? You should then set a timescale for the achievements of the objectives. Ensure you set yourself SMART targets (see above).

4 Discuss your plan with others: it is important to discuss your plan with

colleagues, managers, etc. as they may offer advice and support or have suggestions on how you can gain experience or knowledge.

5 Implement the plan: if you have researched well and your plan is realistic then your plan should be straightforward, although you may need to change your plan or timescale if, for example, the date for a course you were going to attend changes.

Agreeing your personal development plan

You are not expected to be solely responsible for agreeing your own development plan. Your tutor or placement mentor/supervisor should work with you to help you draw up your development plan. He or she should give you advice, time and support to draw up your plan – and then should ensure they are available to discuss any problems or ideas you may have.

Figure 9.1 Your tutor or supervisor will be able to advise you on your personal development plan

AC 2.4 How reflecting on work activities develops knowledge, skills and practice

Self-evaluation is important because it helps you to improve your own practice and to modify plans to meet the learning needs of the children. You can best evaluate your own performance by reflecting on your practice.

Reflective practice

You should get used to reviewing and reflecting on your experiences as part of your everyday learning. In this way, each experience – whether positive or negative – will contribute to your development and personal growth. Ways to reflect include:

- setting yourself some goals or targets when you start studying, and using your tutor's and your placement supervisor's feedback to monitor your progress
- working out what you have achieved and what you still need to work on
- making a record of your thoughts and reflections to help you to keep track of your ideas and see how far they have developed over a period of time

- recording your thoughts on any difficulties or challenges you are facing
- talking things through with another person, such as another student or a trusted friend
- asking yourself questions about what you did and thinking about how you could have done it better
- using evidence to support or evaluate any decision – for example, observations or lecture notes.

It is a good idea to develop the habit of recording your reflections. This will help you to extend your skills in reflective practice.

Progress check

Reflective practice
Reflective practice helps you to review and evaluate your own experiences. General and specific reflective questions will help to organise this evaluation. For example:

General questions
1 Was my contribution to the planning meeting or activity appropriate?
2 Did I achieve my targets? If not, was it because the targets were unrealistic?

3 What other methods could be used?
4 How can I improve my practice?
5 Whom can I ask for advice and support?

Specific questions
For example:

1 How can I help a child to settle into the classroom again after his hospital stay?
2 What is making a child behave inappropriately at meal times?

Reflective practice

Reviewing your learning activities
You may be asked to plan an activity to implement in your work setting, such as a storytelling session using props, or a painting activity. Choose one activity that you have carried out with a group of children and record your answers to the following questions:

1 How suitable was the activity for the group of children?
2 How successful were you in planning the task? Did you consider the following factors: safety, space, children's ages and stage of

development, supervision and availability of resources?
3 How did the children respond during the activity? Were you able to maintain their interest?
4 How might you improve the activity if you did it again? What would you do differently and why?
5 Write a short summary of the activity – perhaps using a format for Observations (see page 256) – and use your findings to help you prepare for the next activity.

AC 2.5 How feedback from others develops own knowledge, skills and understanding

Feedback is structured information that one person offers to another, about the impact of their actions or behaviour – in other words, how you are doing in your study or work role. It is vital to the success of most workplace tasks. Feedback and criticism are different; criticism can make the recipient feel undervalued or angry, which are both unproductive emotions.

The information you hear when receiving feedback from others may be new – and even surprising. You may react with strong emotion. Good feedback is an offer of information, not a diagnosis of your character or potential, so you should not react angrily or 'take it too personally'.

Receiving feedback can:

- help you become aware of how you are getting on – the good and the bad, what is working and what is not
- give you some ideas to help you plan your own development, in order to reach your full potential
- give you a 'reality check' – you can compare how you think you are with what other people tell you.

Feedback from a number of different people helps you make a balanced decision about the information you are hearing. (Remember – not everyone has good feedback skills; you are likely to get a mixed quality of feedback, some perceptive and supportive, some critical and unspecific.)

Apart from the feedback you receive through formal appraisals of your performance, you may receive other forms of feedback, such as:

- informal observations by colleagues, or by the children in your care
- mentoring: a mentor supports you by modelling good practice and guiding you to look critically at your own practice and to decide how it can be improved
- questionnaires: these are useful in obtaining feedback from parents and carers about the setting.

Guidelines for good practice

Receiving feedback

1 **Ask questions:** state what you want feedback about. Be specific about what you want to know. Give the speaker time to think about what they want to say.
2 **Listen:** listen attentively – do not interrupt or digress. Ask for clarification if you are not sure you have understood what you have heard. Try not to be defensive or to reject the information. You need to listen, but not necessarily to agree. Take notes of what is said.
3 **Check:** check what you have heard. Repeat back what the speaker has said and ask for examples of what they mean. Give your reactions to the feedback or ask for time to think about it if necessary. Ask for suggestions on what might work better.
4 **Reflect:** feedback is information for you to use – it is not a requirement to change. If you are unsure about the soundness of the feedback, check it out with other people. Work out the options open to you and decide what you want to do. It is up to you to evaluate how accurate and how useful the feedback is.

AC 2.6 Reflecting on work activities in relation to own professional development

Reflecting on your own work activities
One of the most useful ways to reflect on your activities and experiences in the setting is to keep a reflective diary. Reflective diaries are a personal record of your experiences throughout your placement and so it is important to use them to report thoughts, feelings and opinions rather than simply listing the factual events of the day. Only by

Activity

Accessing support to review your progress and achievements

Work with an appropriate person, such as your tutor or placement/mentor supervisor, to express your opinions and develop an individual plan that includes:

- targets that clearly show what you want to achieve in your learning, work or personal life, and how you will know if you have met these
- the actions you will take (action points) and dates for completing them (deadlines) to help you meet each target
- how to get the support you need, including who will review your progress and where and when this will take place.

Your tutor will help you to discuss your progress; he or she will enable you to reflect on what you learned, how you learned and what has been successful or unsuccessful. You should also aim to:

- identify the targets you have met, by checking your plan to see if you have done what you set out to do
- identify your achievements by finding out what you need to do to improve your performance (the quality of your work, and the way you work)
- use ways of learning suggested by your tutor or supervisor, making changes when needed to improve your performance.

reporting personal feelings following an event can experiences be built upon and improved. It is also important to use your reflective diary to record positive experiences and achievements as well as the not-so-positive ones.

Sources of support

Support for your learning and development is very important and may be provided by people within your work setting and by outside agencies. Before starting a new course of formal study or training, you should discuss the following issues with your tutor or placement mentor/supervisor:

- Where is the course held? Is it easily accessible?
- Does the course meet my learning objectives?
- How will the course be funded?
- How much time will it take? Will you be able to take time out of work to attend? Will there still be time for you to study?

AC 2.6 Progress check

Working as an early years practitioner
Make a list of what you consider to be the most important qualities an early years practitioner should possess.

1 Explain what type of professional development an early years practitioner might expect in his/her first year of employment.
2 Create your own list of ten 'top tips' that you think would be helpful to an early years practitioner about to begin his/her first job.

AC 2.7 Recording progress in relation to personal and professional development

Compiling a portfolio of achievement

A portfolio is a collection of the different types of evidence that can also be used to show successful completion of the course. Examples of evidence include the following:

- completed assignments, observations, projects or case studies, including action plans and evaluations: these can be in written form or word processed, although work in the form of video recordings, audio-tape recordings, photographs, logbooks or diaries may also be acceptable where they contain evidence of the practical demonstration of skills (check with your tutor or supervisor)
- past records of achievement, qualifications, work experience or other evidence of 'prior learning'

- samples of relevant class or lecture notes, lists, personal reading records or copies of letters written (perhaps regarding work experience, to request information or advice, or related to job or further education applications).

Figure 9.2 It is important to keep a record of your personal and professional development

AC 2.7 Progress check

Recording progress

1 Do you keep a record of all training days and staff development events you have attended?
2 Have you included evidence in your portfolio of personal development activities – certificates of attendance, notes and other information?
3 Have you revisited your development plan – reviewed it and reflected on it?

Useful resources

Council for Awards in Care, Health and Education (CACHE)

The specialist awarding organisation for education (CACHE) qualifications in children's care and education.

Family and Childcare Trust

Formerly the Daycare Trust, the Family and Childcare Trust aims to make the UK a better place for families, through research, campaigning and information provision, and working with government, employers and parents to reduce pressures on family life.

www.familyandchildcaretrust.org

National Careers Service

Offers careers information, advice and support to 13–19 year olds between 8 am and 10 pm, seven days a week.

The National Day Nurseries Association

Promotes quality childcare and early years education. Its website profiles people who have chosen to work in childcare and education.

PACEY

The Professional Association for Childcare and Early Years: a standard-setting organisation that promotes best practice and supports childcare professionals to deliver high standards of care and learning.

The Pre-school Learning Alliance

Runs its own courses and publishes information on pre-school work and training.

4Children

Formerly Kid's Club Network, this organisation provides information on jobs and training in out-of-school childcare and playwork.

Skills Active

Gives information on a career in playwork.

Directgov

Provides a search service for jobs, training, careers, childcare and voluntary work (provided by Jobcentre Plus).

www.gov.uk/jobsearch

Unit 10

Supporting children's development

LO1 Understand the stages of child development from birth to seven years

AC 1.1 The expected pattern of development

It is important to keep in mind that every child is unique. By looking at the holistic (or integrated) development of children, we can view the child as a whole person – physically, emotionally, intellectually, morally, culturally and spiritually. Physical growth is different from physical development. Physical growth means that children grow in height and weight, whereas physical development means that children gain skills through being able to control their own bodies.

The whole child may be looked at using four aspects:

- Physical development
- Language and communication development
- Cognitive (or intellectual) development
- Social, emotional and behavioural development

Physical development
Children's physical development follows a pattern:

- From simple to complex: a child will stand before he can walk, and walk before he can skip or hop.
- From head to toe: physical control and coordination begin with a child's head and work down the body through the arms, hands and back and finally to the legs and feet.
- From inner to outer: a child can coordinate his arms using gross motor skills to reach for an object before he has learned the fine motor skills necessary to pick it up.
- From general to specific: a young baby shows pleasure by a massive general response (eyes widen, legs and arms move vigorously, etc.); an older child shows pleasure by smiling or using appropriate words or gestures.

Physical development is the way in which the body increases in skill and becomes more complex in its performance. There are two main areas:

1 Gross motor skills: these use the large muscles in the body and include walking, squatting, running, climbing, etc.
2 Fine motor skills: these include:
  - gross manipulative skills – single limb movements, usually the arm: for example,

throwing, catching and sweeping arm movements

- fine manipulative skills – precise use of the hands and fingers for pointing, drawing, using a knife and fork, writing, doing up shoelaces, etc.

There are wide variations in the ages at which children acquire physical skills, such as sitting, standing and walking. The rate at which children develop these skills will have an effect on all the other areas of development: for example, on the development of language, understanding, self-confidence and social skills. Once a child has learned to crawl, to shuffle on her bottom or to be mobile in other ways, she will be more independent and be able to explore things that were previously out of reach. Adults will make changes to the child's environment now that she is mobile, by putting reachable objects out of her way and making clear rules and boundaries.

Sensory development

The senses of a newborn baby

Newborn babies are already actively using all their senses to explore their new environment. They are:

- sight (or visual development)
- hearing
- taste
- touch
- smell.

Visual development

Newborn babies are very near-sighted at first, and they can focus best on things that are within 25 cm (10 inches) of their faces. This means that they can see well enough to focus on their mother's face when being held to the breast. Their vision is quite blurry outside this range but they can follow a light with their eyes and turn towards lights. Sometimes babies appear to have a squint as their eyes may move independently of each other. This is normal, as they are still gaining control of the eye muscles. Newborn babies prefer to look at:

- people's faces and eyes, especially those of their mothers
- bright colours – they will often reach for colourful objects
- light and dark contrasts and sharp outlines
- patterns, such as stripes or circles, rather than plain surfaces
- things that are moving: they will focus on and follow a moving ball with their eyes, a skill known as tracking.

Hearing

Babies develop very good hearing while in the womb. Ultrasound studies have shown that unborn babies as early as 25 weeks' gestation can 'startle' in response to a sudden loud noise. Newborn babies can distinguish different voices and other sounds, and they can also determine from which direction a sound is coming. For example, if a small bell is rung above a newborn baby's head, he will turn his head in the direction of the sound and watch the object making the sound. Newborn babies prefer to listen to:

- the human voice, especially female voices. They usually recognise their own mother's voice from the start, since this is the voice they have heard, although muffled, throughout their time in the womb. Newborn babies become quiet when they hear their mother's voice, and they turn their heads towards their mother when she speaks. After about a week or so, most newborn babies will prefer their father's voice to that of other men.
- soft, melodic speech. They can tell the difference between a calm, happy tone and an angry voice, and will respond with pleasure to a soft, lilting voice or may cry when they hear a loud, angry voice.

Hearing is an important part of speech development, so it is essential that babies are talked to. Parents and other adults automatically alter the pitch of their voices when talking to babies and use a lot of repetition.

Touch

Newborn babies are very sensitive to touch. They love to be held close, comforted, cuddled, stroked and rocked. Newborn babies prefer:

- stroking of their skin: this action helps newborn babies to sleep, and it helps to encourage closeness between baby and parent
- the feel of soft fabrics
- skin-to-skin contact with their parents, and being cuddled.

Babies who are fed but not touched or held often have problems with their physical and mental development. Gentle stroking is especially beneficial for premature babies. Research shows that it leads to increased weight gain, more alertness and activity and an earlier discharge from hospital.

Taste

Newborn babies also have a well-developed sense of taste. They generally enjoy sweetness and dislike sour liquids. They can detect differences in the taste of their mother's milk, which can change depending on what the mother eats. Babies show that they find tastes pleasant or unpleasant by screwing up their faces and trying to reject the taste from their mouth. See Useful Resources at the end of the chapter.

Smell

Newborn babies are sensitive to the smell of their mother, and they can tell it apart from that of other women. They are attracted not just to the smell of milk, but also to their mother's own unique body scent. Breastfed babies are more aware of their mother's smell compared with babies who are bottle-fed. This may be because breastfed babies spend more time in skin-to-skin contact with their mothers compared with babies who are bottle-fed. Babies will also turn away from a smell they find unpleasant.

Language and communication development

Language development is very closely linked to cognitive development, and a delay in one area usually affects progress in the other. Language development is the development of communication skills. These include skills in:

- receptive speech – what a person understands
- expressive speech – the words the person produces
- articulation – the person's actual pronunciation of words.

Babies are born with a need and a desire to communicate with others before they can express themselves through speaking. Learning how to communicate (to listen and to speak) begins with non-verbal communication, which includes:

- body language, such as facial expression, eye contact, pointing, touching and reaching for objects
- listening to others talking to them
- making sounds (including crying) to attract attention
- copying the sounds made by others.

These skills develop as babies and young children express their needs and feelings, interact with others and establish their own identities and personalities.

Cognitive development

Cognitive (or intellectual) development is the development of the mind – the part of the brain that is used for recognising, reasoning, knowing and understanding. It involves:

- what a person knows and the ability to reason, understand and solve problems
- memory, concentration, attention and perception
- imagination and creativity.

Children learn through play. They need opportunities to:

- learn to predict: children learn to predict that something is about to happen. For example, a baby learns to predict that food will soon appear if a bib is tied around his or her neck.
- learn the consequences of their actions: children understand that they can bring about a result by their own actions. For example, a baby learns that if he or she cries, he or she will be picked up and comforted.
- ask questions: as soon as they can talk, children ask questions to try to make sense of their world and gain information. For example, four-year-old children constantly ask the question 'Why?' whereas a child aged two-and-a-half years often asks 'Who?' and 'What?'
- understand concepts: experiences with real objects help young children to understand concepts and to develop problem-solving skills. For example, mathematical concepts involve understanding number, sequencing, volume and capacity, as well as weighing and measuring.
- use repetition: children learn by repeating activities over and over again. For example, they can learn a song or nursery rhyme by hearing it sung to them many times.
- use imitation: children learn by copying what others do. For example, they learn how to write by copying letters, and in role play children are copying the way they have observed others behave in certain situations.

Emotional, social and behavioural development

These three areas of development are very closely linked. Emotional development involves:

- the growth of feelings about, and awareness of, oneself
- the development of feelings towards other people
- the development of **self-esteem** and a **self-concept**.

Key terms

self-esteem The way in which you feel about yourself (good or bad) leads to high or low self-esteem.

self-concept How you see yourself, and how you think others see you; sometimes called self-image.

Social development

Social development includes the growth of the child's relationships with other people. **Socialisation** is the process of learning the skills and attitudes that enable the child to live easily with other members of the community.

The development of social and self-help skills

As early as six months of age, babies enjoy each other's company. When they are together, they look at each other, smile and touch each other's faces. As their social circle widens, they learn how to cooperate with each other when they play, and they begin to make friends.

What are social skills?

Children need to develop certain social skills (or ways of behaving) in order to fit in – and to get on well – with the people around them (see Figure 10.1).

Key terms

empathy The ability to understand what someone else is feeling and to share the experience with that person.

socialisation The process by which children learn what is expected of them in terms of behaviour and attitudes within society.

behaviour The way in which we act, speak and treat other people and our environment.

Spiritual and moral development

Moral and spiritual development consists of a developing awareness of how to relate to others ethically, morally and fairly. It involves understanding values such as honesty and respect, acquiring concepts such as right and wrong, and taking responsibility for the consequences of one's actions.

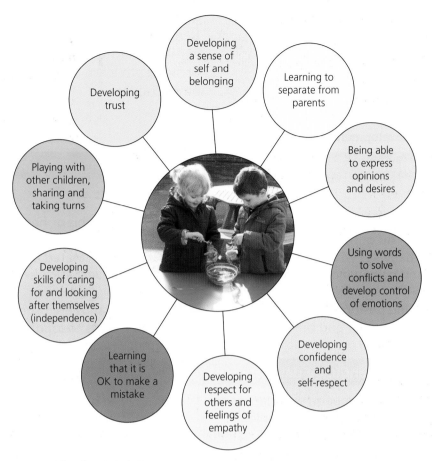

Figure 10.1 Social skills

Case study

Christophe

Christophe is new to the nursery. He is two years old and has a brother, Olivier, who is four-and-a-half years old and has started attending pre-school. Christophe's family have recently moved to the UK from France. Monique, the mother, is fluent in English but speaks French to the boys at home, and has employed a French-Canadian au pair to collect the boys from the nursery two days a week. Antoine, the father, also speaks good English, but is very rarely at the nursery.

The boys are both very lively. Olivier soon picks up English phrases and everyone is delighted and relieved at his speedy progress in becoming bilingual. However, Christophe is struggling with English words, and Monique reports that he has stopped speaking so much French. At nursery, Christophe does not say any recognisable words and will instead 'grunt' answers or start crying. This makes it difficult for nursery staff to communicate with him – he just stares as they address him and does not respond to instructions at all.

He can sometimes be quite destructive and refuses to tidy up after tipping over boxes. Staff members try to show him with actions, but Christophe rarely responds. However, apart from his obvious frustration when trying to communicate, Christophe loves to run around and laughs a lot as he watches other children, and joins in their games. He also joins in with different activities.

1 Why do you think Olivier finds the new language so much easier than Christophe?
2 How has Christophe's difficulty in communicating impacted on other areas of his development?

The stages and sequence of holistic development from birth to seven years

The following pages outline the main features of holistic child development, the ages shown being those at which the average child performs the specific tasks. Remember, however, that children develop at different rates, and some may be faster or slower to learn certain skills than other children.

Table 10.1 Holistic development: the first month

Physical development	
Gross motor skills	**Fine motor skills**
• The baby lies supine (on his or her back). • When placed on his or her front (the prone position), the baby lies with head turned to one side, and by one month can lift the head. • If pulled to sitting position, the head will lag, the back curves over and the head falls forward.	• The baby turns his or her head towards the light and stares at bright or shiny objects. • The baby is fascinated by human faces and gazes attentively at carer's face when fed or held. • The baby's hands are usually tightly closed. • The baby reacts to loud sounds but by one month may be soothed by particular music.

Communication and language development
• Babies need to share language experiences and cooperate with others from birth onwards. From the start babies need other people. • The baby responds to sounds, especially familiar voices. • The baby quietens when picked up. • The baby makes eye contact. • The baby cries to indicate need, e.g. hunger, dirty nappy, etc. • The baby may move his or her eyes towards the direction of sound.

Intellectual development

Babies explore through their senses and through their own activity and movement.

Touch

- From the beginning babies feel pain.
- The baby's face, abdomen, hands and the soles of his or her feet are also very sensitive to touch.
- The baby perceives the movements that he or she makes, and the way that other people move them about through his or her senses.
- For example, the baby gives a 'startle' response if they are moved suddenly. This is called the 'Moro' or startle reflex.

Sound

- Even a newborn baby will turn to a sound. The baby might become still and listen to a low sound, or quicken his or her movements when he or she hears a high sound.
- The baby often stops crying and listens to a human voice by two weeks of age.

Taste

- The baby likes sweet tastes, e.g. breast milk.

→

Table 10.1 Holistic development: the first month   (*continued*)

Intellectual development

Smell

- The baby turns to the smell of the breast.

Sight

- The baby can focus on objects 20 cm (8 inches) away.
- The baby is sensitive to light.
- The baby likes to look at human faces – eye contact.
- The baby can track the movements of people and objects.
- The baby will scan the edges of objects.
- The baby will imitate facial expressions (e.g. he or she will put out their tongue if you do). If you know any newborn or very young babies, try it and see!

Emotional and social development

- A baby's first smile in definite response to carer is usually around 5–6 weeks.
- The baby often imitates certain facial expressions.
- The baby uses total body movements to express pleasure at bath time or when being fed.
- The baby enjoys feeding and cuddling.
- In the first month, babies are learning where they begin and end, e.g. his or her hand is part of them but mother's hand is not.

Table 10.2 Holistic development from one to four months

Physical development

Gross motor skills	Fine motor skills
From four to eight weeks: - The baby can now turn from side to back. - The baby can lift the head briefly from the prone position. - Arm and leg movements are jerky and uncontrolled. - There is head lag if the baby is pulled to sitting position From eight to twelve weeks: - When lying supine, the baby's head is in a central position. - The baby can now lift head and chest off bed in prone position, supported on forearms. - There is almost no head lag in sitting position. - The legs can kick vigorously, both separately and together. - The baby can wave his or her arms and bring his or her hands together over the body.	- The baby turns her head towards the light and stares at bright or shiny objects. - The baby will show interest and excitement by facial expression and will gaze attentively at carer's face while being fed. - The baby will use his/her hand to grasp the carer's finger. - The baby moves his or her head to follow adult movements. - The baby watches his or her hands and plays with his or her fingers. - The baby holds a rattle for a brief time before dropping it. →

Table 10.2 Holistic development from one to four months   (*continued*)

Communication and language development

From four to eight weeks:

- The baby recognises the carer and familiar objects.
- The baby makes non-crying noises such as cooing and gurgling.
- The baby's cries become more expressive.

From eight to twelve weeks:

- The baby is still distressed by sudden loud noises.
- The baby often sucks or licks lips when he or she hears sound of food preparation.
- The baby shows excitement at sound of approaching footsteps or voices.

During the first three months:

- The baby listens to people's voices. When adults close to the baby talk in motherese or fatherese (a high-pitched tone referring to what is around and going on), the baby dances, listens, replies in babble and coo.
- The baby cries with anger to show they are tired, hungry, and to say they need to be changed.
- The baby is comforted by the voices of those who are close to them and will turn especially to the voices of close family members.

Intellectual development

- The baby recognises differing speech sounds.
- By three months, the baby can even imitate low- or high-pitched sounds.
- By four months, the baby links objects they know with the sound, e.g. mother's voice and her face.
- The baby knows the smell of his or her mother from that of other mothers.

Emotional and social development

Four to eight weeks:

- The baby will smile in response to an adult.
- The baby enjoys sucking.
- The baby turns to regard nearby speaker's face.
- The baby turns to preferred person's voice.
- The baby recognises face and hands of preferred adult.
- The baby may stop crying when he or she hears, sees or feels her carer.

Eight to twelve weeks:

- The baby shows enjoyment at caring routines such as bath time.
- The baby responds with obvious pleasure to loving attention and cuddles.
- The baby fixes his or her eyes unblinkingly on carer's face when feeding.
- The baby stays awake for longer periods of time.

Table 10.3 Holistic development from four to six months

Physical development	
Gross motor skills	**Fine motor skills**
• The baby is beginning to use a palmar grasp and can transfer objects from hand to hand. • The baby is very interested in all activity. • Everything is taken to the mouth. • The baby moves his or her head around to follow people and objects.	• The baby now has good head control and is beginning to sit with support. • The baby rolls over from back to side and is beginning to reach for objects. • When supine the baby plays with his or her own feet. • The baby holds his or her head up when pulled to sitting position.

Communication and language development

- The baby becomes more aware of others so he or she communicates more and more.
- As the baby listens, he or she imitates sounds he or she can hear, and reacts to the tone of someone's voice. For example, the baby might become upset by an angry tone, or cheered by a happy tone.
- The baby begins to use vowels, consonants and syllable sounds, e.g. 'ah', 'ee aw'.
- The baby begins to laugh and squeal with pleasure.

Intellectual development

- By four months, the baby reaches for objects, which suggests they recognise and judge the distance in relation to the size of the object.
- The baby prefers complicated things to look at from five to six months and enjoys bright colours.
- The baby knows that he or she has one mother. The baby is disturbed if he or she is shown several images of his or her mother at the same time. The baby realises that people are permanent before realising that objects are.
- The baby can coordinate more, e.g. the baby can see a rattle, grasp the rattle, put the rattle in his or her mouth (they coordinate tracking, reaching, grasping and sucking).
- The baby can develop favourite tastes in food and recognise differences by five months.

Emotional and social development

- The baby shows trust and security.
- The baby has recognisable sleep patterns.

Table 10.4 Holistic development from six to nine months

Physical development

Gross motor skills	Fine motor skills
<ul><li>The baby can roll from front to back.</li><li>The baby may attempt to crawl but will often end up sliding backwards.</li><li>The baby may grasp feet and place them in his or her mouth.</li><li>The baby can sit without support for longer periods of time.</li><li>The baby may 'cruise' around furniture and may even stand or walk alone.</li></ul>	<ul><li>The baby is very alert to people and objects.</li><li>The baby is beginning to use a pincer grasp with thumb and index finger.</li><li>The baby transfers toys from one hand to the other and looks for fallen objects.</li><li>Everything is explored by putting it in his or her mouth.</li></ul>

Communication and language development

- Babble becomes tuneful, like the lilt of the language the baby can hear (except in hearing-impaired babies).
- Babies begin to understand words like 'up' and 'down', raising their arms to be lifted up, using appropriate gestures.
- The baby repeats sounds.

Intellectual development

- The baby understands signs, e.g. the bib means that food is coming.
- From eight to nine months, the baby shows that he or she knows objects exist when they have gone out of sight, even under test conditions. This is called the concept of object constancy, or the object permanence test (child psychologist Jean Piaget's theory). The baby is also fascinated by the way objects move.

Emotional and social development

- The baby can manage to feed herself using her fingers.
- The baby is now more wary of strangers, sometimes showing stranger fear.
- The baby might offer toys to others.
- The baby might show distress when his or her mother leaves.
- The baby typically begins to crawl and this means he or she can do more for him- or herself, reach for objects and get to places and people.
- The baby is now more aware of other people's feelings. For example, he or she may cry if their brother cries.

Table 10.5 Holistic development from nine to twelve months

Physical development

Gross motor skills	Fine motor skills
• The baby will now be mobile – may be crawling, bear walking, bottom shuffling or even walking. • The baby can sit up on her own and lean forward to pick up things. • The baby may crawl upstairs and onto low items of furniture. • The baby may bounce in rhythm to music.	• The baby's pincer grasp is now well developed and he or she can pick things up and pull them towards him or her. • The baby can poke with one finger and will point to desired objects. • The baby can clasp hands and imitate adults' actions. • The baby can throw toys deliberately. • The baby can manage spoons and finger foods well.

Communication and language development

- The baby can follow simple instructions, e.g. kiss teddy.
- Word approximations appear, e.g. hee-haw = donkey or more typically mumma, dadda and bye-bye in English-speaking contexts.
- The tuneful babble develops into 'jargon' and the baby makes his or her voice go up and down just as people do when they talk to each other. 'Really? Do you? No!' The babble is very expressive.
- The baby knows that words stand for people, objects, what they do and what happens.

Intellectual development

- The baby is beginning to develop images. Memory develops and the baby can remember the past.
- The baby can anticipate the future. This gives the baby some understanding of routine daily sequences, e.g. after a feed, changing and a sleep with teddy.
- The baby imitates actions, sounds, gestures and moods after an event is finished, e.g. imitate a temper tantrum he or she saw a friend have the previous day, wave bye-bye remembering Grandma has gone to the shops.

Emotional and social development

- The baby enjoys songs and action rhymes.
- The baby still likes to be near to a familiar adult.
- The baby can drink from a cup with help.
- The baby will play alone for long periods.
- The baby has and shows definite likes and dislikes at meal times and bedtimes.
- The baby thoroughly enjoys peek-a-boo games.
- The baby likes to look at him- or herself in a mirror (plastic safety mirror).
- The baby imitates other people – e.g. clapping hands, waving bye-bye – but there is often a time lapse, so that he or she waves after the person has gone.
- The baby cooperates when being dressed.

Table 10.6 Holistic development from one year to two years

Physical development

Gross motor skills	Fine motor skills
At 15 months: ● The baby probably walks alone, with feet wide apart and arms raised to maintain balance. He or she is likely to fall over and often sit down suddenly. ● The baby can probably manage stairs and steps, but will need supervision. ● The baby can get to standing without help from furniture or people, and kneels without support. At 18 months: ● The child walks confidently and is able to stop without falling. ● The child can kneel, squat, climb and carry things around with him or her. ● The child can climb onto an adult chair forwards and then turn round to sit. ● The child can come downstairs, usually by creeping backwards on her tummy.	● The baby can build with a few bricks and arrange toys on the floor. ● The baby holds a crayon in palmar grasp and turns several pages of a book at once ● The baby can point to desired objects. ● The baby shows a preference for one hand, but uses either. ● The child can thread large beads. ● The child uses pincer grasp to pick up small objects. ● The child can build a tower of several cubes. ● The child can scribble to and fro on paper.

Communication and language development

● The child begins to talk with words or sign language.
● By 18 months: the child enjoys trying to sing as well as to listen to songs and rhymes. Action songs (e.g. 'Pat-a-cake') are much loved.
● Books with pictures are of great interest. The child points at and often names parts of their body, objects, people and pictures in books.
● The child echoes the last part of what others say (echolalia).
● The child begins waving his or her arms up and down which might mean 'start again', or 'I like it,' or 'more'.
● Gestures develop alongside words. Gesture is used in some cultures more than in others.

Intellectual development

● The child understands the names of objects and can follow simple instructions.
● The child learns about things through trial and error.
● The child uses toys or objects to represent things in real life (e.g. using a doll as a baby, or a large cardboard box as a car or a garage).
● The child begins to scribble on paper.
● The child often 'talks' to him- or herself while playing.

Emotional and social development

● The child begins to have a longer memory.
● The child develops a sense of identity (I am me).
● The child expresses his or her needs in words and gestures.
● The child enjoys being able to walk, and is eager to try to get dressed – 'Me do it!'
● The child is aware when others are fearful or anxious for him or her as he or she climbs on and off chairs, and so on.

Table 10.7 Holistic development from two years

Physical development

Gross motor skills	Fine motor skills
• The child is very mobile and can run safely. • The child can climb up onto furniture. • The child can walk up and down stairs, usually two feet to a step. • The child tries to kick a ball with some success but cannot catch yet.	• The child can draw circles, lines and dots, using preferred hand. • The child can pick up tiny objects using a fine pincer grasp. • The child can build tower of six or more blocks (bricks) with longer concentration span. • The child enjoys picture books and turns pages singly.

Communication and language development

- Children are rapidly becoming competent speakers of the languages they experience.
- The child over-extends the use of a word, e.g. all animals are called 'doggie'.
- The child talks about an absent object when reminded of it, e.g. seeing an empty plate, they say 'biscuit'.
- The child uses phrases (telegraphese), 'doggie-gone', and the child calls him- or herself by name.
- The child spends a great deal of energy naming things and what they do – e.g. 'chair', and as they go up a step they might say 'up'.
- The child can follow a simple instruction or request, e.g. 'Could you bring me the spoon?'
- The child increasingly wants to share songs, dance, conversations, finger rhymes.

Intellectual development

- The child has improved memory skills, which helps his or her understanding of concepts (e.g. the child can often name and match two or three colours – usually yellow and red).
- The child can hold a crayon and move it up and down.
- The child understands cause and effect (e.g. if something is dropped, he or she understands it might break).

Emotional and social development

- The child is impulsive and curious about their environment.
- Pretend play develops rapidly when adults encourage it.
- The child begins to be able to say how he or she is feeling, but often feels frustrated when unable to express him- or herself.
- The child can dress him- or herself and go to the lavatory independently, but needs sensitive support in order to feel success rather than frustration.
- By two-and-a-half years, the child plays more with other children, but may not share his or her toys with them.

Table 10.8 Holistic development from three years

Physical development

Gross motor skills	Fine motor skills
<ul><li>The child can jump from a low step.</li><li>The child can walk backwards and sideways.</li><li>The child can stand and walk on tiptoe and stand on one foot.</li><li>The child has good spatial awareness.</li><li>The child rides a tricycle, using pedals.</li><li>The child can climb stairs with one foot on each step – and downwards with two feet per step.</li></ul>	<ul><li>The child can build tall towers of bricks or blocks.</li><li>The child can control a pencil using thumb and first two fingers – a dynamic tripod grasp.</li><li>The child enjoys painting with a large brush.</li><li>The child can use scissors to cut paper.</li><li>The child can copy shapes, such as a circle.</li></ul>

Communication and language development

- The child begins to use plurals, pronouns, adjectives, possessives, time words, tenses and sentences.
- The child might say 'two times' instead of 'twice'. The child might say 'I goed there' instead of 'I went there.' The child loves to chat and ask questions (what, where and who).
- The child enjoys much more complicated stories and asks for his or her favourite ones over and over again.
- It is not unusual for the child to stutter because he or she is trying so hard to tell adults things. The child's thinking goes faster than the pace at which the child can say what he or she wants to. The child can quickly become frustrated.

Intellectual development

The child develops symbolic behaviour. This means that:

- The child talks.
- The child pretend plays – often talking to him- or herself while playing.
- The child takes part in simple non-competitive games.
- The child represents events in drawings, models, etc.
- Personal images dominate, rather than conventions used in the culture, e.g. writing is 'pretend' writing.
- The child becomes fascinated by cause and effect; the child is continually trying to explain what goes on in the world.
- The child can identify common colours, such as red, yellow, blue and green – although may sometimes confuse blue with green.

Emotional and social development

- Pretend play helps the child to decentre and develop theory of mind (the child begins to be able to understand how someone else might feel and/or think).
- The child is beginning to develop a gender role as they become aware of being male or female.
- The child makes friends and is interested in having friends.
- The child learns to negotiate, to give and take, through experimenting with feeling powerful, having a sense of control, and through quarrels with other children.
- The child is easily afraid, e.g. of the dark, as he or she becomes capable of pretending. The child imagines all sorts of things.

Table 10.9 Holistic development from four years

Physical development

Gross motor skills	Fine motor skills
<ul><li>A sense of balance is developing – the child may be able to walk along a line.</li><li>The child can catch, kick, throw and bounce a ball.</li><li>The child can bend at the waist to pick up objects from the floor.</li><li>The child enjoys climbing trees and frames.</li><li>The child can run up and down stairs, one foot per step.</li></ul>	<ul><li>The child can build a tower of bricks and other constructions too.</li><li>The child can draw a recognisable person on request, showing head, legs and trunk.</li><li>The child can thread small beads on a lace.</li></ul>

Communication and language development

- During this time the child asks why, when and how questions as he or she becomes more and more fascinated with the reasons for things and how things work (cause and effect).
- Past, present and future tenses are used more often.
- The child can be taught to say his or her name, address and age.
- As the child becomes more accurate in the way he or she pronounces words, and begins to use grammar, the child delights in nonsense words that he or she makes up, and jokes using words.

Intellectual development

- At about age four, the child usually knows how to count – up to 20.
- The child also understands ideas such as 'more' and 'fewer', and 'big' and 'small'.
- The child will recognise his or her own name when it is written down and can usually write it.
- The child can think backward and forward much more easily than before.
- The child can also think about things from somebody else's point of view, but only fleetingly.
- The child often enjoys music and playing sturdy instruments, and joins in groups singing and dancing.

Emotional and social development

- The child likes to be independent and is strongly self-willed.
- The child shows a sense of humour.
- The child can undress and dress him- or herself – except for laces and back buttons.
- The child can wash and dry his or her hands and brush their teeth.

Table 10.10 Holistic development from five to seven years

Physical development

Gross motor skills	Fine motor skills
From five years: ● The child can use a variety of play equipment – slides, swings, climbing frames. ● The child can play ball games. ● The child can hop and run lightly on toes and can move rhythmically to music. ● The sense of balance is well developed. ● The child can skip. Six and seven years: ● The child has increased agility, muscle coordination and balance. ● The child develops competence in riding a two-wheeled bicycle. ● The child hops easily, with good balance. ● The child can jump off apparatus.	● The child may be able to thread a large-eyed needle and sew large stitches. ● The child can draw a person with head, trunk, legs, nose, mouth and eyes, and with detail, e.g. clothes and eyebrows. ● The child has good control over pencils and paintbrushes. He or she copies shapes, such as a square. ● The child can build a tall, straight tower with blocks and other constructions too. ● The child can write letters of alphabet at school, with similar writing grip to an adult. ● The child can catch a ball thrown from one metre with one hand.

Communication and language development

● The child tries to understand the meaning of words and uses adverbs and prepositions. The child talks confidently, and with more and more fluency.
● The child begins to be able to define objects by their function, e.g. 'What is a ball?' 'You bounce it.'
● The child begins to understand book language, and that stories have characters and a plot (the narrative).
● The child begins to realise that different situations require different ways of talking.

Intellectual development

● Communication through body language, facial gestures and language is well established, and opens the way into literacy (talking, listening, writing and reading).
● The child includes more detail in their drawings – e.g. a house may have not only windows and a roof, but also curtains and a chimney.
● Thinking becomes increasingly coordinated as the child is able to hold in mind more than one point of view at a time. Concepts – of matter, length, measurement, distance, area, time, volume, capacity and weight – develop steadily.
● The child enjoys chanting and counting (beginning to understand number). The child can use his or her voice in different ways to play different characters in pretend play. The child develops play narratives (stories), which he or she returns to over time. The child helps younger children into the play.
● The child is beginning to establish differences between what is real and unreal/fantasy. This is not yet always stable, so the child can easily be frightened by supernatural characters.

Emotional and social development

● The child has developed a stable self-concept.
● The child can hide their feelings once they can begin to control them.
● The child can think of the feelings of others.
● The child can take responsibility, e.g. in helping younger children.

AC 1.1 Activity

Look at the table below. Using the holistic development charts in Tables 10.1–10.10, for each age group in column 1, select three significant 'milestones' of development, using each category of development in columns 2, 3, 4 and 5.

For example, for the age group 'Birth to one year (physical development)', you could choose to include the following three milestones:

- At eight to twelve weeks, the baby can now lift head and chest off bed in prone position, supported on forearms.
- At four to six months, the baby is beginning to use a palmar grasp and can transfer objects from hand to hand.
- At nine to twelve months, the baby will now be mobile – may be crawling, bear walking, bottom shuffling or even walking.

Age group	Physical development	Language and communication development	Cognitive development	Social, emotional and behavioural development
Birth to one year				
One to three years				
Three to five years				
Five to seven years				

AC 1.2 The difference between the sequence of development and rate of development

Sequence of development

Children across the world seem to pass through similar sequences (or order) of development, but in different ways and different rates according to their culture. The work of Mary Sheridan on developmental sequences has been invaluable, but she suggests that children move through rigidly prescribed stages that are linked to the child's age: the child sits, then crawls, then stands, then walks. In fact, this is not the case. Not all children do crawl. Blind children often do not. Some children, like Mark in the case study below, 'bottom shuffle', moving along in a sitting position. A traditional approach to child development study has been to emphasise normative measurement. This is concerned with 'milestones' or stages in a child's development. These show what most children can do at a particular age. In reality, there is a wide range of normal development, and this will be influenced by genetic, social and cultural factors. Because of this, normative patterns of development should only be used as a guide. Children have been labelled as 'backward' or 'forward' in relation to the so-called 'normal' child, which is not always helpful.

Rate of development

It is important to be aware that normative measurements can only indicate general trends in development in children across the world. They may vary quite a bit according to the culture in which a child lives. It is important to understand that while the sequence of development is fairly general to all children, the rate – or speed – of development can vary a great deal. When children do things earlier than the milestones suggest is normal, it does not necessarily mean that they will be outstanding or gifted in any way. Parents sometimes think that because their child speaks early, is potty-trained early or walks early, he or she is gifted in some way.

Case study

1 Mark moved around by bottom shuffling and did not walk until he was two years old. He went on to run, hop and skip at the normal times. Walking late was not a cause for concern, and he did not suffer from any developmental delay.

2 African children living in rural villages estimate volume and capacity earlier than European children who live in towns. This is because they practise measuring out cups of rice into baskets from an early age as part of their daily lives. Learning about volume and capacity early does not mean that children will necessarily go on to become talented mathematicians. Children who learn these concepts later might also become good mathematicians.

Children with special educational needs often seem to 'dance the development ladder': they move through sequences in unusual and very uneven ways. For example, they might walk at the normal age, but they may not talk at the usual age. As researchers learn more about child development, it is becoming more useful to think of a child's development as a network that becomes increasingly complex as the child matures and becomes more experienced in their culture. So, instead of thinking of child development and learning as a ladder, it is probably more useful to think of them as a web.

AC 1.2 Activity

In your own words, describe the difference between the sequence of development and the rate of development.

LO2 Understand influences on children's development

There are many factors that affect the healthy growth and development of children. These factors work in combination and so it is often difficult to estimate the impact of any single factor on holistic child development.

AC 2.1 Factors that may influence children's development

Scientists believe that both our environment and our genes influence the person we become.

Genetic influences

Genes are found in our chromosomes and parents pass these on to offspring in their sex cells (the egg and the sperm). Different versions of the same gene are called alleles, and these can determine features such as eye colour, and also the inheritance of disorders such as cystic fibrosis. A baby's development can also be affected during pregnancy, at the time of birth and after the birth. In the very early weeks of pregnancy, a woman may not even know she is pregnant, but the first 12 weeks of life in the womb (or uterus) are the most crucial as this is when all the essential organs are being formed.

- Antenatal – the time from conception to birth: the mother's diet, whether she smokes and consumes alcohol and whether she is fit and healthy are all factors which can affect the development of the child.
- Perinatal – the actual time of the birth: a baby who is born prematurely (before

37 weeks' gestation) may need intensive care and may have problems that affect development. Difficulties around the birth itself – such as the baby lacking adequate oxygen – can also affect future development.

The child's background

Parental health and lifestyle

Children who live with one or both parents who have a mental health problem, such as depression, sometimes suffer as their parents may lack the necessary support to deal with their condition. Also, some older children may find themselves in the role of carer for younger children.

Parents not available to their children

This may occur when parents have substance misuse and are often absent both physically (because they are out looking for drugs) and emotionally (because they are intoxicated). Either way, they are not available to the child. Parents who work long hours may also be unavailable to their children.

Poor parenting skills

Substance misuse is often, but not always, associated with poor or inadequate parenting. This can show itself in a number of ways, including physical neglect, emotional neglect or unpredictable parental behaviour: for example, lurching between 'too much' or 'not enough' discipline and mood swings – being very affectionate or very remote. This leads to inconsistent parenting that can be confusing and damaging to the child. Some parents have poor parenting skills, such as being unable to cook.

Economic influences

According to the children's charity Barnardo's, poverty is the single greatest threat to the well-being of children in the UK. Growing up in poverty can affect every area of a child's development: physical, intellectual, emotional, social and personal.

- **Accident and illness**: children growing up in poverty are four times more likely to die in an accident, and have nearly twice the rate of longstanding illness of those living in households with high incomes.
- **Quality of life**: a third of children in poverty go without the meals, clothes or toys that they need.
- **Poor nutrition**: living on a low income means that children's diet and health can suffer.
- **Space to live and play**: poorer children are more likely to live in substandard housing and in areas with few shops or amenities, where children have little or no space to play safely.
- **Growth**: children in poverty are also more likely to be smaller at birth and shorter in height.
- **Education**: children who grow up in poverty are statistically less likely to do well at school and have poorer school attendance records.
- **Long-term effects**: as adults, they are more likely to suffer ill health, be unemployed or homeless. They are statistically more likely to become involved in offending and with drug and alcohol abuse. They are statistically more likely to become involved in abusive relationships.

Reflective practice

Supporting parents and carers
The great majority of parents are concerned to do their best for their child, even if they are not always sure what this might be. How might ineffective parenting skills affect a child's development? Find out what support is available for parents in the community.

Health

Infection

During childhood, there are many infectious illnesses that can affect children's health and development. Some of these infections can be controlled by childhood immunisations: these are diphtheria, tetanus, polio, whooping cough, measles, meningitis, mumps and rubella. Other infections can also have long-lasting effects on a child's health.

Diet

There are various conditions that may occur in childhood that are directly related to a poor or unbalanced diet:

- failure to thrive (or faltering growth) – poor growth and physical development
- dental caries or tooth decay – associated with a high consumption of sugar in snacks and fizzy drinks
- obesity – children who are overweight are more likely to become obese adults
- nutritional anaemia – due to an insufficient intake of iron, folic acid and vitamin B12
- increased susceptibility to infections – particularly upper respiratory infections such as colds and bronchitis.

Sleep

Sufficient sleep is essential for all aspects of children's development. Being tired all the time because of insufficient sleep at night can affect their ability to learn as well as causing emotional, social and behavioural problems.

Immediate and wider environment

Pollution

Pollution of the environment can have a marked effect on the health and development of children. The three main threats to health are water pollution, air pollution and noise pollution. Children are particularly vulnerable to air pollution. This is partly because they have a large lung surface area in relation to their small body size; this means that they absorb toxic substances more quickly than adults do and are slower to get rid of them. The effects of air pollution from factory chimneys, the use of chemical insecticides and car exhausts include:

- lead poisoning – children are particularly susceptible to lead poisoning, mostly caused by vehicle exhaust fumes; even very low levels of lead in the blood can affect children's ability to learn
- asthma – air pollution can act as a trigger for asthma and can make an existing condition worse; the incidence of asthma is much higher in traffic-polluted areas.

Housing

Poor housing is another factor that affects healthy holistic development. Low-income families are more likely to live in:

- homes which are damp and/or unheated – this increases the risk of infection, particularly respiratory illnesses
- neighbourhoods which are densely populated, with few communal areas and amenities – children without access to a safe garden or play area may suffer emotional and social problems
- overcrowded conditions – homeless families who are housed in 'hotels' or bed and breakfast accommodation often have poor access to cooking facilities and have to share bathrooms with several other families; often children's education is badly disrupted when families are moved from one place to another.

Accidents

Some accidents have lasting effects on a child's healthy growth and development, and many are preventable.

Emotional and social influences

A child who is miserable and unhappy is not healthy, although he or she may appear physically healthy. Children need to feel secure and to receive unconditional love from their primary carers. Child abuse, although not common, is bound to affect a child's health and well-being, and can have long-lasting health implications.

Cultural influences

Each family and community has certain values, customs and beliefs (or culture) that affect the way children are related to, treated and encouraged to behave. Religion and spiritual beliefs are also part of this culture. The culture in which a child grows up will shape their emotional and social development. In some families, there are marked differences in the way in which boys and girls are treated, and this too may affect the child's developing sense of identity.

Recognising and responding to concerns about children's development

Practitioners are ideally placed to recognise when a child's development is not following the expected norms. Often the parents will have expressed their own concerns and you need to respond to these.

At any point in their lives, children may need extra support in nursery or school. This may be for any reason, at any time and for any length of time. Some developmental concerns are temporary (such as a hearing impairment that is corrected by an operation) and therefore only require temporary support.

AC 2.1 Progress check

Concerns about development
The following factors can affect the way in which a child develops holistically.

- Family circumstances: family breakdown, e.g. separation of parents or arrival of a new partner; a child being a carer for another family member; being looked after by the local authority or recently having left care.
- Social or emotional problems: bereavement; behavioural difficulties; being involved in a bullying situation or subject to some form of discrimination.
- Disability or health needs: hearing or visual impairment; language and communication difficulties; autistic spectrum disorder; chronic illness leading to frequent hospitalisation; conditions requiring a surgical operation.

A child whose development is giving cause for concern will need to be supported. Practitioners should try to identify the child's particular developmental needs and respond quickly; the sooner the need is identified, the more likely that the support offered will be effective. Parents or carers should be consulted so that the support needed can then be tailored to the individual child.

AC 2.2 How to support the development of children from birth to seven years

As an early years practitioner, you will be involved in providing activities to support children's holistic development. The Early Years Foundation Stage provides guidance for early years settings to structure their routines and activities to support the development of children aged from birth to five. For children aged five to seven, Key Stage 1 of the national curriculum covers specific developmental aims as well as placing a need for schools to 'promote the spiritual, moral, cultural, mental and physical development of pupils at the school and of society'.

Helping children to learn: active learning

What is active learning?

Active learning is learning that engages and challenges children's thinking using real-life and imaginary situations. It takes full advantage of the opportunities for learning presented by:

- spontaneous play
- planned, purposeful play
- investigating and exploring
- events and life experiences
- focused learning and teaching.

These opportunities for learning are supported when necessary through sensitive intervention to support or extend learning. All areas of the framework can be enriched and developed through play.

The importance of play in active learning

The provision of well-planned play is important for the following reasons. Play:

- helps children to think and make sense of the world around them
- develops and extends their linguistic skills
- enables them to be creative
- helps them to investigate and explore different materials
- provides them with opportunities to experiment and predict outcomes.

Children need opportunities to follow their own interests and ideas through free play. Children's learning is most effective when it arises from **first-hand experiences** (whether spontaneous or structured) and when they are given time to play without interruptions and to a satisfactory conclusion.

> ### Key term
>
> **first-hand experience** One that is lived through personally rather than experienced by someone else and seen or heard about.

Play underlies a great deal of young children's active learning. In order to promote active learning through play, practitioners need to provide:

- a carefully planned and organised environment – with varied resources
- challenging and interesting play opportunities appropriate to children's needs, interests and abilities
- opportunities for creative play – intervening only when necessary to avoid repressing language or imagination
- sufficient time for children to develop their play
- opportunities for social interaction: promoting cooperation , turn-taking and sharing
- links between play activities and real-life situations (e.g. shop play linked with real shopping trips)
- opportunities to observe children's activities in order to plan for the future and to enable regular assessment.

Providing an environment that supports and encourages children's learning

All children will flourish in a good learning atmosphere – or ethos – in which adults support and extend the development and learning of all the children. Every child needs full access to the curriculum in order to learn effectively. This applies to all children, regardless of their ethnic background, culture, gender, language, special educational (or additional) needs or economic background.

The factors that can affect the child's ability to learn

Recently there have been many advances in the way we understand the brain and its functions – and particularly in our understanding of how children learn. It used to be accepted that the structure of our brains is fixed from birth – as a result of the genes we inherit from our parents. Neuroscientists now believe that while the basic brain structure is determined by our heredity, this serves only as a framework. Cognitive development is influenced by many factors; these include:

- genetic factors (e.g. sensory impairments, Down's syndrome)
- physical factors: general health, quality of nutrition, opportunities for physical activity, the development of physical skills (e.g. fine motor skills for hand–eye coordination)
- environmental factors: the effects of poverty, provision for play and active learning
- emotional factors: self-esteem and confidence, effects of trauma – such as bereavement, abuse, a new baby in the family, etc.
- social factors: role models, number of opportunities to socialise, stability of relationship with adults
- cultural factors: different cultural experiences and expectations.

One factor may affect another; for example, physical factors such as a hearing impairment may affect a child socially and emotionally – which in turn may lead to lack of confidence and motivation. If children lack stimulation in their environment, in any area of development, they will miss out on important learning experiences that help in the formation of concepts.

The skills children need to learn effectively

In order to learn effectively, children need to develop skills in:

- thinking
- perception
- memory

- language and communication skills – reading and writing
- concentration
- reasoning and problem-solving
- imagination and creativity
- understanding concepts.

The frameworks for learning for children from birth to 16 in the UK are designed to promote these skills and to assess each child's skills throughout their schooling.

Helping children to learn: scaffolding

Jerome Bruner, a psychologist, believed in the importance of scaffolding in helping children to learn. Adults can help develop children's thinking by being like a piece of scaffolding on a building. At first, the building has a great deal of scaffolding (i.e. adult support of the child's learning), but gradually, as the children extend their competence and control of the situation, the scaffolding is progressively removed until it is no longer needed.

Scaffolding can be described as anything a teacher can provide in a learning environment that might help a student learn. This includes anything that allows the student to grow in independence as a learner, such as:

- clues or hints
- reminders
- encouragement
- breaking a problem down into smaller steps
- providing an example.

The same scaffolding may be provided to all students, or teachers may offer customised scaffolding to individual learners.

How to encourage concentration and attention in children

An important part of the learning process is being able to concentrate and to keep attention focused on one activity at a time, without being distracted by other things. We all use

Discussion point

Scaffolding an activity

Daniel and his father were out shopping. Daniel stopped walking and was obviously struggling to do up the zip on his jacket, but was becoming increasingly frustrated. His father stood behind him and, using his own hands to guide Daniel's, helped him to insert the end of the zip into the metal fitting. When Daniel had managed to slot it in, he was easily able to pull the zip up by himself and was delighted.

In class, think about the following scenarios and discuss how you could scaffold the child's learning:

- learning to ride a two-wheeled bike
- learning how to tie shoelaces.

our attention and concentration skills every day, often without really noticing them. These skills help us to:

- select and focus on what is important (e.g. what the teacher is saying)
- ignore irrelevant things that we don't need to pay attention to (e.g. what you can hear going on outside)
- maintain our effort or attention over time (e.g. concentrate for the necessary amount of time).

There are two types of concentration required in different situations:

1 active concentration: construction, creative activities, imaginative play, sand and water play, problem-solving in maths, and science and literacy activities
2 passive concentration: watching television or videos, listening to stories, sitting in assemblies, etc.

Some children can concentrate passively for fairly long periods, while others are better able to concentrate actively when building a model or taking part in imaginative play.

Difficulties with attention and concentration

All children have times when they find it difficult to concentrate. This could be because they:

- are tired or unwell
- are unable to focus in a busy environment, e.g. with other children talking to them or around them
- are easily distracted by things going on around them
- are easily distracted by thoughts or feelings which are unrelated to the task at hand (daydreaming)
- are easily overwhelmed by large amounts of information
- are emotionally distressed
- have attention deficit hyperactivity disorder (ADHD).

Promoting self-reliance

Children need to learn to be capable and independent in order to learn new skills. The child who is self-reliant will be more active, independent and competent: he or she will have the confidence necessary to cope with situations on his/her own and to become an effective learner. All children should be allowed and encouraged to do the things that they can do from an early age – and be praised and rewarded for their efforts.

Allow children to do things for themselves

Even very young children begin to show an interest in doing things for themselves.

- Encourage independence by letting children do things for themselves as soon as they express a desire to do so.
- Focus on the effort made by the child and avoid being critical of the 'end product'.
- Always praise children for doing things on their own. As children grow and mature, they will naturally want to do more and more for themselves.
- Encourage children to help with challenging tasks. This helps to promote self-confidence.
- Encourage children to try to do new things and to face new challenges; this will promote self-confidence. Remember to choose tasks that children can accomplish.

In practice

Helping children to concentrate

There are many ways in which you can help children to concentrate. These include the following:

- Minimise distractions: children need a quiet area for activities which require more concentration; carpets and rugs can be used to keep noise levels down.
- Respond to individual needs: some children react badly when they feel rushed in their learning – others become bored and may disrupt others if given too much time for one activity.
- Time activities appropriately: avoid situations where the students are passive listeners for long periods of time. Keep activities brief or structure them into short blocks; provide a clear beginning and end.
- Provide children with hands-on activities: for example, experiments, orienteering activities, projects, etc.
- Use children's names and make eye contact: when giving instructions, get the child's attention by calling their name and making eye contact.
- Use memory games and encourage participation in classroom discussions and other collaborative activities.
- Use songs and rhymes: these will improve memory and concentration.
- Use praise and positive feedback: children benefit from having targets to improve their concentration and incentives or rewards when they reach them.

Encourage children to make decisions

Children learn to make good choices by being given choices. At first, choices should be kept simple, like allowing children to choose what to wear out of two outfits. As children get older, encourage them to make more and more complex decisions.

Be a good role model for responsibility and independence

Children learn by watching adults. Let children see you making decisions without wavering, and also taking care of responsibilities in an appropriate manner.

Help and encourage children to solve their own problems

Problem-solving is a skill that must be learned. Encourage children to come up with their own solutions to their problems. The ability to problem-solve is a skill that will be useful throughout children's lives. It will also help in the development of confidence and independence.

Encourage children to take risks

Taking risks involves facing potential failure. Many parents – and other adults – try to shield children from the disappointment of failure. However, children need to take risks in order to grow. Children must experience failure in order to learn how to cope with it.

Be there to provide support, when needed

Even the most independent-minded children need adult support on certain occasions. Make an effort to be available to the children in your care and to provide support when needed. Children who are secure in their relationships will have the confidence needed to explore the world.

Praise children

Children should receive praise when they display responsible and independent behaviour. Adults who praise such behaviour are letting children know that they notice and appreciate their efforts.

Give children responsibilities

One of the best ways for children to learn how to behave responsibly is to be given responsibilities. Make sure that the tasks assigned to the children match their capabilities. Take the time to show them how to do their assigned tasks properly. However, how well children perform a task is not as important as what they are learning about responsibility.

AC 2.2 Activity

Find out how daily routines, such as snack time, meal time, washing hands, sleep and rest, outdoor play, etc., are carried out in your early years setting/placement. For each routine, write a brief description of the ways in which each child's holistic development is supported by early years practitioners.

LO3 Understand the needs of children during transition

A **transition** is a passage of change from one stage or state to another. Children naturally pass through a number of stages as they grow and develop. Often they will also be expected to cope with changes such as movement from nursery education to primary school, and from primary to secondary school. You may have just made the transition from secondary school to a tertiary college or sixth form. Along with the excitement of a new course and possibly making new friends, you are likely to have felt some apprehension about the change to your life. This is likely to affect you more if you have experienced many changes in your life.

These changes are commonly referred to as transitions. Some children may have to cope with personal transitions that, unlike the transition to school at a certain age, are not necessarily shared or understood by all their peers.

transition Any significant stage or experience in the life of a child that can affect his or her behaviour and/or development.

AC 3.1 Transitions a child may experience

Types of transitions

Transitions can affect all areas of the development of children:

- emotional: personal experiences, such as parents separating, bereavement, entering or leaving care
- physical: moving to a new educational setting, a new home or care setting
- intellectual: moving from nursery to primary school, or primary to secondary school
- physiological: changes in growth, hormonal influences or a long-term medical condition.

Expected transitions

Many transitions are universal – they are experienced by almost everyone – and can usually be anticipated, or expected. Babies experience transitions when they:

- are weaned onto solid food
- are able to be cared for by others, such as at nursery or a childminder's home
- progress from crawling to walking
- move from needing nappies to being toilet-trained.

Children experience transitions when they:

- start nursery or change between different settings
- move up to primary school.

Unexpected transitions

Not every transition is experienced by every child, and not all transitions can be anticipated. These unexpected transitions include:

- the birth of a new baby in the family (although this is a very common transition, it is not always expected)

- an unexpected change of school or childcare provider
- moving house
- violence or abuse within the family
- parents separating or divorcing; having a new step-parent and perhaps new step-family
- serious illness, accident or death in the family.

Before we can fully understand the importance of transitions in children's lives, we need to explore the concepts of attachment, separation and loss.

Attachment

Attachment means a warm, affectionate and supportive bond between a child and his or her carer, which enables the child to develop **secure relationships**. When children receive warm, responsive care, they feel safe and secure.

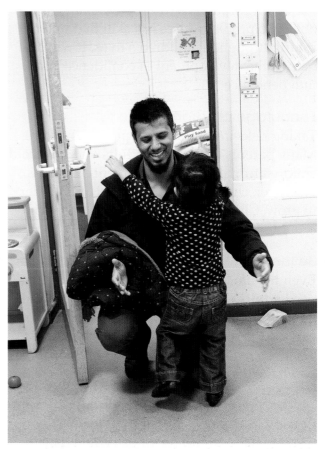

Figure 10.2 Babies need to have a strong attachment with their primary carers

Secure attachments are the basis of all the child's future relationships. Because babies experience relationships through their senses, it is the expression of love that affects how they develop and that helps to shape later learning and behaviour.

Children who are securely attached will grow to be more curious, get along better with other children and perform better in school than children who are less securely attached.

With children who have a strong attachment to their parent or primary carer, the process of becoming attached to the key person is easier, not harder, than it is for children with a weaker attachment. Remember, though, that all parents find separation difficult, whether they have formed a strong attachment with their child or not.

The role of the key person
Each family is given a key person at nursery who gets to know them well, and this helps everyone to feel safe. A baby or young child knows that this special person and the important people at home often do the same things for them:

- They help you manage through the day.
- They think about you.
- They get to know you well.
- They sometimes worry about you.
- They get to know each other.
- They talk about you.

The Sure Start programme was launched in the late 1990s, but continues in the form of Children's Centres around the country. Sure Start makes a distinction between the key worker role and the key person role. The term 'key worker' is often used in nurseries to describe how staff work, to ensure liaison between different professionals and to enhance smooth organisation and record-keeping. The key person role is defined as a special emotional relationship with the child and the family.

Separation
Many of the times that are difficult for children have to do with separation. Going to bed is separation from the main carer and is often a source of anxiety in children. Some young children can be terrified as a parent walks out of the room. How children react to separation is as varied as children are themselves. For some children, each new situation will bring questions and new feelings of anxiety. Other children love the challenge of meeting new friends and seeing new things.

Loss
Children who have had to make many moves or changes may feel a sense of loss and grief. These changes may have a profound effect on their emotional and social development. Reasons for transitions include the following:

- divorce or separation: children whose parents have separated or divorced may have to live and get along with several 'new' people (e.g. stepfathers, stepmothers, half-brothers and sisters)
- changes in childcare arrangements: children may experience many different childcare arrangements (e.g. frequent changes from one nanny or childminder to another)
- being cared for by the local authority – either in residential children's homes or in foster care
- moving house – for example, for employment reasons or as travellers.

How transitions may affect children's development and behaviour
Children who have experienced multiple transitions need to feel supported each time they enter a new setting. They may feel:

- disorientated – no sooner have they settled in one place and got to know a carer than they may be uprooted and have to face the same process again
- a sense of loss – each time they make a move, they lose the friends they have made and also the attachments they have formed with their carers
- withdrawn – children may withdraw from new relationships with other children and with carers because they do not trust that the separation will not happen again.

As children become older, they start to cope better with being separated from their parents or main carers; however, the way they cope will still depend on their early experiences of separation and how earlier transitions were managed. Children who have had to change schools many times – maybe because of a parent's job – often find it harder to settle in and make new friends and relationships.

> ### AC 3.1 Activity
>
> The key person system is the cornerstone of effective early years practice. Find out how the key person system is implemented in your setting. What happens, for example, when a child's key person is absent through illness or on holiday? How does the key person get to know the children assigned to him or her?

AC 3.2 Preparing a child for a planned transition

Being separated from our loved ones is difficult at any age, and a feeling of bereavement can be experienced. In situations where children are repeatedly separated from their families, through home circumstances or war and conflict, it helps when the adults with whom the child is left understand the elements discussed in this chapter, so that vulnerable children feel a sense of belonging and well-being, and feelings of being valued, loved and respected.

Supporting times of transition

- Remember that if the parent is anxious about leaving their child, the child will be anxious about being separated from the parent. Make sure that every adult and child is welcomed. Put notices in the languages of the community as well as in English.
- A noticeboard with photographs of staff and their roles helps people to feel familiar with the environment.
- An attractive display of some of the recent experiences gained by the children helps people to tune in to the setting's way of working.

- A notice with the menu for the week gives valuable information to parents and carers.
- Something for children to do is vital; watching fish in a fish tank or having a turn on a rocking horse are popular examples.

Anna Freud, who worked with children who had experienced the Holocaust (see Useful Resources), found that children's friendships with each other were very important, and so was having a normal childhood with opportunities for sensitively supported play. Play seemed to have a self-healing power.

> ### AC 3.2 Activity
>
> Choose a child who you know is about to experience a transition – for example, who is moving from nursery class to infant school. How would you prepare the child to promote his or her well-being and to make the transition as smooth as possible?

AC 3.3 Supporting the needs of children during transition

The first few days at a nursery or playgroup can be very daunting for some children. They may not have been left by their parents or primary carers ever before, and some children will show real distress. You need to be able to recognise their distress and to find ways of dealing with it. Children show their distress at being separated from their carer by crying and refusing to join in with activities. Parents too can feel distressed when leaving their children in the care of others; they may feel guilty because they have to return to work, or they may be upset because they have never before been separated from their child.

You can help a child to settle in by following the suggestions given below:

- Trying to plan for the separation: nursery staff can help by visiting the child and their parents at home. This gives both parents and children the opportunity to talk about their fears and helps them to cope with them. When children know in advance what is going to happen and not happen, they can think about and get used to their feelings about it. Parents can be encouraged to prepare their child for the change by:

- visiting the nursery with their child so that they can meet the staff
- reading books about starting at a nursery or going to hospital
- involving their child in any preparation, such as buying clothing or packing a 'nursery bag'.

- Encouraging parents to stay with their child until the child asks them to leave: this does not mean that the parents should cling to their child. Children can always sense a parent's uncertainty. Although young children do not have a very good sense of time, parents and carers should make it very clear when they will be back (e.g. saying 'I'll be back in one hour.').

- Allowing the child to bring a comforter – for example, a blanket or a teddy bear – to the nursery. If it is a blanket, the parent could cut a little piece and put it in the child's pocket if they think they might be embarrassed about it. Then the child can handle the blanket and feel comforted when feeling lonely. This object is often called a **transitional object** as it helps the child to make the transition from being dependent on family for comfort to being able to comfort him- or herself.

- Having just one person to settle the child: hold and cuddle the child and try to involve him or her in a quiet activity with you (e.g. reading a story). As part of the EFYS all settings must employ a key person who will be responsible for one or two children during the settling-in period.

- Contacting the parent or primary carer if the child does not settle within 20 minutes or so: sometimes it is not possible to do this, and you will need to devise strategies for comforting and reassuring the child. Always be honest with parents regarding the time it took to settle their child.

Key term

transitional object Often a soft toy or blanket to which a child becomes attached, a transitional object is used by a child to provide comfort and security while he or she is away from a secure base, such as a parent or home.

Other transitions

When children are facing other transitions or changes in their lives, such as bereavement or loss, or the arrival of a new sibling, their key person will need to be especially sensitive to their feelings and always take time to talk with them about how they are feeling. Opportunities should be provided for children to express their feelings in a safe and unthreatening environment. For example, some children may be encouraged to use play dough to release pent-up feelings of frustration; others may choose to use role play.

Reflective practice

Thinking about your own behaviour
Reflect on your practice by asking yourself the following questions:

1 Do I know why the child is behaving as he or she is?
2 Have I considered the child's needs? Is he or she tired, hungry or simply needing a hug?
3 Have I talked with and listened to the child?
4 Have I been consistent in dealing with unacceptable behaviour and been a positive role model?
5 Would it be appropriate for a child to say or do what I have just done?
6 Is there anything I could change in the physical environment to create a more relaxed, comfortable environment, one that is conducive to meeting the child's needs?

Comfort objects

1 Do you remember having a special comfort object? What did this object mean to you?
2 Using examples from your setting, discuss how, in early childhood, such objects help to comfort young children coping with separation and transitions.

In practice

Helping children to settle in

This activity will help a child who is new to the setting to realise that he or she is not alone and that other children also feel shy and alone at times.

- Introduction: choose a teddy and introduce him to the group, saying something like 'Teddy is rather shy and a little bit lonely. How can we help him to feel better?'
- Discussion and display: take photos of Teddy – using a digital camera if possible – with different groups of children and in different places in the nursery (e.g. playing in the sand, reading a book, doing a puzzle), and use them later for discussion and display.
- Circle time: in circle time, pass Teddy round and encourage each child to say something to him – for example, 'Hello, Teddy, my name is Lara,' or 'Hello Teddy, I like chocolate…'.
- Taking Teddy home: each child takes it in turns to take Teddy home. Include a notebook and encourage parents to write a few sentences about what Teddy did at their house that evening. The children can draw a picture.
- Story time: read and act out the story of 'Goldilocks and the Three Bears', with the different-sized bowls, beds and chairs.
- Cooking: use a shaped cutter to make teddy-shaped biscuits or dough teddies.
- Teddy bears' picnic: arrange a teddy bears' picnic where each child brings in a favourite bear: 'What does your teddy like to eat?', 'Are there enough plates, biscuits and cups for all the bears?'
- You can probably think of many more teddy-related ideas that will help children gain a sense of belonging.

In practice

Transitions

How does your setting help children to cope with transitions? Does it have a settling-in policy? Find out how children new to the setting are helped to separate from their parents or carers.

Assessment practice

1 Why is it important to look at a child's development 'in the round' or holistically?
2 Identify the different aspects of child development.
3 What is meant by the sequence of development and the rate of development?
4 Describe the factors which affect child development.
5 What is meant by active learning?
6 Why is play so important in the early years?
7 Describe how you can promote children's self-reliance and independence.
8 Explain what is meant by the term 'transition'. Why is it important to be able to identify when a child is going through a transition?
9 Describe the different transitions that a child may experience. Give examples of how each type of transition might affect the child.
10 Explain how you could support a child through the transition phase.

Useful resources

Meggitt, C. (2012) *Child Development: An Illustrated Guide* (3rd edn), Harlow, Essex: Pearson Education.

Research on the benefits of touch for premature babies

http://tinyurl.com/o9bhdwg

Feldman, Ruth, Rosenthal, Zehava, Eidelman, Arthur I.'Maternal-Preterm Skin-to-Skin Contact Enhances Child Physiologic Organization and Cognitive Control Across the First 10 Years of Life'. *Biological Psychiatry* (2014); 75 (1)

Anna Freud's work with children who survived the Holocaust

http://tinyurl.com/pbw4wsm

Unit 11

Use observation, assessment and planning

Learning outcomes

By the end of this unit, you will:

1 Understand the role of observation when working with children.

2 Be able to use observation methods.

LO1 Understand the role of observation when working with children

Why observe children?

Parents, babysitters and early years practitioners automatically watch the children in their care. They want to know that the children are safe, happy, healthy and developing well. Watching or observing closely can often reassure all concerned that everything is all right, but may also alert them to concerns or illness. Any discussion about a child usually relates to what has been seen, heard or experienced, and leads to conclusions about his/her personality, likes, dislikes and difficulties.

Anyone who works with children needs to develop the skill of observing them (sometimes to be written/recorded) to check that a child is:

- safe – not in any physical danger from the environment, from him- or herself or from others
- contented – there are many reasons why a child might be miserable; some may relate to physical comfort (e.g. wet nappy, hunger, thirst) or emotional comfort (e.g. main carer is absent, comfort object is lost) or lack of attention and stimulation

- healthy – eats and sleeps well and is physically active (concerns about any of these aspects may indicate that the child is unwell)
- developing as expected – in line with general expectations for his/her age in all areas; there will be individual differences but delays in any (e.g. crawling/walking or speaking) may show a need for careful monitoring and, perhaps, specialist help; any particular strength or talent may also be identified and encouraged.

A series of observations – particularly if they are written or recorded in some way (e.g. photos) – can provide an ongoing record of progress, which can be very useful to parents and other professionals involved with a child's care and education.

AC 1.1 How observations are used when working with children

Becoming skilled in observation and assessment is one of the most important parts of your training and developing practice.

- Observation means closely watching, listening to and generally attending to what a child is doing, and recording your findings as accurately as you can. While you are observing, you should try to avoid drawing any conclusions, and to stay as focused on the child as possible.

- Assessment means making judgements about what your observation says about the child's development, learning, health and well-being.

The importance of careful observations

Observations can provide valuable information about:

- individual children – their progress and how they behave in particular situations
- groups of children – the differences between individuals in the same situations
- adults – how they communicate with children and how they deal with behaviour
- what activities are successful and enjoyed by children.

How observations are used to plan for individual children's needs

All early years practitioners must consider children's individual needs, interests and levels of development, and must use this information to plan a challenging and enjoyable experience for each child in all seven areas of learning and development. For example, you might notice that a child is making lots of progress in their communication, but you have no observations of their exploratory play and early scientific learning. You will need to plan to look out for the child's play and learning in that area. You might need to think of ways of encouraging the child to participate in those sorts of experiences.

How observations are used for early intervention

Throughout the early years, if a child's progress in any of the prime areas of learning gives cause for concern, practitioners must discuss this with the child's parents and continue to provide focused support in that area, enabling the child to be full prepared for starting Key Stage 1. Practitioners should consider using observations and assessments to determine if a child is gifted and talented, has an underlying developmental delay or if there is a concern that a child may have

a special educational need or disability which is affecting their development. Early identification should reduce the risk that the child will continue to struggle in certain areas. The importance of early intervention is discussed in Unit OP 1.

How observations are used to review the environment

When observing children in the setting, focused observations can help you to analyse such issues as the use of different play areas. Event sampling and time sampling will enable practitioners to assess the quality of the setting in providing for children's learning in all the EYFS areas. Sometimes settings might identify that there are significant patterns in their observations and assessments:

- If there are many observations of boys in the block play area, but none of girls, you will need to think how you will encourage girls to take part in construction play.
- If boys spend little time in the book area, you might need to change the types of books on display, or try adding homemade books about children's play and interests.
- If the bilingual children in the setting make less progress than those who speak English as a first language, you will need to focus on whether your setting is providing appropriate support.

How observations are used during transition

When a young child is experiencing a transition, such as starting a new nursery or adapting to a new sibling in the family, observations can help practitioners to build up a picture of the child's needs during transition. The practitioner could, for example, visit the child's home before he or she starts at the nursery to observe their behaviour and to find out about any worries that the parents or carers might have. This will make it easier to plan for the separation and so ease the transition.

How observations are used when working in partnership

Even the most experienced early years practitioners may find that, although they have observed a child and made efforts to adapt their provision, they need help from outside the setting. This is particularly true if there is a specific medical condition or developmental delay. In these cases, the people who know the child best – almost always the parents or main carer – will provide the most valuable suggestions, alongside the advice and guidance of other expert or specialist professionals.

The development of an individual 'care plan' or special educational programme will take account of evidence gathered from different sources – for example, from parents, early childhood practitioners, health visitors, doctors, social services, speech and language therapists, and so on. These provisions can only meet the child's needs when there is cooperation between all the services involved, and those who are competent to do so make accurate assessments. This is called partnership working.

AC 1.1   Progress check ✔

It is important to become skilled in observing and assessing children so that you can:

- get to know the children
- have purposeful discussions with parents, carers and colleagues
- think about what to plan next
- identify children's strengths and also their areas of difficulty
- monitor children's progress and offer help if a child does not seem to be accessing a particular area of the curriculum or does not seem to be making good progress
- reflect on the quality of your work as a practitioner and the overall quality of your setting.

LO2 Be able to use observation methods

There are many different methods of observing children, but the principles underlying them remain the same:

- Every observation should have a clear purpose or aim.
- Appropriate observation methods must be used for both the child and the setting.
- Observations must be in line with current frameworks and the setting's own policies.
- Confidentiality must be maintained.
- It must be clear how the assessment outcomes will be distributed and to whom.

AC 2.1 Observation methods

Checklists

This form of recording has its limitations, including the following:

- They give no detail or supporting evidence.
- They are narrow in focus.
- They make practitioners feel that they have more information than they really do.
- They are time-consuming to create.

However, if these limitations are appreciated and the checklist is well thought out, it can be a very straightforward method of recording your observation. However, it should only be used in addition to other methods. It can be used to help:

- monitor developmental progress of an individual child or several children
- assess children on a regular basis over a period of time
- staff to plan for children's changing needs
- consider one area of development
- assess a child's behaviour.

	CHILD 1		CHILD 2		CHILD 3	
	yrs	m	yrs	m	yrs	m
1. WALKING						
Looks ahead						
Walks upright						
Avoids objects						
Small steps						
Strides						
Walks heel to toe						
Arms by side						
Arms swinging						
Other observation						
2. BALANCE						
Stands on one foot						
Balances for 3–4 seconds						
Balances for longer						
Leans to one side						
Arms stretched out						
Arms by side						
Arms folded						
Can walk on narrow line						
Other observation						
3. RUNNING						
Runs on tiptoe						
Runs flat-footed						
Swings arms						
Arms by side						
Arms folded						
Able to change speed						
Changes direction						
Runs round corners						
Other observation						

You can add to this chart for other gross motor skills, such as skipping, hopping, climbing, swinging, etc., by identifying the important components of the action.

Figure 11.1 Example of a gross motor skills checklist

Free description

Perhaps the most common observation method for working with children is the narrative or free descriptive observation. This type attempts to record everything that happens, as it happens, with plenty of detail. Methods that fit into this framework are:

- descriptive/running record
- detailed
- target child
- diary description
- anecdotal record
- tape and transcript (may be considered to fit into this category so long as the section focused upon and used for evaluation purposes is continuous and not a series of edited extracts)
- video recording (as for tape and transcript).

Target child observation

The target child observation (Sylva *et al.*, 1980) is a technique based on narrative observation, which also includes a coding system to help you interpret your findings. The target child observation involves observing individual children for 10–20 minutes, allowing you to gain in-depth information about each child. You need time for the observation and then at least the same amount of time again for the coding and analysis of your results. The target child observation approach was used in the Oxford Preschool Research project in the 1970s and the EPPE (Effective Provision of Pre-School Education) project, which has been in progress since 1997.

Time sampling

Time sampling involves making a series of short observations (usually up to two minutes each) at regular intervals over a fairly long period. The intervals between observations and the overall duration are up to you, depending on exactly what you are observing and why. For example, you may choose to record at 20-minute intervals over the course of a whole day, or every 15 minutes during a half-day session.

It can be a useful way of finding out how children use particular toys or resources, to monitor how a new child has settled in or to observe the behaviour of an individual child. When observing an individual child's

Possible use: for monitoring reading skills
Title of book used: *The Birthday Cake*   Date:

Skill	Child 1	Comment	Child 2	Comment
1. **Holds book right way up**	✓	Held book correctly in both hands	✓	Took book from me and turned it right way
2. **Knows which is the front of a book**	✓	Looked at front cover before opening book	✓	Pointed to character on cover picture
3. **Follows text/pictures left to right**	✓	Followed pictures as story was read	✓	Head movements showed was doing this
4. **Knows text 'works' top to bottom**	✓	As above	✓	As above
5. **Can point to known characters in illustrations**	✓	Pointed to Chip and Floppy	✓	Named characters as they appeared in illustrations
6. **Can talk about illustrations**	✓	Did so when prompted	✓	Pointed to things in pictures which he found funny
7. **Can recap the story partway through**	✗	Needed prompting and had to turn back through pages	✓	Good recall of what had happened
8. **Can suggest what might happen next**	✗	Could offer no ideas	✓	Good suggestions with reasons
9. **Identifies some individual letters**	✓	Named and pointed to 'c', 'd' and 'a'	✓	Named and pointed to 'c', 'd', 'a', 'g', 'h', 'l', 'b', 'n', 'w', 't', 's', 'r', 'y', 'p'
10. **Can identify a capital (upper-case) letter**	✓	Named and pointed to 'C' – own initial letter	✓	Named and pointed to 'C', 'F', 'B', 'H', 'T', 'R'
11. **Can identify a full stop**	✗		✗	

Figure 11.2 Example of an expanded checklist showing reading development

behaviour, time sampling can raise awareness of positive aspects which may be overlooked in the normal run of a busy day. Staff can then make a point of noticing and appreciating the incidents of positive behaviour and encourage these as part of a strategy to reduce unwanted aspects.

It is difficult to keep stepping away at regular intervals from whatever else you are doing, in order to make the record. Negotiation with colleagues is essential so that children's safety is not put at risk.

You can choose your own headings for the chart format to match the detail you need to include. Usual headings are 'Time', 'Setting or location', 'Language' and 'Social group',

but you may want to include 'Actions' and 'Other'.

Event sampling

This involves the observation of specific actions, incidents or behaviour. The event to be observed is usually decided in advance, and a chart format is most often used to record events as they happen.

Diary description

This is usually kept to monitor the learning and development of an individual child (but can also be used for a group) and provides a day-to-day account of significant events. It may include anecdotal records (see below) and other forms of observation. A diary is time-consuming

RP = role play, SOL = solitary, SG = small group, LG = large group, TC = target child, C = child, A = adult, BC = book corner, SW = small world, W = waiting

Child initials: JG   Gender: M   Age: 3 yrs 10 mths   Date/Time: 1/10/05 2.15 p.m.

ACTIVITY RECORD	LANGUAGE RECORD	TASK	SOCIAL
1 min TC on carpeted area, playing with farm animals and buildings.	TC→C My cow wants to come in your field. C→TC No. You'll have to wait till my tractor has finished.	SW	SG
2 min TC sitting at edge of carpet, looking at wall display.		W	SOL
3 min Now in dressing-up area, putting on a floppy hat and laughing.	C→TC You look funny in that. TC→C Let me see. Where's the mirror?	RP	SG
4 min Sitting in a small chair at a table, holding a knife and fork in his hands.	TC→C Where's my tea? I want my tea. Not fish fingers again!	RP	SG
5 min Standing at 'cooker' and stirring something in a pan.	A→TC What are you cooking? TC→A I'm a good cooker. It's basgetti.	RP	SG
6 min Taking off hat and tidying equipment.		RP	SOL
7 min Sitting in story corner, looking at book.		BC	LG

Figure 11.3 Example of a target child observation

to keep and you need to be sure that the information gathered is helpful and remains objective, rather than being mundane, repetitive and subjective. This type of observation can help to record the progress of every child in a group over time.

Anecdotal record

This is a brief description of an incident written soon after it occurred. This is a widely used method of observation and is useful because it is recorded only a short time after the incident. The adult records a significant piece of learning, perhaps the first steps a baby takes unaided or an important development in relationships with other children. Anecdotal observations can be made in a different coloured pen, to show that they are not 'on-the-spot' but recalled events.

Observing children: what should be recorded?

There is some information that should be included in any observation, but other aspects will depend on the purpose of the observation. If it is to consider the child's fine motor skills then the detail will probably be different from one that is to find out about his/her social development – even if the same activity or situation is being observed. You should also record some introductory information (see below).

Child observed = HR   Teacher = T   Other children = A, B, C, D, E.
LG = large group, SG = small group, P = pair of children
Aim: To find out how well a child, newly arrived from another school, has settled in, looking particularly at interaction with other children.

Time	Setting	Language	Social group	Other
9.00	Registration – sitting on carpeted area.	None	LG	At back of class group, fiddling with shoelaces and looking around the room.
9.20	At a table, playing a language game.	HR: 'It's *not* my turn.'	SG	One parent helper and 3 other children.
9.40	On floor of cloakroom.	HR: 'You splashed me first and my jumper's all wet, look.'	P	Had been to toilet and is washing hands.
10.00	In maths area, carrying out a sorting activity using coloured cubes.	T: 'Can you find some more cubes the same colour, HR?' HR: 'There's only 2 more red ones.'	SG	Concentrating and smiling as he completes the task.
10.20	Playground – HR is standing by a wall, crying.	Sobbing sounds – won't make eye contact with or speak to T on duty.	SOL	Small group of children look on.
10.40	Music activity – playing a tambour to beat the rhythm of his name.	Says his name in 2-syllable beats.	LG	Showing enjoyment by smiling – T praises him.
11.00	Tidying away instruments with another child.	A→HR: 'We have instruments every week. It's good, isn't it?' HR → A: 'Yeh. I liked it.'	P	
11.20	Playing with construction equipment with A and B.	B→HR + A: 'I've got loads of Lego at home.' HR→B + A: 'So have I. I like the technical stuff best.' B→HR: 'What's that like?'	SG	Children working together to build a garage for toy cars.
11.40	HR fetching reading book to read to T.	Humming to himself.	SOL	
12.00	Lining up with other children to go for lunch.		LG	Nudging A, who is standing in front of him. A turns round and grins.

Figure 11.4 Example of a time sample in a Year 1 class

When you carry out a written observation, it is usually because you want to find out something about an individual child or a group of children. This provides an aim, which should be identified at the start of your work. For example:

Aim: 'To see what gross motor skills Child R uses in a PE lesson and consider how confident he is on the apparatus.'

A clear aim explains what you want to find out and the activity or context that you have decided will best give you this information. This is better than saying you will watch Child R in a PE lesson. The aim you identify should affect what information you write in your introduction and in the actual observation.

As well as an aim, your observation should include:

- the date the observation was carried out
- start and finish times
- who gave permission
- where it took place (setting)
- number of children present
- number of adults present
- age/s of child/ren

- names or identification of children (remember confidentiality)
- method used (brief reason for choice)
- signature of supervisor or tutor.

How should it be recorded?

Your tutors will have their own preferences for how they want you to present your work but, generally, each observation should include the following sections: Introduction; Actual observation; Evaluation; Bibliography.

Introduction

In this section, you must state where the observation is taking place (e.g. 'At the sand tray in a Reception class') and give some information about what is happening (e.g. 'The children had just returned to the classroom from assembly…'). If there is any relevant information about the child, you might include it here (e.g. 'Child R has been ill recently and has missed two weeks of school'). Include information that is relevant to your aim – for example, it may be important to know whether the child is of average build if you are dealing with physical skills, but this would not be particularly relevant if you are dealing with imaginative play.

Actual observation

There are many different methods of recording and your tutors will help you decide which one is best – perhaps a 'chart' format, a checklist or a written record describing what you see as it happens. Remember only to write what you see and, if appropriate, hear. Do not write your judgements, opinions, assessments and so on. Make sure you include information about other children or adults involved, if it is relevant.

When recording your observation, remember to maintain confidentiality by only using a child's first name or initial, or some other form of identification (e.g. Child R). You may use 'T' or 'A' for 'teacher' or 'adult'.

Evaluation

An evaluation is an assessment of what you have observed. This section can be dealt with in two parts.

1 You need to look back at your recorded information and summarise what you have discovered. For example:
'Child R was looking around the classroom and fidgeting with his shoelaces during the story, and appeared bored and uninterested. However, he was able to answer questions when asked so he must have been listening for at least part of the time.'
This is a review of what you saw.

2 You then need to consider what you have summarised, and compare your findings to the 'norm' or 'average' or 'expected' for a child of this age and at this stage of development. What have you yourself learnt about this particular child/group of children, and how has this helped you to understand children's development more widely? Use relevant books to help you and make reference to them – or quote directly if you can find a statement or section that relates to what you are saying or the point you are making. Your tutor or assessor wants to know what you understand, not information he or she could read in a book, so use references carefully.

As observation of children can help carers to plan for individual needs, try to suggest what activity or caring strategy might be needed next. You may also, in this section, give your opinion as to reasons for the behaviour, and so on – take care not to jump to conclusions about the role of the child's background, and never make judgements about the child or the child's family.

Bibliography

The bibliography is a list of the books you have used when reading and researching for information relating to your observation.

Guidelines for good practice

Using cameras, camcorders and MP3 recorders

- Before you make an audio or video recording of a child, or take photographs, check the policy of the setting.
- Think about how you will store data safely and with parental consent. It is not advisable to download photos or video onto your personal computer, for example. Best practice would be to keep everything on a computer in the setting, with password protection or encryption.
- Think about how you will position yourself. You will need to be quite close to the children to pick up their voices clearly, for example.
- Analysing video and audio recordings is extremely time-consuming. You may get the best results if you record for just a minute or two at the right moment – when a child is really engaged in his play or in full conversational flow. Accurately transcribing even a few minutes of children's conversation can take half an hour or more.
- Think about how you will display and share information:
  - Digital slideshows of well-taken photos can be a powerful and accessible way of showing a child's learning story, for example, or how a range of children play and learn in a particular area.
  - Many settings put together profile books of individual children. These usually consist of photos with written observations and assessments. You will need to take care that a profile book is not merely a scrapbook of photos, without any commentary on the child's learning and development.

AC 2.1 Progress check ✔

Using a range of tools for observation and assessment

- Experiment with different ways to observe a child's development.
- Talk as a team about any checklists that you use and consider whether these are useful.
- Share different types of observations and assessments with parents in order to develop a dialogue about children's progress and areas of difficulty.

AC 2.2 Observing an individual child and provision in line with current frameworks

Sharing of information

Most settings provide clear guidance (sometimes in a booklet or sheet written especially for students) about working with children. Some settings now also have an observations policy. As a student, you should also be given information that will help you understand what a particular setting is trying to achieve and how it goes about it. You will always need to gain permission to carry out an observation and your placement supervisor may well wish to read your work. This is not only to check it through, but also out of interest, to find out more about the children, activity or safety aspects that you observed. Remember, information accurately observed by you can be just as valuable to the setting as that gathered by staff.

Cooperation between professionals requires sharing of information. However, in a work setting, observations and records must be kept confidentially and access given only to certain people – these may include the individual child's parents or legal guardian, supervisor, teacher or key worker and other involved professionals (e.g. the health visitor).

Remember: any information about a child may be shared only if the parent or legal guardian gives consent.

The importance of confidentiality and objectivity

Maintaining confidentiality is an important aspect of your role, but it is particularly important when carrying out observations, especially those that are written and recorded. For your own training and assessment purposes, the identity of the child and setting is not important. It must, therefore, be protected (see below). You are developing your observational and record-keeping skills as you learn more about children in general, children as individuals and the various work settings.

Objectivity in observations

When you record your observational findings, you need to be as objective as possible. This means that you must record factual information – what you actually see and hear – rather than information you have already begun to interpret.

By including plenty of detail to describe what you see, you are providing yourself (and any reader) with a lot of information for analysis. For example, Observation A in the activity below presents a much fuller picture of the situation than Observation B, and may lead you to a different conclusion about G's interest and attention. It is often difficult to describe facial expressions and actions accurately, which is why many students produce work in the style of Observation B rather than in the style of Observation A.

Guidelines for good practice

How to maintain confidentiality in your observation

- Ensure you have permission for making an observation – from your supervisor and the parent/main carer (this is confirmed by an authorising signature).
- Use codes rather than names to refer to the individuals involved – you should never use a child's first name. An initial or some other form of identification (e.g. Child 1) is sufficient. (You may use 'T' or 'A' for 'teacher' or 'adult'.)

- Understand and abide by policies and procedures in the setting.
- Take extra care when sharing observations with fellow students – they may have friends or family involved in a work setting and could easily identify individuals.
- Never discuss children or staff from your work setting in a public place (e.g. when sitting on a bus or in a café).
- Never identify individuals when talking at home about your daily experiences (e.g. they could be neighbours' children).

Activity

Observations

Read the two brief examples below and identify where the observer has substituted a conclusion or interpretation for what was actually seen.

Observation A

'...G is sitting on the floor with her legs crossed and her left hand in her lap. She is twiddling her hair with her right hand and staring at a picture on the wall display behind the teacher's head. She is smiling. The teacher says,

"G, what do you think will happen to the cat next?" G stops fiddling with her hair and looks at the teacher. "I think it will hide," she says and laughs as she turns to N next to her...'.

Observation B

'...G is sitting cross-legged on the floor in front of the teacher. She is fiddling with her hair and looking bored. The teacher asks her a question, "G, what do you think will happen to the cat next?" G says, "I think it will hide."'

For information on developing your skills in observation and assessment see page 103.

For information on developing your skills in observation and assessment see page 103.

AC 2.2 Activity

Using the guidelines above, and possibly with extra guidance from your tutor, carry out observations on:

- an individual child
- indoor provision
- outdoor provision.

AC 2.3 Reflecting on outcomes of observations carried out in own setting

Reflect on:

- the ways in which you communicate with children
- the variety of activities you provide for children – both indoors and outdoors
- the ways in which you use regular observations to find out about children's needs and interests.

Think about these aspects of your work in relation to supporting children's developmental needs. For example:

- Do you vary your method of communication to account for the individual child's needs and stage of development?
- Do you provide a wide range of activities which are designed to promote particular skills?
- Do you plan activities to promote development for individual children?
- Do you use observations to build up a picture of children's interests and needs?

- Do you involve parents in the observations you carry out with their children?

AC 2.3 Progress check

After considering the questions above, can you think of ways in which you could improve your practice?

AC 2.4 Working with others to plan next steps in relation to the needs and interests of a child

Early years practitioners need to share information gained from observation and assessment to:

- inform their future planning
- group children for particular activities and interests
- ensure that the curriculum meets the needs of all children
- promote continuity and progression.

Information should be shared between the setting and the home, so that a holistic picture of the child's needs, preferences and skills emerges. Parents have important information about their child's competence at home which will help practitioners to plan for their next stage of learning.

AC 2.4 Progress check

For each of the observations carried out for AC 2.2, you should work with others to plan the next steps in relation to the children's needs and interests.

Assessment practice

1 Explain how observations are used to plan for individual children's needs.
2 How can observations help in early intervention?
3 What is the role of observations in reviewing the early years environment?
4 How can observations help during transition?
5 How would you use observations when working in partnership?
6 Describe the different observation techniques. For each method of observation, give an example of its possible application.
7 Why is it important to be objective when carrying out observations?
8 How do you practise confidentiality when carrying out observations?
9 Reflect upon your own role in meeting the needs and interests of children in the setting.
10 How can you work with others to plan next steps in relation to the needs and interests of an individual child?

Useful resources

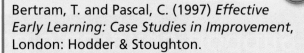

Bertram, T. and Pascal, C. (1997) *Effective Early Learning: Case Studies in Improvement*, London: Hodder & Stoughton.

Harding, J. and Meldon-Smith, L. (1996) *How to make Observations and Assessments*, London: Hodder Arnold.

Sylva, K., Roy, C. and Painter, M. (1980) *Childwatching at Playgroup and Nursery School*, London: Sage Publications.

Unit 12

Support children's positive behaviour

Learning outcomes

By the end of this unit, you will:

1 Understand policies and procedures relating to children's positive behaviour.
2 Be able to support positive behaviour.
3 Be able to respond to inappropriate behaviour.

4 Be able to reflect on own role in relation to managing children's behaviour in own setting.

LO1 Understand policies and procedures relating to children's positive behaviour

Behaviour is the way in which we act, speak and treat other people and our environment. Children who develop well socially and emotionally at an early age are more likely to make friends, settle well into school and understand how to behave appropriately in different situations. They have strong self-esteem and a sense of self-worth, but also have a feeling of empathy for others. They understand what the boundaries are, and why they are necessary. A child with poor social and emotional development may be at risk of developing poor relationships with peers and problem (or unwanted) behaviour.

AC 1.1 Policies and procedures relating to children's positive behaviour

Every setting should have a policy on the management of behaviour in the setting. This should be specific to the aims and needs of the setting and include guidelines for managing the behaviour of both children and adults involved with the setting. A good behaviour policy will help new staff to learn how to promote positive behaviour, by explaining that children need to develop the following positive skills and attributes:

- self-respect and self-esteem
- pro-social behaviour, including consideration and empathy for others
- social skills, such as negotiation and problem-solving.

The policy also needs to address adult strategies in two important areas:

- promoting the behaviour that you would like from the children
- discouraging behaviour that you do not want from the children.

Specific procedures for staff to follow which help in achieving these aims should also be included, such as:

- being a good role model: showing what you want from children by setting a good example in your own behaviour
- praising children: when they have shown wanted behaviour – for example, when they have been helpful to another child
- organising the environment: to make it easier for children to be patient or to take turns

- intervening calmly: to stop children hurting each other or behaving in an unsafe way
- setting boundaries: to teach children what sort of behaviour is acceptable and what is not
- giving a simple explanation or alternative: to the child who is finding it difficult to observe boundaries.

The policy should also detail the strategies that will definitely never be used in the setting and also explain why. For example:

- Adults will not hit or shake children – this is a misuse of your adult strength and is contrary to the ground rules for children's behaviour.
- Adults will not use verbal humiliation or insults – this would undermine children's self-esteem and set a very poor example to all children.

In practice

Behaviour policy
Find out about the policy and procedures in your setting. Why is it important for settings to have a behaviour policy?

Codes of conduct
Each behaviour policy applies to a particular setting and so will vary according to the type of setting. The Early Years Foundation Stage requires that 'children's behaviour must be managed effectively and in a manner appropriate for their stage of development and particular individual needs'. Schools are also legally required to have policies and procedures in place to identify and prevent bullying. Codes of conduct generally form part of a setting's behaviour policy. These relate to the behaviour of staff as well as to the behaviour of children.

The code of conduct for staff in an early years setting may provide extra guidance for staff on dealing with inappropriate behaviour:

- keeping calm when dealing with inappropriate behaviour

- listening to both sides of the story when there is conflict – and apologising if you have made a mistake
- being consistent when dealing with inappropriate behaviour
- making sure that you do not make any negative comments in front of the children.

The main features of a code of conduct for children deal with issues such as fairness and taking turns, playing safely and not bullying. It will also describe use of the following measures to promote positive behaviour.

Rewards and sanctions
Most settings have ways of rewarding positive behaviour and of using sanctions to discourage inappropriate behaviour. The use of rewards and sanctions is discussed in the next section.

Dealing with conflict and inappropriate behaviour
Everyone working with children needs to be clear about what is meant by inappropriate behaviour; this is why it is so important to have a behaviour policy. Practitioners must follow the code of conduct by dealing with conflict in a fair and consistent way.

AC 1.1 Activity

Find out about the behaviour policy in your setting. Answer the following questions:

- What positive strategies does the setting use?
- How does the setting deal with a child's challenging or inappropriate behaviour?
- How does the setting approach dangerous and harmful behaviour – such as biting and hitting?
- How does the nursery approach repeated difficult behaviour?
- What is the setting's view on the role of parents in supporting children's positive behaviour?

AC 1.2 The need for a consistent approach in applying boundaries and guidelines for behaviour

The importance of being fair and consistent

It is important that everyone in the setting is both fair and consistent when dealing with children's behaviour. When you are fair and consistent in your response to inappropriate behaviour, the child's sense of security and knowledge of right from wrong will be reinforced. The adult response to inappropriate behaviour should be the same every time that behaviour occurs.

Consistency in applying the boundaries is important, especially in the work setting, where children need to relate to several adults. They will check that the rules have not changed and that they still apply regardless of which adult is present. If you are supervising an activity, the children will expect you to apply the same rules as other staff. It undermines your own position if you allow unacceptable behaviour and another staff member has to discipline the children you are working with.

Setting rules and boundaries

If children are to understand what is regarded as acceptable behaviour at home, in the work setting and in society, then they must be given very clear and consistent guidelines. Work settings will have a policy relating to behaviour and discipline, which all staff should follow and which is regularly reviewed.

Rules

The policy will explain the rules that are applied, and how children will be helped to understand and learn to keep them. In most cases, the rules are simple and reflect the concerns for safety and for children to be considerate of others and their environment. They should be appropriate for the age and stage of development of the children and for the particular needs of the work setting. Rules apply to the forms of behaviour that are encouraged, and cover physical, social and verbal aspects.

Rules, or targets, should be realistically set for the child's age and stage of development. Examples of rules for a child aged four to five years are to:

- say 'please' and 'thank you'
- share play equipment
- tidy up
- be quiet and listen for short periods (such as story or register time).

Boundaries

These are the limits within which behaviour is acceptable – they identify what may, and may not, be done or said. Children need to understand the consequences of failing to act within those boundaries. It is important that the boundaries are appropriate for the age and stage of development.

Examples of boundaries for young children are that they may:

- play outside – but must not tread on the flowerbeds
- watch television – but only until tea is ready
- use the dressing-up clothes – if they put them away when they have finished.

> **Discussion point**
>
> Discuss what you think is positive behaviour and what is inappropriate behaviour.
>
> Think of the behaviour you have observed of young children you know, who are related to you, who you have worked with and those you see out in public.

LO2 Be able to support positive behaviour

The ways in which children behave will depend to a large extent on their developmental stage. Before looking at how to support positive behaviour, we need to understand what is expected behaviour at certain ages.

Figure 12.1 Children need to know what behaviour is expected of them; they need boundaries

Stages of behavioural development

The following stages of behavioural development are, of course, linked only loosely to the ages shown. As with any normative measurements, they serve as a rough guide to help understand children's behaviour and how best to respond to it. Much will depend upon children's experiences and the way in which they have been helped to develop effective relationships.

Aged one to two years

At this age, children:

- have developed their own personalities and are sociable with close family and friends
- still become shy and anxious when parents or carers are out of sight
- are developing their speech, and can attract attention by calling out or crying

- can become possessive over toys, but can often be distracted with something else
- are discovering that they are separate individuals
- are self-centred (see things from their own point of view)
- are gaining mobility, improving their ability to explore their surroundings – this results in conflicts, often regarding safety
- begin to understand the meaning of 'No,' and firm boundaries can be set
- can be frustrated by their own limitations, but resist adult help (perhaps saying 'me do it').

Aged two to three years

At this age, children:

- are developing greater awareness of their separate identities
- are not yet able to share easily

- are developing their language abilities; they begin to communicate their needs and wishes more clearly and to understand 'in a minute'
- can still be distracted from the cause of their anger
- have tantrums (usually when parents or main carers are present) when frustrated – possibly caused by their efforts to become self-reliant (such as feeding or dressing themselves) or having ideas that the adult does not want them to carry out
- experience a range of feelings – being very affectionate and cooperative one minute and resistant the next
- are aware of the feelings of others and can respond to them.

Aged three to four years

At this age, children:

- are very aware of others and imitate them – especially in their play; their developing speaking and listening skills allow them to repeat swear words they hear
- are more able to express themselves through speech and, therefore, there is often a reduction in physical outbursts; however, they are still likely to hit back if provoked
- can be impulsive and will be less easily distracted
- become more sociable in their play and may have favourite friends
- can sometimes be reasoned with and are just becoming aware of the behaviour codes in different places or situations
- like and seek adult approval and appreciation of their efforts.

Aged four to five years

At this age, children:

- can behave appropriately at meal times and during other 'routine' activities and may begin to understand why 'please' and 'thank you' (or their equivalents) are important
- are able to share and take turns, but often need help

- are more aware of others' feelings and will be concerned if someone is hurt
- are becoming more independent and self-assured, but still need adult comfort when ill or tired
- will respond to reason, can negotiate and can be adaptable, but can still be distracted
- are sociable and becoming confident communicators, able to make more sense of their environment; there will continue to be conflicts that they cannot resolve on their own and with which they will need adult help
- can sometimes be determined, may argue and may show aggression.

Aged five to six years

At this age, children:

- understand that different rules apply in different places (such as at home, school, grandparents' house) and can adapt their behaviour accordingly
- are developing control over their feelings – they argue with adults when they feel secure and need to feel there are firm boundaries in place
- will respond to reason and can negotiate, but are less easily distracted – anger can last longer and they need time to calm down
- are able to hide their feelings in some situations
- can cooperate in group play, but are not yet ready for team games
- may show off and boast (for example, when they celebrate an achievement)
- will continue to need adult support to resolve conflicts
- will share and take turns, and begin to have an understanding of what is 'fair' if given an explanation.

Linking behaviour to child development

When assessing children's behaviour, it is important to bear these developmental stages in mind and to view the behaviour in the context of overall or holistic development.

Here are two examples:

1 It is well known that tantrums are a common, even expected, feature of a two-year-old child's behaviour. There is bound to be some cause for concern, however, if they are a regular feature of a six-year-old child's behaviour. However, some adults have unrealistic expectations of children and express surprise when inappropriate behaviour occurs.

2 A five-year-old child becomes restless and upset during a Christmas pantomime. The adults will view the occasion as a treat and may feel resentment that their child is complaining, but it is reasonable that a five-year-old should lose concentration, be unable to sit still for a lengthy period or understand all of what is going on.

Factors affecting behaviour

It is well known that behaviour is commonly affected by certain factors. There are some factors that stem from the children themselves:

- illness
- accident and injury
- tiredness.

Other factors result from situations:

- arrival of a new baby
- moving house
- parental separation or divorce
- change of carer – either at home or in a setting
- loss or bereavement
- change of setting – such as transition from home to nursery or nursery to school.

Individual children will respond to these situations differently but regression is common (usually temporary) when they revert to behaviour that is immature for them. Events that they do not understand will leave them confused, leading to frustration and aggressive outbursts, or they may blame themselves, which could result in withdrawn behaviour and the development of inappropriate habits through anxiety.

Generally, any factor that causes stress may result in the child:

- needing more comfort and attention
- being less sociable
- being unable to cope with tasks that they would normally manage
- being subject to mood swings
- being unable to concentrate (this includes listening to instructions) and less able to cope with challenging situations and difficulties.

AC 2.1 The benefits of encouraging and rewarding positive behaviour

Positive behaviour management is about using positive rather than negative approaches to encourage children to behave appropriately. Promoting positive behaviour involves:

- setting clear boundaries, which are applied in a calm and consistent way
- encouraging children to make their own choices about behaviour – and to understand the negative consequences if they choose inappropriate behaviour
- setting 'positive' rules rather than 'negative' ones. Negative rules tend to begin with the word 'Don't' and tell children what they must not do, but do not guide them as to what they may or should do.

AC 2.1 Activity

What do you think the benefits are of providing consistent boundaries and guidelines for children's behaviour?

Skills and techniques for supporting and encouraging positive behaviour

In trying to understand behaviour, it is helpful to note whether there are particular incidents or situations that seem to trigger inappropriate behaviour. Some of these can be avoided altogether by minor changes in routine or approach, but others, such as siblings teasing each other, will occur frequently; children therefore need to be given strategies and support to be able to cope with them effectively. It is important never to reject the child but only what the child has done (for example, 'That was an unkind thing to say' rather than 'You are unkind').

The A-B-C of behaviour

- **Antecedent**: what happens before, or leads up to, the observed behaviour.
- **Behaviour**: the observed behaviour – what the child says and how he or she acts (this is any behaviour, both positive and negative).
- **Consequence**: what happens following the observed behaviour.

Part of your role as an early years practitioner is to observe children's behaviour, whether or not you make a written record, so that you can contribute to discussions about a child's behaviour and develop good practice in managing unacceptable aspects. In your work setting, you should try to see not only how other staff and parents deal with incidents, but also which methods seem to be effective with which children.

AC 2.1 Progress check ✓

By tuning in to children and responding to them, you can help them to become aware of how they are feeling.

Work with your team to set and maintain clear and agreed boundaries, so that children know what sort of behaviour is acceptable.

AC 2.2 How modelling positive behaviour impacts on children's behaviour

Children learn a lot of their behaviour from those around them. Children who develop well socially and emotionally at an early age are more likely to make friends, to settle well into school and to understand how to behave appropriately in different situations. They have strong self-esteem and a sense of self-worth, but also have a feeling of empathy for others. They understand what the boundaries are, and why they are

necessary. A child with poor social and emotional development may be at risk of poor relationships with peers and unwanted behaviour. Early years practitioners must be good role models, by modelling positive behaviour; this includes showing respect, being polite, showing consideration for others and waiting with patience. For more information on modelling positive behaviours, see Unit 6, page 149.

AC 2.3 Modelling positive behaviour

For information on modelling positive behaviour, see Unit 6, page 149.

AC 2.4 Using positive reinforcement with children

Positive reinforcement is the most effective way to promote positive behaviour and to minimise inappropriate behaviour. It is based on the idea that, if children receive approval and/or a reward for behaving acceptably, they are likely to want to repeat that behaviour. If one child is praised (e.g. for tidying up), others are often influenced to copy or join in so that they, too, will receive praise and attention. For young children, the reward must be immediate so they understand the link between it and the positive behaviour. It is of little value to promise a treat or reward in the future. Similarly, star charts and collecting points are not appropriate for children younger than five years old.

The use of positive reinforcement encourages the development of self-confidence and self-esteem in young children, which in turn helps them to become active learners and to feel confident as they grow and develop.

Positive reinforcement is achieved through the use of positive feedback. This includes:

- positive body language and a warm tone of voice
- physical touch
- praise and compliments
- encouragement and attention
- rewards and privileges.

Figure 12.2 Positive reinforcement is the most effective way to promote positive behaviour

Using rewards

There are different forms of rewards:

- verbal praise (such as 'Well done')
- attention – this could be non-verbal (smile of approval, a nod)
- sharing success by telling other staff and parents
- own choice of activity or story
- tangible rewards, such as stickers.

There are problems associated with rewards in that some children may behave in a particular way purely to receive the reward rather than from an understanding of the need to consider safety, others and their environment, or enjoying what they have achieved for its own sake. The type of reward also needs to be considered; for example, is it desirable for children to be given sweets as rewards? Some parents may have strong views about this.

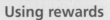

Case study

Using rewards

In an infant school, a new head teacher introduced the regular practice of listening to children read to her. This involved children being sent individually to her office where she would reward them with a jelly bear if they read well or tried hard. One mother was surprised, when talking to her daughter about the school day, that she was upset to have read to her class teacher instead of to the head teacher. The girl explained that everyone was asking to read to the head teacher and she was not chosen – so she missed out on a jelly bear!

The parent was alarmed, firstly that sweets were being given as a reward without parents knowing, and secondly that children were not rewarded by the experience itself and the head teacher's appreciation of children's efforts.

LO3 Be able to respond to inappropriate behaviour

AC 3.1 Identifying inappropriate behaviour

Inappropriate behaviour conflicts with the accepted values and beliefs of the setting and of society. Inappropriate behaviour may be demonstrated through speech, writing, non-verbal behaviour or physical abuse and includes:

- attention-seeking
- aggression (both physical and verbal) towards others
- self-destructive behaviour or self-harming.

Attention-seeking

Children will do just about anything to get the attention they crave from parents and carers. This is often shown through disruptive (making noises, not responding to an instruction) or aggressive behaviour and needs managing as identified below. Sometimes children who are trying to please can be just as disruptive. Those who desperately want adults to notice them will call out, interrupt, ask questions and frequently push in front of other children to show something they have made or done.

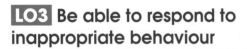

Case study

A lack of consistency

Callum is in nursery class. He is an energetic, popular and sociable boy, aged two-and-a-half years. The room leader, Joanne, has a particular soft spot for Callum as she was friends with his mum before he started at the nursery. Lately, Callum has begun to disrupt the class by running around during quieter times and meal times. He has recently dropped his afternoon nap at Mum's request, and is very noisy and boisterous when the other children are trying to sleep. Joanne is usually in the office during this naptime after lunch and leaves Fiona in charge of the running of the room.

Fiona adopts a firm line with Callum. She takes him aside, gets down to his level and tells him clearly why he cannot make noise and run around, and what behaviour she expects from him. She also takes the opportunity to go with him to find quiet games to play while the others are asleep. This works well for a little while, but usually Callum needs a few reminders before he accepts. Occasionally, as a treat, he is allowed to go and play outside with the pre-school children (if they have room for him) but Fiona will not allow this unless Callum is behaving well.

However, Fiona has noticed that when Callum is being disruptive and Joanne is in the room, she adopts a different approach. First Joanne will tell him to stop, but when he does not respond, she leaves the room, taking him with her to 'help' her run errands, saying to the other staff members that he is bored and that is why he is not behaving well. Fiona views this as rewarding inappropriate behaviour and finds that, after it has happened a few times, Callum becomes increasingly difficult to control and easily upset and tearful. He stops responding so positively to Fiona's technique and requires one-to-one attention at a time when staff members are trying to settle 10 other children for their naps, as well as supply play for the few children who, like Callum, no longer have daytime naps.

1 What do the staff need to do to rectify this situation?
2 Why do you think that Callum is now becoming upset easily?
3 Do you think that Callum's 'treat' of running errands is making him happy in the long run?
4 Why is it unfair on children when there is inconsistency in discipline techniques?

Physical aggression

This usually results from strong feelings that are difficult to control. Hitting, kicking, spitting, biting, swearing and disrupting other children's activities are behaviours that children use to demand attention. When children behave like this, they can soon become labelled as naughty or impossible to manage, and it is only a short step to these children starting to live up to their label, and staff starting to speak and act towards them in an anxious or hostile way. So it is important to break this cycle, to try to hold on to the positive aspects of the child's behaviour and appeal to these.

Self-destructive behaviour

This includes head banging and forms of self-mutilation (e.g. tearing out hair, excessive nail-biting causing pain and bleeding). It usually signals some emotional difficulty that needs expert intervention. Staff and parents need to discuss their concerns and agree a common approach based on the advice they are given.

Unacceptable language

This includes swearing and name-calling, which often result from children repeating what they have themselves heard. Sometimes they are unaware that it is unacceptable in one setting but not another. In these cases, they need to be told firmly not to say those words 'here' – you cannot legislate for language they may use at home or criticise their families. Some children will deliberately use unacceptable language to shock or seek attention. In these cases, you should state the rule calmly and firmly.

Name-calling

Name-calling must always be challenged and dealt with firmly, particularly if it is discriminatory (regarding race, creed, disability, family background, appearance, etc.). Explain that it is hurtful and that we are all different. This behaviour is best combated through good example and through anti-discriminatory practices in the work setting, which will help children to value other people as individuals.

Temper tantrums

These are usually associated with two-year-olds but can occur in older children. In fact many people would not describe tantrums as inappropriate behaviour in toddlers. They may happen particularly when a child is ill or tired, but often build from a confrontational incident when he or she is asked to do something, or not to do something, and a battle of wills begins! Temper tantrums often involve shouting and crying, refusal to cooperate and mounting anger – shown through kicking, hitting, screaming, stamping – and, on occasions, self-harm. In younger children, tantrums can be over very quickly but older children can take longer to reach a peak and calm down afterwards.

AC 3.1 Progress check

During the next few days you spend in your setting, think about any inappropriate behaviour that you have seen and note how other members of staff deal with it.

AC 3.2 Procedures for reporting inappropriate behaviour

Sometimes the behaviour management strategies outlined above fail to be effective, or are only effective for a short period of time. So when behaviour is inappropriate for the child's stage of development or is persistently challenging, there are other professionals who may be called upon to help all those involved. It is useful to attend meetings which allow everyone to contribute information about a child; these will help to create an overall view of progress, development and behaviour and it is here that recorded observations will be especially useful.

Some of these professionals are art, music or play therapists and child psychotherapists.

In contrast to the behavioural modification approach outlined above, a therapeutic approach will generally involve an attempt to find the underlying causes of the child's difficult behaviour. Through play, art, music or talking in a free way, the child can be helped to express his or her feelings. The therapist can help by giving the child a safe space for expression, and by interpreting the child's communications in a way that makes it possible for the child to live with feelings of anger, loss or unhappiness. As the child is increasingly able to express and find ways of living with difficult emotions, he or she becomes more able to develop and grow throughout childhood, instead of being 'stuck'.

Professionals who may become involved include the following:

- Health visitors work primarily with children up to five years and their families, checking for healthy growth and development.
- Physiotherapists assess children's motor skills and development and might be asked to advise on appropriate activities and equipment.
- Speech therapists assess mouth movement as well as speech/language itself, and may suggest ways of supporting children who experience communication difficulties.
- Play therapists, art therapists and music therapists have specialist training and work with children through play, art and music to help them feel emotionally secure.
- Paediatricians are doctors who specialise in the care of children up to the age of 16, to check for normal development and diagnose difficulties.
- Educational psychologists assess children who have special needs and give advice, particularly for those with emotional and behavioural difficulties.
- Child psychiatrists and psychotherapists work with children and their families to help them to express their thoughts and feelings.

> **In practice**
>
> **Reporting incidents**
> It is important to follow correct procedures for reporting incidents. Check that you know what these procedures are in your work setting.

AC 3.3 Agreed strategies for dealing with inappropriate behaviour

Strategies for dealing with attention-seeking behaviour

Children who seek attention challenge patience but, with some reminding about turn-taking and clear expectations, they can learn to wait for their turn. It is important to give attention when they have waited appropriately so that they are encouraged to do so again. Practitioners could try the following strategies:

- whenever possible, ignoring attention-seeking behaviour, unless their attention is drawn to it (perhaps by another child), as the message sent then is that it is acceptable to behave in that way
- giving attention and praise to another child who is behaving acceptably
- distracting the child's attention (particularly appropriate with younger children) or removing him or her to another activity or group
- expressing disapproval – verbally and/or non-verbally through body language, facial expression (frowning) and shaking of the head
- using a sanction – withdrawal of a privilege (such as removing a toy or activity).

Strategies for dealing with aggressive behaviour

How to respond when a child bites

Try to think why the child has bitten. Ask the following questions to help you to understand why it has happened:

- When and where did it happen?
- Who with?

Guidelines for good practice

Strategies for dealing with temper tantrums

- Try to avoid them – if you can anticipate them, try distracting the child with a game or another activity.
- Try to ignore them – apart from safety concerns, try to give as little attention as possible during the tantrum.
- Be consistent – if children think, from past experience, that the adult will not keep the boundary firmly, they will continue to tantrum; clear boundaries are essential.
- A firm hug may help the child feel secure and under control until they calm down – this is useful in situations where you cannot walk away.
- Talk about them – this may help older children to express their feelings calmly.
- Provide experiences and activities that the child finds interesting; this usually helps children to become involved in positive ways.
- Do not give in and let the boundary go – this almost certainly leads to more rather than fewer tantrums because children are confused by inconsistency.

Guidelines for good practice

Strategies for dealing with a child who bites

- Comfort and take care of the child who has been bitten, in a 'low-key', calm way. Tell the bitten child, 'That must be sore, let's get a cold cloth.'
- To the biter, say firmly, but gently, 'It's not OK to bite, because biting hurts. If you want to bite, you can bite a biscuit or a toy, but I can't let you bite Martha.'
- Encourage the biter to 'make amends' in some way – to help get the cold cloth or a teddy for comfort.

Managing the behaviour of a child who bites

- Try to offer positive attention and affection to the 'biter' throughout the day.
- Provide snacks and drinks regularly.
- Make sure there is more than one of a favourite toy so there is a smaller chance of the child becoming frustrated.
- Arrange the room to make space for play.
- Show the child how to negotiate and take turns.
- Be aware of any changes taking place at home and help the child to deal with these by talking sensitively with them about it.

- What happened before?
- What happened afterwards?
- How do you think the child feels?

Many settings develop a 'biting policy' and produce a leaflet with guidelines to support both parents and practitioners.

The use of sanctions

A **sanction** is designed to discourage inappropriate behaviour. To be effective, however, it must protect the practitioner's relationship with the child and safeguard the child's self-esteem. Examples of sanctions to be used with young children include:

- a non-verbal signal: for example, a frown or shake of the head can be very effective
- a minute's withdrawal (timed with a timer to ensure fairness) from the activity or group
- time out: it is important that 'time out' is used appropriately and only when essential (see 'Guidelines for good practice' below).

When children misbehave, the adult responsible at the time should deal with it and, whenever possible, issue rebukes and sanctions in private. Children should always receive a warning before a sanction is imposed, to give them the chance to cooperate.

Time out

This involves the child who has been aggressive being taken to an identified place away from the incident – a corner or chair. 'Time out' allows for a calming-down period and for other children to be reassured. This method can work but needs positive follow-up by a staff member to explain why the behaviour was unacceptable and suggest how the child might have behaved otherwise; for example, they should have asked instead of snatched, or listened to the apology for the toy being broken. Unless this is done, there is a danger that the chair (or area) becomes known to the children as the 'naughty chair' and staff begin to use it as a way of 'grounding' a child who is causing annoyance without really addressing the issues. Many adults do not like to use this approach for this reason.

Guidelines for good practice

Using time out

If time out is used, the supervising adult should:

- ignore the child, offering no eye contact or conversation: this gives the child time to calm down – to think and reflect on his or her behaviour
- time the time out: the length of time out should ideally match the age of the child; for example, for a three-year-old child, use three minutes
- invite the child to return: the child should be invited to return after the time out and to agree to behave appropriately if he or she wants to rejoin the wider group
- praise the child: if the child then behaves appropriately in the next few minutes, the adult should offer approval and praise.

Guidelines for good practice

Dealing with inappropriate behaviour

- Try to remain calm: it is easier to control a difficult child or situation if you are in control of yourself. Listen to both sides of the story when there is conflict and apologise if you have made a mistake.
- Ignore attention-seeking behaviour: children who desperately want adults to notice them will call out, interrupt, ask questions and frequently push in front of other children to show something they have made or done. It is important to ignore such behaviour as much as possible and to reward them by giving them attention only when they have waited appropriately, so that they are encouraged to do so again.
- Use a distraction or diversion: if two children are arguing over a toy, you could distract them by offering an alternative activity: 'Shall we go and play with the blocks instead?' Or you could use a volunteer task as a distraction, such as helping with handing out resources.
- Blame the behaviour, not the child: when you need to talk to children about their behaviour, it is important for them to feel that it is not personal – that you do not dislike the child, only his or her behaviour. For example, you might say, 'Bailey, throwing toys is dangerous behaviour; I want you to stop right now!'
- Give the child a choice: explain that the child can choose how to behave. For example, you might say: 'Bailey, you now have a choice. You can stop throwing the toys and play nicely with them, or I'm afraid I will have to take them away.' Allow the child a few minutes to decide what to do. If he or she refuses to comply, follow through with the sanction by removing the toys.

LO4 Be able to reflect on own role in relation to managing children's behaviour in own setting

AC 4.1 Reflecting on own role in relation to managing children's behaviour

Being able to reflect on your practice in relation to managing children's behaviour will help you to understand which things have worked well – and which have not worked so well. This will help you to think of ways to improve your practice. There are various ways to reflect on your practice. These include:

- observing the children's behaviour and reflecting on possible triggers of inappropriate behaviour
- reviewing which strategies for promoting positive behaviour worked well and which did not work so well
- asking colleagues for feedback.

When reflecting on your own role, try the following exercises in self-awareness and empathy:

1 Try to imagine what it is like to be a child in the setting.
   Does it sometimes feel like there is a great mass of children, all demanding attention and seeking the same equipment? You can help by taking time with individual children, listening to them and observing them, encountering them as special individuals and not just one of many in the group.

2 Try to become aware of your own feelings. Angry children provoke angry responses from adults. Can you work on your responses and become calmer and clearer, and reduce confrontations? Saying 'I can wait a minute, but then I really do need you to come and sit down' will often work much better than demanding 'Sit down now!'

3 Look for patterns in children's behaviour. If a child is often angry at a particular time of the day, during a particular activity or in response to particular children, try to plan the day to minimise these times.

Whatever the cause – and it may be provocation – the adult should deal with it calmly and ensure that the needs of all the children involved are met. A child who has lost control frightens him- or herself and the other children.

Reflective practice

Sharing experiences
Discuss how staff in your setting deal with inappropriate behaviour. Do you feel that the methods used are generally effective?

Assessment practice

1 Identify policies and procedures relating to children's positive behaviour.
2 Why is it important to have a consistent approach in applying guidelines and boundaries for children's behaviour?

(Learning outcomes 2 and 3 must be assessed in real work environments by a qualified vocationally competent assessor. Simulation is not permitted.)

Useful resources

Axline, V. (1971) *Dibs, In Search of Self: Personality Development in Play Therapy*, London: Penguin.

Dowling, M. (2010) *Young Children's Personal, Social and Emotional Development* (3rd edn), London: Sage Publications.

Paley, V.G. (1981) *Wally's Stories*, Cambridge, MA: Harvard University Press.

Sylva, K. and Lunt, I. (1982) *Child Development: A First Course*, Oxford: Blackwell.

Tovey, H. (2007) *Playing Outdoors: Spaces and Places, Risk and Challenge*, Oxford: Oxford University Press.

Anna Freud Centre

The centre was established in 1947 by Anna Freud to support the emotional well-being of children through direct work with children and their families, research and the development of practice, and training mental health practitioners.

www.annafreud.org

HighScope

HighScope is an American approach to early education and care, with several decades of

research into its effectiveness. The website includes books, DVDs and news of training events and conferences in the UK.

Kate Greenaway Nursery School and Children's Centre

This website includes news and policies for a centre based in central London.

www.kategreenaway.org

Kidscape

This charity was established specifically to prevent bullying and child sexual abuse. The website includes resources for parents, children and professionals, and details of campaigns and training events.

www.kidscape.org.uk

The National Strategies (Early Years)

The government's programme for developing practice in the early years, including statutory requirements, advice on best practice, and research findings. Go to the following website and search for 'early years'.

www.foundationyears.org.uk

Optional units

Unit OP1

Support children with additional needs

Learning outcomes

By the end of this unit, you will:

1 Understand factors which may result in children needing additional support.
2 Understand how personal experiences, values and beliefs impact on practice.

3 Understand inclusive practice.
4 Understand the role of early intervention in partnership working.
5 Be able to support the additional needs of children.

LO1 Understand factors which may result in children needing additional support

Children with additional needs have needs that are 'in addition' to the general needs of children. Some children have a very obvious and well-researched disability, such as Down's syndrome or cerebral palsy; others may have a specific learning difficulty, such as dyslexia or giftedness. What defines them as children with additional needs is the fact that they need additional support in some area of development, care or education compared with other children.

It is important to remember that children are more alike than they are different. Every child needs:

- to feel welcome
- to feel safe, both physically and emotionally
- to have friends and to feel as if they belong
- to be encouraged to reach their potential
- to be celebrated for his or her uniqueness.

In other words, children are always children first; and the additional need is secondary.

Main categories of additional needs

Children with additional needs may be grouped into the following categories:

- physical **disability**: needs related to problems with mobility or coordination, such as cerebral palsy, spina bifida or muscular dystrophy
- speech or communication difficulties: needs related to communication problems such as delayed language, difficulties in **articulation** or stuttering
- specific learning difficulties (SLD): needs related to problems usually confined to the areas of reading, writing and numeracy; dyslexia is a term often applied to difficulty in developing literacy skills
- medical conditions: needs related to medical conditions such as cystic fibrosis, diabetes, asthma, chronic lung disease or epilepsy
- sensory impairment: needs related to problems with sight or hearing
- complex needs: many of these needs involve problems resulting from a **genetic disorder** or from an accident or trauma
- behavioural difficulties: needs related to aggression, challenging behaviour, hyperactivity, attention deficit hyperactivity disorder (ADHD) or antisocial behaviour
- life-threatening illness: needs related to a serious or terminal illness, e.g. childhood cancer, HIV, AIDS and leukaemia
- emotional and social difficulties: needs related to conditions such as anxiety, fear, depression or autistic spectrum disorder (ASD).

AC 1.1 Factors that may result in children needing additional support

Additional support needs may be of short duration, perhaps a few weeks or months, or could be long term, over a number of years. The factors that may give rise to additional support needs are wide and varied because they relate to the circumstances of individual children, and an individual may have additional support needs arising from more than one of the factors listed below.

Short-term factors
A child may need additional support in the short term – that is, have a temporary additional need – because they:

- are being bullied or are bullying
- have sustained an injury or illness requiring hospitalisation
- are temporarily hearing impaired – for example, have 'glue ear' or recurrent ear infections
- are highly able – or gifted – and may not be challenged sufficiently
- have specific reading or writing problems and may not be receiving the appropriate support
- have been bereaved
- are experiencing difficulties during a transition – for example, a change in family living arrangements

- have a home life disrupted by poverty, homelessness, domestic abuse, parental alcohol or drug misuse or parental mental or physical health problems
- are looked after by a local authority.

The same factor may have different impacts on individual learning. For example, one child may find that difficulties at home have an adverse impact upon them. Another child in apparently similar circumstances may experience a minimal impact.

Long-term factors
A child may need additional support in the long term because they have:

- a disability caused by a genetic defect, e.g. Down's syndrome
- a physical disability: difficulty with movement, e.g. cerebral palsy
- a visual or hearing impairment
- a specific language impairment
- autistic spectrum disorder
- learning or attention difficulties, such as attention deficit hyperactivity disorder
- a chronic illness.

AC 1.1 Progress check
Describe factors which may affect children's development in the short term and the long term.

LO2 Understand how personal experiences, values and beliefs impact on practice

AC 2.1 How personal experiences, values and beliefs impact on practice

Your own personal experiences, values and beliefs impact on your work with young children and their parents.

Your attitudes, values and behaviour should demonstrate your commitment to diversity, inclusion and participation. You need to be able to think clearly and fairly about issues related to diversity, inclusion and participation. This will enable you to care for young children with due attention to their individual needs as well as promoting their development and early learning in ways which open up opportunities for their future. It is important to be aware of the effect that your use of language can have on others:

- The words you use to express yourself affect the development of your own attitudes, values and behaviour.
- The language you use shapes the way you think and may lead you to distorted or limited opinions. Language reflects and influences how you think about yourself and others.
- Language can reinforce the development of stereotyped and prejudiced ideas or it can help you to think more constructively and treat others respectfully.

See Unit 4, AC 4.2 (page 130) for more on the impact of your own attitudes, values and behaviour on practice.

AC 2.1 Activity

A hearing problem

Carla, a baby of 15 months, has just been diagnosed with a severe hearing impairment. Mary, the baby room supervisor, notices that Laura, one of the early years practitioners, changes Carla's nappies in silence, although she always smiles, chats and plays with the other babies during nappy-changing routines. When Mary asks her why she doesn't do the same with Carla, Laura replies that she doesn't see the point because Carla can't hear anything.

1 Why is Mary concerned about Laura's childcare practice?
2 Discuss ways in which practitioners could promote Carla's development and support her holistic needs.

LO3 Understand inclusive practice

The principles of inclusive practice

Inclusive practice is a term used within education to describe the process of ensuring equality of learning opportunities for all children and young people, whatever their disabilities or disadvantages. This means that all children have the right to have their needs met in the best way for them. They are seen as being part of the community, even if they need particular help to live a full life within the community. So, while integration is about bringing people who are different together, inclusion is about providing the support that is needed to enable different people to be together in a community.

Inclusive practice is important in early years settings because:

- it promotes equality of opportunity for all children
- it encourages the development of more flexible attitudes, policies and everyday practices
- it promotes community integration through understanding of and respect for others
- it recognises and celebrates diversity.

AC 3.1 The requirements of current legislation and frameworks in relation to inclusive practice

Inclusive schools are those that welcome all pupils and develop values which promote pupils' educational, social and cultural development.

Despite the moves towards inclusion, there are arguments for keeping a minority of children in special schools. Inclusion is about much more than the type of setting that children attend – it is about the quality of their experience and how they are welcomed, helped to learn and enabled to participate fully in the life of the school or setting.

Excluded from an outing

The nursery manager at a private nursery explains to a child's parents that their son, Thomas, will not be able to join the rest of his group on a visit to a local children's theatre production of *The Gruffalo's Child*. Thomas has Down's syndrome and learning difficulties. The nursery staff had met to discuss the problem and had concluded that there was no point in Thomas going as he would not appreciate the show and would probably disrupt the other children. Thomas's mother is very unhappy with their decision and has accused the nursery of discriminating against Thomas on account of his disability.

Discuss the following questions in a group:

1 Do you think the nursery staff were justified in their decision?
2 What could the nursery staff have done in order to enable Thomas to join the others?
3 Do you believe the nursery has discriminated against Thomas?

Inclusion is about the child's right to:

- attend the local mainstream setting
- be valued as an individual
- be provided with all the support needed to thrive in a mainstream setting.

Inclusive provision should be seen as an extension of the early years setting's equal opportunities policy and practice. It requires a commitment from the entire staff, parents and children, to include the full diversity of children in the local community. This may require planned restructuring of the whole environment to ensure equality of access.

With reference to inclusive practice, the EYFS framework makes it clear that all providers have a responsibility: 'to ensure that diversity of individuals and communities is valued and respected and that no child or family is discriminated against. Settings need to provide individualised opportunities based on each child's needs, particularly those related to ethnicity, language and disability.'

Current legislation in relation to inclusive practice is discussed in Unit 4, including new legislation introduced in 2014 relating to children with special educational needs and disabilities.

AC 3.1 Activity

Identify the requirements of current legislation and frameworks in relation to inclusive practice.

AC 3.2 Examples of inclusive practice

Kidsactive defines inclusive provision as: 'provision that is open and accessible to all, and takes positive steps in removing disabling barriers, so that disabled and non-disabled people can participate' (Douch, 2004).

The following inclusion indicators may help you to identify whether inclusion is being put into practice in your setting.

Inclusion indicators

1 Visitors can see that:
   - nobody makes a fuss about the presence of children with a disability or additional need
   - activities are designed around the interests and enthusiasm of all children who attend and with regard to any dislikes or impairments they may have
   - each person, adult or child, is welcomed on arrival
   - all children, including those with disabilities, have choices and are able to exercise those choices.
2 The leader/manager:
   - has sought out families, schools and services for disabled children and built

links to promote the involvement of disabled children

- runs regular staff meetings designed to enable staff to reflect on their practice together and develop good future practice

- can identify action taken and progress made towards inclusion, and also the things he or she still needs and plans to do to make the setting more inclusive.

3 The staff:
- have received disability equality training and/or attitudinal training and continue to undertake other training relating to inclusion

- feel that they are consulted and informed by the leader/manager.

4 Disabled and non-disabled children:
- report being involved in making rules/policies or 'having a say in what goes on'

- say they are generally happy with the setting.

5 Parents of disabled and non-disabled children:
- feel welcome and valued

- say they are consulted about how best to meet their children's needs.

6 Policies and paperwork indicate that:
- a commitment to inclusion is explicit in public and internal documentation

- staff that have particular support roles with individual disabled children are full members of the team and have job descriptions which stress the inclusion of the child, rather than just one-to-one support. (Douch, 2004)

AC 3.2 Activity

Using the inclusion indicators above, give examples of the ways in which inclusive practice is demonstrated in your setting.

LO4 Understand the role of early intervention in partnership working

The range of additional needs is enormous, from severe to relatively minor, from temporary or short-term to permanent. Young children with an additional need will often arrive in an early years setting or school with difficulties that have not yet been understood or assessed. Sometimes parents have not noticed the difficulties, but it is more usual that there is a general anxiety or sense that all is not well with the child.

AC 4.1 Reasons for early intervention in order to meet children's additional needs

If a child has a diagnosed special need, or if an assessment reveals a special need, they are likely to be in need of some kind of intervention. This will offer support for them and for their family. Sometimes parents are unaware that their child's development is delayed compared with other children of the same age, especially in the case of their first or oldest child. On other occasions, parents may have felt that 'something is not quite right', but have either been anxious about sharing their worries or have talked to other professionals but not been fully understood.

Sometimes a child can appear to be developing well during a check-up, but have difficulties in less structured environments or in the company of other children. Early identification means that the child can be helped while still very young. In many cases, prompt intervention and support early on can prevent or minimise later difficulties.

AC 4.1 Progress check

Describe the reasons for early intervention when meeting children's additional needs.

Case study

The importance of early recognition

When Matthew, Emma and their three-and-a-half-year-old daughter, Chloe, went on holiday to Portugal with another family, they found themselves in a nightmare situation. During the holiday, Chloe had not only pushed another child into the deep end of a swimming pool, where he had to be rescued by lifeguards, but she had also shoved an entire restaurant table into the harbour.

Matthew and Emma had been concerned for some time that Chloe's development was slower than other children her age, her hearing variable and her speech poor. But whenever they raised their anxieties with health professionals, they were told not to worry. Chloe had failed her first hearing test but had passed a subsequent one and a speech test at 18 months. After the disastrous holiday, Matthew and Emma were so desperate that they consulted a child psychologist, who recommended ignoring Chloe for two hours every time she 'misbehaved'. After a few weeks, Chloe was transformed into a calm, compliant child. Now Emma believes it was the cruellest thing she has ever done and feels guilty about the whole episode.

What Matthew and Emma now know is that Chloe is deaf. In fact, she was born deaf. But even after numerous tests, Chloe's deafness was not diagnosed until she was nearly four years old. Chloe had somehow taught herself to lip-read. Matthew and Emma began to do their own hearing tests on Chloe; when they hid from her while speaking, they realised that she failed to respond – it was obvious she couldn't hear them.

Chloe was just about to start school at four when she was diagnosed with a moderate to severe hearing loss after a thorough hospital hearing check. She was fitted with hearing aids. Matthew remembers the moment well: 'She smiled the most enormous smile of her whole life,' he says. Now six years old, Chloe is still struggling to catch up with her 'normal hearing' peers. Matthew and Emma just wish they had known what to look for in those early years.

(Chloe's is a true story. Since she was born, the otoacoustic emissions test (OET) – a hearing screen that might have identified her hearing impairment – has been routinely offered to all babies in the UK within a few days of birth.)

AC 4.2 Reasons for working in partnership with others to meet children's additional needs

The earlier a need for additional support is identified, the more likely it is that early intervention can prevent certain aspects of a child's development or behaviour developing into a persistent difficulty. At this point, partnership working involving all the adults in a child's life becomes very important.

Working in partnership with parents and families

Parents and carers find that getting a diagnosis for their child is important. Being given a name for their child's condition or special need enables them to discuss their child's development needs with health, social services and education professionals. Getting information about what they and their children are entitled to, as early as possible, is very important. This applies to the benefits they are entitled to as well as the services.

Working in partnership with families is particularly important when a child has additional support needs. Each parent should be made to feel welcome and valued as an expert on their child, and that they play a vital role in helping practitioners to enable their child to participate and learn.

Figure OP1.1 Parents play a vital role in informing practitioners about their child's additional needs

Parents and families:

- have a unique knowledge and expertise regarding their children, and local authorities need this to help them to provide the best education possible
- should be encouraged to participate in the decisions that affect their children and their education
- should be provided with the information they need to be informed about changes to legislation and practice in education
- should be given a named contact person for more detailed information; this person will provide them with details of local and national organisations that can offer more help, if required
- should be able to choose the extent to which they are involved in their child's setting. Not all parents have the time or the confidence to become involved in activities within the setting.

Providing support for children and families

Each family will respond in their own way when they find out that their child has a disability or an additional need. Common reactions of parents to having a child with additional needs include the following.

- A sense of tragedy: parents who give birth to a child with a disability experience complex emotions. They may grieve for the loss of a 'normal' child, but they have not actually been bereaved – they still have a child with a unique personality and identity of their own. Relatives and friends can be embarrassed if they do not know how to react to the event, and their awkward response can leave parents feeling very isolated at a time that is normally spent celebrating.
- A fear of making mistakes: sometimes there is an over-reliance on professional help. If the disability seems like the most important aspect of the child's personality, parents may believe that only a medical expert can advise on the care of their child. The reality is that the parent almost always knows what is required for their child. A great deal of what the child needs is not related to their disability in any case.
- Being overprotective: a desire to cocoon the child can be counterproductive. The child needs to be equipped for life and can learn only by making mistakes. In addition, siblings may resent the disabled child who is seen as spoilt or never punished.
- Exercising control: parents may take freedom of choice away from the child, so disempowering them. Parents and carers often dictate where and with whom the child plays, thus depriving them of an opportunity for valuable social learning.

There are other factors that will have an impact on family life. These include:

- financial worries, especially when parents have to juggle work commitments with childcare
- feeling guilty that other children in the family are missing out on family fun because of their child's special needs
- parents feeling tired and stressed because of the extra attention required by their child, especially during bouts of illness.

Information and advice

Parents find that getting a diagnosis for their child is important. Being given a name for their child's condition or special need enables them to discuss their child's development needs with health, social services and education professionals.

● Shared experiences: parents often find that the most helpful sources of information and advice are others with shared experiences. There are many organisations that exist to provide support and answer questions.
● Examples: Contact a Family, the Down's Syndrome Association, Mencap and the Royal National Institute of Blind People. There are hundreds more – most with their own website and helpline.
● Service provision: getting information as soon as possible about what parents and their children are entitled to is very important.

Communicating with parents

The principles of effective communication are discussed in Unit 2.1.

One of the main purposes of communicating with parents is to provide and to share information about the child and about the setting – the care and education setting as well as the home. Practitioners need to build up a partnership with parents, and to do this they need to promote a feeling of trust.

Parent partnership services

The Parent Partnership Scheme (PPS) is a statutory service that offers the following support:

● information, advice and support for parents of children and young people with special educational needs (SEN)
● putting parents in touch with other local organisations
● making sure that parents' views are heard and understood – and that these views inform local policy and practice.

Some parent partnerships are based in the voluntary sector, although the majority of them remain based in their LEA (local education authority) or Children's Trust. All parent partnerships, wherever they are based, work separately and independently from the LEA; this means that they are able to provide impartial advice and support to parents. For more information, visit the IASS Network (Information, Advice and Support Services) website at www.iassnetwork.org.uk.

Every Disabled Child Matters (EDCM)

Every Disabled Child Matters is a campaign to make sure disabled children and their families get the same rights as everyone else. The aims of the campaign are for disabled children and their families to:

● have the same rights as everyone else so that they are fully included in society
● get the services and support they need to live their lives in the way they want
● stop living in poverty
● receive education that meets their needs
● have their say about services for disabled children.

The Early Support programme

Early Support is an integral part of the delivery of the EYFS for babies and young children under five with disabilities or emerging special educational needs. It helps staff in early years settings to identify impairments early and to work in partnership with families and other services to provide the best possible care and support for young disabled children. An important part of the Early Support programme is the Family File, which the family holds. The Family File:

- is used by the professionals and the family together, to plan appropriate support to be provided for the child
- informs the family about the different professionals they may meet and what their role is
- explains how the different health, education and social services can provide support
- allows parents and carers to share information about their child with the professionals they meet, without having to say the same things to every new person
- provides information about sources of financial support and childcare.

Under the provisions of the Children and Families Act 2014, there is a new graduated approach to supporting children with SEN called SEN support. Information on SEN support is available in the 0-25 SEND Code of Practice, starting at paragraphs 5.36: www.gov.uk/government/publications/send-code-of-practice-0-to-25.

Working in partnership with other agencies and professionals

In addition to liaising with parents, you may need to liaise with other professionals in order to support children with additional needs and those with specific requirements, as well as providing effective support for colleagues in the setting. Statutory services include health, education and social services. A number of different services or agencies may work together to support children and their families. Some areas provide a single multi-agency service for young children and families which bring together health, education and social services, e.g. Children's Centres.

Agencies and professionals involved in the care and education of children with additional needs include the following:

Local education authority:

- educational psychologists
- special needs advisers
- specialist teachers
- **portage home visitors**
- education welfare officers
- **special educational needs coordinators (SENCO)** and special needs support teachers.

Health services:

- paediatricians
- dieticians
- health visitors
- physiotherapists
- occupational therapists
- health play specialists
- speech and language therapists
- play therapists
- school nurses
- clinical psychologists.

Social services:

- social workers
- specialist social workers: sensory disabilities, physical disabilities, mental health or children and families.

Charities and voluntary organisations – for example, AFASIC, British Dyslexia Association, Council for Disabled Children, National Autistic Society, RNIB, Action on Hearing Loss, SCOPE.

Key terms

portage home visitor Portage is an educational programme for children who have difficulty in learning basic skills due to either physical or behavioural problems. Portage will offer a framework of support with regular home visits, generally weekly or fortnightly, by a trained portage home visitor. Parents share with the home visitor their understanding of their child's individual gifts, abilities and support needs. Portage home visitors are specially trained in understanding child development and come from a variety of professions, ranging from nurses and other health professionals to school teachers.

special educational needs coordinator (SENCO) A SENCO is a person (not necessarily a staff member) in a school or maintained nursery school who has responsibility for coordinating SEN provision. In a small school, the head teacher or deputy may take on this role. In larger schools, there may be a team of SENCOs. Other early years settings in group provision arrangements are expected to identify an individual to perform the role of SENCO. Under the new SEND (Special Needs and Disability) Code of Practice 2014, childminders are 'encouraged' to identify someone who would cover a number of childminders, whether that is the local authority area SENCO or someone working for one of the new childminder agencies.

LO5 Be able to support the additional needs of children

AC 5.1 Identifying the individual needs of children in own setting

Early years practitioners need to actively seek out information about a possible underlying additional need. When you have worked with lots of children in a particular age group, your experience will help you to notice those who appear to have specific difficulties which lie outside the range of typical child development. By working closely with the parents and other specialist professionals, you may be able to help identify that a child has an additional need or disability. The support that can follow early identification can make a real difference to a child's well-being, quality of life and later achievement and enjoyment in school.

You need to know and understand the details about particular additional needs as they affect the children in your setting and your ability to provide a high-quality service. Children with additional needs and those with specific requirements in your setting may include children with:

- a hearing impairment
- a visual impairment
- physical disabilities
- behavioural difficulties
- emotional difficulties
- communication difficulties
- learning difficulties.

Some children may require support in the setting due to specific requirements, such as additional sensory and/or physical needs as a result of hearing, visual and/or physical impairment. As children with sensory or physical impairments may be dependent on others for some of their needs, it is essential to provide opportunities for them to be as independent as possible. Give them every chance to join in, to express opinions and to interact with their peer group. Remember to focus on each child as a unique person with individual strengths – focus on what they can do rather than what they cannot.

AC 5.1 Progress check

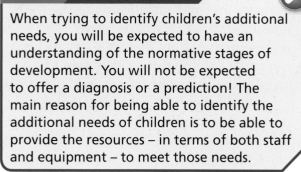

When trying to identify children's additional needs, you will be expected to have an understanding of the normative stages of development. You will not be expected to offer a diagnosis or a prediction! The main reason for being able to identify the additional needs of children is to be able to provide the resources – in terms of both staff and equipment – to meet those needs.

AC 5.2 Planning activities with others to meet children's additional needs

When working with children, you should maintain a balance between flexibility and consistency in your approach to time allocation to ensure that the needs of individual children are met. An individual support plan will ensure that this time allocation takes into account:

- the individual child's learning, play or leisure needs in terms of staffing, resources and equipment – for example, mobility and communication aids
- the management of medical issues and personal care routines – for example, epilepsy or difficulties with eating and drinking
- approaches to minimising the impact of sensory and physical impairments – for example, the use of specialised lighting or appropriate positioning of equipment
- individual counselling and the management of difficult emotions and behaviour – for example, helping the child recognise what triggers outbursts and how to respond
- the use of therapeutic treatments – for example, speech and language therapy, physiotherapy, hydrotherapy, etc.

An effective individual support plan:

- builds on the child's understanding of their own support needs, as well as the views and contributions of parents, carers, families and others
- uses the expertise and involvement of a range of professionals from different agencies that may include therapists, nursing staff, social workers and representatives from the voluntary sector
- can make a significant contribution to an effective and inclusive environment for a disabled child by ensuring that parts of therapeutic programmes are successfully integrated in the activities of the setting.

Your contribution to an individual support plan will depend on your exact role and responsibilities within the setting. You may be involved in developing a plan with an individual child to support learning, play or leisure needs. You may be involved in a variety of planning sessions and meetings, or simply be required to implement the plans of others, such as teachers and/or specialists.

An individual support plan may be either short term (e.g. a week, a month or half term) or long term (e.g. a term, several months or a whole year) and can cover a range of developmental and learning needs, including social, physical, intellectual, communication or emotional. A plan for several months or the whole year will, of course, require more work than a plan for a week or two. An individual support plan should be based on detailed observations and assessments of the child's learning and development. These assessments will include information from parents and appropriate professionals, as well as the observations and assessments made by you and your colleagues.

In practice

Observe a child with additional needs over a period of time (e.g. a week, a month or a half term) which is appropriate to your role in the setting. Using your observations, assess the child's development and make suggestions for the child's future learning needs.

As part of your role in the planning process, you may be involved in making suggestions for the specific content of an individual support plan. You will work in conjunction with colleagues, the special educational needs coordinator (SENCO) and possibly a specialist, such as an educational psychologist, speech and language therapist, physiotherapist or occupational therapist.

The individual support plan should include:

- the child's age and level of development
- the specific area of impairment or special need
- the intended length of the plan
- where and when the plan is to be implemented (e.g. at home, in the setting or both)
- details of the activities to be provided to support learning, play or leisure needs
- who will provide the activities and any necessary support
- the resources required, including any specialist equipment.

AC 5.3 Working with others to provide activities to meet children's additional needs

As appropriate to your own role and responsibilities, you will implement the individual support plan, including providing activities to support the child's learning, play or leisure needs. It is essential that you understand your own role (and that of colleagues) in the planning and carrying out of the programme.

In addition to following the general information on promoting learning and development (see Unit 8), you also need to consider implementing activities in ways that maximise benefit to the child. For example:

- implement activities at a time when the child is receptive
- avoid unnecessary distractions for the child
- keep disruptions to the usual routines of the setting to a minimum
- use appropriate resources, including any specialised learning materials and/or equipment.

Techniques for supporting the learning of children with additional needs

Many children with additional needs will have personal priority needs which are central to their learning and quality of life. Some

---

In practice

Developing a support plan for a child with additional needs

Develop a possible individual support plan for a child with additional needs, based on your observations and assessments from the previous 'In practice' activity (AC 5.2).

Your outline plan could include the following:

- spidergram of activities and/or skills to be developed using headings appropriate to your setting and the child's learning, play or leisure needs (e.g. the Early Years Foundation Stage)
- list of the planning and preparation for the activities, including resources and organisation
- inclusion of the child's activities into the usual routines of the setting, including any necessary modifications
- your role in supporting the child during the activities
- any health and safety issues
- timetable of the first week's activities from the plan
- detailed description of the implementation of at least one activity from the plan (remember to review and evaluate this activity afterwards)
- review and evaluate the whole plan.

If you have never done an outline plan before, ask your tutor for guidance on a format which might be most appropriate to your role within the setting.

---

children may need the provision of a specific therapy or may require paramedical care. Others need to have existing equipment or activities modified or adapted to suit their particular needs. This might involve:

- adapting standard equipment – for example, by having a tray on the table so that objects stay on the table and a child with a visual impairment does not 'lose' objects that fall off

- providing the opportunity to learn sign languages – for example, Makaton or PECS (see pages 61 and 71)
- helping children to maintain good posture, appropriate muscle tone and ease of movement, and promoting skills in independent mobility
- helping children to manage eating and drinking – there is a wide range of specialist aids for eating and drinking, such as angled spoons and suction plates
- promoting relaxation and support to help children manage stress and anxiety – some settings use a sensory room, but a quiet, comfortable area will benefit all children
- providing pain-relieving treatments for painful conditions to ensure children's health and well-being
- promoting children's independence through the use of specialist aids and equipment – for example, non-slip table mats and specially designed cutlery for eating
- developing children's self-esteem (e.g. by encouraging and praising effort as well as achievement)
- allowing children's behaviour and alternative ways of communicating to be acknowledged and understood
- providing appropriate therapies – for example, speech and language therapy, occupational therapy or physiotherapy (support from health services is generally set out as non-educational provision in a child's statement; however, speech and language therapy may be regarded as either educational or non-educational provision)
- planning the use of music, art, drama or movement therapy: these therapies may play a complementary role in the curriculum for individual children and will need to be planned as part of the whole curriculum
- using specialist environments – for example, ball pools, warm-water pools or light and sound stimulation rooms
- providing ramps for wheelchair users
- providing thick pencils and brushes for children with poor fine motor skills

- positioning children so that they learn effectively – for example, by making sure the light falls on the adult's face, so that a child wearing a hearing aid is able to lip-read and a child with a visual impairment can use their residual eyesight to see facial expressions.

Figure OP1.2 Using a multisensory room

The use of a sensory curriculum for profound needs

The multisensory curriculum

All teachers differentiate the curriculum (that is, they provide different learning experiences) in order to meet the range of learning needs in their class. Children who are multisensory impaired are likely to need the curriculum differentiated individually because each child's combination of hearing impairment, visual impairment, other disabilities and learning characteristics will be different.

Case study

Providing for Holly's needs

When Holly, a partially sighted baby, joined the nursery, her key person, Simon, discussed her needs with her parents and contacted the RNIB for information about ways of supporting her development. Simon decided to plan a set of activities that could be used by Holly – and by sighted babies too – based on his research, which found that for profoundly blind and partially sighted babies, it is important to consider the following:

● Offer as wide a range of tactile experiences as possible right from the beginning. So Simon started collecting tactile objects, such as a foil survival blanket to scrunch and reflect, a flat silky cushion containing polystyrene beads, and a pan scourer, lemon reamer, pasta strainer, dishwashing brush.
● Encourage movement: helping babies to become aware of whole-body movements and to learn to tolerate different positions, such as being placed on their stomach. So Simon provided some brightly lit and sound-producing toys to provide the motivation to roll and reach, rearranged the nursery furniture to provide a logical sequence to support the baby when moving – and to help 'mental mapping' of her environment.
● Encourage exploration of sound, rhythm and timing. So Simon provided tactile nursery rhyme prompt cards: he made these using A4 cards and stuck on different fabrics to link touch to a particular song – for example, a piece of fur fabric stuck on card to make a link with 'Round and Round the Garden like a Teddy Bear' or a single shiny silver star stuck onto dark blue card to make a link with 'Twinkle, Twinkle Little Star'; a handbell, rolling chime ball, musical xylophone and a drum.
● Simon also used some of the tactile objects in a treasure basket that could be enjoyed by all the babies in the setting.

Some settings have a multisensory room, which provides opportunities for children with a wide range of special needs. This room features a variety of lights, smells, sounds and touch sensations which help to stimulate each sense. Staff need to be trained in the use of a sensory room so that it works optimally for each child.

Reflective practice

Supporting children with special needs

1 How well does your setting provide for the special needs of children?
2 Is there effective communication between the child's parents or carers and the setting?
3 Do the play experiences and activities avoid stereotyping and ensure that each child has an equal opportunity to take part in activities?

AC 5.3 Progress check

Provide examples of how you have supported children with additional needs to enable them to participate in the full range of activities and experiences in your setting – for example, encouraging the child to participate in activities or modifying activities to meet the child's individual learning, play or leisure needs.

AC 5.4 Encouraging parents/carers to take an active role in their child's development

Working in partnership with families is particularly important when a child has additional support needs. Each parent or carer should be made to feel welcome and valued as an expert on his or her child, playing a vital role in helping practitioners to enable their child to participate and learn.

When liaising with parents about the additional needs of their children, you should consider the family's home background and the expressed wishes of the parents. You must also follow the setting's policies and procedures with regard to specific requirements (e.g. inclusion strategies, policies, procedures and practices). You may need to give parents positive reassurance about their children's care, learning and development. Any concerns or worries expressed by a child's parents should be passed immediately to the appropriate person in the setting. If a parent makes a request to see a colleague or other professional, then you should follow the relevant setting policy and procedures.

Parents and carers often find that the most helpful sources of information and advice come from those with shared experiences. As shown in AC 4.2, there are many organisations that provide support and can answer questions, such as Contact a Family, The Down's Syndrome Association, Mencap and the RNIB.

Communicating with parents and carers
The principles of effective communication are discussed in Unit 2.1.

One of the main purposes of communicating with parents and carers is to provide and to share information about the child and the setting – both about the early years setting and about the home. Practitioners need to build up a partnership with parents and carers, and to do this they need to promote a feeling of trust.

Providing flexible support for the family
Parents and carers want support that is flexible enough to respond to their particular family's needs, both that which is available in an emergency and that which can be planned in advance. Children want support that enables them to do the kinds of things their peers do: this can vary from going swimming with their siblings to spending time away from home with their friends. The most popular services are generally those developed by parents or carers themselves, or by local disability organisations.

Coordinating the support
A single point of contact for the family (such as a key person, link worker or care coordinator), with a holistic view of the child and family, can help the family to find out about what services are available and the roles of different agencies, and help professionals to understand their needs. Families with a single point of contact report better relationships with services, fewer unmet needs, better morale, fewer feelings of isolation and burden, better provision of information about services, greater satisfaction and more parental involvement. Care coordination should ensure that the family's needs for information, advice and help are identified and addressed.

Types of support and information for families include:

- information about communication aids, such as learning to use sign language, Makaton, speech boards
- social and emotional support, such as coming to terms with the impact of disability on the family
- financial support, such as claiming benefits
- information about services and availability, such as housing adaptations
- information about children's and families' rights
- information for parents about their child's condition and how they can support their child's development
- information for children and their family about the condition and treatment, about how to live with the condition and how to overcome disabling barriers
- support that enables families to do activities together, as a whole family
- short-term breaks and domiciliary services
- accessible and appropriate play and leisure services.

AC 5.4 Activity

Find out about the services available to provide support and information for families with children with additional needs in your local area. Visit your local authority website for more information. Examples may include domiciliary services, special nursery provision, play and leisure services, portage and Home-Start.

AC 5.5 Reflecting on own practice in meeting children's additional needs

You should be able to reflect on your own practice as part of your everyday learning. In this way, every experience – whether positive or negative – will contribute to your development and personal growth.

In relation to meeting children's additional needs, reflect upon the following questions:

- Have you regularly observed individual children to help you to identify their holistic needs?
- Have you found out more about a child's particular additional need?
- Have you established a good relationship with the child's parents?
- Do you understand your own role within the setting in planning for children's additional needs?
- Are you able to plan activities to meet the play and learning needs of a child with additional needs?
- Do you regularly review and evaluate your plans and activities?
- Have you identified what you have achieved and what you still need to work on?

Assessment practice

1 Describe factors which may result in children needing additional support in the short term and in the long term.
2 How do your personal experiences, values and beliefs impact on your professional practice?
3 What is meant by inclusive practice? Give examples of inclusive practice.
4 Identify the requirements of current legislation and frameworks in relation to inclusive practice.
5 Why is early intervention important in meeting children's additional needs, and what strategies are in place to facilitate early intervention?
6 Describe the principles of working in partnership with other professionals and agencies to meet children's additional needs.
7 Describe how you have been able to identify the individual needs of children in your own setting.
8 Write a brief summary of the ways in which you have been able to plan (with others) to meet children's additional needs.
9 How can practitioners encourage parents and carers to take an active role in their child's play, learning and development?
10 Show that you have been able to reflect on your own practice when meeting children's additional needs in your setting.

Useful resources

Alcott, M. (2002) *An Introduction to Children with Special Needs*, London: Hodder & Stoughton.

Contact a Family (2004) *Caring for Disabled Children: A Guide for Students and Professionals*, available at www.cafamily.org.uk

Department for Education (2014) *Early Years: Guide to the 0 to 25 SEND Code of Practice*, available at www.gov.uk/government/ publications/send-guide-for-early-years-settings.

Horwath, J. (2001) *The Child's World: Assessing Children in Need*, London: Jessica Kingsley Publishers.

Lindon, J. (2005) *Understanding Child Development: Linking Theory and Practice*, London: Hodder Arnold.

Mortimer, H. (2001) *Special Needs and Early Years Provision*, London: Continuum International Publishing Group.

Wall, K. (2006) *Special Needs and Early Years: A Practitioner's Guide*, London: Paul Chapman Publications.

Wilson, R. (2003) *Special Educational Needs in the Early Years*, London: Routledge Falmer.

Action on Hearing Loss

Action on Hearing Loss is the new name for the Royal National Institute for Deaf People. It is the largest charity in the UK offering a range of services for people who are deaf or have a hearing impairment, and providing information and support on all aspects of deafness, hearing loss and tinnitus.

Advisory Centre for Education

ACE provides independent advice and information for parents on education issues in England.

www.ace-ed.org.uk

Alliance for Inclusive Education

The Alliance for Inclusive Education is a national campaigning organisation led by disabled people.

British Dyslexia Association

The BDA is a national charity working for a 'dyslexia-friendly society' that enables dyslexic people of all ages to reach their full potential.

www.bdadyslexia.org.uk

Early Support

Early Support provides materials for families and professionals, including a service audit tool, a family pack, information for parents and developmental journals on the deaf, Down's syndrome and visual impairments.

www.councilfordisabledchildren.org.uk/what-we-do/networks-campaigning/early-support

Every Disabled Child Matters

www.edcm.org.uk/

Information, Advice and Support Services Network

The IASS Network provides training and support to Information, Advice and Support Services across England.

www.iassnetwork.org.uk

KIDS

KIDS works for disabled children, young people and their families.

National Association of Special Educational Needs

NASEN aims to promote the education, training, advancement and development of all those with special and additional support needs.

www.nasen.org.uk

National Autistic Society

The NAS aims to champion the rights and interests of all people with autism, and to provide individuals with autism and their families with help, support and services.

Royal National Institute of Blind People

The RNIB has produced an excellent booklet, Focus on Foundation, which offers practical advice on the inclusion in early years settings of children who are blind and partially sighted.

www.rnib.org.uk

Scope

Scope is a charity that supports disabled people and their families. Its vision is a world where disabled people have the same opportunities as everyone else. Scope specialises in working with people who have cerebral palsy.

www.scope.org.uk

Unit OP2
Support creative play

Learning outcomes

By the end of this unit, you will:

1 Understand creative play.
2 Be able to support children's creative play.

3 Be able to reflect on own contribution to children's creative play.

LO1 Understand creative play

AC 1.1 What 'creative play' means

Creative play is about experimenting with materials and music. It is not about producing things to go on display or to be taken home; for example, when children are involved with messy finger play with paint, nothing is left at the end of the session once it has been cleared away.

It is often thought that being creative is about the arts. It is, but it is also possible to be creative in scientific and problem-solving ways.

Creative play involves children:

- taking risks and making connections
- exploring their own ideas and expressing them through movement
- making and transforming things using media and materials such as crayons, paints, scissors, words, sounds, movement, props and make believe
- making choices and decisions about their own learning
- responding to what they see, hear and experience through their senses.

The requirement for play in the Development Matters 2012 document states that:

'Play is a key opportunity for children to think creatively and flexibly, solve problems and link ideas. Establish the enabling conditions for rich play: space, time, flexible resources, choice, control, warm and supportive relationships.'

AC 1.2 The role of creative play in children's learning and development

Creative play is made up of the following aspects:

- Being creative: responding in a variety of ways to experiences – what children see, hear, smell, touch or feel. It is also about expressing and communicating their ideas, thoughts and feelings.
- Exploring media and materials: finding out about (by themselves or being guided) and exploring a widening range of media and materials; thinking about and working with colour, texture, shape, space and form in two and three dimensions.
- Creating music and dance: exploring (by themselves or being guided) sound, movement and music; focusing on how sounds can be made and changed and how sounds can be recognised and repeated from a pattern; it includes ways of exploring movement, matching movements to music and singing simple songs from memory.

- Developing imagination and imaginative play: how children are supported to develop and build their imaginations through stories, role play, imaginative play, dance, music, design and art.

Adults can encourage creative play by offering children a range of materials and play opportunities in dance, music, messy play, drawing, collage, painting, model-making and woodwork, sand (small-world scenarios), water (small-world scenarios) and miniature garden scenarios.

Creative play helps children to express their feelings and ideas about people and objects and events. It helps children to:

- be physically coordinated (physical development)
- develop language (language and communication development)
- develop ideas or concepts (intellectual – or cognitive – development)
- develop relationships with people (social development)
- be more confident and boost their self-esteem (emotional development).

AC 1.2 Activity

Explain what 'creative play' is and how it helps children's learning and development.

AC 1.3 How creative play links to learning and development within current frameworks

The Early Years Foundation Stage and creative development

The EYFS guidance for effectively implementing creative development asks practitioners to pay particular attention to the following themes: positive relationships; enabling environments; and learning and development.

Positive relationships

- Ensure that children feel secure enough to 'have a go', to learn new things and to be adventurous.
- Value what children can do and children's own ideas rather than expecting them to reproduce someone else's picture, dance or model, for example.
- Give opportunities for children to work alongside artists and other creative adults so that they see first-hand different ways of expressing and communicating ideas and different responses to media and materials.
- Accommodate children's specific religious or cultural beliefs relating to particular forms of art or methods of representation.

Enabling environments

- Provide a stimulating environment in which creativity, originality and expressiveness are valued.
- Include resources from a variety of cultures to stimulate new ideas and different ways of thinking.
- Offer opportunities for children with visual impairments to access and have physical contact with **artefacts**, materials, spaces and movements.
- Provide opportunities for children with a hearing impairment to experience sound through physical contact with instruments and other sources of sound.
- Encourage children who cannot communicate by voice to respond to music in different ways, such as gestures.

Learning and development

- Present a wide range of experiences and activities that children can respond to by using many of their senses.
- Allow sufficient time for children to explore and develop ideas and finish working through these ideas.
- Create opportunities for children to express their ideas through a wide range of types of representation.

'Early Years Outcomes' (2013) is a non-statutory guide for practitioners and inspectors to help inform understanding of child development through the early years. (This document is available for download at www.gov.uk/government/publications/early-years-outcomes.)

Early learning goals: creative play
Exploring and using media and materials:

- Children sing songs, make music and dance, and experiment with ways of changing them.

Figure OP2.1 Working alongside creative artists in a woodworking activity

- They safely use and explore a variety of materials, tools and techniques, experimenting with colour, design, texture, form and function.

Being imaginative:

- Children use what they have learnt about media and materials in original ways, thinking about uses and purposes.
- They represent their own ideas, thoughts and feelings through design and technology, art, music, dance, role play and stories.

LO2 Be able to support children's creative play

AC 2.1 Planning creative play activities for children

Equipment and activities used to support creative development
Children learn about play from natural and recycled materials as well as specially designed toys and equipment. They need a balance of the two – for example, hollow wooden blocks and cardboard boxes.

Natural materials
These should be attractively presented. They are important for children living in a world where plastic is found everywhere. Natural materials help children to learn about sand, water, wood and clay. They also show children how they can find materials for themselves, and they are cheap to provide.

Recycled materials

These cost nothing to provide. Margarine tubs, bottle corks and plastic bottles, for example, need to be set out in attractive containers, easy to reach and use. Children need enough space and table room for creative play with these materials.

Commercially made equipment

These can be expensive and need to be chosen carefully. Many toys are pre-structured, which means that children can only use them in a narrow way. Open-ended equipment, which can be used in a variety of ways, is better value for money – for example, wooden blocks, Lego or Duplo. If there are plenty of these, children can build exciting models. It is best to have all the same brand, so these can be added to over the years.

Key term

play prop Using objects in dramatic play or role play – for example, a cardboard box might represent a car or an oven; play dough might be made into cakes to go in the oven.

Figure OP2.2 Playing with recycled materials allows children the choice of what to make

Guidelines for good practice

Equipment for creative play

- Check equipment for safety marks.
- Can it be cleaned easily?
- Can it be mended easily or are there replacement parts?
- Is it open-ended so that it can be used in many different ways – for example, doll's house, farm, home area equipment, wooden blocks.

Choosing play materials

Adults need to choose play materials carefully and to create:

- play opportunities
- time to play

- space for play indoors and outdoors
- places for dens, physical play, manipulative play and creative play
- **play props** and clothes for dressing up and role play
- an adapted play environment for children with disabilities.

Adults who provide open-ended materials create more play possibilities for children. You should provide:

- recycled junk materials (string, boxes, wood)
- natural materials (clay, woodwork, sand, water, twigs, leaves, feathers)
- traditional areas (home area, wooden blocks, workshop area with scissors, glue, etc.).

Providing a variety of resources

A painting or drawing activity that allows children to develop their creativity and their fine manipulative skills can be adapted to provide variety by using:

- different-quality paper – sugar, cartridge, 'newsprint', wall lining paper, etc.
- paper of different colours
- different sizes of paper
- different media – pastels, wax crayons, colouring crayons, chalk, etc.
- different types of paint – ready-mixed, powder, thick, thin, fluorescent, pearlised, etc.
- different techniques – finger, bubble, printing, marble rolling, string, etc.

While using such a variety, the children are also learning about textures and colours, and are developing concepts about materials – how runny paint 'behaves', how chalk smudges, etc. Other types of activity – construction, water, sand, small world, role play, etc. – can easily be varied to broaden children's experience.

Progress check

Materials for creative play

1 What is the meaning of 'open-ended' materials?
2 Why is it important to provide open-ended materials?
3 Give three examples of open-ended material provision and three examples of pre-structured material provision.

Creative activities with children

When children are playing creatively – or being creative – they must not be expected to 'make something'. Creative play is about experimenting with materials and music.

Adults can encourage creative play by offering children a range of materials and play opportunities in:

- imaginative play
- messy play
- music, dance and movement.

Imaginative play

In imaginative play, children use their own real-life experiences and rearrange them. It provides opportunities for children to express emotions, such as jealousy, frustration or anger, in a safe and unthreatening way. Imaginative play links with:

- creative play
- role play
- dramatic play
- domestic play
- fantasy play
- play with dolls and small-world objects.

Imaginative play (or pretend play) requires children to invent scenarios and tell stories. Children make play scenarios – for example, about a shop or a boat, a garage, an office, a swimming pool. The important thing to remember about pretend play is that there will be nothing left to show anyone when the play finishes. Pretend-play scenarios do not last. This is why it is sometimes difficult to explain to parents the importance of pretend play.

Playing with hand puppets helps young children to develop creative skills by forcing them to use their imaginations. They make up the roles, the rules, the situations and the solutions by themselves. It is through imaginative play that children come to understand the differences between fantasy and reality. The real world becomes more real to children who have opportunities to pretend.

Imaginative play links with the Early Years Foundation Stage Profile and is part of all seven areas of learning. Pretend play also links with all areas of a child's development: emotional development; social development; language development; cognitive (thinking) development; and physical development.

Whether playing with a friend or with an imaginary character, imaginative play requires children to look beyond their own needs and desires. It encourages children to learn compassion, empathy and understanding.

Activities that support imaginative play

- Role play (or pretend play): children act out roles, usually pretending to be parents or characters from TV programmes or books. They benefit from having access to a home area, with scaled-down cooker, table and chairs, etc.
- Small-world play: small-scale models of people, animals, cars, doll's houses and fake food are useful in imaginative play. Children are familiar with these objects and playing with them helps them to relax and also to extend their language skills.
- Dressing-up activities: playing with dressing-up clothes stimulates imaginative play and pretending to be an adult (parent, superhero, king or queen) allows children to feel in control and empathise with others.
- Puppets and dolls (or teddies): these can often help a withdrawn or shy child to voice their hidden feelings – by using the puppet's voice. This type of play may also help children to vent their powerful emotions (e.g. jealousy of a new baby) by shouting at the teddy.

Home area

The home area is one of the most important areas in early years settings. The home area should ideally have:

- some items that are like those in the child's home, e.g. cups, cooking pots
- objects from a range of cultures
- a proper place for everything, and children should be encouraged to tidy up carefully
- a large dresser – with hooks for cups and cupboards to store dishes and saucepans
- big, middle-sized and small dolls, representing children of different cultures
- a cooker (this can be homemade, e.g. from a cardboard box)
- wooden boxes, which can be used as beds, tables, chairs
- food that is pre-structured (plastic fruit), transformable (dough), real (a salad) or pretend
- clothes that can be kept in a chest of drawers, labelled with pictures and words
- magazines, notepads and writing implements, which can be put by the telephone, and perhaps a bookcase with books
- adaptations for children with disabilities – for example, a child who is a wheelchair user will need a low table so that they can use the bowls and plates, etc.

Outdoors, the home area could be a den.

- Old furniture can be used outside to make a home area. An old airer (clothes horse) with a sheet or blanket over it makes good walls.
- Children can make pretend food using sand, water and messy materials.

- A rug can be put in the den and furniture can be made by collecting spare cardboard boxes (e.g. they can become tables or beds for dolls).
- Cushions can make seats or beds.
- A box on its side can become a cupboard with flaps as the cupboard doors.
- Cups and saucers can be made out of old yoghurt pots and margarine containers.

Home area safety

- Wooden equipment should be checked regularly for rough edges and splinters.
- Cutlery must be carefully introduced. Ask your supervisor for advice.
- Glass and china break easily and should not be used in the home area.

Figure OP2.3 Playing in the home area

As children get older, their home area play changes:

- At one to two years: children carry materials such as pots, pans, dolls, etc. about; they put them in and out of boxes and prams and put them in rows.
- At two to three years: they begin to make play scenarios, often about food.
- At three to five years: stories develop about a wider range of events and people.

Dressing-up clothes

Children enjoy wearing dressing-up clothes indoors and outdoors.

- The clothes need to be simple and flexible in use.
- A basic cape, some basic hats, including 'uniform' hats such as a firefighter's helmet, scarves and drapes, saris, tunic, shoes and baggy trousers help children in role playing. Clothing needs to reflect different cultures.
- Fastenings should be varied to give children different experiences of connecting clothes together, e.g. zips, buttons, tying bows, buckles and Velcro.
- The clothes need to be hanging on a rack, with separate boxes for shoes and hats. A large safety mirror at child height is useful.

Dressing-up safety

- There should be no strings, ribbons or purses on strings around the neck, which might strangle a child.
- Beware of children tripping over clothes that are too long.
- Make sure children wear suitable footwear – for example, no high heels when playing on climbing frames or running outdoors.
- Clothes should be washed regularly.

As children get older, their dressing-up play changes:

- At one to two years: children wear hats and shoes.
- At two to three years: children wear hats, shoes, capes and scarves.
- At three to five years: children are more adventurous – they begin to wear whole outfits and want more accuracy to look right for the role they play.

Small-world play

Garages, farms, zoos, space scenes, domestic scenes, hospitals, boats and castles all feature in small-world play.

Children can easily create play scenarios with pretend people and make up imaginative stories using small-world materials to help them. These are best set out on a floor mat or carpet, or in a sand tray (see 'Sand and water play').

- Miniature gardens make a good play scene; these can be made in seed trays from garden centres and put on tables.
- Children can make their own gardens and make up stories using them – pots of moss, gravel, twigs, pebbles and feathers.
- They can also make paths, trees, grass and hills.
- Older children begin to use doll's houses, garages and castles.

Small-world play safety

- Check that the pieces are not so small that a younger child might choke.

As children get older, their small-world play changes:

- At one to two years: children mainly put toys in rows and make constructions.
- At two to four years: they make more complex constructions, e.g. a house, simple everyday stories.
- At four to six years: children use play scenarios, e.g. going shopping, and stories with different people, e.g. hospital scenes, outer space, garage scenes.

Messy play

When children are given the opportunity to engage in messy play, they are able to use all their senses to explore materials, moulding, manipulating and combining them to make exciting discoveries about their world. By emphasising the sensory and exploratory aspects of messy play, each child is able to enjoy and explore the materials rather than aiming to produce something at the end of it. Messy play involves:

- children using all their senses in the process of exploration, especially the sense of touch
- offering children plenty of opportunity to mould and manipulate materials
- not having a focus on making or producing something.

The outdoor play area offers all sorts of opportunities for messy play. Children can make the most of natural resources and work on a larger scale than is possible indoors. For example, children can:

- dig deep in sand and soil
- make and explore mud – in particular, making mud pies
- splash in puddles and explore water in paddling pools
- move water using guttering, pumps and pipes
- mix large amounts of sand and water.

Activities which support messy play

Indoor messy play includes the following activities:

- Water: for babies, use flannels, sponges and baby bath bubbles. Older children can use different-sized containers for filling and pouring, plastic balls, small toys, tea sets, plastic bottles.
- Gloop: add water to cornflour and mix to make a runny, milkshake consistency. Food colouring can be added. Children of all ages love to play with it as it can appear 'solid' but as soon as it is handled, it runs like water through the fingers. It can be played with indoors or outside if you put it on a tray.
- Pasta: cook spaghetti in water with a few drops of cooking oil to stop the pasta sticking together.
- Paint: use large stubby brushes, toothbrushes, house decorating brushes and different types of paper (or paint outside with water).
- Glue: thin down PVA glue as this makes it easier to spread. Stick large items such as ribbons, string, cake cases and fabric.
- Shaving foam (for sensitive skin), whipped cream: use in shallow containers and use fingers to make patterns. Using a large tray will allow a baby or toddler to sit or stand in it and experience the textures through their feet or body.

Figure OP2.4 Messy play

- Cereals: lift cereal up and let it trickle through the child's fingers. Toddlers will enjoy stamping on it in bare feet or pouring and scooping it in and out of cups and bowls.
- Jelly: mash up green jelly to make a swamp and add toy animals.

Messy play safety

- Check that paints, glues and other substances are designed for children.
- Do not use tiny things that could become a choking hazard – for example, lentils.
- Supervise these activities at all times.

Sand and water play

Sand can be offered in a commercial sand tray, in seed boxes from a garden shop or in washing-up bowls on tables. It can be poured on to a plastic mat and used as a 'beach' experience with shells, buckets, spades and pebbles. The mat can be rolled up at the end of the session and the sand poured into a sand tray to use again. There should always be both wet and dry sand on offer – for example, dry sand in bowls on tables and wet sand in a sand tray. Provide jugs, scoops, funnels, sponges, small-world scenarios, farms, tubes, spades, small buckets and rakes. Miniature gardens can be made adding twigs, moss and leaves.

Sand and water play outside is similar to indoors. However, the following equipment can also be used outdoors:

- hoses
- watering cans
- water-washable paint for use on tarmac (using buckets of water and giant brushes)
- large, covered sandpit where several children can play.

Sand and water play safety

- Make sure that sand and water play is carefully supervised.
- Be alert as children can drown in very shallow water, get sand in their eyes or slip on wet floors.
- Outdoor sandpits need covers to keep animals and insects out.
- Place the indoor water tray near to the sink (because it is heavy and in case people slip).
- Change the water every day.
- Always sweep the floor after sand play.
- Use a mop to ensure floors are not slippery after water play.

As children get older, their sand and water play changes:

- At one to two years: children begin by pouring and carrying water and sand and by putting these materials in and out of containers.
- At three to five years: children begin to enjoy practical problems and to solve them as they develop their learning – for example, how to make a strong jet of water, how to make sand keep its shape.
- At five to seven years: children's play scenarios have more of a story than before. They use a variety of play people and cooperate more with other children.

Clay, dough and mud patches

Children often do not make anything in particular because this is creative play.

Clay can be brown or grey. It is stored by rolling it into a ball, the size of a large orange, pressing a thumb into it, pouring water into the hole, and covering the hole full of water with clay. It should then be stored in a bin with a well-fitting lid.

A mud patch for digging is a popular area outdoors. Spades and rakes with short handles are useful. Children love to bury things and fill holes with water. They enjoy planting flowers and vegetables.

Clay and dough play safety

- Play dough must be made using salt and cream of tartar if it is to be stored and used more than once.
- Deter children from putting the dough in their mouths. Be extra vigilant with children who have coeliac disease as they must not consume any gluten (present in ordinary flour).

As children get older, their play with clay and dough changes:

Figure OP2.5 This girl was fascinated by the water-filled balloons and received a big surprise when exploring one with her teeth!

- At one to three years: children bash and bang clay.
- At three to five years: they learn to pinch, pull and roll it as well. They can make shapes. They choose their tools or use their hands more carefully. They begin to design and make models, which they sometimes like to keep and display, but not often.

Painting and drawing

For drawing, children need a variety of materials to draw with (fat and thin felt pens, chubby crayons, pastels, chalks, charcoal and pencils). Different sizes, textures, shapes and colours of paper should be attractively set out and stored on shelves or in boxes or trays.

Figure OP2.6 Children painting

For painting, provide a variety of paints – freshly mixed every day – and brushes, clean water, non-spill paint containers, and pots to mix colours.

- Children need a range of paintbrushes (thick, medium and thin), ideally made from good-quality hog's hair. Poor-quality brushes lead to poor-quality paintings and are frustrating to use.
- Flat tables are easier for younger children to use than easels.
- Children should choose which paper and tools to use.
- A well-designed paint dryer which stacks paintings while allowing them to dry is ideal, but you can spread paintings out on

the floor under a radiator, or hang with pegs to dry from a washing line.
- Mixing colours: it is best only to provide primary colours (red, blue and yellow paints) and to make shades by adding white or black to lighten or darken the colours:

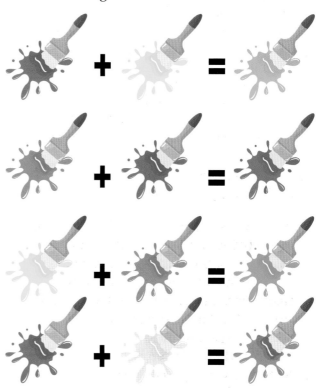

Figure OP2.7 Colour mixing chart

- Children can mix their own colours if these are presented in large tins in the middle of the table, with a spoon in each tin. Patty pan pallets can be used for mixing, and water can be scooped with a small ladle from a large bowl in the centre into small, easily manageable jugs. In this way, children can pour small amounts and learn to mix the colours and shades of paint they need with a paintbrush.
- Children need encouragement to wear aprons. Those they step into using their arms first are the most popular, as aprons over the head can be frightening for very young children.
- If children want to keep their paintings or drawings, they need to be kept in a safe place. They might like to see them displayed on the wall. They must have the right to say if they do not want this.

- Painting is a messy activity, which is probably why it is not always done in the home. Protect the floor, easels and tables with newspaper.
- Young children should always be given the opportunity to express themselves through painting, undisturbed by adults. Adults should never interrupt, ask questions about the child's painting or make their own suggestions; these actions will discourage creativity and may stop the children from valuing their own work.
- Many children are not interested in the product of their paintings. At this stage, they are interested in the process.

Painting and drawing safety

- Children should be discouraged from walking around with pencils or brushes in their mouths, in case they fall and injure themselves or someone else.
- Mop up any major water spills quickly to avoid floors becoming slippery.

Music, dance and movement

Although different cultures have their own traditions, music is a 'universal' language and is, therefore, accessible to everyone. Our bodies have a natural rhythm – the heartbeat and pulse – and even those with hearing impairments can be aware of rhythms and vibrations caused by sound.

Nursery, finger and action rhymes are often the first songs that children participate in and each family will use its own favourites. Work settings usually introduce an even wider range to children. These rhymes help to develop children's sense of rhythm as well as increasing their vocabulary and, perhaps, encouraging their number skills (counting up and down) or naming of body parts, etc.

Activities to support music, dance and movement

Listening to music – live or taped

Try to introduce a wide range, including music from different cultures – East Asian folk tunes, pan pipes from South America, unaccompanied vocal music from other continents, as well as military band music and western styles. The extracts should not be too long and you can encourage active listening by asking children to focus on one aspect, such as the tempo (speed), the tune or the rhythm.

Singing

This can be well-known rhymes or games that involve children imitating a short tune sung by an adult (or – with older, confident children – a child). Regular singing games develop children's listening skills and ability to discriminate sound, particularly helping them to 'pitch' a note more accurately.

Playing instruments

This involves many skills – physical, listening, social and intellectual. The best, and most available, instruments are our own bodies. Body percussion involves hitting, flicking, tapping, thumping, etc. different parts of the body to produce a wide range of sounds – try chests, fingernails, teeth, cheeks with mouths open; in fact, anything, not forgetting the human voice! Children learn to control their movements to create loud and soft sounds, fast and slow rhythms.

Any bought instruments available should be of good quality and produce pleasing sounds. Cheap ones are not sufficiently durable and often create a poor sound. Although tuned percussion instruments (i.e. xylophone, glockenspiel, metallophone) are likely to be found in schools, individual, child-friendly instruments are better for younger children who may not be ready to share. A good range could include untuned percussion – tulip blocks, cabasa, guiro (or scraper), maracas, tambour (hand-held drum), tambourine (a tambour but with the metal discs around the side), castanets (on a hand-held stick), claves (or rhythm sticks), click-clacks, bongo drums, as well as Indian bells, triangle and beater, individual chime bars and beaters, cow bells and hand-held bells. A group of instruments can be placed in a 'sound' corner for children to experiment with on their own or in pairs – perhaps all 'wooden' instruments on one occasion or 'ones which are struck with a beater' another time.

Playing musical instruments in a group

Large group sessions can be difficult to organise but some simple rules can make them enjoyable and worthwhile for all:

- Sitting in a circle and reinforcing the names of instruments as they are given out helps to keep things under control. Even three-year-olds can understand that they must leave their instrument on the floor in front of them until asked to pick it up, although this is not easy in the first instance.
- Having a go: it is usually a good idea to allow children to 'have a go' with their instruments before doing a more focused activity. The whole point of the games is for children to experience music making so there must be plenty of playing and experimenting and not too much sitting around waiting!
- Taking turns to listen to each child make as many different sounds on her instrument in as many ways as she can is a good way of building her confidence and understanding that there is no right or wrong way.
- Offer choices: children can choose the sounds they like best. Similarly, work can focus on dynamics – loud and soft – and children can be asked to play as loudly as they can and as quietly as they can. Which instruments were difficult to do this with? Why?
- Taking turns to play: another activity involves each child having an instrument – this time, make sure there are some which resonate (i.e. go on sounding after they have been played or struck) as well as the wooden percussion instruments. Going around the group, one child plays her instrument and the next child cannot play until the sound has died away. Discuss which instruments had 'long' sounds and which 'short' ones.

Moving to music

This allows children to respond creatively to different sounds and rhythms. A wide variety should be available, as for listening. Circle singing games such as 'The farmer's in his den', 'Ring-a-ring o' roses' and 'Here we go round the mulberry bush' all encourage children to move in time with the pulse or beat.

Composing music

Choosing sounds and putting them together in patterns around silence to create their own tunes and rhythms can develop listening and intellectual skills.

Using homemade instruments

This adds variety and interest. The most successful of these are shakers made from 'found materials' using different containers – tins, plastic pots, boxes (these must be clean and have close-fitting lids) and choosing contents which will produce interesting sounds. These could be rice grains, lentils, chickpeas, black-eyed beans, runner bean seeds, dried pasta, stones and sand. Under supervision, children can experiment and choose the contents, the amount and the container. If they are to be used continually, it is a good idea to glue the lids on to avoid the danger of children putting small items in their mouths. They can also be decorated or covered in patterned sticky-backed plastic.

AC 2.1 **Progress check**

Using the information in this section, plan creative play activities for children in each of the following areas: imaginative play, messy play, and music, dance and movement.

AC 2.2 Implementing creative play activities with children

Providing opportunities for creative play

Helping children to be creative is as much about encouraging attitudes of curiosity and questioning as about skills or techniques. Children notice everything and closely observe the most ordinary things that adults often take for granted.

- Building on children's interests can lead to them creating amazing inventions or making marks on paper that represent for them an experience or something they have seen.
- Encouraging children to choose and use materials and resources in an open-ended way helps them to make choices and to have confidence in their own ideas.
- Retaining childhood confidence in their ideas and skills can easily be lost if others 'take over' and try to suggest what the child is making, thinking or doing. Just expressing an interest in the process a child has gone through is often enough, or asking open questions such as 'Can you tell me about it – that looks interesting' may be all that is required to help a child hold on to their remarkable creativity.

AC 2.2 Progress check

Using the information in AC 2.1, use the plans you made and implement creative play activities with children that support imaginative play, messy play, and music, dance and movement.

AC 2.3 Encouragement and praise during creative play activities

One of the best ways to help children to develop their creative skills is to talk about what they have done. By talking with children about their activity, you are showing that you value their art or creative thinking. Adults should not interrupt the child during the activity or make suggestions. It is not helpful to ask a child 'What is it?' when he or she brings a model or drawing to show you. However, encouraging children to talk about what they have already done will promote language development as well as letting children know that you appreciate their efforts.

Children need confidence to learn anything, and knowing that you value what they do can help them to be more adventurous. Most settings display children's work or put them in a personal folder. This helps children to feel that their work is valued and encourages them to try the experience again.

Displaying children's work

Displaying work imaginatively is one way of showing children that their contribution and creativity are valued.

Displays need not be static or one-dimensional. If you have the space, plan displays that children can easily see, interact with and enjoy. Music, dance, drama and the visual arts can all be recorded or photographed and easily shared with the help of digital technology

LO3 Be able to reflect on own contribution to children's creative play

AC 3.1 How professional practice contributes to children's learning during creative play

As a practitioner, you need to think about the following questions:

- Do you ensure that there is enough time for children to express their thoughts, ideas and feelings in a variety of ways, such as in role play, by painting and by responding to music?
- Do you encourage children to discuss and appreciate the beauty around them in nature and the environment?
- Do you provide a wide range of materials, resources and sensory experiences to enable children to explore colour, texture and space?
- Do you provide a place where work in progress can be kept safely?
- Do you provide open-ended resources that can be used, moved and combined in a variety of ways?

- Do you introduce vocabulary to enable children to talk about their observations and experiences – for example, smooth, shiny, rough, prickly, flat, patterned, jagged, bumpy, soft and hard?
- Do you provide experiences that involve all the senses and movement?

Reviewing your own working practice

Reflection on your own practice is important because it allows you to assess what you are doing well and to identify areas where you might like or need more training or guidance to ensure:

- you are performing to the best you can
- you are meeting all standards and expectations within the setting's policies and procedures.

It also helps you to think about what you are doing and to be aware at all times of how you work with children, families and colleagues.

> ### Progress check ✔
>
> **Reviewing your practice**
> 1 Using the questions above, think of three examples when you have successfully supported children's creative play.
> 2 Explain why those particular activities were successful.
> 3 Use the questions to explore areas where you feel activities were not successful and think of reasons for this.

> ### Reflective practice ❓
>
> **Creative development**
> - What open-ended activities do you provide for children in your setting?
> - Do you give children the experience of playing with paint and glue before expecting them to use them to make a product, such as a greetings card?
> - Have you ever taped or filmed your interactions with children to see how you support their creative development?

Adapting your own practice to meet individual children's needs

Every setting is different and, of course, every child is unique. Most children love the opportunity to be creative, but you may have children in your setting who have difficulties in a particular area. For example, some children might not like getting dirty when painting or modelling with clay. Others might be too angry or fearful to act out their feelings through dramatic play. However, they may be able to draw a picture that expresses their emotions. A child with poor fine motor skills may become frustrated when trying to express herself creatively. It is important that you know how to **review** and adapt your own practice to meet the needs of each individual child.

> ### In practice
>
> **Meeting individual needs**
> 1 Choose a child in your setting who requires additional help with some aspect of creative play.
> 2 Make an assessment of the child's needs.
> 3 Plan a programme or activity that will help to meet those needs.
> 4 Implement the activity.
> 5 Evaluate the activity.

> ### Key term 🔑
>
> review Look back over the topic or activity and make or identify adjustments, changes or additions that would improve the topic or activity.

AC 3.2 How to identify next steps for children's learning and development

The EYFS places strong emphasis on meeting children's individual needs in the setting. Practitioners are expected to meet children's individual needs and to support them in taking the next steps in their development.

Assessment practice

1 Explain what is meant by the term 'creative play'.
2 Why is creative play so important in children's learning and development?
3 How does creative play link to areas of learning and development within the EYFS?
4 Plan and implement creative play activities for children that support imaginative play.
5 Plan and implement creative play activities for children that support messy play.
6 Plan and implement creative play activities for children that support music, dance and movement.
7 How can you use encouragement and praise when supporting children during creative play activities?
8 Reflect on how your own professional practice has contributed to children's learning and development during creative play.
9 How can you ensure that you identify next steps for children's learning and development through creative play?

- Children feel secure when they take part in activities which interest them – for example, role play or stories. You can help children to build on prior learning by pitching the play or story at a level that is demanding but still within the child's reach.
- Conversation, open-ended questions and thinking out loud are important tools in developing vocabulary and in challenging thinking. For example, you can find out about a child's learning by asking questions such as 'How can we make a noise like rain falling?' 'Can you find a way to make the two pieces into just one piece?' 'Can you think of another way to do that?'
- Encouraging children to reflect on and tell others what they have been doing – 'I wonder if…?' – helps them to give voice to what they know and to practise creative thinking and new vocabulary.
- Practitioners need to share information gained from assessment to develop:
  - the planning for individual children to promote progression – that is, the next steps in their learning
  - the systems for observing and assessing what the children know and can do and then use the information to plan effectively for the next steps in their learning

- skills in observation and assessment in order to plan to meet young children's individual needs.
- the ability to group children for particular activities and interests

In practice

Sometimes a child naturally revisits a previous activity and – with a bit of support – achieves the next step. As long as you are aware of what the next step is, and appropriate resources are provided for the child to revisit their activity or progress it quite naturally, then the child can 'lead' his or her own activity and achieve the next step in learning. This encourages enjoyment and spontaneity.

Useful resources

Bruce, T. (2011) *Cultivating Creativity: Babies, Toddlers and Young Children*, London: Hodder Education.

5x5x5=creativity

An independent, arts-based action research organisation that supports children in their exploration and expression of ideas, helping them to develop creative skills for life.

EFYS and associated document links

www.foundationyears.org.uk/eyfs-statutory-framework

Unit 1.1

Support healthy lifestyles for children through the provision of food and nutrition

Learning outcomes

By the end of this unit, you will:

1 Understand the impact of food and nutrition on children's health and development.
2 Understand how food choices impact on health and development during pre-pregnancy, pregnancy and breastfeeding.
3 Understand the nutritional needs of children.

4 Understand the impact of poor diet on children's health and development.
5 Understand individuals' dietary requirements and preferences.
6 Be able to support healthy eating in own setting.

LO1 Understand the impact of food and nutrition on children's health and development

AC 1.1 What is healthy eating?

A healthy diet consists of eating a variety of foods from the four main food groups every day (potato and cereals, fruit and vegetables, milk and milk products and high-protein foods like meat, fish, eggs or nuts), to help the body to grow and to provide energy. It must include enough nutrients (proteins, fats, carbohydrates, vitamins, minerals and fibre) as well as water to fuel and maintain the body's vital functions. See the NHS eatwell plate, Figure 1.1.2.

Key term

nutrients The essential components of food which provide the individual with the necessary requirements for bodily functions.

Good nutrition, or healthy eating, is important for children under five to:

- ensure that they get enough energy (calories) and nutrients when they are growing rapidly
- but not too much as this may lead to children becoming overweight or obese
- encourage them to eat a wide variety of foods and to develop good dietary habits to take with them into later childhood and adulthood.

A healthy diet for very young children should:

- offer plenty of choice and balance
- contain lots of fruit and vegetables
- contain lots of starchy foods, bread, rice, potatoes and pasta
- contain calcium and iron-rich foods – milk and dairy, and other sources of protein, such as meat, fish, eggs and beans
- include regular healthy meals and snacks
- be low in salt and added sugar.

AC 1.1 Activity

Check that you know which nutrients are needed for a healthy diet and explain what is meant by healthy eating. In a group, discuss what you think is meant by healthy eating. What are the main features of a healthy diet?

AC 1.2 National and local initiatives which promote healthy eating

The Eat Better, Start Better programme
This programme is run by The Children's Food Trust and aims to help early years providers meet children's nutritional needs more consistently and to help families with young children to develop the cooking skills and confidence they need to cook and eat more healthily. Their practical guide includes the government-backed *Voluntary Food and Drink Guidelines for Early Years Settings in England*, as well as advice on encouraging children to eat well, including managing fussy eating and special dietary requirements.

The Schools Fruit and Vegetable Scheme (SFV)
It is recommended that children – like adults – eat at least five portions of fruit and vegetables every day. Children aged between four and six who attend a fully state-funded infant, primary or special school are entitled to receive a free piece of fruit or vegetable each school day.

Feeding Young Imaginations
The Pre-school Learning Alliance's campaign, Feeding Young Imaginations, supports parents and early years groups by providing information to promote a balanced diet for under-fives.

The Children's Food Campaign
Sustain (the alliance for better food and farming) launched the Children's Food Campaign. It wants to improve young people's health and well-being through:

- good food and real food education in every school
- protecting children from junk food marketing
- clear food labelling that everyone, including children, can understand.

Cool Milk
Cool Milk works in partnership with local authorities and early years groups to supply free and subsidised school milk to children in

1 medium apple 2 broccoli florets 2 halves of canned peaches

1 handful of grapes 1 medium banana 3 heaped tablespoons of peas

1 medium glass of orange juice 7 strawberries 3 whole dried apricots

5 A DAY

Just Eat More (fruit & veg) 3 heaped tablespoons of cooked kidney beans 16 okra NHS

Figure 1.1.1 'Just eat more' portion poster for the NHS Five a day programme

pre-schools, nurseries and primary schools. Cool Milk aims to make the provision of milk easier for schools, nurseries, local authorities and parents, while promoting the important health benefits and learning opportunities that school milk offers.

Change4Life
The School Food Trust supports the NHS Change4Life programme by ensuring that as many children as possible are eating healthy school food. All school lunches must now meet nutrient-based standards to ensure that they provide children with the fuel they need to lead a healthy, active lifestyle. Change4Life also provides guidance and resources on the following:

- healthier breakfast clubs
- healthier tuck shops

- water provision
- healthier vending machines
- healthier lunchboxes
- dining room environment
- healthier cookery clubs.

The Nursery Milk Scheme

The Nursery Milk Scheme enables:

- children under five to receive free of charge 189 ml (one-third of a pint) of milk for every day they attend approved day care facilities for two hours or more
- babies aged under 12 months to receive dried baby milk made up to 189 ml (one-third of a pint)
- day care providers who have been approved to supply milk under the scheme to be reimbursed for the cost of the milk they supply.

Eat Smart, Play Smart

Eat Smart, Play Smart is a Food Standards Agency teaching resource developed for primary school teachers throughout the UK to use with children aged five to seven years. Eat Smart, Play Smart materials have been developed to:

- help children to understand the need for healthy diets and to choose appropriately from different food groups for their meals
- encourage children to be more active in their everyday lives and to understand the benefits of being active; strategies for increasing activity in the home and at school are suggested in fun, energetic and easy-to-follow ways.

AC 1.2 Activity

Find out about and evaluate local initiatives to promote healthy eating in your area. See, for example, the information for Change4Life in the 'Useful resources' section on page 336.

AC 1.3 Food and drink requirements in relation to current frameworks

The statutory framework for the Early Years Foundation Stage (EYFS) states the following:

- Where early years settings give children meals, snacks and drinks, these must be healthy, balanced and nutritious.
- Before a child is admitted to the setting, the provider must obtain information about any special dietary requirements, preferences and food allergies that the child has, and any special health requirements.
- Fresh drinking water must be available and accessible at all times.
- Providers must record and act on information from parents and carers about a child's dietary needs.
- There must be an area which is adequately equipped to provide healthy meals, snacks and drinks for children as necessary.
- There must be suitable facilities for the hygienic preparation of food for children, if necessary including suitable sterilisation equipment for babies' food.
- Providers must be confident that those responsible for preparing and handling food are competent to do so. In group provision, all staff involved in preparing and handling food must receive training in food hygiene.

Food requirements vary according to age, gender, size, occupation or lifestyle, and climate. Different foods contain different amounts of energy per unit of weight; foods that contain a lot of fat and sugar have high energy values.

Food energy is traditionally measured in calories (kcal) or kilojoules (kJ).

- 1 kcal = 4.2 kJ
- 1000 kJ = 1 MJ (mega joule) = 239 kcal

An excess of calories will result in weight gain, as the surplus 'energy' is stored as fat; an insufficient intake of calories will result in weight loss, as the body has to draw on fat reserves to meet energy requirements. Babies and young children have relatively high energy requirements in relation to their size. The food and drink requirements for young children are discussed in LO3 on page 313.

AC 1.3 — Progress check ✔

Read through the statutory framework requirements for food and eating. Does your setting comply with all the requirements? For example, is fresh drinking water available and accessible at all times?

LO2 Understand how food choices impact on health and development during pre-pregnancy, pregnancy and breastfeeding

AC 2.1 The impact of food choices during pre-pregnancy, pregnancy and breastfeeding

Pre-pregnancy diet

Following a healthy balanced diet before a woman becomes pregnant will allow her to build up reserves of the nutrients vital to the unborn baby in the first three months. Guidelines for a healthy pre-pregnancy diet include the following:

- Eat something from the four main food groups every day (potato and cereals, fruit and vegetables, milk and milk products, and high protein foods).
- Cut down on sugary foods and eat fresh foods where possible.
- Avoid pre-packed foods and any foods which carry the risk of **salmonella** or **listeria** – such as soft or blue-veined cheeses, pâté, liver and raw meat.
- Do not go on a slimming diet: follow your appetite and do not eat more than you need.
- Vegetarian diets which include milk, fish, cheese and eggs provide the vital protein the baby needs.

- Vegans should eat soya products and nuts and pulses to supply protein, and vitamin B12 may need to be taken as a supplement.
- Folic acid tablets and a diet rich in folic acid taken both pre-pregnancy and in pregnancy help the development of the brain and spinal cord and also help to prevent defects such as **spina bifida**. Sources of folic acid include broccoli, nuts and wholegrain cereals.

Key terms 🔑

listeria and **salmonella** Bacteria that can cause food poisoning.

spina bifida This occurs when the spinal canal in the vertebral columns is not closed (although it may be covered with skin). Individuals with spina bifida can have a wide range of physical disabilities. In severe forms, the spinal cord bulges out of the back, the legs and bladder may be paralysed, and obstruction to the fluid surrounding the brain causes it to build up around the brain.

Diet during pregnancy

Every pregnant woman hears about 'eating for two' but the best information available today suggests that this is not good advice. Research shows that the quality (not quantity) of a baby's nutrition before birth lays the foundation for good health in later life. Therefore, during pregnancy women should eat a well-balanced diet. See the guidelines in the box below.

Foods to avoid during pregnancy

During pregnancy, women should avoid certain foods. Sometimes this is because they cause problems such as food poisoning. At other times, certain foods contain harmful bacteria and toxins which can cause serious problems for the unborn baby.

Nutrition for mothers who breastfeed their baby

If the mother is going to breastfeed her baby, she should follow the principles for the healthy diet in pregnancy. Both calcium and

Guidelines for good practice

A healthy diet in pregnancy

- Lean meat, fish, eggs, cheese, beans and lentils are all good sources of nutrients. Eat some every day.
- Starchy foods like bread, potatoes, rice, pasta and breakfast cereals should – with vegetables – form the main part of any meal.
- Dairy products, like milk, cheese and yoghurt, are important as they contain calcium and other nutrients needed for the baby's development.
- Citrus fruit, tomatoes, broccoli, blackcurrants and potatoes are good sources of vitamin C, which is needed to help the absorption of iron from non-meat sources.
- Cut down on sugar and sugary foods like sweets, biscuits and cakes, and sugary drinks like cola.
- Eat plenty of fruit and vegetables that provide vitamins, minerals and fibre. Eat them lightly cooked or raw.
- Green, leafy vegetables, lean meat, dried fruit and nuts contain iron, which is important for preventing anaemia.
- Dairy products, fish with edible bones like sardines, bread, nuts and green vegetables are rich in calcium, which is vital for making bones and teeth.
- Margarine or oily fish (e.g. tinned sardines) contain vitamin D to keep bones healthy.
- Include plenty of fibre in the daily diet; this will prevent constipation, and help to keep the calorie intake down.
- Cut down on fat and fatty foods. Reducing fat has the effect of reducing energy intake; it is important that these calories are replaced in the form of carbohydrate. Fat should not be avoided completely, however, as certain types are essential for body functioning, as well as containing fat-soluble vitamins.
- Folic acid is a B vitamin which is very important throughout pregnancy, but especially in the first 12 weeks when the baby's systems are being formed. (Most doctors recommend that pregnant women take a folic acid supplement every day, as more folic acid is required than is available from a normal diet.)
- Department of Health advice is to eat according to appetite, with only a small increase in energy intake for the last three months of the pregnancy (an extra 200 kcal a day).

Table 1.1.1 Foods to avoid during pregnancy

Foods to avoid	Reasons

- Soft and blue-veined cheese, such as Camembert, Brie, Stilton and chèvre, goat's cheese
- Pâté (any type, including liver pâté and vegetable pâté)
- Prepared salads (such as potato salad and coleslaw)
- Ready-prepared meals or reheated food, unless they are piping hot all the way through
	Listeria:
	
	- High levels of the listeria bacteria are occasionally found in prepared foods.
	- Some ready-prepared meals are not always heated at a high enough temperature to destroy the bacteria.
	- Listeriosis (infection with listeria bacteria) can cause problems for the unborn child, such as:
	   - miscarriage - meningitis
	   - stillbirth - pneumonia.

- Raw or partially cooked eggs, such as homemade mayonnaise, and some mousses and sauces - Unpasteurised milk (both goats' and cows' milk)	Salmonella: - Salmonella is found in unpasteurised milk, raw eggs and raw egg products, raw poultry and raw meat. - Eggs should only be eaten if they are cooked until both the white and the yolk are solid. - Salmonella food poisoning could cause miscarriage or premature birth.

→

Table 1.1.1 Foods to avoid during pregnancy (*continued*)

Foods to avoid	Reasons
• Some types of fish, such as shark, swordfish and marlin	High levels of mercury: • High levels of mercury can harm a baby's developing nervous system. • Women should eat no more than two tuna steaks a week (or four cans of tinned tuna). • High levels of mercury can cross the placenta and may cause delayed development.
• Unwashed raw fruit and vegetables • Raw or undercooked meat	Toxoplasmosis: • Toxoplasmosis is an infection caused by a parasite found in cat faeces. It can also be present in raw or undercooked meat, and in soil left on unwashed fruit and vegetables. • Although rare, the infection can occasionally be passed to the unborn baby, which can cause serious problems, such as miscarriage, stillbirth, eye damage and hydrocephalus.
• Liver and liver products (e.g. liver pâté)	Too much vitamin A: • Women should avoid eating liver and liver products such as pâté and avoid taking supplements containing vitamin A or fish liver oils (which contain high levels of vitamin A). • If high levels of vitamin A build up in the body, they can cause serious problems, including birth defects.
• Peanuts and foods that contain peanuts	Peanut allergy: • Avoiding foods like peanuts – and foods that contain peanuts – may reduce the baby's chances of developing a potentially serious peanut allergy. • This is especially true if there is a history of allergies, such as hay fever or asthma, in the family.

energy requirements increase dramatically when the woman is lactating (producing milk) and most women find that breastfeeding is also one of the most effective ways of regaining their pre-pregnancy weight. The mother should have at least half a litre of milk and a pot of yoghurt or some cheese each day to satisfy her body's need for extra calcium and should try to drink 1.5–2 litres of water a day. The Food Standards Agency recommends that breastfeeding mothers take supplements containing 10 micrograms (mcg) of vitamin D each day.

AC 2.1 Activity

1 Why is it important to eat a healthy diet before conceiving a baby?
2 Why is folic acid an important part of the diet during pregnancy?
3 List five foods that should be avoided during pregnancy – and explain the reasons why.
4 Explain the impact on health and development of food choices before and during pregnancy and during breastfeeding.

LO3 Understand the nutritional needs of children

AC 3.1 The nutritional value of the main food groups

A healthy diet for young children combines foods from all of the four food groups in Table 1.1.2.

> ### AC 3.1 Activity
>
> Explain the nutritional value of the main food groups. How does your setting ensure that all snacks and meals are healthy and nutritious? Have a look at your setting's food policy.

The eatwell plate

Use the eatwell plate to help you get the balance right. It shows how much of what you eat should come from each food group.

Fruit and vegetables

Bread, rice, potatoes, pasta and other starchy foods

Meat, fish, eggs, beans and other non-dairy sources of protein

Foods and drinks high in fat and/or sugar

Milk and dairy foods

Department of Health in association with the Welsh Government, the Scottish Government and the Food Standards Agency in Northern Ireland

Figure 1.1.2 The eatwell plate

Table 1.1.2 The four food groups and the nutrients they provide

Food groups	Examples of food included	Main nutrients provided	Recommended servings
Starchy foods	Bread, potatoes, sweet potatoes, starchy root vegetables, pasta, noodles, rice and other grains, breakfast cereals	Carbohydrate, fibre, B vitamins and iron	Four portions each day Provide a portion as part of each meal (breakfast, lunch and tea) and provide as part of at least one snack each day
Fruit and vegetables	Fresh, frozen, canned, dried and juiced fruit and vegetables, and pulses	Carotenes (a form of vitamin A), vitamin C, zinc, iron and fibre	Five portions each day Provide a portion as part of each main meal (breakfast, lunch and tea) with some snacks
Meat, fish, eggs, beans and non-dairy sources of protein	Meat, poultry, fish, shellfish, eggs, meat alternatives, pulses, nuts*	Protein, iron, zinc, omega 3 fatty acids, vitamins A and D	Two portions each day Provide a portion as part of lunch and tea (two to three portions for vegetarian children)
Milk and dairy foods	Milk, cheese, yoghurt, fromage frais, custard, puddings made from milk	Protein, calcium and vitamin A	Three portions each day provided as part of meals, snacks and drinks

* Nuts: children under five should not be offered whole nuts as they may cause choking. Nut butters and ground or chopped nuts in recipes are fine. However it is important to check if a child has a nut allergy before offering nuts. See p 328, 'Food allergies'.

AC 3.2 Government guidance on the nutritional needs of babies until they are fully weaned

The way in which babies are fed involves more than simply providing enough food to meet nutritional requirements; for the newborn baby, sucking milk is a great source of pleasure and can also be enjoyable for the mother. The ideal food for babies to start life with is breast milk, and breastfeeding should always be encouraged as the first choice in infant feeding; however, mothers should not be made to feel guilty or inadequate if they choose not to breastfeed their babies. The health visitor and National Childbirth Trust can support mothers who are breastfeeding but it is important to remember that the decision to breastfeed will depend on the mother and their individual circumstances.

Breastfeeding

During pregnancy, the breasts produce **colostrum**, a creamy, yellowish fluid, low in fat and sugar, which is uniquely designed to feed the newborn baby. Colostrum also has higher levels of antibodies than mature milk and plays an important part in protecting the baby from infection. Mature milk is present in the breasts from around the third day after birth. Hormonal changes in the mother's bloodstream cause the milk to be produced, and the sucking of the baby stimulates a steady supply.

Key term

colostrum This is the first 'milk' that the breasts produce, as a precursor to breast milk. It is lower in fat, but higher in protein and antibodies, which protect the baby against infection and kick-start the immune system.

The advantages of breastfeeding

- Human breast milk provides food constituents in the correct balance for human growth. There is no trial and error to find the right formula to suit the baby.
- The milk is sterile and at the correct temperature; there is no need for bottles and sterilising equipment.
- Breast milk initially provides the infant with maternal antibodies and helps protect the child from infection – for example, against illnesses such as diarrhoea, vomiting, chest, ear and urine infections, eczema and nappy rash.
- The child is less likely to become overweight, as overfeeding by concentrating the formula is not possible, and the infant has more freedom of choice as to how much milk he or she will suckle.
- Generally, breast milk is considered cheaper, despite the extra calorific requirement of the mother.
- Sometimes it is easier to promote mother–infant bonding by breastfeeding, although this is certainly not always the case.
- Some babies have an intolerance to the protein in cows' milk (which is the basis of formula milk).

Bottle-feeding

Commercially modified baby milks (formula milks) must be used for bottle-feeding. Any other type of milk, such as cows' milk or goats' milk, will not satisfy a baby's nutritional needs and should not be given to babies under one year of age. A young baby's digestive system is unable to cope with the high protein and salt content of cows' milk, and this milk is likely to cause an adverse reaction. Soya-based milks can be used if the baby develops an intolerance to modified cows' milk (this happens very rarely). For the first four to six months, the baby will be given infant formula milk as a substitute for breast milk; he or she may then progress to follow-on milk, which may be offered until the age of one year.

Government guidelines state that as each baby will have his or her own individual requirements, it is best to let them feed on demand. Newborn babies may take quite small volumes of infant formula milk to start with, but by the end of the first week of life most babies will ask for approximately 150–200 ml per kg per day – although this will vary from baby to baby – until they are six months old.

Figure 1.1.3 Bottle-feeding

AC 3.2 **Progress check** ✔

Explain the nutritional needs of babies from birth to the end of the weaning process.

AC 3.3 How to plan a weaning programme

The principles of weaning and its importance to the baby's development

Weaning is the gradual introduction of solid food to the baby's diet. The reasons for weaning are to:

- meet the baby's nutritional needs – from about six months of age, milk alone will not satisfy the baby's increased nutritional requirements, especially for iron
- satisfy increasing appetite
- develop new skills – for example, use of feeding beaker, cup and cutlery
- develop the chewing mechanism – the muscular movement of the mouth and jaw also aids the development of speech
- introduce new tastes and textures – this enables the baby to join in family meals, thus promoting cognitive and social development.

When to start weaning

Department of Health guidelines advise parents to wait until their baby is around six months before starting him or her on solid food. When the following three key signs are present together, it means that the baby is ready for solid food:

- The baby can stay in a sitting position while holding his or her head steady.
- The baby can coordinate his or her eyes, hands and mouth – that is, look at food, grab it and put it in his or her mouth him- or herself.
- The baby can swallow his or her food – if the baby is not ready, most of it will be pushed back out.

Babies who are born prematurely should not be introduced to solid foods just because they have reached a certain age or weight. They will need individual assessment before weaning.

Giving solids too early – often in the mistaken belief that the baby might sleep through the night – places a strain on the baby's immature digestive system. It may also make the baby fat and increases the likelihood of allergy.

If parents do choose to introduce solid foods before 26 weeks, they should consult their health visitor or GP first. There are also some foods they should avoid giving their baby. These include:

- foods containing gluten, which is in wheat, rye, barley, oats
- eggs
- fish and shellfish
- liver
- citrus fruit juices
- nuts and seeds.

Babies under one year old should not be given honey because it is not pasteurised and can cause infant botulism – a rare but very serious illness which occurs when *Clostridium botulinum* or related bacteria produce toxins in the intestines of babies under one year old.

Stages of weaning

Every baby is different. Some enjoy trying new tastes and textures, moving through weaning quickly and easily, while others need a little more time to get used to new foods.

Stage 1 (around six months)

Give puréed vegetables, puréed fruit, baby rice and finely puréed dhal or lentils. Milk continues to be the most important food.

Stage 2 (about six to eight months)

Increase variety; introduce puréed or minced meat, chicken, liver, fish, lentils and beans. Raw eggs should not be used, but cooked egg yolk can be introduced from six months, along with wheat-based foods – for example, mashed Weetabix and pieces of bread. Milk feeds decrease as more solids rich in protein are offered.

Stage 3 (about nine to 12 months)

Cows' milk can safely be used at about 12 months, along with lumpier foods such as pasta, pieces of cooked meat, soft cooked beans, pieces of cheese and a variety of breads. Additional fluids can be given – for example, diluted unsweetened fruit juice or water. Three regular meals should be taken, as well as drinks.

Methods of weaning

Some babies take to solid food very quickly; others appear not to be interested at all. The baby's demands are a good guide for weaning – meal times should never become a battleground. Even very young children have definite food preferences and should never be forced to eat a particular food, however much thought and effort have gone into the preparation. Table 1.1.3 offers guidelines on introducing new solids to babies.

The best baby food is homemade from simple ingredients, with no sugar, salt or spices. Any leftovers can be frozen in ice cube trays. Puréed, cooked vegetables, fruit and ground cereals such as rice are ideal to start weaning. Chewing usually starts at around the age of six months, whether or not the baby has

teeth, and slightly coarser textures can then be offered. The baby should be fed in a bouncing cradle or highchair – not in the usual feeding position in the carer's arms.

Food can be puréed by:

- rubbing it through a sieve using a large spoon
- mashing it with a fork (for soft foods such as banana or cooked potato)
- using a mouli-sieve or hand-blender
- using an electric blender (useful for larger amounts).

Guidelines for good practice

Weaning

- Try to encourage a liking for savoury foods.
- Only introduce one new food at a time.
- Be patient if the baby does not take the food – feed at the baby's pace, not yours.
- Do not add salt or sugar to feeds.
- Make sure that food is the right temperature.
- Avoid giving sweet foods or drinks between meals.
- Never leave a baby alone when he or she is eating.
- Limit the use of commercially prepared foods – they are of poorer quality and will not allow the baby to become used to home cooking.
- Select foods approved by the baby's parents or primary carers.

Finger foods

Finger foods are any foods that can be given to a baby to manage by him- or herself. After weaning, encourage the baby to chew – even if there are no teeth – by giving finger foods or foods that have a few lumps. Examples of finger foods include:

- wholemeal toast
- pitta bread
- banana or peeled apple slices
- cubes of hard cheese – for example, Cheddar
- chapatti
- breadsticks
- cooked carrots or green beans.

Table 1.1.3 Introducing new solids to babies

Age	You can give or add	How	When	Why	Not yet
4–6 months	• Finely puréed fruit • Finely puréed vegetables • Thin porridge made from oat or rice flakes or cornmeal	Offer the food on the tip of a clean finger or on the tip of a clean (plastic or horn) teaspoon	A very tiny amount at first, during or after a milk feed	The start of transition from milk to solids	• Cows' milk – or any except breast or formula milk • Citrus fruit • Soft summer fruits • Wheat (cereals, flour, bread, etc.) • Spices • Spinach, swede, turnip, beetroot • Eggs • Nuts • Salt • Sugar • Fatty food
6–8 months	• A wider range of puréed fruits and vegetables • Purées which include chicken, fish and liver • Wheat-based foods, e.g. mashed Weetabix • Egg yolk, well cooked • Small-sized beans such as aduki beans, cooked soft • Pieces of ripe banana • Cooked rice • Citrus fruits • Soft summer fruits • Pieces of bread	On a teaspoon	At the end of a milk feed	To introduce other foods when the child is hungry	• Cows' milk, except in small quantities mixed with other food • Chillies or chilli powder • Egg whites • Nuts • Salt • Sugar • Fatty food

➜

Table 1.1.3 Introducing new solids to babies (*continued*)

Age	You can give or add	How	When	Why	Not yet
9–12 months	• An increasingly wide range of foods with a variety of textures and flavours • Cows' milk • Pieces of cheese • Fromage frais or yoghurt • Pieces of fish • Soft cooked beans • Pasta • A variety of breads • Pieces of meat from a casserole • Well-cooked egg white • Almost anything that is wholesome and that the child can swallow	On a spoon or as finger food	At established meal times	To encourage full independence	• Whole nuts • Salt • Sugar • Fatty food

Always stay near to the baby during feeding to make sure he or she does not choke and to offer encouragement.

Baby-led weaning

Some parents use a technique for weaning their babies called baby-led weaning. This involves letting the baby select those items of food that can be held or grasped by the baby and taken to his or her mouth. Starter foods may include pieces of broccoli, carrot or fruit cut into 'chip' shapes and offered to the baby on a tray. The use of bowls and weaning spoons is discouraged. The principles behind this way of feeding babies are that baby-led weaning:

• offers the baby the opportunity to discover what other foods have to offer, as part of finding out about the world around him or her
• utilises the baby's desire to explore and experiment, and to mimic the activities of others

• enables the transition to solid foods to take place as naturally as possible – by allowing the baby to set the pace of each meal, and maintaining an emphasis on play and exploration rather than on eating.

For more information, visit this website: www.babyledweaning.com.

Progress check

• Weaning is the gradual introduction of solid food to the baby's diet.
• Giving solids too early places a strain on the baby's immature digestive system.
• The Department of Health recommends that babies be started on solid food at around six months.
• Babies usually start chewing food at around the age of six months, whether or not they have teeth.

A.C 3.3 Activity

Using the information in this section and the guidelines below, plan a weaning programme for a baby at each stage of the process – first stage: around six months; second stage: six to eight months; third stage: nine to 12 months.

Key term

anaemia A condition in which your blood can't carry enough oxygen to meet the needs of your body, either because you don't have enough red blood cells or because you don't have enough of a protein called haemoglobin in your red blood cells.

AC 3.4 The nutritional requirements of children aged one to seven years

Children need a varied energy-rich diet for good health and growth. For balance and variety, choose from the four main food groups (see Table 1.1.2).

A healthy diet should also include foods rich in calcium, iron and vitamin D.

Iron, calcium and vitamin D in children's diets

Iron

Iron is essential for children's health. Lack of iron often leads to **anaemia**, which can hold back both physical and mental development. Children most at risk are those who are poor eaters or on restricted diets. Iron comes in two forms, either:

- found in foods from animal sources (especially meat), which is easily absorbed by the body, or
- found in plant foods, which is not quite so easy for the body to absorb.

If possible, children should be given a portion of meat or fish every day, and kidney or liver once a week. Even a small portion of meat or fish is useful because it also helps the body to absorb iron from other food sources.

If children do not eat meat or fish, they must be offered plenty of iron-rich alternatives, such as egg yolks, dried fruit, beans and lentils, and green leafy vegetables. It is also a good idea to give foods or drinks that are high in vitamin C at meal times, as this helps the absorption of iron from non-meat sources.

Calcium and vitamin D

Children need calcium for maintaining and repairing bones and teeth. Calcium is:

- found in milk, cheese, yoghurt and other dairy products
- absorbed by the body only if it is taken with vitamin D.

The skin can make all the vitamin D that a body needs when it is exposed to gentle sunlight. Sources of vitamin D are shown in Figure 1.1.4.

The Department of Health recommends that from six months to five years of age, children should be given a vitamin supplement containing vitamins A, C and D unless they are drinking 500 ml of infant formula a day or are eating a varied diet with a wide range of foods to provide an adequate intake of vitamins and minerals.

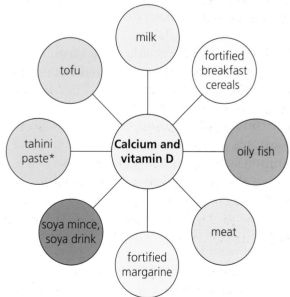

(* Tahini is made from sesame seeds; these may cause an allergic reaction in a small number of children.)

Figure 1.1.4 Sources of calcium and vitamin D

Dietary fibre

Dietary fibre, or roughage, is found in cereals, fruits and vegetables. Fibre is made up of the indigestible parts or compounds of plants, which pass relatively unchanged through our stomach and intestines. Fibre is needed to provide roughage to help to keep the food moving through the gut. A small amount of fibre is important for health in pre-school children but too much can cause problems as their digestive system is still immature. It could also reduce energy intakes by 'bulking up' the diet. Providing a mixture of white bread and refined cereals, white rice and pasta as well as occasionally a few wholegrain varieties helps to maintain a healthy balance between fibre and nutrient intakes.

Foods that contain fat and sugar

Young children under two years old need more energy from fat than older children and adults. Once the child is two years old, you can gradually reduce the amount of fat in their diet. The amount of saturated or 'bad' fat should be limited and some unsaturated fats – from vegetable oils and fish – should be provided. Cheap burgers, crisps, chips, biscuits, cakes and fried foods are all high in saturated fat. Meanwhile, sugary food and drinks will lead to tooth decay. Sweet foods such as cakes, biscuits and sweets should be avoided wherever possible. Dried fruit and diluted fruit juice can be provided but only during meal times.

How much food should children be given?

Children's appetites vary enormously, so common sense is a good guide to how big a portion should be. Always be guided by the individual child:

- Do not force them to eat when they no longer wish to.
- Do not refuse to give more if they really are hungry.

Some children always feel hungry at one particular meal time. Others require food little and often. You should always offer food that is nourishing and that satisfies their hunger. Table 1.1.4 gives examples of foods to provide for a balanced diet.

Providing drinks for children

An adequate fluid intake will prevent dehydration and reduce the risk of constipation. The best drinks for young children are water and milk and they are also the best drinks to give between meals and snacks as they do not harm teeth when taken from a cup or beaker.

Milk is an excellent nourishing drink which provides valuable nutrients. Cows' milk should not be given to children under the age of one, as it does not contain enough nutrients for them – they should have infant formula and/or breast milk. All toddlers should drink whole (full-fat milk) until they are two years old. Children above this age who are eating well can change to semi-skimmed milk. However, skimmed milk should not be given to children under the age of five.

Other drinks

All drinks which contain sugar can be harmful to teeth and can also affect children's appetites. Examples are flavoured milks, fruit squashes, flavoured fizzy drinks and fruit juices (containing natural sugar).

Unsweetened diluted fruit juice is a reasonable option – but not as good as water or milk – for children, but should only be offered at meal times. Low-sugar and diet fruit drinks contain artificial sweeteners and are best avoided. Tea and coffee should not be given to children under five years, as they prevent the absorption of iron from foods. They also tend to fill children up without providing nourishment.

Providing drinks for children aged one to three

The normal fluid requirement for children aged one to three years is 95 mls per kg of

Table 1.1.4 Providing a balanced diet

Breakfast	Diluted orange juice	Milk	Diluted apple juice	Milk	Yoghurt
	Weetabix, buttered toast	Cereal, e.g. corn or wheat flakes, toast and jam	1 slice of toast with butter or jam	Cereal with sliced banana or scrambled egg on toast	Porridge, slices of apple
Morning snack	Diluted apple juice	Blackcurrant and apple drink	1 glass of fruit squash	Peeled apple slices	Diluted apple juice
	1 packet raisins	Cheese straws	1 biscuit	Wholemeal toast fingers with cheese spread	Chapatti or pitta bread fingers
Lunch	Chicken nuggets or macaroni and cheese	Thick bean soup or chicken salad sandwich	Vegetable soup or fish fingers	Sweet potato casserole	Bean casserole or chicken drumstick, noodles
	Broccoli	Green beans	Carrot sticks (raw)	Sweet corn	Peas or broad beans
	Fruit yoghurt	Fresh fruit salad	Kiwi fruit	Spinach leaves	Fruit yoghurt
	Water	Water	Water	Chocolate mousse	Water
				Water	
Afternoon snack	Diluted fruit juice	Milkshake	Diluted fruit juice	Hot/cold chocolate drink	Lassi (yoghurt drink)
	Cheese cubes with savoury biscuit	Fruitcake or chocolate biscuit	Thin-cut sandwiches cut in small pieces	1 small packet of dried fruit	1 banana
					1 small biscuit
Tea or supper	Baked beans on toast or ham and cheese pasta	Fish stew or fish fingers	Baked potato with fillings	Home-made burger or pizza	Lentil and rice soup
	Lemon pancakes	Mashed potato	Broccoli	Green salad	Pitta or wholegrain bread
	Milk or yoghurt	Fruit mousse or fromage frais	Ice cream	Pancakes	Rice salad
		Milk or yoghurt		Milk	Milk

body weight per day. The guidelines for early years settings state the following:

- Children must have access to drinking water throughout the day and be encouraged to help themselves to water.
- Children need six to eight drinks (each of 100–150 mls) a day to make sure they get enough fluid.
- Children may need extra drinks in hot weather or after physical activity as they can dehydrate quite quickly.

Sweetened drinks, including diluted fruit juice, should only be consumed with, rather than between, meals to lessen the risk of dental decay. Consumption of sugar-free fizzy or fruit-based drinks, although not recommended, should also be confined to meal times because the high acidity level of these drinks can cause dental decay.

Providing drinks for children aged four to seven years

The normal fluid requirement for children aged four to seven years is 85 mls per kg of body weight per day.

- The following drinks are recommended: still water, milk, plain or flavoured, diluted pure fruit juice, fruit and milk/yoghurt smoothies, vegetable juices, and no-added-sugar (sugar-free) squashes – well diluted.
- In between meals and snacks, water and plain milk are still the best drinks as they will not damage teeth as acidic and sugary drinks do.

Recent research shows that some parents never offer children water to drink as they do not drink water themselves; some parents even consider it cruel to offer water in place of flavoured drinks. So it is important that children get into the habit of drinking water in the setting.

Providing nutritious snacks

Some children really do need to eat between meals. Health guidelines recommend children should not go longer than three hours without refreshment. Children's stomachs are relatively small and so they fill up and empty faster than adult stomachs. Sugary foods should not be given as a snack because sugar may spoil the child's appetite for the main meal to follow. Healthy snack foods include:

- fruit – banana, orange, pear, kiwi fruit, apple or satsuma
- dairy foods such as cheese or plain yoghurt with added fruit
- fruit bread or wholemeal bread with a slice of cheese

- milk or homemade milkshake
- raw vegetables such as peeled carrots, sweet pepper, tomato, cucumber or celery (all well washed)
- wholegrain biscuits, breadsticks, cream crackers, matzos, melba toast, crispbread, oatcakes or sesame seed crackers
- any type of bread, including fruit bread, crumpets, teacakes, muffins, fruit buns, malt loaf, bagels, pitta bread or sandwiches. Suitable fillings for sandwiches might be cheese, yeast extract, banana, salad or combinations of these.

The Children's Food Trust does not recommend giving dried fruit, such as raisins or dried apricots, or diluted fruit juices in between meals because they are high in sugar and can cause tooth decay.

The dangers of too much salt

On average, children are eating twice the recommended amount of salt. The recommended nutrient intake (RNI) for infants aged between one and three years is not more than 1.25 g of salt each day; four- to six-year-olds should consume no more than 1.75 g. A lot of manufactured foods are marketed at children, and some of these can exceed their daily salt requirement in a single serving – a bag of crisps, for example. A small can (200 g) of pasta shapes in tomato sauce contains twice the daily RNI of salt for a one- to three-year-old and a third more than the daily RNI for a four- to six-year-old.

Guidelines for good practice

Reducing salt in children's diets
- Cut down gradually on the amount of salt used in cooking so that children become used to less salty foods.
- If preparing baby food at home, do not add salt, even if it tastes bland. Manufactured baby food is tightly regulated to limit the salt content to a trace.
- Try using a low-salt substitute, such as LoSalt, Solo or a supermarket's own-brand low-sodium salt in cooking or at the table. These products substitute up to 70 per cent of the sodium chloride with potassium chloride.

Foods to avoid giving to children

- Salt: there is no need to add salt to children's food. Even when buying processed food made specifically for children, remember to check the information given on the labels to choose those with less salt.
- Nuts: do not give whole or chopped nuts to children under five years old because of the risk of choking.
- Raw eggs: avoid food that contains raw or partially cooked eggs because of the risk of salmonella, which causes food poisoning. Make sure that eggs are always cooked until both the white and the yolk are solid.
- Undiluted fruit juice: these contain natural sugars which are known to cause tooth decay; they are best only given at meal times and should be diluted when given to young children.
- High-fibre foods like brown rice and wholemeal pasta are too bulky for children under five; too much fibre can also make it more difficult for the body to absorb some essential nutrients, like calcium and iron.
- Shark, swordfish and marlin should not be given because these fish contain relatively high levels of mercury, which might affect a child's developing nervous system.
- Raw shellfish: to reduce their risk of getting food poisoning.

AC 3.4 | Activity

Make sure you know the current guidelines and nutritional requirements concerning the provision of a healthy diet, including guidelines for providing drinks and avoiding extra salt and sugar. Find out about the food policy in your setting.

AC 3.5 Strategies to encourage healthy eating

The early years setting is an ideal place to provide meal and snack times that make eating an enjoyable social event. When children positively enjoy their food-related experiences, they are less likely to develop food-related problems. Also, children are more likely to try new foods if they see their friends trying them in a relaxed and happy atmosphere. There will be opportunities to talk about food, their likes and dislikes and the texture, colour and smell of different foods. Every child is unique; they gradually develop a whole catalogue of likes, strong dislikes and mild preferences regarding food and meal times. For example:

- some like their food bathed in sauces, while others prefer it dry
- some like every food kept separate from the others on the plate
- many do not like 'tough' meat or foods that are difficult to chew.

It is important to respect a child's likes and dislikes and offer alternative foods from the same food group where necessary.

Introducing new foods

When introducing children to new foods, the following points are important:

- They should have the chance to try the same food on more than one occasion. The first time they try a food it can be the fact that it is new or that they do not like the texture that makes them not want to eat it. The second time they try it, it is not so unfamiliar and their preferences may change.
- When trying new foods, children need to know that they do not have to swallow the food. If they know they can spit it into a tissue, they are less likely to be worried about putting a new type of food into their mouth.

AC 3.5 | Activity

What strategies are used in your setting to promote healthy eating? Are parents kept informed and involved in the planning of meals and snacks for their children?

Guidelines for good practice

The role of the practitioner in promoting healthy eating

- Set an example: children will imitate both what you eat and how you eat it. It will be easier to encourage a child to eat a stick of raw celery if you eat one too! If you show disgust at certain foods, young children will notice and copy you.
- Offer a wide variety of different foods: give babies and toddlers an opportunity to try a new food more than once; any refusal on first tasting may be due to dislike of the new rather than of the food itself.
- Be prepared for messy meal times: present the food in a form that is fairly easy for children to manage by themselves (for example, not difficult to chew).
- Do not use food as a punishment, reward, bribe or threat: for example, do not give sweets or chocolates as a reward for finishing savoury foods. To a child this is like saying, 'Here's something nice after eating those nasty greens.' Give healthy foods as treats, such as raisins and raw carrots, rather than sweets or cakes.
- Introduce new foods in stages: for example, if switching to wholemeal bread, try a soft-grain white bread first. Always involve the children in making choices as far as possible.
- Teach children to eat mainly at meal times and avoid giving them high-calorie snacks (such as biscuits and sugary drinks) which might affect their appetite for more nutritious food. Most young children need three small meals and three snacks a day.
- Ensure that children sit down at a table to eat their snacks, that they are supervised during these times and that they are monitored to ensure they eat an appropriate amount of food safely to reduce the risk of choking.
- Presentation is important: food manufacturers use a variety of techniques to make their children's food products exciting – colours, shapes, themes and characters. Using these tactics can make meal times more fun.
- Allow children to follow their own individual appetites when deciding how much they want to eat. If a child rejects food, never force-feed them. Simply remove the food without comment. Give smaller portions next time and praise the child for eating even a little.
- Never give a young child whole nuts to eat – particularly peanuts. Children can very easily choke on a small piece of the nut or even inhale it, which can cause a severe type of pneumonia. On rare occasions, a child may have a serious allergic reaction to nuts. Always check whether a child has any known allergies.

LO4 Understand the impact of poor diet on children's health and development

AC 4.1 The impact of poor diet on children's health and development

Healthy eating – or good nutrition – during childhood makes it easier to maintain a healthy weight and has been shown to improve children's concentration and behaviour. It can also help to reduce the risk of developing many common diseases, including heart disease, cancer, diabetes, obesity, osteoporosis and dental decay.

Malnutrition and under-nutrition

In recent years, there has been increasing public concern about the quality of children's diets, rapidly increasing rates of child obesity, diet-related disorders and low consumption of fruit and vegetables by children. There are various conditions that may occur in childhood that are directly related to a poor or unbalanced diet; these are a result of either **malnutrition** or **under-nutrition** and include:

- failure to thrive* (or faltering growth): poor growth and physical development
- dental caries or tooth decay: associated with a high consumption of sugar in snacks and fizzy drinks

- obesity: children who are overweight are more likely to become obese adults
- nutritional anaemia: due to an insufficient intake of iron, folic acid and vitamin B12
- increased susceptibility to infections: particularly upper respiratory infections, such as colds and bronchitis.

*Failure to thrive can also result from child abuse: physical abuse, emotional abuse, neglect and sexual abuse. This subject is discussed in Unit 2.

> **Key terms**
>
> **malnutrition** A person's diet is lacking the necessary amounts of certain elements that are essential to growth, such as vitamins, salts and proteins.
>
> **under-nutrition** This occurs when people do not get enough to eat.

Food refusal

Many children go through phases of refusing to eat certain foods or not wanting to eat much at all. This is particularly common in children up to the age of five and is a normal part of growing up and asserting their independence. Eating can quickly become a focus for conflict and tension at home, with parents feeling anxious and out of control. Food refusal often starts because it is one of the few ways in which children can exert influence over their parents. Reasons for food refusal in young children include the following:

- Slower growth and small appetites: growth slows down in a child's second year. This means that toddlers often have small appetites and need less food. Children eat according to their appetite, and this can vary from day to day. Some children eat in spurts; they may eat much one day and very little the next. It also depends on how active they have been during the day.
- Distraction: young children have no concept of time. Their world has become an exciting place to explore and food can

seem less important when there are so many other things to do.

- Grazing and snacking: toddlers rarely follow a traditional meal pattern. They tend to need small and regular snacks. Parents may offer sweets or crisps throughout the day so that children 'won't go hungry'. Children then become even less inclined to eat their meals when they know that they can fill up on their favourite snacks. Large quantities of milk or other drinks throughout the day also affect a child's appetite.
- Fussy eating and food fads: showing independence is part of normal child development, and this often includes refusing to eat foods 'to see what will happen'. It is quite normal for children to have certain times when their food choices become very limited. For example, they will only eat food prepared and presented in a certain way. Some decide they do not like mixed-up food or different foods touching each other on the plate, and they develop strong likes and dislikes that frequently change.
- New textures and tastes: children are experimenting with, or being asked to try, new textures and tastes. Rejecting a food does not always mean the child does not like it; they may eat it the very next day.
- Seeking attention: children may seek to gain attention in different ways – they may test their parents' reactions and learn the effects of their uncooperative behaviour. They may have learnt to say 'no' and may welcome all the attention they get by, for example, refusing to eat (or taking a long time to eat) a meal.

How to cope with food refusal

Research shows that one-third of all parents worry that their child is not eating enough, but unless they are ill, young children will never voluntarily starve themselves. If a child seems to be healthy and energetic, they are almost certainly eating enough. There is plenty of advice for parents and carers from health experts and child dieticians on how to cope with their child's refusal of food, including the following tips:

- Never force-feed a child, either by pushing food into his mouth or by threatening punishment or withdrawal of a treat.
- Keep calm and try not to make a fuss about whether the child is eating or not. Instead, try to make meal times pleasant, social occasions, because if children associate meal times with an enjoyable event, they will want to repeat it.
- Encourage self-feeding and exploration of food from an early age, without worrying about the mess.
- Offer alternative foods from every food group: if a child dislikes cheese, they may eat yoghurt.
- Provide healthy, nutritious snacks between meals as these play an important part in the energy intake of young children. Ideas include fresh fruits, yoghurt, biscuits with cheese or peanut butter.
- Do not give sweets and crisps between meals to children who refuse food at meal times.

AC 4.1 Activity

Arrange to observe a group of children during meal time. Note, in particular, children who seem reluctant or 'fussy' eaters. Note also each child's food preferences.

LO5 Understand individuals' dietary requirements and preferences

AC 5.1 Reasons for special dietary requirements and keeping dietary records

Multicultural dietary customs

The UK is a multicultural society. Dietary customs of different cultures are wide and varied but some may be related to the beliefs of religious groups, including Muslims, Hindus and Sikhs.

Apart from the dietary implications of multicultural food provision, there may be several other dietary requirements – some

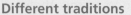

Research activity

Different traditions
Find out about the dietary requirements and restrictions in one cultural or religious group different from your own. Choose from:

- Jewish
- Christian
- Muslim
- Hindu
- Rastafarian.

based on family preferences or because the child has a disorder or allergy.

Children on vegetarian diets

Children who are on a vegetarian diet need an alternative to meat, fish and chicken as the main sources of protein. Alternatives might include:

- milk
- cheese and eggs
- pulses (lentils and beans).

They also need enough iron. As iron is more difficult to absorb from vegetable sources than from meat, a young child needs to obtain iron from sources such as:

- leafy green vegetables – such as spinach and watercress
- pulses (beans, lentils and chickpeas)
- dried fruit (such as apricots, raisins and sultanas) – although some dentists believe that dried fruit contributes to dental decay, and so it should be given sparingly and only at meal times
- some breakfast cereals.

It is easier to absorb iron from our food if it is eaten with foods containing vitamin C, such as fruit and vegetables, or with diluted fruit juices at meal times. Do not give young children tea or coffee, especially at meal times, because this reduces the amount of iron they can absorb.

Table 1.1.5 Multicultural provision and dietary implications

Muslim diets	Hindu diets	Jewish diets
Muslims practise the Islamic religion, and their holy book, the Koran, provides them with their food laws. Unlawful foods (called haram) are: pork, all meat which has not been rendered lawful (halal), alcohol and fish without scales. Wheat based foods and rice are the staple foods. The Koran recommends that children should be breastfed up to the age of two years, but this is considered optional. Fasting: during the lunar month of Ramadan, Muslims fast between sunrise and sunset; fasting involves abstinence from all food and drink, so many Muslims rise early to eat before dawn in order to maintain their energy levels. Pre-pubescent children and the elderly are exempt from fasting.	Wheat is the main staple food eaten by Hindus in the UK; it is used to make types of bread called chapattis, puris and parathas. Orthodox Hindus are strict vegetarians as they believe in Ahimsa – non-violence towards all living beings – and a minority practise veganism. Some will eat dairy products and eggs, while others will refuse eggs on the grounds that they are a potential source of life. Even non-vegetarians do not eat beef as the cow is considered a sacred animal, and it is unusual for pork to be eaten as the pig is considered unclean. Ghee (clarified butter) and vegetable oil are used in cooking. Fasting: common for certain festivals, such as Mahshivrati (the birthday of Lord Shiva).	Jewish people observe dietary laws which state that animals and birds must be slaughtered by the Jewish method to render them kosher (acceptable). Milk and meat must never be cooked or eaten together, and pork in any form is forbidden. Shellfish is not allowed as it is thought to harbour disease. Only fish with fins and scales may be eaten. Fasting: the most holy day of the Jewish calendar is Yom Kippur (the Day of Atonement), when Jewish people fast for 25 hours.

Sikh diets	Rastafarian diets	Afro-Caribbean diets
Most Sikhs will not eat pork or beef or any meat that is killed by the halal method. Some Sikhs are vegetarian, but many eat chicken, lamb and fish. Wheat and rice are staple foods. Fasting: devout Sikhs will fast once or twice a week, and most will fast on the first day of the Punjabi month or when there is a full moon.	Dietary practices are based on laws laid down by Moses in the Book of Genesis in the Bible. These laws state that certain types of meat should be avoided. The majority of followers will only eat Ital foods, which are foods considered to be in a whole or natural state. Most Rastafarians are vegetarians and will not consume processed or preserved foods. No added salt; no coffee.	The Afro-Caribbean community is the second-largest ethnic minority group in the UK. Dietary practices within the community vary widely. Many people include a wide variety of European foods in their diet alongside the traditional foods of cornmeal, coconut, green banana, plantain, okra and yam. Although Afro-Caribbean people are generally Christian, a minority are Rastafarians.

Table 1.1.5 Multicultural provision and dietary implications (*continued*)

Festivals from different cultures

- Shichi-go-san (Japanese festival for young children) – 15 November
- Chinese New Year – late January/ early February
- Shrove Tuesday (Mardi Gras) – 40 days before Easter
- Rosh Hoshanah (Jewish New Year) – usually September
- Holi (Hindu Spring festival) – February or March
- Id Al Fitir (major Muslim festival) – at end of Ramadan
- Diwali (Hindu New Year) – October or November
- Rastafarian New Year – 7 January

The vegan diet

A vegan diet completely excludes all foods of animal origin; that is, animal flesh, milk and milk products, eggs, honey and all additives which may be of animal origin. A vegan diet is based on cereals and cereal products, pulses, fruits, vegetables, nuts and seeds. Human breast milk is acceptable for vegan babies.

Food intolerance

Food intolerance is an adverse reaction to some sort of food or ingredient that occurs every time the food is eaten, but particularly if larger quantities are consumed. Food intolerance is not the same as:

- a food allergy because the immune system is not activated
- food poisoning, in which toxic substances would cause symptoms in anyone who ate the food.

Food intolerance does not include psychological reactions to food; it is much more common than food allergy.

Some babies develop an intolerance to cows' milk protein; the most common symptoms are vomiting, diarrhoea and failure to thrive. After weaning, foods most likely to cause an adverse reaction in babies are:

- hens' eggs
- fish

- citrus fruits
- wheat and other cereals
- pork.

Sometimes an adverse reaction will be temporary, perhaps following an illness, but the offending food should always be removed from the baby's diet. Dietetic advice should be sought before any changes to a balanced diet are made.

Food allergies

A food allergy is an abnormal response (an allergic reaction) of the immune system to otherwise harmless foods. Up to 5 per cent of children have food allergies. Most children outgrow their allergy, although an allergy to peanuts and some other tree nuts is considered lifelong.

There are eight foods that cause 90 per cent of all food allergic reactions. These are:

- peanuts
- soy
- tree nuts (such as almonds, walnuts, pecans, etc.)
- wheat
- milk
- shellfish
- eggs
- fish.

Milk is the most common cause of food allergies in children, but peanuts, nuts, fish and shellfish commonly cause the most severe reactions.

What are the symptoms of an allergic reaction?

Symptoms of an allergic response can include:

- vomiting
- hives (or urticaria) – an itchy raised rash usually found on the trunk or limbs
- itching or tightness in the throat
- diarrhoea
- eczema
- difficulty breathing
- cramps
- itching or swelling of the lips, tongue or mouth
- wheezing.

Allergic symptoms can begin within minutes to one hour after ingesting the food.

Anaphylaxis

In rare cases of food allergy, just one bite of food can bring on anaphylaxis. This is a severe reaction that involves various areas of the body simultaneously. In extreme cases, it can cause death.

Anaphylaxis is a sudden and severe, potentially life-threatening, allergic reaction. It can be caused by insect stings or medications, as well as by a food allergy. Although potentially any food can cause anaphylaxis, peanuts, nuts, shellfish, fish and eggs are foods that most commonly cause this reaction.

Symptoms of anaphylaxis may include all those listed above for food allergies. In addition, the child's breathing is seriously impaired and the pulse rate becomes rapid. Anaphylaxis is fortunately very rare, but is also very dangerous:

- Symptoms can occur in as little as five to fifteen minutes.
- As little as half a peanut can cause a fatal reaction in severely allergic individuals.
- Some severely allergic children can have a reaction if milk is splashed on their skin.
- Being kissed by somebody who has eaten peanuts, for example, can cause a reaction in severely allergic individuals.

Emergency treatment of anaphylaxis

- Summon medical help immediately. The child will need oxygen and a life-saving injection of adrenaline.
- Place the child in a sitting position to help relieve any breathing difficulty.
- Be prepared to resuscitate if necessary.

In some settings attended by a child or children known to be at risk from anaphylaxis, the staff will be trained to give the adrenaline injection.

How can food allergies be managed?

The only way to manage food allergies is strictly to avoid the foods to which the child is allergic. It is important to learn how to interpret ingredients on food labels and how to spot high-risk foods. Many children outgrow earlier food-allergic symptoms as they get older, but parents will need professional support and advice to ensure that their child is receiving a safe, balanced diet.

> **Key term**
>
> **allergy** Abnormal sensitivity reaction of the body to substances that are usually harmless.

Keeping and sharing coherent records with regard to children's special dietary requirements

Information about special dietary needs and allergies should be recorded on each child's registration document – and should be regularly checked to ensure that the information is kept up to date. Most settings display this information clearly in the food preparation area, thus ensuring that the information is accessible to all staff involved in food provision. Each practitioner should take responsibility to report and record any new information they receive regarding children's special dietary requirements, and parents and carers should be involved in the recording process.

AC 5.1　Progress check

Each setting will have its own method for recording and sharing information – some have a separate policy for this aspect of care. Find out how such information is recorded in your setting. How is the information shared with other practitioners? How often are these records updated?

AC 5.2 Your role in meeting children's dietary requirements and preferences

Meeting children's individual dietary requirements and preferences

All staff in early years settings should be aware of the identities of children who have food allergies and should have clear instructions on how to deal with each case. In particular, lunchtime supervisors need to be kept informed. Most settings display a photograph of any child with a special dietary requirement or allergy in the food preparation area to ensure that permanent and supply staff are aware of each individual child's needs. Some settings have developed a system of personalised children's food mats which display the relevant information for each child's needs and preferences.

In practice

Special dietary requirements

Find out about the policy in your work setting covering special dietary requirements. In particular, find out about:

- special diets (which have been medically advised)
- preference diets (where there is no degree of risk attached)
- food allergies.

How does your setting ensure that any special dietary requirements are identified and that every child is offered the appropriate food and drink?

When a child has been diagnosed as having a severe allergy to a particular food, staff may

decide to minimise the risk of exposure by avoiding having the food or ingredient in the setting. In severe cases, it is essential that there is regular access to up-to-date advice from a registered dietician because ingredients in processed foods change frequently. Everybody involved in the care of children with known allergies should know:

- how to recognise the symptoms of a food allergy or intolerance
- how to avoid the foods that the child is sensitive to
- what to do if the child has an allergic reaction
- how to use the child's adrenaline injector or EpiPen, if they have one
- when and how to record and report any suspicion of food allergy or intolerance.

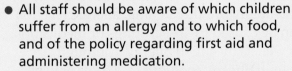

Figure 1.1.5 An EpiPen

Progress check

Allergies and intolerances

- All staff should be aware of which children suffer from an allergy and to which food, and of the policy regarding first aid and administering medication.
- All staff involved in the care of that child must be aware of the foods and ingredients being offered to the child.
- Care must be taken in the preparation and serving of food not to cross-contaminate food being served to a child with an allergy.
- If you ever notice swelling of a child's mouth or face or breathing difficulties when eating, seek medical advice immediately. Symptoms such as a rash or vomiting after eating may also suggest that there has been a reaction to a food. Always inform the parent or carer.
- To lessen the risk of peanut allergies, peanut-containing foods should not be given to children under three years of age if the child has a parent or sibling with a diagnosed allergy. Whole nuts should not be given to any child under the age of five years because of the risk of choking.

Food allergies and intolerances
In your setting:

- Find out how many (if any) children have food allergies or intolerances.
- How is information displayed about children's allergies?
- Is there a policy document relating to reporting and recording allergies and intolerances?

AC 5.3 Benefits of working in partnership with parents/carers

Many early years settings have written procedures for children with special dietary needs. This helps practitioners to work in partnership with parents to find out more about their child's requirements and to reassure them that their child's needs will be met. A procedure may include the following points:

- Before a child starts the nursery, the child's parents will be asked by the key person to outline the child's dietary needs.
- If the child has a food allergy or requires a special diet, the parents will be asked to identify in detail any food allergies or special dietary needs that their child has.
- The key person will ensure the nursery manager and all members of staff who may come into contact with the child know about the child's individual needs and any actions required.
- The nursery manager will ensure that a suitable individual menu is drawn up for the child (expert advice will be sought if necessary).
- Parents should advise the setting manager which foods can be given as alternatives, ones to be avoided and any triggers. They should also provide confirmation in writing.
- The child's parents will be given a copy of the individual menus and asked to sign an agreement that their child may have all the foods and drinks listed.

- The cook will be given a copy of the child's signed menu and will inform all other staff who may be involved in preparing the child's food about the child's individual needs and any actions required.
- The child's parents will be asked to give permission for their child's individual allergies or individual dietary needs to be displayed discreetly in the nursery to ensure that all staff members are aware of what the child may and may not be given to eat and drink.
- If a child is provided with particular products on prescription – for example, gluten-free bread – it may be possible for parents to provide a quantity of these to the setting for cooks to use when preparing a meal.

AC 5.3 Progress check

Find out about the policy or procedures for children with special dietary requirements in your setting. Why is it beneficial to children when staff work in partnership with parents in relation to special dietary requirements?

LO6 Be able to support healthy eating in own setting

AC 6.1 Planning an activity to support healthy eating

Raising awareness of healthy eating
Almost all children have some experience of cooking, or at the very least food preparation, in their own homes. This experience can range from watching tins being opened and the contents heated, seeing fruit being peeled and cut or bread being put in a toaster and then spread, to a full meal being cooked.

Food preparation and cooking activities are also useful in raising children's awareness of healthy and nutritious foods, educating them about diet and choice. For example, by discussing the need for an ingredient to sweeten food, children can be introduced to the variety available and be made aware of healthy options.

Children learn through active involvement so any cooking activity must be chosen carefully to ensure that children can participate. There is very limited value in them watching an adult carry out the instructions and occasionally letting them have a stir!

Other learning outcomes include:

- development of physical skills through using the equipment – pouring, beating, whisking, stirring, etc.
- aspects of counting, sorting, measuring – size and quantity – sharing, fractions, ordinal number (i.e. first, second), sequencing and memory through following and recalling the recipe instructions
- independence skills through preparation, controlling their own food and equipment, tidying up
- expressing their ideas, opinions, likes and dislikes
- understanding how to present food attractively through arrangement and decoration.

Planning a cooking activity with young children

When selecting a cooking activity, remember:

- that parental wishes must always be respected
- to check that all children can eat the food being cooked
- to check that there are no problems regarding allergies or religious dietary restrictions
- to follow basic food safety and hygiene guidelines.

Ideas for planning and implementing a cooking activity include:

- cutting and preparing fruit, vegetables, salad items or cheese
- spreading breads, crackers or crispbreads with a variety of foods – butter, jam, cream cheese, yeast extract, etc.
- making biscuits or cakes – although as these are never part of a healthy diet this activity should be an occasional treat.

AC 6.2 Implementing an activity to support healthy eating

Having planned your activity, make sure you allow plenty of time for preparation, and follow the guidelines below.

Guidelines for good practice

Implementing a cooking activity with children

- Always prepare surfaces with antibacterial spray and clean cloths.
- Always ensure children have washed their hands and scrubbed their fingernails.
- Always provide protective clothing and, if necessary, roll up long sleeves.
- Always tie back long hair.
- Always check equipment for damage.
- Always follow the safety procedures and policies of the work setting.
- Always ensure adequate supervision.
- Always remind children not to cough over food or put their fingers or utensils in their mouths when handling food.
- Always check the use-by dates of food items and store them correctly.
- Always check for 'E' numbers and artificial ingredients in bought food items.
- Always check any allergies and dietary requirements of the children involved. Remember that a child can have an allergic reaction just by touching something they are allergic to.

Evaluation

After the activity, evaluate your activity. How successful were you in achieving your aims? Were all the children involved? What do you think the children learned about healthy eating?

AC 6.3 Reflecting on own role when supporting healthy eating

Consider your own role when supporting healthy eating in your setting. Try to answer the following questions to help you reflect on your own experiences:

- Am I a good role model for the children?
- Do I always seek to promote healthy eating – through a thorough understanding of what constitutes a healthy diet?
- Are meal times and snack times enjoyable for all the children?
- Do I encourage children to help themselves to water throughout the day?
- Do I observe children to ensure they are eating a healthy diet?
- Am I aware of the food preferences of individual children or of their needs for a particular diet?
- Do I consult with parents or carers about their child's dietary needs?
- Do I try to involve both children and their families when planning food-related activities?

AC 6.4 Making recommendations for healthy eating

AC 6.4 Activity

1 Create a weekly plan that shows all the meals, drinks and snacks for the children in your setting.
2 Identify how your plan meets the children's nutritional needs, using the guidelines in Table 1.1.2.
3 Describe the methods you have used to identify each child's needs and preferences.
4 Describe the steps you would take to cope with a child who refuses to eat.

Assessment practice

1 What is meant by healthy eating? Describe the nutrients that make up a healthy diet.
2 How far do you think national and local initiatives have succeeded in promoting healthy eating?
3 Why is it so important that young children have access to drinking water throughout the day? What are the food and drink requirements in early years settings?
4 Why is a healthy diet important in the pre-conceptual period, during pregnancy and when breastfeeding?
5 What are the main food groups? Why do children require vitamins, iron and calcium?
6 Why is breast milk best for a baby? When is it safe to give cows' milk to a baby?
7 What is weaning? How could you plan a weaning programme to meet the nutritional needs of babies?

8 Describe the nutritional requirements for children aged between one and seven years. Which foods should be avoided and what sorts of food should be limited as part of a healthy diet?
9 Describe some strategies you could use to promote healthy eating.
10 Explain the short-term and long-term impact of poor nutrition on children's health and development.
11 Describe the need for special dietary requirements. What is your role in meeting children's individual dietary needs and preferences?
12 Describe ways in which you can promote healthy eating in your setting.

Useful resources

National initiatives

England – Change4Life: **www.nhs.uk**

Northern Ireland – Get a life, get active: **www. getalifegetactive.com**

Scotland – Take life on, one step at a time: **www.takelifeon.co.uk**

Wales – Change4Life Wales: **www. change4lifewales.org.uk**

The Eat Better, Start Better programme

Voluntary Food and Drink Guidelines for Early Years Settings in England – A Practical Guide.

Vegan Society

The Vegan Society provides information, support and advice to individuals, health professionals, caterers and manufacturers.

Vegetarian Society

The Vegetarian Society aims to influence, inspire and support people to embrace and maintain a vegetarian lifestyle.

www.vegsoc.org

Support healthy lifestyles for children through exercise

Learning outcomes

By the end of this unit, you will:

1 Understand children's need for exercise.
2 Understand inclusive practice in relation to the use of provision for children's exercise.

3 Be able to support children's exercise in an outdoor space.

LO1 Understand children's need for exercise

AC 1.1 The benefits of exercise for children

The importance of physical activity for young children's holistic development

Physical activity and the development of movement skills help children to develop holistically in the following areas:

- Expressing ideas and feelings: children become aware that they can use their bodies to express themselves by moving in different ways as they respond to their moods and feelings, to music or to imaginative ideas.
- Developing skills requiring coordination of different parts of the body: for example, hands and eyes for throwing and catching, legs and arms for skipping with a rope.
- Exploring what their bodies can do and becoming aware of their increasing abilities, agility and skill. Children's awareness of the space around them and what their bodies are capable of can be extended by climbing and balancing on large-scale apparatus, such as a climbing frame, wooden logs and a balancing bar, and by using small tricycles, bicycles and carts.

- Cooperating with others in physical play and games. Children become aware of physical play both as individuals and as a social activity: in playing alone or alongside others, in playing throwing and catching with a partner, in using a seesaw or push cart, or in joining a game with a larger group.
- Developing increasing control of fine movements of their fingers and hands (fine motor skills). For example, playing musical instruments and making sounds with the body, such as clapping or tapping, help develop fine motor skills in the hands and fingers, while also reinforcing the link between sound and physical movement. Helping with household tasks – washing up, pouring drinks, carrying bags – also develops fine motor skills.
- Developing balance and coordination, as well as an appreciation of distance and speed; energetic play that involves running, jumping and skipping helps children to develop these skills.
- Developing spatial awareness: for example, dancing and moving around to music develop a spatial awareness while also practising coordination and muscle control.

Effects on short- and long-term health and well-being

Physical activity and exercise are no longer a regular feature in many children's lives. Some children never walk or cycle to school, or play sport. Children need to be physically active in order to prevent harmful effects on their health, in both the long and short term.

Short-term health

Physical activity boosts energy and helps to alleviate stress and anxiety. Children who are physically active are more likely to fall asleep easily and to sleep for longer. They are also less likely to develop infections, such as colds and flu, because their immune system is made stronger by having regular exercise and sufficient sleep.

Long-term health

Physical activity in young children also helps, in the long term, with:

- controlling weight – and so preventing obesity: a recent study found that teenagers who carry a gene for obesity are less likely to become overweight or obese if they are physically active for an hour a day; if an overweight child becomes an overweight or obese adult, they are more likely to suffer from health problems, including diabetes, stroke, heart disease and cancer
- increasing bone density in children and helping to maintain strong bones in adolescents: it also slows down bone degeneration later in life; this can help to prevent osteoporosis, a condition when bones become brittle and more prone to break
- reducing blood pressure: if you have high blood pressure, you are more likely to have a stroke or heart attack
- reducing the risk of diabetes: keeping active can help lower the risk of developing type 2 diabetes later on in life
- reducing the risks of some kinds of cancer.

General well-being

Children who are physically active have improved psychological well-being. They gain more self-confidence and have higher self-esteem. Children benefit from playing outdoors in the fresh air and having lots of space in which to move freely. They also benefit socially from playing alongside other children and making friends. See Public Health England's paper 'How healthy behaviour supports children's wellbeing' for more details on these ideas.

AC 1.1 Activity

Describe the benefits of physical exercise in terms of children's holistic development.

AC 1.2 The requirements of current frameworks for outdoor access and regular exercise

The Early Years Foundation Stage (EYFS) states that in order to give all children the best opportunities for effective physical development, practitioners should give particular attention to:

- planning activities that offer appropriate physical challenges
- providing sufficient space, indoors and outdoors, to set up relevant activities
- giving sufficient time for children to use a range of equipment
- providing resources that can be used in a variety of ways or to support specific skills
- introducing the language of movement to children, alongside their actions
- providing time and opportunities for children with physical disabilities or motor impairments to develop their physical skills, working as necessary with physiotherapists and occupational therapists
- using additional adult help, if necessary, to support individuals and to encourage increased independence in physical activities.

In addition to the EYFS framework guidelines, there are also the following UK physical activity guidelines specifically aimed at children under five years old.

UK physical activity guidelines

The introduction of UK early years physical activity guidelines reflects a growing awareness of their importance and follows the lead of other major international countries. They are based on evidence from research and the combined input from experts in this field of study. All children under five years old should minimise the amount of time spent being sedentary. Sedentary means being restrained (children in harnesses/prams/highchairs or a child that is in a playpen or bouncer) or sitting for extended periods (except for time spent sleeping). These guidelines are relevant to all children under the age of five and are aimed at the following groups.

For early years (under fives) – infants who cannot yet walk unaided

Physical activity should be encouraged from birth, particularly through floor-based play and water-based activities in safe environments. From birth, babies need to have daily opportunities to move freely on their stomach or back in a variety of safe spaces, without being constrained for long periods by clothing or straps (e.g. in car seats, baby chairs or bouncers). They need opportunities to practise important movements such as:

- 'tummy time' – this includes any time spent on the stomach, including rolling and playing on the floor (remember, 'tummy time' is only for when babies are awake and supervised; babies should always be placed on their backs to sleep)
- reaching for and grasping objects
- turning the head toward stimuli
- pulling, pushing and playing with other people, objects and toys.

Pre-school children who can walk unaided

Children of pre-school age who are capable of walking unaided should be physically active daily for at least 180 minutes (three hours), spread throughout the day. The 180 minutes can be activity of any intensity. For this age group, the amount of physical activity is more important than the intensity.

Physically active play is the best way for young children to be physically active. Physically active play opportunities should encourage young children to:

- use large muscle groups, e.g. back, shoulders, legs, arms, etc.
- engage in more energetic forms of physical activity, e.g. running and chasing games; these need to be encouraged through short bouts of activity, rather than be expected to take place for extended periods of time
- practise a wide range of different movements, e.g. locomotor, stability and object control skills
- experience a variety of play spaces and equipment
- have fun and feel good about themselves and what they can do.

Key term

physically active play Play that involves movements of all the major muscle groups, e.g. legs, arms. It can range from activities with small intermittent movements, e.g. clapping hands, to large movements involving the whole body, e.g. climbing and running. It tends to be used to describe young children's physical activity.

AC 1.2 Activity

Find out more about the UK physical activity guidelines for children from birth to five years from the British Heart Foundation website (www.bhfactive.org.uk).

AC 1.3 National and local initiatives which promote children's exercise

Play England

Play England campaigns for all children to have the freedom and space to play throughout childhood. As the national organisation for children's play, Play England works with all those who have an impact on children's lives to support and champion play as an essential part of childhood.

Love Outdoor Play

Love Outdoor Play is led by Play England and supported by the Free Time Consortium, a growing collective of local and specialist organisations working together to increase freedom to play.

Play4Life

Play4Life is a sub-brand of the Change4Life programme backed by the Department of Health. It aims to help every family in England eat well, move more and live longer.

> #### AC 1.3 Activity
> Find out about a specific national or local campaign and evaluate its effectiveness in promoting children's exercise.

AC 1.4 Benefits of working in partnership with parents/carers

Early years settings can do a great deal to promote children's exercise. Apart from promoting this aspect of development in their everyday practice, it is important to involve parents as much as possible.

Physical activity begins at home. Research suggests that parental physical activity impacts positively on how much physical activity their children participate in. Children who are physically active usually have parents or carers who:

Figure 1.2.1 Play4Life outdoor play leaflet cover

- encourage them to participate in physical activity
- participate in physical activity with them
- watch them play or compete
- transport them to physical activity and sports events.

Practitioners should work with parents to promote the importance of physical activity for their child or children and to encourage them to interact with them in a physically active way. This will encourage a child to be more active, to enjoy the experience and stimulate further participation. Parents and carers are important role models for their children and being physically active themselves has many health benefits too.

AC 1.4 **Progress check**

Describe the benefits of working in partnership with parents in relation to supporting children's exercise. Older schoolchildren often travel to school in a 'walking bus' – run by parents who want to promote their children's physical exercise. How do you think parents could be more involved in their children's daily physical exercise, and how could the setting help?

LO2 Understand inclusive practice in relation to the use of provision for children's exercise

AC 2.1 Evaluating a local indoor provision in relation to inclusive practice

Both the indoor and the outdoor environments should be carefully planned and prepared to provide opportunities for physical activity and the development of movement skills.

The following factors are important in planning for physical activity that is inclusive (that is, it includes all children and uses the indoor provision effectively):

- Time: you will need to allow sufficient time for babies and children to become familiar with newly introduced equipment and activities, and also to practise both new and existing skills.
- Space: you need to plan for sufficient space to set up appropriate activities for physical play. Movement is important but it does require a lot of room. Additional space may be necessary for children who have physical disabilities or motor impairments and you need to take into account the specialised equipment and extra professional support required, such as physiotherapy or occupational therapy.
- Indoor environments: opportunities for physical activity should ideally be provided both indoors and outdoors. Regular sessions

Figure 1.2.2 Playing hopscotch involves many movement skills, such as jumping, skipping, hopping, turning and balancing

of indoor physical play are particularly important when the weather limits opportunities for outdoor play.

Providing variety, risk and challenge in play

Play England states that: 'All children both need and want to take risks in order to explore limits, venture into new experiences and develop their capacities, from a very young age and from their earliest play experiences.' Physically challenging activities that involve safe risk-taking help children to build and extend their strength and fitness levels. You need to plan activities that are interesting to children and that offer physical challenges and plenty of opportunities for physical activity. When assessing risk and challenge in physical play, you need to decide whether the activity is developmentally appropriate. Children quickly become frustrated if activities are too challenging or difficult, but they also lose interest in activities that are lacking in challenge or that they find too easy.

Problem-solving in physical play

Children need to develop the skills of making assessments and solving problems. Any conscious movement involves making judgements or assessments. Assessment of the situation and of your ability (speed, power, etc.) will help you to make the appropriate movement. For example, a child might make an assessment of:

- how hard to throw
- how fast to run
- how much effort to use to jump so high
- when to begin to stop.

Inclusive practice: meeting the needs of all children

Girls and boys

Boys are routinely offered more opportunities for energetic play – for example, rough-and-tumble games with parents and early introduction to football games. You need to offer the same opportunities for physical play to boys and girls.

Children with disabilities

Some children may need special equipment for physical play or they may need to have existing equipment adapted; for example, a child with cerebral palsy may have limited control over his or her body movements and need to use a tricycle with differently positioned handles or pedals.

Children with additional needs

A child with a hearing impairment can be encouraged to dance to music as they can usually feel the vibrations through the floor. Practitioners must ensure that hearing aids are looked after carefully as sand and dirt can damage them.

Children of different ages

Babies need physical play just as much as older children. From just a few weeks old, babies can be placed on the floor and encouraged to kick their legs freely. Activities need to be planned that are developmentally appropriate for every child or group of children.

AC 2.1 Activity

Choose a particular indoor activity in your setting and evaluate it in relation to inclusive practice.

AC 2.2 Evaluating a local outdoor provision in relation to inclusive practice

The outdoor environment can provide the scale and freedom for a type of play that is difficult to replicate indoors. For example, outdoors there are opportunities for children to:

- dig a garden
- explore woodland and climb trees
- run on the grass and roll down a grassy slope
- pedal a car across a hard surface.

Keeping children safe

Children who play in a physically safe environment are more likely to develop confidence, self-esteem and self-reliance. In modern society, it is often dangerous for children to play outside in the street. Safety considerations have had a huge impact on what parents and carers allow their children to do, and the freedom to play outdoors out of a carer's sight is now extremely rare.

It is therefore very important that, when children attend group settings, they can be physically safe. Safety issues should always be in mind when working with young children so that accidents are prevented. This is called risk assessment because adults are thinking ahead about possible physical dangers to

Case study

A child-centred outdoor environment
The design of Cowgate Under 5s Centre in Edinburgh reflects the centre's philosophy inspired by the educationalist Friedrich Froebel, who believed that children learn best through spontaneous child-centred play and that they should be surrounded by kindness, understanding and beauty. (See 'Useful resources' for a link to more information on Friedrich Froebel.)

Good design has enabled a wide range of experiences to be offered within a small space. Nearly all of the resources are made from natural materials, have been chosen to enhance the children's curiosity and provide both challenge and risk. There are two timber houses at either end of the site (one of which is two storeys high), a pergola with climbing

plants, bird boxes, feeders and insect homes, a sandpit, a rabbit run with a rabbit, planted beds with sensory plants such as rosemary and lavender, an adventure playground with a rope climb, wobbly bridge and tyre swing, a greenhouse for growing, large-scale musical instruments, a raised wet area and a seating area with a storytelling seat.

The children are allowed to use all the equipment at all times as a member of staff is always present. First thing in the morning, the doors are opened wide and the children are free to move between the indoors and outdoors.

1 How does the Cowgate Under 5s Centre provide for children's physical activity?
2 Why is it important for children to play outdoors?

children. Children need to be supervised carefully; it is important for adults never to sit with their back to the group, either indoors or outdoors. Without supervision, children might become involved in unacceptable or inappropriate behaviour, such as throwing stones at a window or snatching a tricycle from another child.

The importance of natural outdoor environments

We have seen how important movement is and how it requires a lot of room. The natural outdoor environment – such as woodland, fields and beaches – provides young children with a wonderful and constantly varying 'playground'. An exciting outdoor space provides an opportunity for children to explore the environment at their own individual levels of development.

Planning and implementing physical activities
Opportunities for physical activity
When planning physical activities, you need to consider the following factors:

Reflective practice

Managing risks and challenges
Think about the way in which risk and challenge are managed in your setting.

● Have you encouraged a child to assess the risks involved in a particular activity, and to work out for themselves how to manage the risk? Did you have to intervene to support the child?
● Have you encouraged a child to try a more challenging activity?
● Have you helped a child to talk through potential problems during a play activity?
● How could you improve the way in which you support children to understand and assess risks?

● Observation: before planning how to provide physical activity, take some time to observe children's natural and spontaneous movements. You should observe:
● how they move
● their object control skills
● their coordination and balance skills
● which activities individuals prefer.

You can observe their movement and object control skills and plan their physical play by extending an activity: for example, a baby who is sitting but not yet moving (crawling or bottom shuffling) could be supported in trying to move if you provide some exciting objects that are just out of reach.

- Balance of **child-initiated activities** and **adult-led activities**: the EYFS in England requires that a balance be maintained between those activities initiated by the child and those that are adult led.
- Range of skills and movements: you need to consider the wide range of motor skills, movement skills and balance and coordination skills when planning activities.
- Time: children need to be allowed to play at their own pace. Some children are slow to begin and may need support to attempt a new skill.
- Interests: children need to have their interests valued and taken into account when planning. This is where your observations of children playing will be useful.

Developmentally appropriate activities

Table 1.2.1 suggests a range of developmentally appropriate activities. For children with

disabilities or special needs, you may need to seek advice from other professionals and their parents when planning play for them.

Key terms

child-initiated activities These activities are wholly decided upon by the child, based on the child's own motivation, and remain under the child's control. They may involve play of many types, or they may be seen by the child as activities with a serious purpose to explore a project or express an idea, which the child may not see as pure play.

adult-led activities Adult-led activities are those that adults initiate. The activities are not play, and children are likely not to see them as play, but they should be playful – with activities presented to children which are as open-ended as possible, with elements of imagination and active exploration that will increase the interest and motivation for children. As well as focused activities with groups of children, adult-led activities can include greeting times, story times, songs and even tidying up.

AC 2.2 Activity

Choose a local outdoor provision and evaluate its effectiveness in relation to inclusive practice.

Table 1.2.1 Activities that are developmentally appropriate for babies and young children

Motor skills development	Activities for movement skills	Activities for fine manipulative skills
By six months		
• grasps adult finger • arm and leg movements jerky and uncontrolled • holds a rattle briefly	• gentle bouncing games on the carer's knee to songs • encourage baby to kick, lying on back and front, to build muscles in neck and back • swinging in a baby swing to promote balance	• rattles and soft, squashy toys • books • waterproof books in bath

Table 1.2.1 Activities that are developmentally appropriate for babies and young children (*continued*)

Motor skills development	Activities for movement skills	Activities for fine manipulative skills
By nine months		
• rolls from front to back • sits up unsupported • may crawl or bottom shuffle • grasps object and passes it from one hand to other	• encourage balance by placing toys around seated baby • encourage mobility by placing objects just out of reach • play 'rolling over' games with baby	• picture books • toys to transfer safely to the mouth • simple musical instruments, e.g. xylophone
By 12 months		
• sitting for longer periods • mobile – crawling or rolling • may be walking, usually with hand/s held • stands, holding on to furniture	• push and pull brick trolleys • roll balls to and from baby • low climbing frames • swimming sessions	• stacking and nesting toys • messy play • painting and drawing
By 18 months		
• walking independently • bends and squats to pick up objects • climbs up and down stairs with help • uses pincer grasp to pick up small objects	• walker trucks, pull-along animals, etc. • low, stable furniture to climb on • space to run and play • trips to parks and woodland • low climbing frames • swimming sessions	• posting toys and shape sorters • threading toys • jigsaw puzzles • hammer and peg and pop-up toys • messy play, sand and water play • play dough
By two years		
• runs and jumps • rides a tricycle propelling with feet • walks up and down stairs	• toys to ride and climb on • space to run and play • ball play: throwing and catching • trips to parks and woodland • swimming sessions	• threading toys • jigsaw puzzles • messy play, sand and water play • play dough • models to build (e.g. Duplo)
By three years		
• rides a tricycle using pedals • walks and runs • jumps from a low step • stands on one foot and walks on tiptoe	• climbing frames • scooters and tricycles • trips to parks and woodland • swimming sessions • dancing to music	• creative activities: painting, drawing, modelling • jigsaw puzzles • messy play, sand and water play • play dough →

Table 1.2.1 Activities that are developmentally appropriate for babies and young children (*continued*)

Motor skills development	Activities for movement skills	Activities for fine manipulative skills
By three to four years		
• walks with arms swinging • climbs upstairs with one foot on each step and downwards with two feet on each step • catches, throws, kicks and bounces a ball • can stand, walk and run on tiptoe	• balls and bean bags for throwing and catching • simple running games • rope swings, climbing frames, slides, suitable trees • party games such as musical statues • running to music: fast or slow, loudly or quietly according to the music • trips to parks and woodland • swimming sessions • bikes with stabilisers	• creative activities: painting, drawing, modelling • jigsaw puzzles • messy play, sand and water play • small-world play
By four to five years and beyond		
• good sense of balance • catches, throws and kicks a ball • runs up and down stairs, one foot per step • can run and dodge lightly on the toes • climbs, skips and hops forwards on each foot separately • shows good coordination and fine motor skills	• climbing frames, rope swings • skipping ropes and hoops • hopping and jumping • action songs and games • riding tricycles, bikes, with or without stabilisers • trampoline • simple running games • team sports • trips to parks and woodland • obstacle courses for bike riders	• practising dressing and undressing • creative activities: painting, drawing, modelling • small-world play • construction toys

LO3 Be able to support children's exercise in an outdoor space

AC 3.1 Planning an activity which supports children's exercise outdoors

Planning for physical activities

Children need to feel motivated to be physically active. You can support them to develop movement skills through:

• valuing and following their interests (letting them initiate an activity)
• praise

• encouragement
• appropriate guidance.

Your plan should:

• meet the individual movement skill needs of babies and children
• promote the development of movement skills
• encourage physical play.

Whenever possible, you should involve children in your planning – by finding out what they would like to do and what equipment they would like to use.

Case study

Taking your cue from children

Rebecca, Shana and Chris work in a pre-school setting with children aged three to five years. On quieter days, they like to take the children to the local park. One day, they plan an outing with ten children. Rebecca, the room leader, ensures that they have drinks, a first aid kit and mobile phones with them. She has checked that all the parents and carers have signed up-to-date outing permission slips. As they walk through the park, four-year-old twins Chloe and Oscar run ahead to a fallen tree. The other children are delighted by their find and rush to join them. Rebecca decides that they will stop here to let the children play. The staff help the children to climb and balance, and encourage them to jump off the lower end of the tree trunk onto the soft grass. The children love the activity and it promotes much discussion when they return to the setting.

The next time they plan to go to the park, Rebecca includes Shana and Chris in thinking of ways to promote the children's movement skills as they play. They decide to take rubber rings, markers and a canvas tunnel, and they set about making an obstacle course that incorporates the fallen tree as a central obstacle. The children are shown the course and how to complete it and are supported to have a go, one at a time. The children waiting for their turn join in with the staff, shouting encouragement. Chris decides to vary the course after every child has had a turn, and he involves the children in helping him. The children are encouraged to offer their ideas and are supported in working as a team to put the objects in the right places.

1 List the areas of development being promoted.
2 How are the children being empowered during this activity?
3 This activity can be extended in many ways to promote children's movement and balance skills. Think of other activities that could be used with the children, incorporating the children's interests, such as the fallen tree.

Figure 1.2.3 This girl enjoys playing on the slide

AC 3.1 Activity

Plan an outdoor activity which promotes children's exercise.

AC 3.2 Implementing an activity which supports children's exercise outdoors

Again, careful observation is vital to the successful implementation of a plan. You will need to observe the way in which children are playing and be ready to adapt the activity if it does not seem to be meeting the children's needs and stimulating their interest. Sometimes your plan might be 'taken over' by the children. They may find a different way of playing with a piece of equipment, or they may introduce other play props into their play. You need to be flexible and prepared to adapt or even abandon the activity to enable children to initiate their own play.

Building opportunities for physical activity into everyday routines

Children need to have opportunities for physical activity every day. They need opportunities to walk, run, jump, climb and swing. Most of these activities will take place outdoors, but there are other ways in which you can build in opportunities for physical activity in the setting. Everyday routines are those that are usually built in to a setting's provision.

The importance of physical activity in everyday routines

Helping children to develop physical skills in everyday routines will promote their confidence and self-esteem, as well as providing a positive pattern for later in life. Children also need to have opportunities to go for a walk every day, so that being outside and walking in the fresh air become a regular, enjoyable experience.

How to provide opportunities in practice

It is important to stand back and consider how physical activity is built into your own practice. It is often quicker and easier to do things ourselves, but children can be encouraged to develop self-help and social skills if we build opportunities into our practice. Toddlers can be asked to fetch their own coat or shoes, for example, or you could make a game out of tidy-up time, involving children in sweeping up and putting away the toys they have been playing with.

Reflective practice

Physical activity in everyday routines
Think about a session in your setting:

- How many opportunities are there for children to be engaged in everyday routines that could involve physical activity?
- How much time do children spend outdoors? Are these opportunities limited by rainy or cold weather?
- How could you improve the provision of physical activity opportunities?

AC 3.2 Activity

Implement your planned activity from AC 3.1.

AC 3.3 Reflecting on an activity which supports children's exercise outdoors

When evaluating the effectiveness of our provision and practice, we need to be able to identify and record ways of continually improving our practice.

Assessing the effectiveness of planned provision

The main way of evaluating our practice is by observing children's participation and assessing whether their needs have been met.

Observing and assessing children

Select one child (or a group of children) and carry out a structured observation over a number of sessions or a few weeks. Your aims are to find out:

- how their physical activity has been supported – in particular, their progression in movement skills
- how their confidence has improved.

Obtaining feedback
From the child or children

You can obtain direct feedback from the child or children by listening to them and noting their comments or by asking them questions. It is usually easy to see whether children have enjoyed a physical activity, as they will often be clamouring to do it again.

From colleagues and parents

Parents know their own child best and they are often able to provide valuable insight into the effectiveness of activities. Colleagues are often well placed to give feedback as they may be able to observe children during an activity. Feedback can also be obtained by filming the children during the activity and observing the children's reactions and comments.

AC 3.3 Activity

Reflect on the activity you have planned and implemented.

AC 3.4 Making recommendations for the outdoor provision for own setting

Identifying and recording areas for improvement

Having obtained feedback, you now need to identify areas for future development. This can be recorded as an action plan. You should draw up a plan that identifies:

- areas for improvement
- reason for action
- details of action to be taken
- equipment and resources needed
- date for implementation.

Reflecting on your own practice

Reflect on your daily practice and think about how well you provide appropriate physical play experiences for the children you work with. For example:

- How do you consider the balance between child-initiated activity and adult-led activity?
- Do you join in with physical activity?
- How do you enable children and their parents to express opinions and be listened to?
- How confident are you in planning for children's individual needs and in observing and assessing their progress?

- How do you ensure that there is sufficient challenge in the activities you provide?
- How can you improve your practice?

AC 3.4 Activity

Using reflective practice, make recommendations for the outdoor provision in your setting.

Assessment practice

1 What are the benefits of exercise for children?
2 What are the requirements of current frameworks for outdoor access and regular exercise for children?
3 Evaluate the success of campaigns which seek to promote children's exercise.
4 Evaluate a local indoor provision in relation to inclusive practice, using the guidelines for inclusive provision.
5 Evaluate a local outdoor provision in relation to inclusive practice, using the guidelines for inclusive provision.
6 Plan an outdoors activity which promotes children's exercise.
7 Implement an outdoors activity which promotes children's exercise.
8 Reflect on an outdoors activity which promotes children's exercise.
9 Make recommendations for the outdoor provision in your own setting.

Useful resources

Hughes, B. (1996) *Play Environments: A Question of Quality*, London: PLAYLINK.

Meggitt, C. (2012) *An Illustrated Guide to Child Development* (3rd edn), Oxford: Heinemann.

British Heart Foundation National Centre (BHFNC)

The BHF publishes the UK physical activity guidelines for early years.

www.bhfactive.org.uk

Froebel Trust

For more information on educationalist Friedrich Froebel.

www.froebeltrust.org.uk/

JABADAO

JABADAO is a national charity which works in partnership with the education, health, arts and social care sectors to bring about a change in the way people work with the body and movement.

Northern Ireland Curriculum: physical development and movement

A selection of resources giving ideas on how to develop movement skills for Reception-aged children.

www.nicurriculum.org.uk/foundation_stage/areas_of_learning/physical_development

Play England

Play England campaigns for all children to have the freedom and space to play throughout childhood.

www.playengland.org.uk

Public Health England

www.gov.uk/government/publications/how-healthy-behaviour-supports-childrens-wellbeing

Start4Life and Play4Life (Department of Health)

The early years section of the Department of Health's Change4Life campaign. Active play resources can be downloaded from the following website.

www.nhs.uk/Change4Life/Pages/change-for-life.aspx

Index